Karel Appel

Psychopathological Notebook

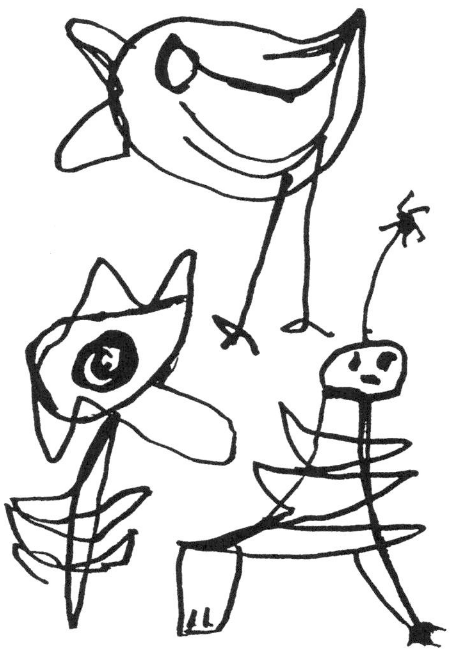

Karel Appel

Psychopathological Notebook

Drawings and Gouaches
1948–1950

with contributions by

Donald Kuspit
Rudi Fuchs
Johannes Gachnang

Verlag Gachnang & Springer
Bern - Berlin

Contents

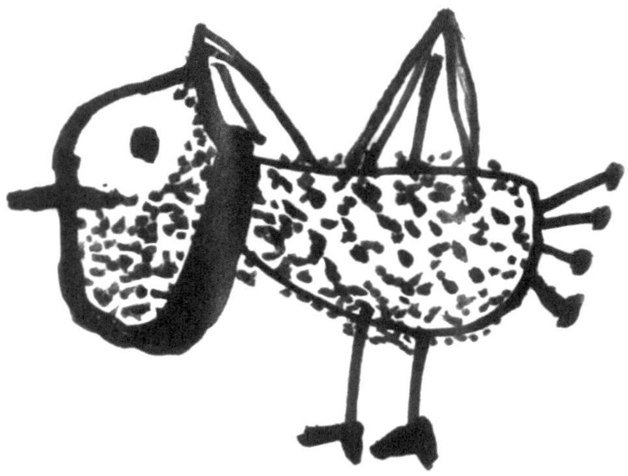

La griffe de l'artiste

Rudi Fuchs

Almost imperceptibly, a childhood word or an expression from a local dialect can crop up, and (should that be noticed) the question is then what to do with it. The poet Seamus Heaney speaks about this in an essay and gives an example of such a word, which he had changed into a more ordinary word that was part of the general language and not the narrow context of the dialect. Why had he seen this? "Because I thought twice," he says. He interrupted, shall we say, the course of the inspiration, looked about and saw the word whose appearance and sound were foreign, exotic; the word did not fit in its surroundings.

To make art is to reconsider the context again and again, to see whether the whole is coherent. At least that is the impression I get when I quietly and patiently survey the history of art. Nonetheless one has to force oneself to look for all those moments, in all those paintings, where one sees the painter place things very cautiously—weigh things, groping for the right spot. Nowadays it is possible to X-ray paintings, so that one can see where and how the artist did this groping, how the position of a hand, for instance, was drawn many times, with small variations, before it was right. Actually it isn't fair to make these X-rays; what they show, the trying and the searching, was later concealed by the painter, because he was eager to create the impression of being accurate. In this century, though, we prefer to look for the grace and the sponaneity of paintings. Vermeer produced only a few paintings; all of them are rather small, all planned and executed with the utmost precision. Nothing was left to chance. He also had all the time in the world. Fast painting was invented by the Impressionists. The motif that they had in front of them, while sitting in the landscape, had to be put down on canvas before the light changed. They worked quickly and intently with fresh colors. There was no time to mix colors and find the right hue. Once they had started, they could not allow themselves too many second thoughts. Painting became impulsive during that period. Compared to the slowly constructed compositions in classical art, Impressionist paintings are slapdash and fragmentary. The Impressionists undermined and disrupted classical perfection; from that disruption there eventually arose what we call "Modern Art."

Impressionist paintings were considered shameless by some, yet refreshing and spontaneous by others. Other artists, in particular, could sense their liberation from old rules. Such aspects (freedom, shamelessness, speed) were so attractive, because they promised adventure. And so, after Modern Art had indeed become that adventure through the many interventions of brilliantly spontaneous artists, the young Karel Appel discovered in Paris in 1950 an exhibition of "art" by mentally disturbed people, and this exhibition was accompanied by a simple catalogue, a booklet without illustrations: *Psychopathological art*. Psychiatrists were interested in such expression, as it could provide clues to the nature of an individual's mental illness; the fact that psychiatrists saw the drawings of disturbed people as being expressive, and that their expressiveness was spontaneous and direct (that the ill would not think twice), was supported as a theory by the developments in Modern Art. The exhibition in Paris and Karel Appel's interest in the psychopathological material was a fortunate but not a coincidental juncture.

Freedom and spontaneity were part of the great legend of Modern Art. The artist was to allow his imagination to roam free; any interpretation of this rich flow of images, coming directly and spontaneously from the subconscious, would interfere with human authenticity. In some movements, especially Surrealism of course, such views became ideologies—but no matter how they all painted (as Cubists, Expressionists, Fauvists and so on), the idea that things had to be spontaneous, by which they became purer and more honorable, played a pervasive role and formed the heart of the modern consciousness. Modern art had to be open and even raw; it claimed to be the great reversal and the antithesis of the contrived and enchanting illusionism of classical art. The point was to find methods that would heighten and intensify spontaneity—and to keep the painter from thinking twice. This, of course, was not without problems. It was one thing to dream of an image at night and then to remember that image, from the subconscious realm of the dream, in the morning. The process of making a painting gave rise, however, to all sorts of matters about which a painter did need to think. How big should it or could it be? The size determines the distance from which the painter will work and the nature of the brushstroke. There is a film (by Jan Vrijman) in which we see Karel Appel, from beginning to end, producing a painting. The true theme of this film is unbridled impulsiveness. We see the artist working, rapidly and tensely. "I do not paint. I hit," he says, flogging the canvas with paint. But sometimes he is still for a moment. He peers at the painting. He is thinking it over again. Then he walks back to the canvas in order to put down another stroke somewhere, where he had been before. No matter how spontaneous the painter tries to be, no matter what technique he uses for this (extreme speed, for instance), his head is also full of memories of other art. There is an awareness of specific qualities in works of art. Having emerged at one time, they live on invincibly in history: balance, harmony, clarity, density, a great deal more. Spontaneity is incompatible with that historical awareness; the envisioned image and its realization in matter thus battle with each other. The artist makes his own particular decisions within that area of tension. Picasso chose to be wild and not to have too many second thoughts, and Mondrian opted for that long, slow deliberation with himself and with the painting. A greater difference between two artists can scarcely be imagined. Even so, they are both representatives of the eminent new version of Modern Art; both of them seek to express their artistic sincerity as spontaneously as character permits, without allowing themselves to be distracted from this.

The mentally ill person who makes a drawing is not distracted, because he is entirely confined by his obsession. The artist must resist distraction through concentration and self-control. Examples—and a method that can suggest examples—are helpful in that. When Karel Appel came to Paris, he was a member of the CoBrA group, in which like-minded artists from Denmark, Belgium and the Netherlands had found each other. In post-war Europe they came across each other, most of them still quite young, and they discovered a shared ambition. Modern Art had become quieter during the 1930s (as though the oncoming war could be sensed), and the post-war youth felt rebellious. Art had to become spontaneous again. In order to arrive at this, they began to acquaint themselves with expressive statements from areas outside art: with the carefree drawings of children, with primitive forms of folk art, with the art of primitive peoples far from Europe and so, too, with the creations of the mentally ill. The major exhibition of CoBrA, fabulously installed by the young architect Aldo van Eyck, took place in 1949 at the Stedelijk Museum in Amsterdam. It demonstrated the verve of a new generation. The fact that Karel Appel went to look at the expressions of the mentally ill in Paris in 1950 was entirely consistent with the state of his emotion at that time—and with his curiosity. He went to look a number of times and, in the meantime, read through the catalogue. He then started to draw in order to find out what it was that made the expressions of the mentally ill so unique. The drawings gave him access to the dynamism of these expressions. He tried to draw without second thoughts, but nevertheless, being a restless artist, he was unable to prevent his vocabulary in these intimate drawings from becoming gradually clearer. With spontaneity he came to grips with himself.

Translation: Beth O’Brian

Karel Appel's "Psychopathological Notebook"

Donald Kuspit

Psychopathological art is a brochure that was published on the occasion of the International Congress of Psychiatry held in Paris 1950. Karel Appel was inspired by this brochure—by the idea of art that expressed psychopathology—and drew and painted on its pages. The result is a major, unique document of 20th century avant-garde art. Appel in effect illustrates a text on psychopathological art with his own psychopathological imagery. Attuned to the text, he offers a reading so close as to become its visual equivalent. At the same time, there is something defiant in Appel's imagery, as though to assert that to label an art psychopathological is to betray it. It is to stigmatize, even ghettoize its creativity: it is to smear the artists as insane.

It is of course those who are the keepers of everyday sanity—they call themselves normal—who pass the judgment of insanity on those who do not accept their version of the world. Thus they justify themselves, and self-righteously defend themselves against the idea that they in fact may be the really insane ones, for they accept the world as it is, in a conspiracy of self-serving compliance to it. Insane people represent the threat of another idea of the world than the one that is officially the case, and thus they must be locked away in a world of their own, a world completely discontinuous with the everyday world, as though their world—the insane asylum—has no relevance to the larger world, when in fact it may contain the hidden truth about it. There are always more ostensibly sane people than openly insane people—people openly professing an alternative vision of the world—because it is hard to sustain such an alternative vision and to know what to do with it and make of it. Thus the supposedly sane have power over the obviously insane, and suppress their vision of the word by labelling it mad.

But this vision is irrepressible: it demands to be seen. Thus one thing the insane do in insane asylums is to express their insane vision in art, compulsively project their alternative vision, without understanding its meaning and value, the import and power of its difference. They have to get their vision off their chests, out into the open, to relieve the pressure it puts on their lives. The vision oppresses and possesses them, and they decompress by expressing it. They use whatever means they have—often a confused mix of conventional communication codes—to articulate their vision, making it seem stranger than it is (for unconsciously it is not at all strange). Indeed, on the social surface, the results seem triply baffling and disturbing:

1. The feelings they convey are those ordinarily not admitted to oneself.

2. When they are, one dares not talk about them in public (1. and 2. make one sane).

3. When one does dare acknowledge them as one's own and make them public, one tends to do so in an incoherent, even incomprehensible way. This is in part because they are hard to sort out, and in part because they are inherently conflicted, self-contradictory. This makes them slippery and wild—elusive and uncontrollable; and, however much one tries to represent them, feelings seem peculiarly unrepresentable. Every representation seems unequal to their strength and subtlety, no doubt because it is necessarily conscious (in part), and because feelings are rooted in the unconscious, however conscious of them we are. Thus their representation puts the artist in a double bind, parallel to that created by daring to admit feelings that are ordinarily inadmissible. Indeed, to do so in polite society is a serious faux pas. (3. makes one insane).

Now people in insane asylums are there because they don't know how to keep their insanity to themselves—how to accept the doubleness that is necessary to survival. They don't know how to navigate in the two worlds we all inhabit: the world of our inner "insane" vision, and the everyday world in which no one admits to insanity (which, as I have tried to suggest, is the greatest insanity). They do not know how to accommodate themselves to the ordinary vision of things that is common currency in the world. But certain kinds of artists do: artists like Appel. He lives in both worlds; both worlds appear in his art. He intuitively understands the difference between them, as well as their underlying similarity and continuity. Appel's psychopathological vision is a brilliant compromise formation, like a dream: it seamlessly fuses ordinary objective vision and extraordinary subjective vision. This vision creates a perfect ambiguity, as it were. It ostensibly uses ordinary images, recognizable as faces and figures, but it gives them a strange twist, which suggests that they are insane. Like an undertow, they drag us into the unconscious, despite our resistance.

Through their remarkable spontaneity, they drive us mad, as it were. They introduce us to the unstructured psyche: the psyche at its most fluid and fundamental, the psyche with no brakes on its process, with no rules except those innate to it. Appel's figures and faces quickly lose the logic of their conventional appearance and dissolve into a stream of irrational gestures and colors, dancing to another logic, the logic of "sensational" feelings. The figures and faces are no more than frames for raw sensations, evocative of dangerous feelings. To put this another way, the figures and faces are constituted by an incredibly rapid, protean flow of color gestures, at once libidinal and aggressive—passionate and violent. At first glance, they obey the rules of secondary process, as the psychoanalysts call it, but at second glance they become projections of primary process. The figures become raw expressions of the body ego, the faces become variations on the *Urgesicht*—the primordial inner face. Appel's images are eloquently self-contradictory, sane and insane—bright and dark—at once: familiar figures and faces, perhaps a little strange and all too colorful, like toys or clowns; but also unfamiliar and uncanny, grimly funny fantasy characters, at once nightmarish and comic, playful and terrorizing. They are personifications of the haunting, tragicomic emotional truth: the truth ordinary consciousness denies, but that we glimpse in dreams and in certain unexpected emotions.

Let us look at Appel's achievement more carefully. It is not without its ironies: he draws a colorful owl of wisdom, comically wide-eyed, on the title page. Thus he appropriates and mocks the book's contents at the same time, as though refusing to be appropriated himself: the artist who makes psychopathological art, he in effect says, is wiser than the psychiatrist who writes about it. Defiantly, Appel declares himself to be a psychopatholgical artist—identifies with the psychopathological artists the book examines. It is as though he is daring the psychiatrists to write about his art. He also gives us an example of psychopathological art, as though to say one picture is worth a thousand scholarly words, a hundred ideas. And a multitude of examples is worth a treatise. In other words, he counters the intellectuality of the book with the emotional reality of his art: he undoes the book's efforts to deal in a systematic, scientific—ultra-sane—way with the art of the insane by spontaneously making it. He undoes the book's sophisticated conceptualization of psychopathological art with his own psychopathologically raw art. His art is a kind of defensive secretion on the surface of an irritating psychiatric text, unexpectedly turning it into a pearl.

In fact, Appel proceeds to cover the pages of the book with his images. It is an aggressive act of art, a witty reversal—perversion—of the usual order of things: unconscious expression covers over and "tops"—literally covers (sometimes completely) or is placed of top of—conscious statement. The spontaneous replaces the reasoned. The neat black lines of the text are obscured by colorful, wildly drawn, almost amorphous figures and faces. When the drawings are in black ink—a very black ink—the destructive intention toward the text is even more evident, particularly in marginal figurative drawings, and in the drawings which use the page as an "aura."

Pages 17, 18, 45, 51, 52 and 53

Pages 41, 42, 43, 44, 47 and 48

In every case, Appel's emphatic figures and faces render the text secondary, even irrelevant: it is not Appel's art that illustrates the text, as first seemed to be the case, but the text that illustrates the art, and that in a rather poor, inconsequential way—so much so that we need not pay attention to it, as Appel seems to be suggesting. (And couldn't if we wanted to, because it has become impossible to read with all the images superimposed on it.)

Appel is finally saying: "Who cares about all this technical writing? Look at my spontaneous images. They're the real psychopathological thing." Even more, he implies that it is psychopathological to write a text about psychopathological art rather than to enjoy it, to enter into its spirit, to be emotionally liberated by it, to play along with it, to try to be as playful and alive as it is. It is better to live it than to analyze it.

Appel's images are strong, daring stuff. They take their important place in the history of works of Modern Art influenced by psychopathological art. But they seem more important than the usual examples: Appel does not simply copy and vary the art of the insane, as many other modern artists do, but creates an original psychopathological art, that is nonetheless an art historical advance. His "psychopathological drawings" carry automatism to a heroic extreme: it is a truly independent exploration of psychotic process, not merely a stylish, flashy, literary technique. Also, the drawings reveal the disintegrative potential in the irrational anatomies of Surrealism: Appel's figures all but come apart. They hold together only because they have outlines. Internally, they are catastrophes. Compared to the French Surrealists, Appel's line is wild, his figures are monstrous and his line is vigorous. The figures of color, as well as the numerous black and white drawings, are more instinctive, like the animals Appel sometimes renders. Above all, they are not bound by theory—not inhibited by the need to serve an abstract idea. Stylized absurdity is not the point of Appel's imagery, but the power of the unconscious to appropriate, overrun, and finally destroy consciousness. His "Psychopathological Notebook" offers a less pretentious, more incisive insight into human existence than overtheorized French Surrealism.

Pages 7, 8, 10, 47 and 48

Appel's wild faces are in a class by themselves—virtually unprecedented, if not unrelated to the distortions of Picasso and Miró, the two major role models for artists during the period between the world wars. The 1948–1950 date of Appel's psychopathological drawings is of course important: they are among the first major productions of European art immediately after the second world war. No doubt they were kept private—they were never exhibited until the "Parallel Visions" show in Los Angeles (1992)—because they are particularly personal works. Also, they are a virtual encyclopedia and inventory of Appel's imagery, a resource from which he drew in later years—in effect, his whole development in concentrated form. They are his most basic images, which he later elaborated and built on. In other words, they were a working tool, a direct stimulus to his ceativity. In fact, and no doubt ironically, they became a text for his own private use, like the more public text that stimulated his creativity to produce them.

Indeed, the psychopathological figures and faces are perhaps the most elemental and elementary Appel ever made. In the "Psychopathological Notebook" he works and reworks them, until he can reduce them no further. The Notebook is a remarkable example of a sustained creative process. Appel zeroes in on his themes, but remains extraordinarily responsive to them. His fertility is truly astonishing.

Interest in the art of the insane has been enormous since the publication in 1921 of Walter Morgenthaler's "Adolf Wölfli—Ein Geisteskranker als Künstler" and 1922 of Hans Prinzhorn's "Bildnerei der Geisteskranken." They are virtually the first in depth study of such art. In 1948 André Breton, the Pope of Surrealism, officially endorsed the art of the insane in his essay on "The Art of the Insane: Freedom to Roam Abroad" (L'art des fous, la clé des champs). That same year Jean Dubuffet published his Art brut manifesto, declaring the inherent fascination of art created by "people considered mentally ill and confined in psychiatric establishments." John M. MacGregor's "The Discovery of the Art of the Insane" (1989) is the climax of this long, ambitious attempt to mainstream and esthetically legitimate the art of the insane. What all of these writings miss, and what Appel's "Psychopathological Notebook" makes clear, is that it is possible to make an art of the insane without being confined in a psychiatric hospital—a genuine art of the insane, not simply an imitation or stylized art of the insane.

Even in retrospect—half a century after their production—Appel's psychopathological drawings do not seem compromised by esthetic pretentions, by the exploitative determination to distill a genuine innovation into a high style. They remain authentically insane where so much other self-styled insane art has become merely art. Appel did not try to displace their creativity with his own, or learn lessons from it to enrich his own. Appel's "psychopathological drawings" pay homage to the insane the only way it is really possible to do so: they show him becoming one of them, and thus as creative as they are. They show him discovering his own insanity, and with it his own creativity.

In his "psychopathological drawings" Appel shows that he truly understands the point of insanity: to discover a new reality in the dregs of the old reality, a more extraordinary reality than the ordinary one. He realizes that in fantasy there is a different, bolder, hitherto unsuspected reality.

But unlike the insane he shows that he has the ego strength to survive the chaos—the sense of nothingness and disorientation—that results from abandoning and dissolving the old order of reality, and the resources to describe the new order that emerges from the chaos. Thus he is not victimized by his insanity. It is a deliberate risk he takes, not an involuntary suffering. His "psychopathological drawings," then, avoid the Scylla of helpless insanity and the Charybdis of simulated insanity. And because they do they can reclaim what is in fact everyone's birthright: the land under the sea of one's suffering. Appel's "Psychopathological Notebook" shows it when it is still raw, not yet farmed by art, the first step in its domestication, civilization.

His is a genuine regression in the service of the European ego that was destroyed by the trauma of the second world war, not a mock regression simply to find a new source for art. Like the art of the insane, his "Psychopathological Notebook" is a remarkable pearl that grew around the intrusion of a unwelcome reality, undermining his sense of safety, yet giving him a strong sense of his own reality, indeed, forcing him to use all his creative power to survive. Appel's "psychopathological drawings" are remarkably unsafe in a world of safe art. They are a tour de force of remarkable conviction.

Donald Kuspit and Karel Appel in Conversation*

March 29, 1994

I think the book with the "psychopathological drawings" is extremely important for a number of reasons. First, it really represents the earliest, one of the earliest, productions of Karel Appel. And perhaps most important of all, it's like a kind of encyclopedia of all his imagery. Everything will come out of it. But even more to the point, it is really a very early articulation of the post-war period, of an ongoing interest in the art of the insane, outsider art, art that seems to have a kind of freedom and directness of expression which is otherwise not found. And what's interesting about it is that it is not just an effort to be influenced by the art of the insane, by outsider art; but it is an effort to produce insane art in some sense, by an artist who is hopefully not insane, who is not mad. So I think this is quite unusual. It shows the extraordinary psychic and artistic flexibility that Appel has in being able to enter this art in spirit. The book contains texts about the various types of patients who produce the imagery and what Appel does, in effect, is enter into the spirit of that text and try to produce an image that on the one hand would seem to be of the patient, but also by the patient. So I think it's on a very deep psychological level, it's extraordinarily spontaneous, and it is a rather amazing figuration produced spontaneously. In my opinion that is its basic importance. It is also historically important for continuing the tradition of spontaneous automatist art and continuing it in a direction which I think is quite new or at least was not fully explored and articulated as thoroughly before.

* The following conversation was conducted in English and recorded, and then a transcript was made from the tape. In order to preserve the authenticity of the exchange of ideas between Karel Appel and Donald Kuspit, no grammatical or lexical corrections have been made in the transcript.

Donald Kuspit: I wonder if you could tell me the circumstances of the making of this notebook and what you thought of the booklet when you saw it? Why this particular book? And how did you respond to the text and the images in it?

Karel Appel: When I began to live in Paris in 1950, I visited Sainte-Anne's, a psychiatric hospital.

DK: You just decided to visit it?

KA: No, there was an exhibition, an exhibition from the people, the sick people, the mad people. So, I visited that exhibition several times and then I bought a catalogue. It was a simple catalogue, only text, no images. And I started to read it and I kept the catalogue and little by little, I went back to look at the exhibition and it gave me a sort of inspiration, different than when I saw other artists.

DK: But this imagery is your own imagery, in response to the imagery in the exhibition and the book, yes?

KA: Yes, then I started to work spontaneously, like you see, with a pen.

DK: Are there any memories of the images that you saw in your mind when you were doing this? Or is it just kind of a general kind of influence?

KA: No, it gave me the kind of inspiration to do sometimes more directly and simply. Like here for instance, that face, I did it absolutely without thinking. You know, the complete freedom I have, the stimulation of freedom for spontaneity.

DK: Do you think the madness, that these were images produced by mentally disturbed people, by so-called "mad people" outside society, was important to you? Did you in any way identify with them?

KA: Yes.

DK: And also, wasn't this the beginning of your trip, your move to Paris, when you were just getting started?

KA: No. I was already in Paris.

DK: For how long were you in Paris?

KA: I visited Paris in 1947, 1948 and 1949, and then I decided to stay to live in Paris in 1950. And I was busy already in that same field. I saw more of these paintings and drawings before in the Netherlands and Belgium. I saw exhibitions in Paris in some closed houses. Then began the big show which gave a lot of inspiration to be rid of the past, the classical European past. I know from Holland, as a Dutch artist, you learn so much about the classical arts and to make you lose that you needed the stimulation.

DK: So there was a negative purpose to it as well, yes?

KA: Yes.

DK: It was antagonistic to do this.

KA: Yes, it was antagonistic. It looks antagonistic, but I think the deconstruction, that I am still doing in a way like my "Hybrids," feeling with all of the pieces from several cultures, the hybrid deconstruction is the style. You could say, is the new expression. And I always had that feeling. And that was helping very much these people to show, as "outsider art," that it is sometimes fresher, and more direct, and in fantasy what we don't have.

DK: The fantasy element of this was very important, yes?

KA: Yes. And sometimes it was also very sad for me, it put you down too. You feel behind and ill, a sick spirit. But between the spirit and the material is the body, is the brain. The brains are sick, not the spirit, I found out. I think the spirit is the spirit but it goes in a sick body, let's say simply. It is not the spirit that is ill, it is the instrumentation, what it goes through, that is sometimes disturbed.

DK: Are all these figures, all of the images here figural?

KA: All are figural.

DK: What interested you so much about the figure?

KA: I tell you that is maybe the only aspect left over from my classical base. If you see classical art: Egyptian, Roman, Greek or European art, there was always the human being. With the human being you can do everything, there is always the image which was always deformated. And every culture had its own deformation. The Greek style is different from the Renaissace style. Or different than the style of the Egyptians or German Expressionists.

We say always, still today, that the human being, and this world and this earth is the most important. That is why we paint human beings. And every culture, we say that is Renaissance style, that is Egyptian style, that is Fauvism, that is Dada. But is always the same, a human being. And it is a deformation. Every style I think is a deformation of the human being. That is why the psychopathological art belongs to it too. It is a deformation of the human being, only by a sick instrumentation, we call it. It becomes not a style, it becomes not a culture, it is only partly in the culture, here and there.

DK: A lot of this imagery though looks very abstract. It can be taken as non-figuration. I remember you once said that CoBrA and Abstract Expressionism in America were the two major movements of the post-war, you saw an affinity between them. But, Abstract Expressionism, say in Pollock, moves away from the figure. At least that is officially ... why did you never move away from the figure?

KA: I did move away from the figure.

DK: You have moved away completely from the figure? Total abstraction?

KA: Total abstraction for three and a half years. I could show you the brushstroke, the disciplined brushstroke. I left the scene. I left the theater. I left the image, the human being and went in the space where the human being is no longer there, it was not available anymore in my spirit, not for about three years.

DK: Why was the human being not available at that particular time, at that period? Were you disillusioned? Bothered by human beings? Too deformed?

KA: No, absolutely not. It was more, in this country (in the United States) the human being is not so important. Here, is always important the empty space, the color field, the abstraction, always the emptiness. When I saw the first work of Pollock, for instance in this country in 1957, I saw the work from him during the war which was so close to the CoBrA movement. It had the same sprit behind it. He makes it loose, he makes it free, but still using the human being. Which always happens, it is the classical aspect left over, to use the human being.

That was the early Pollock, during the war he was making that. I saw it after the war here. And then he went to direct, spontaneous work. At that moment which I also felt, he jumped into complete freedom by spontaneity. He lost the human being.

DK: So he influenced you in some way?

KA: No, he didn't influence me, he was experiencing the same phenomenon. Franz Kline was the same.

DK: I'm interested still in this period where you stopped doing the figure. This was in the United States more or less from 1957–1960, and it had something to do with the effect of New York on you and the effect of the Abstract Expressionists. You had mentioned previously in conversation that it had to do with these empty spaces that you saw everywhere in New York or perhaps in America in general, and that you were unconsciously picking that up, responding to that?

KA: For me, it was a new discovery. Before, I finished my painting with oil paint, even the white canvas I fill in with white paint. But then I realized the beauty of the unfinished canvas. I kept the white canvas like it is, white, without touching it. But I found out that the raw unfinished space was beautiful too. In between the painting color and between the lines from the oil painting, like Franz Kline who was doing only that. Even De Kooning was very influenced by Franz Kline for a moment.

DK: What was your relation to Kline like? Did you see each other regularly, did you look at each other's works?

KA: I met him for the first time in the evening in the Cedar Bar, third avenue somewhere, where I met De Kooning and other artists too. I talked with him a lot. He was a very simple man, no pretensions at all.

Most American artists were not pretentious, very easy to talk with, the opposite of the French.

DK: The French are very pretentious.

KA: Yes, they feel themselves so fantastic. That you cannot, in a bistro, talk with them like we do now. That was also with Franz Kline and De Kooning and other artists, many artists. So, it was not a club, but you had more human contact, so you could talk more easily about your work.

DK: Was this also the time of your interest in jazz?

KA: Yes, absolutely. Thelonious Monk was playing in the Five Spot every night.

DK: Did that affect your visual art in any way, your production?

KA: Music was always my big inspiration. Before in Europe it was the classical music, like European classical music. Later, I came here and discovered the big jazz, musicians as stars, in Central Park and in Rendall Stadium. And that was a big influence for me too. Even the smaller bands in the bistros, where they played to make money.

DK: Is there any continuity between the psychological drawings and your experience with the voids in New York and then of jazz, which is a kind, or was a kind of outsider music before it was assimilated into the mainstream. I mean jazz was the music of black people who had been oppressed.

KA: I don't have a separated feeling for here is black and here is white. It is not for me. I come from Holland and we don't have that feeling. For me, the blacks are more spontaneous, more open and spontaneous in the music and in the talk. Not intellectual talk but spontaneous talk. So, that was also a stimulation. I discovered, like Lao-tse, the complete freedom of your spirit.

DK: Why did you leave Holland? Did you feel it was not so spontaneous?

KA: No, for me it was claustrophobic. Holland has the best organization, but that is it, not more. I need the enormous freedom feeling which I discovered, for real, for the first time in my life in the United States. When I stepped off of the boat, from Paris, there was a complete freedom feeling in that time in the fifties, it was enormous. Plus the jazz music was open and free, and the artists painted with big brushstrikes, said to hell with the image, we paint our space. That is what they said. And that was the same stimulation I was looking for. I was looking for the feeling, which I was able to feel in psychopathological art. You know, freedom is the most stimulating for the artist.

DK: But is that also a Dutch phenomenon, to want to be free? I mean, you have this extraordinary group of artists out of the Netherlands if you just think, say, of these big names Rembrandt, Van Gogh, even Mondrian, and then yourself in your own way is very different. You are somehow liberating yourself from this claustrophobic world, as you call it. I mean, does that make sense, that one needs this tight world in order to break out. Is that what your art is about? A perpetual breaking out, in some sense?

KA: I think so, yes. If you see, I just spoke about it recently, for instance, Mondrian started to live in Paris and got the same claustrophobic feeling. And by force he had to leave Paris and go to London, then New York, during the war.

DK: And when he comes to New York and makes these works called "New York City" and "Broadway Boogie Woogie," very open with the colors and the light coming in them, he gets even more liberated, in a way.

KA: Yes, then he painted "Victory Boogie Woogie," the bigger size. The color was more dense and more moving. And when I saw these paintings, after the war in the Amsterdam museum, I discovered the Van Gogh in Mondrian. Not that he paints as Van Gogh, but he had the same feeling of freedom. Like Van Gogh painted the "Potato Eaters" and then went to the South of France. You feel the difference. He discovered the light. That contrast was visible to me, from Mondrian I discovered that contrast. But Van Gogh had the same, he discovered the enlightenment of the light. That is typically Dutch, I must say. Rembrandt, Van Gogh, Mondrian, myself.

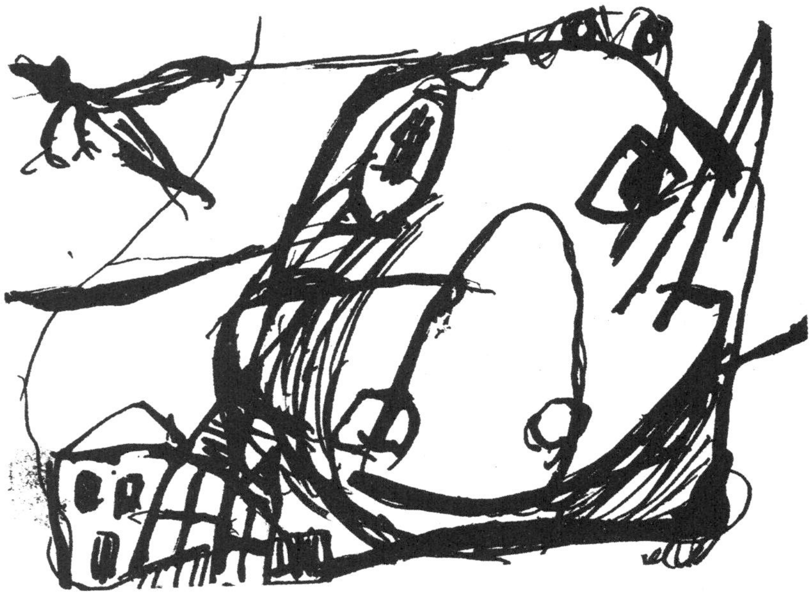

Psychopathological Notebook

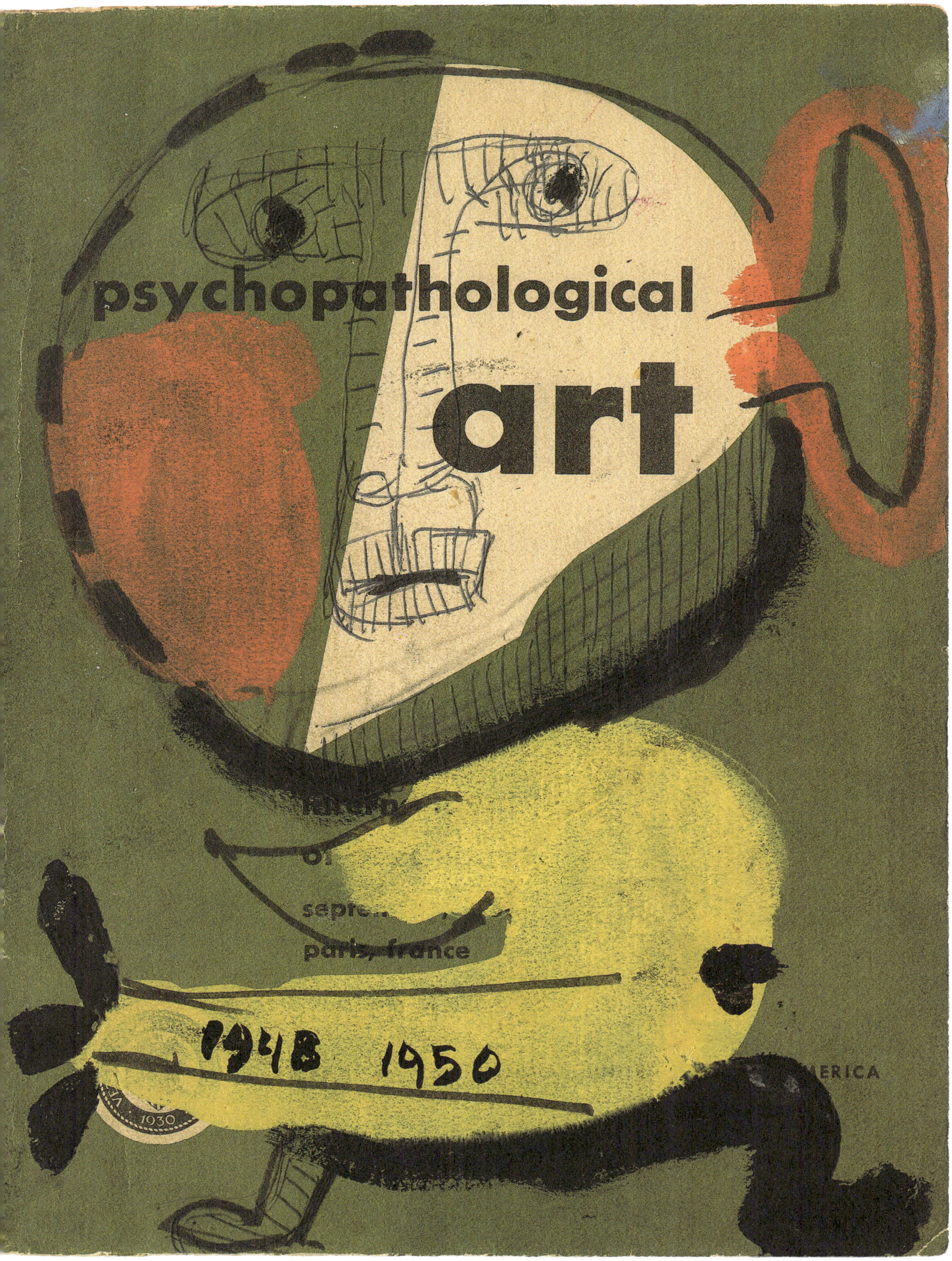
psychopathological
art
paris, france
1948 1950
1930

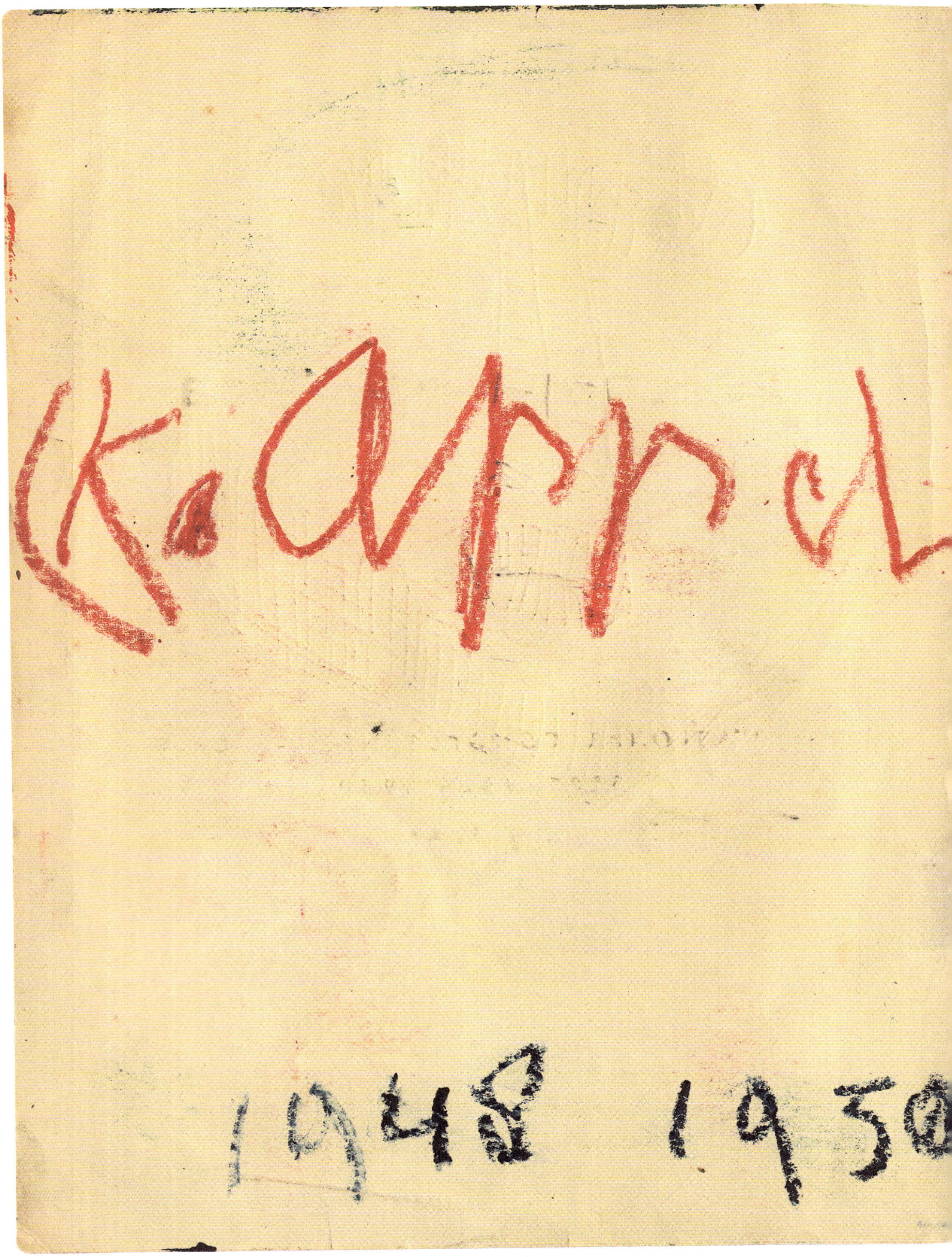
K.appel
1948 1950

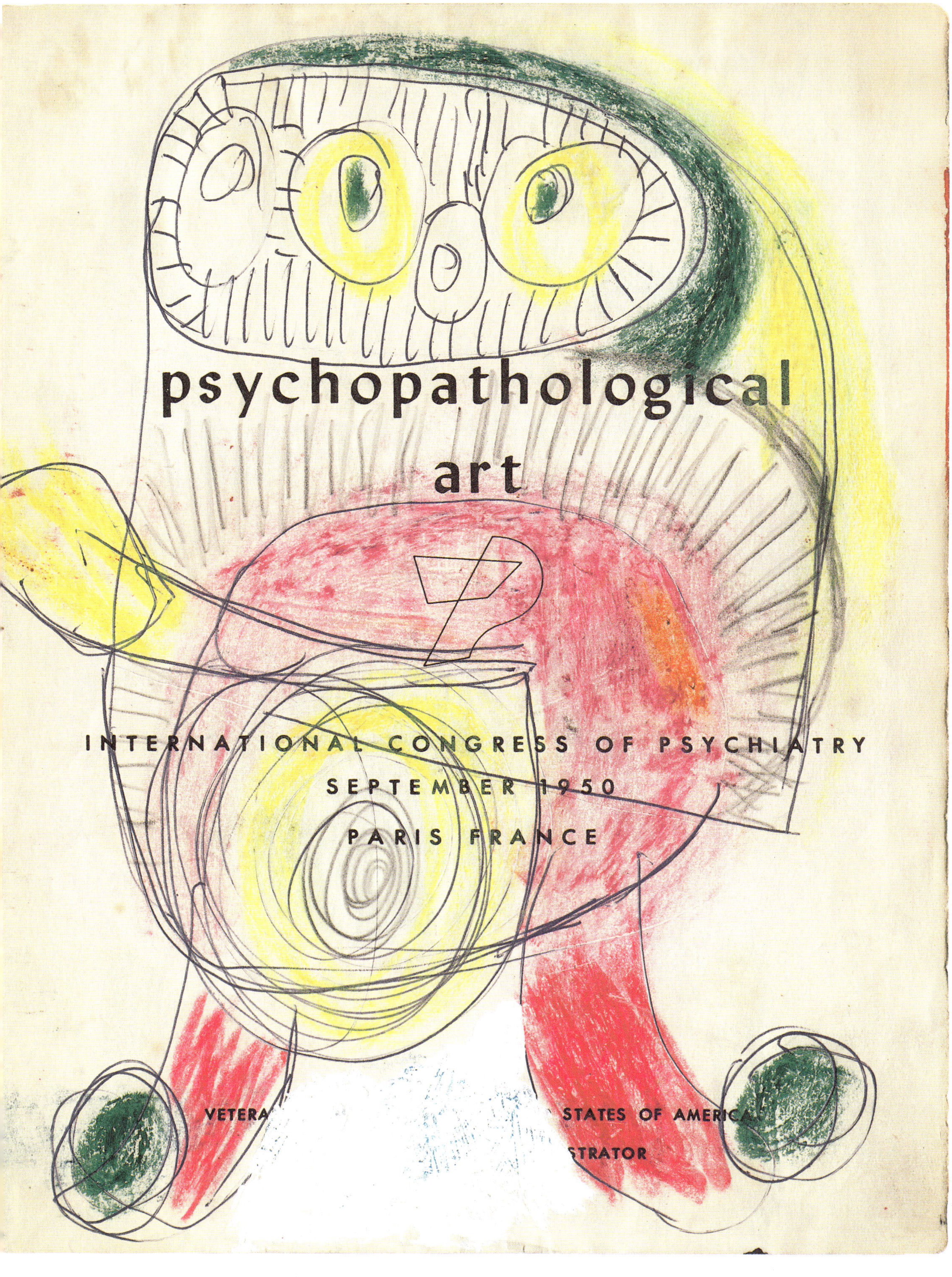

psychopathological art

INTERNATIONAL CONGRESS OF PSYCHIATRY

SEPTEMBER 1950

PARIS FRANCE

VETERA STATES OF AMERICA

STRATOR

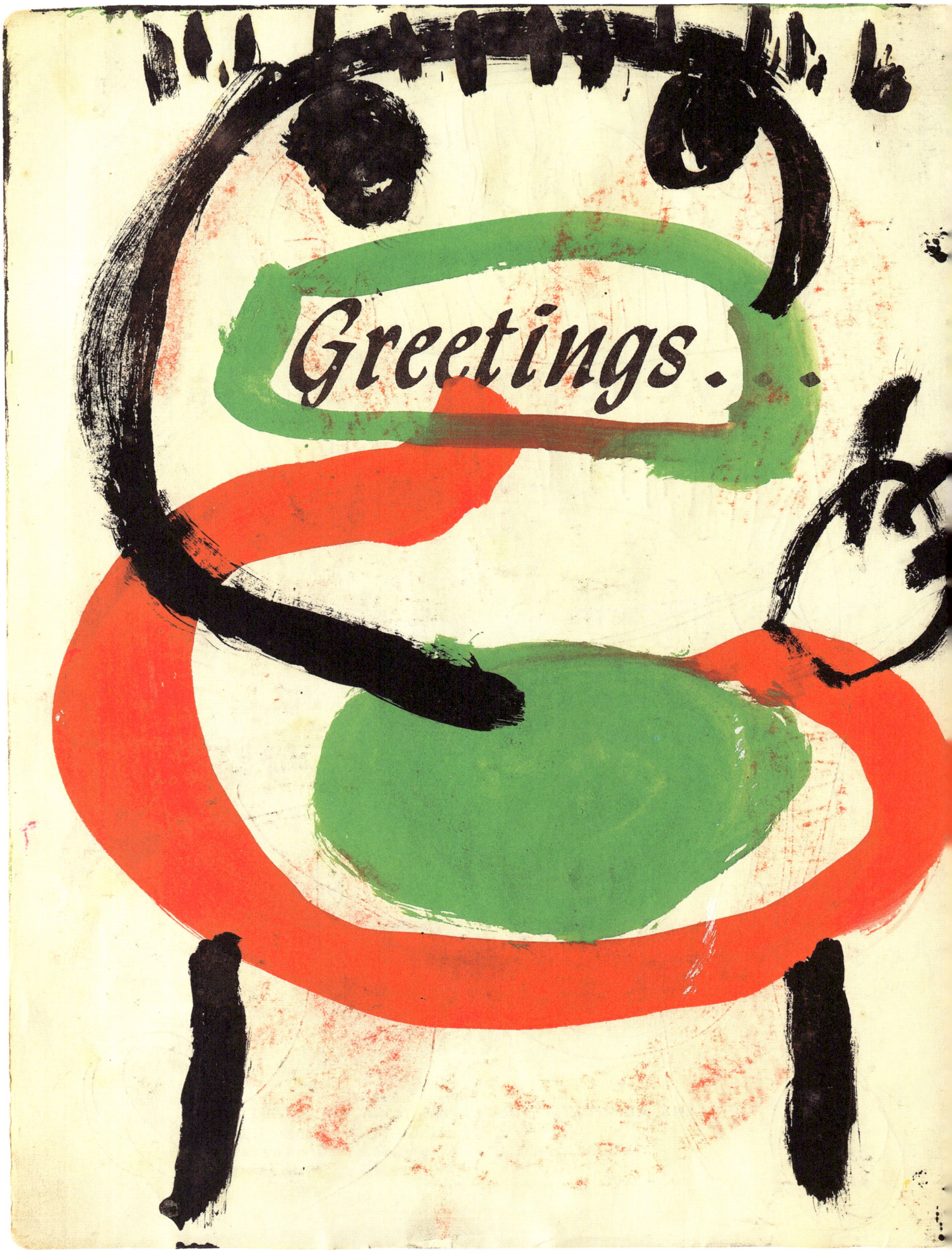
Greetings.

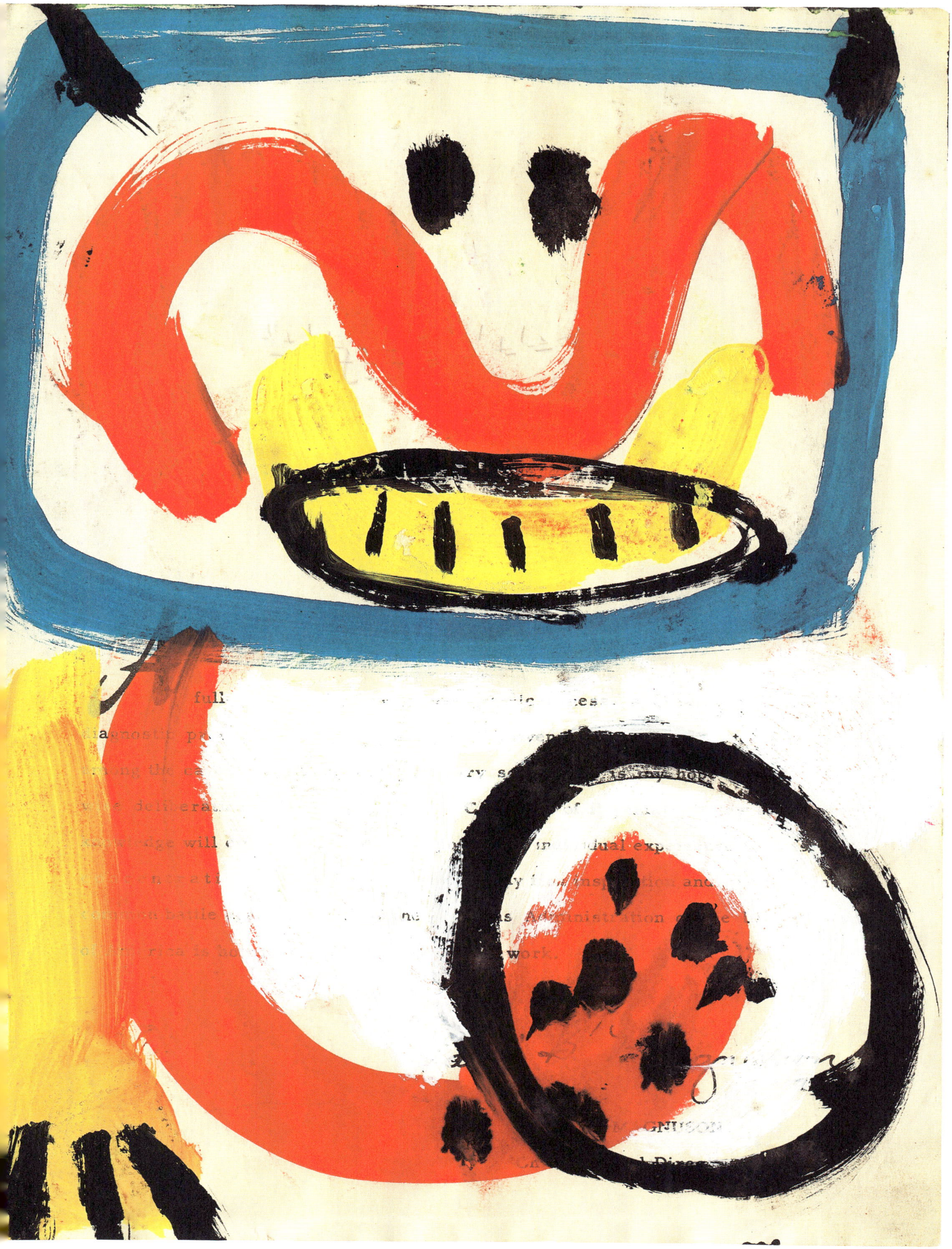

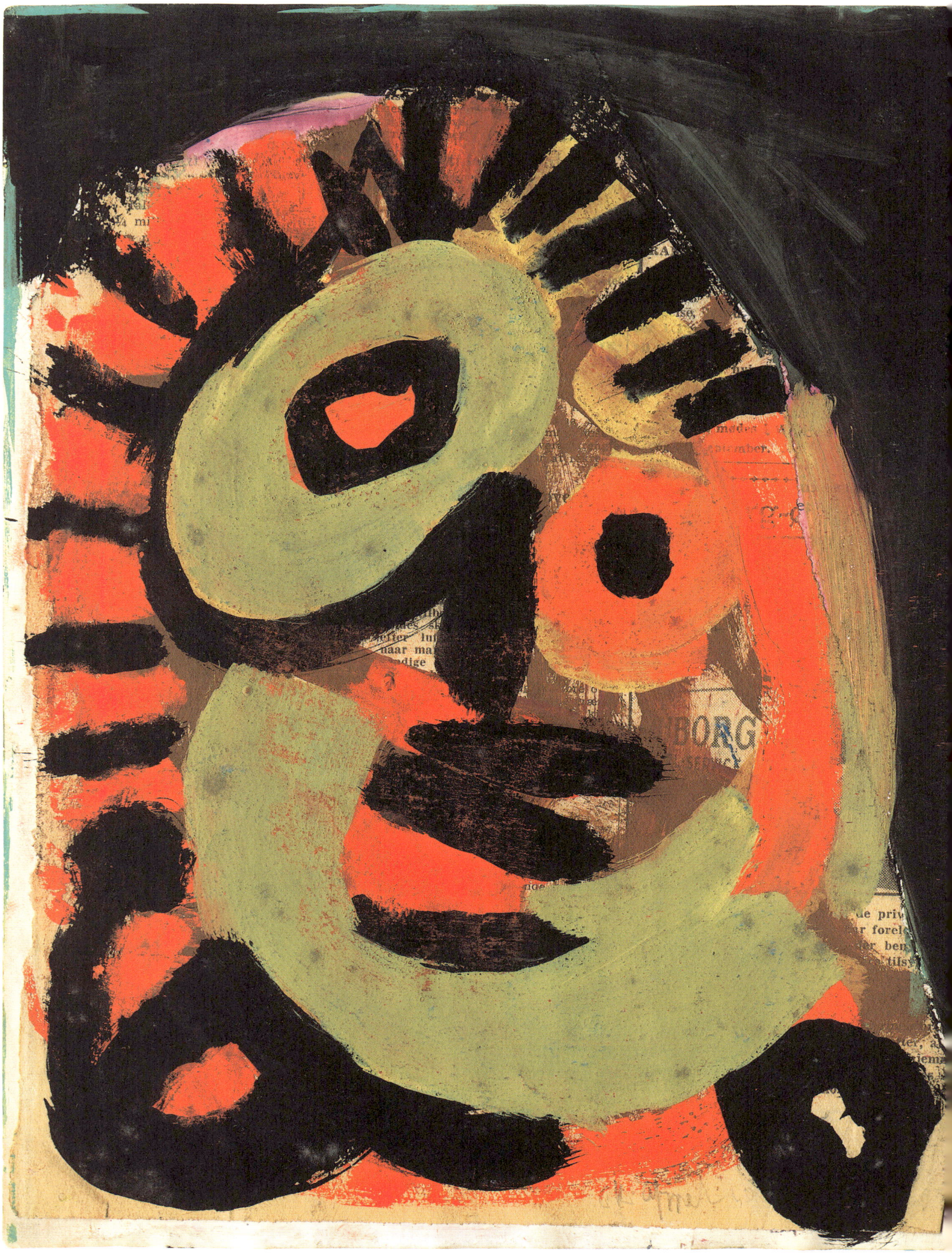
BORG

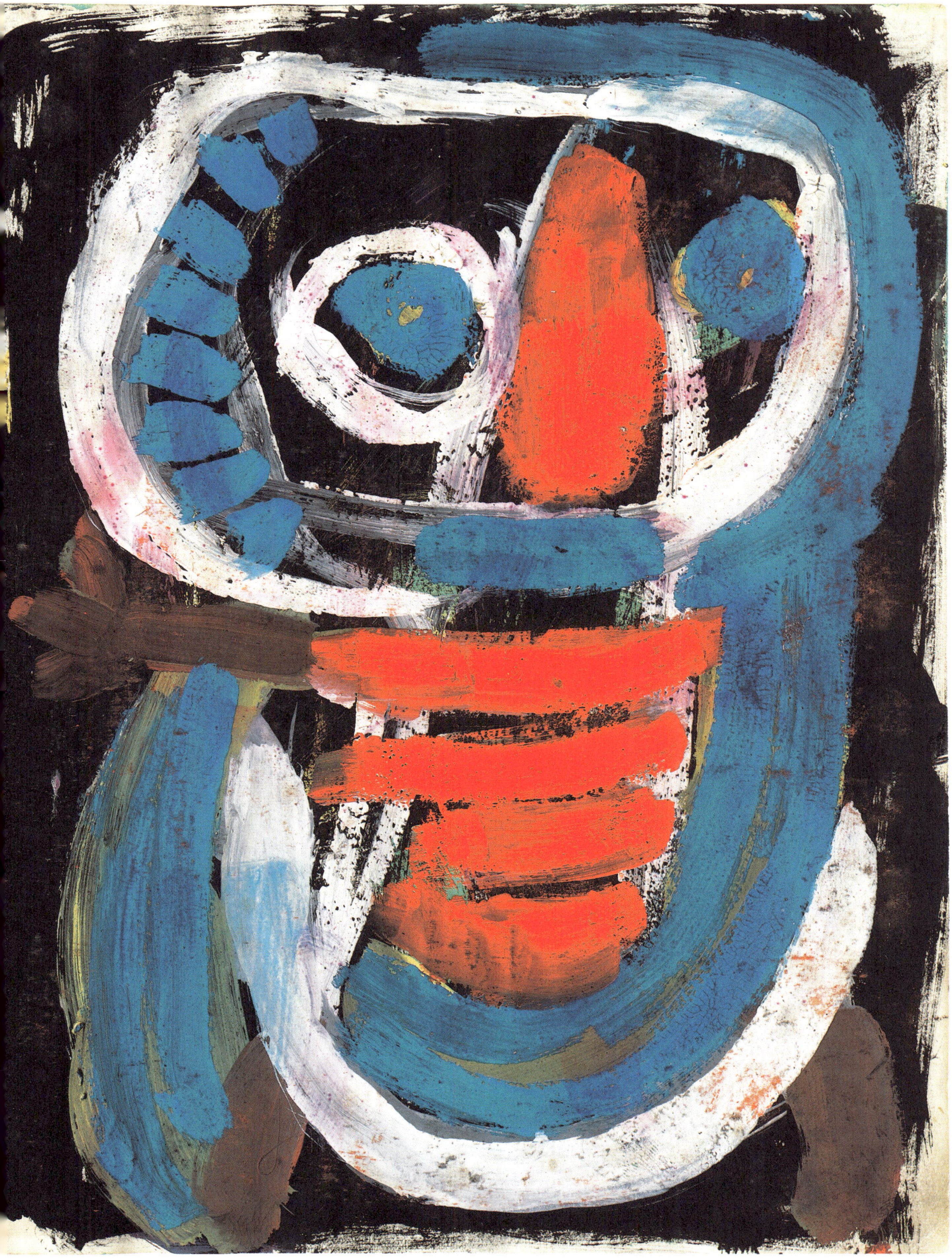

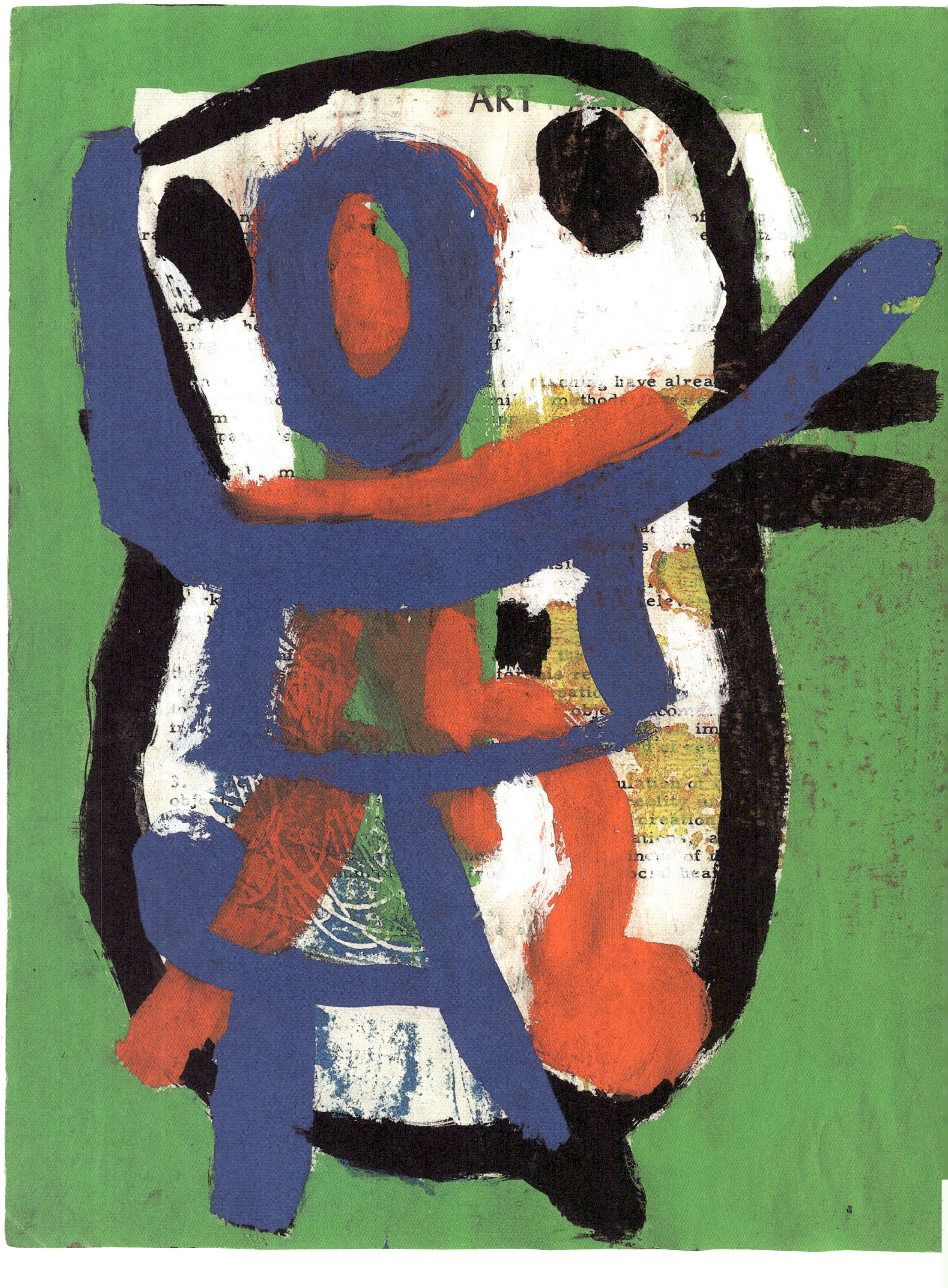

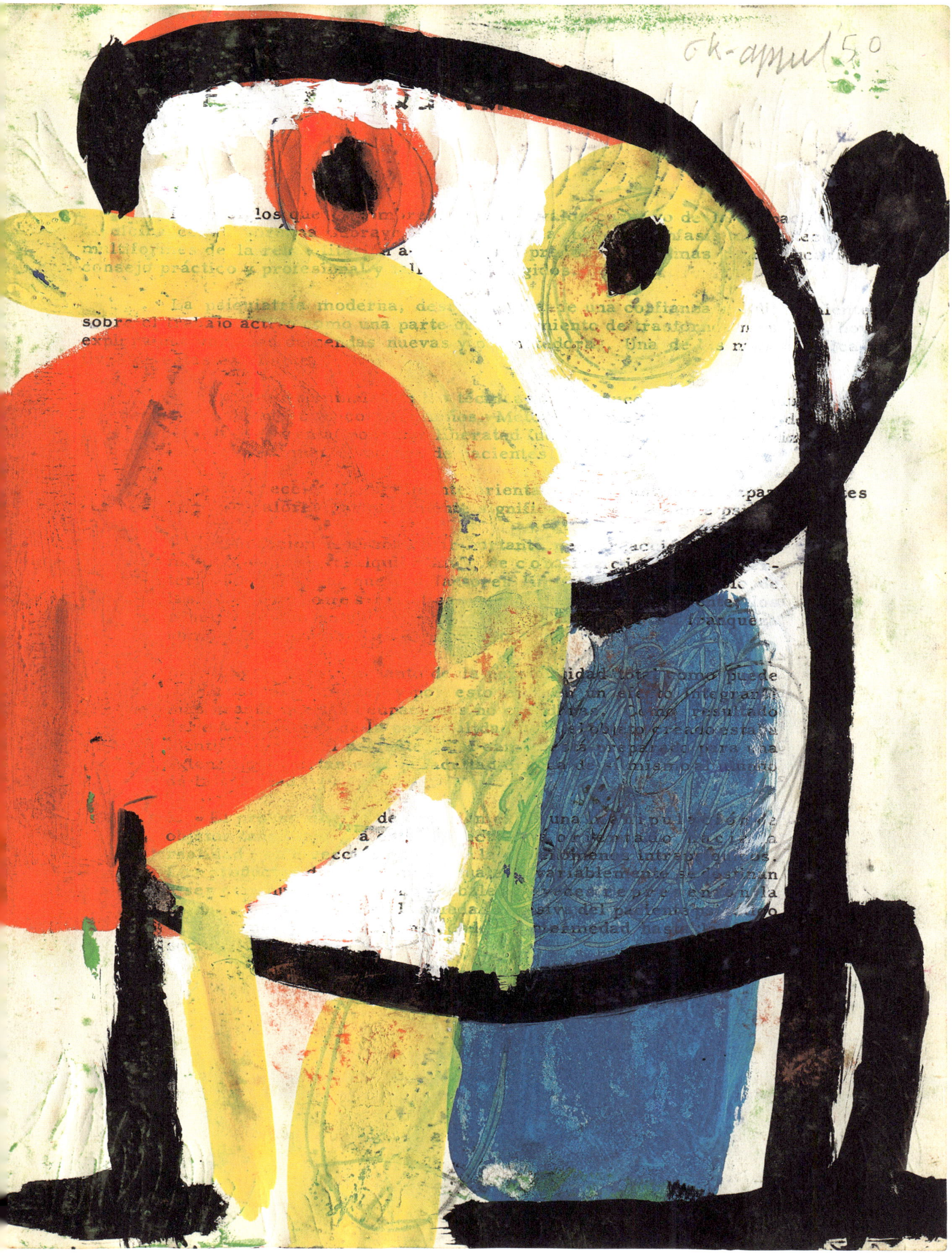

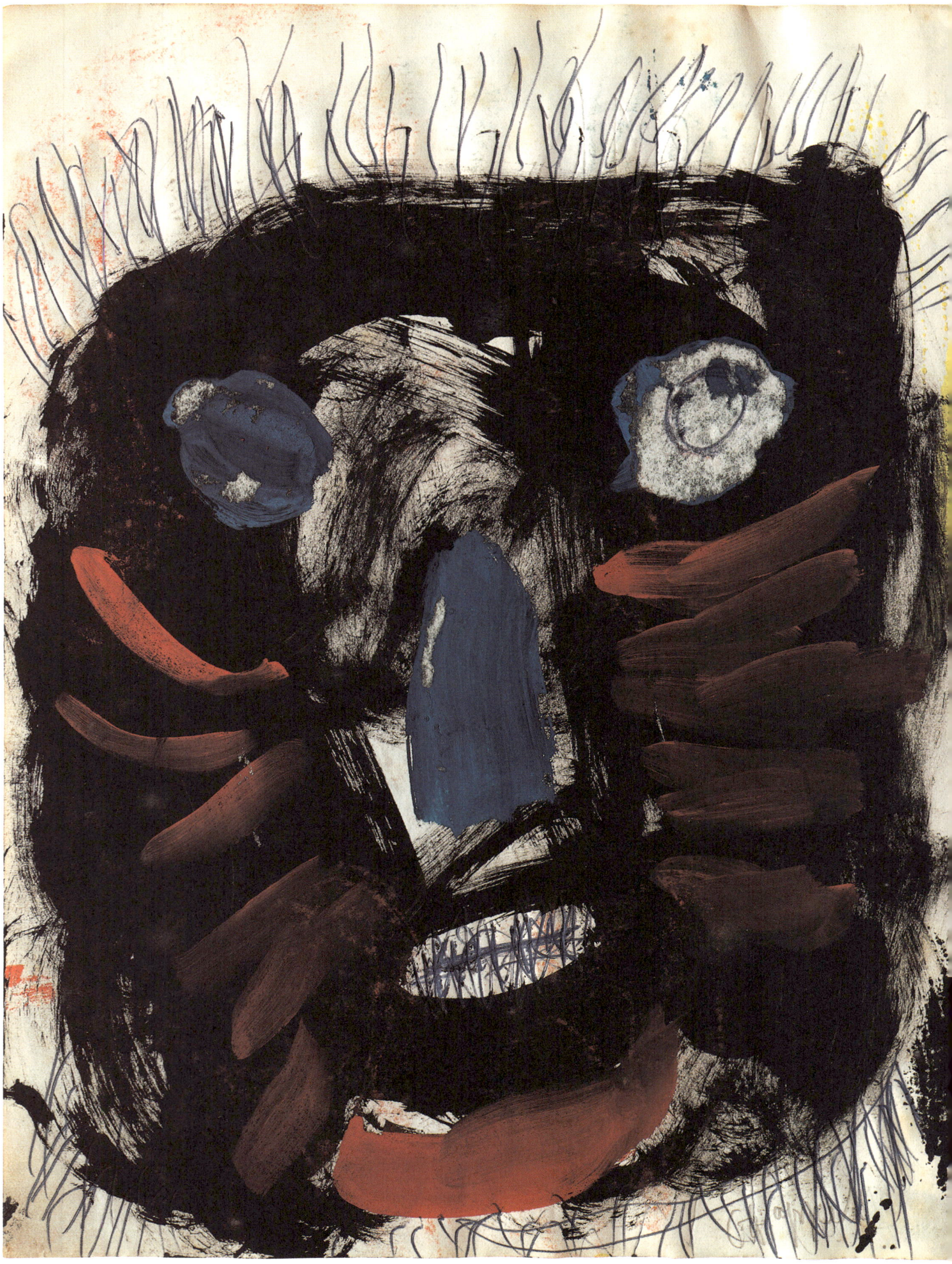

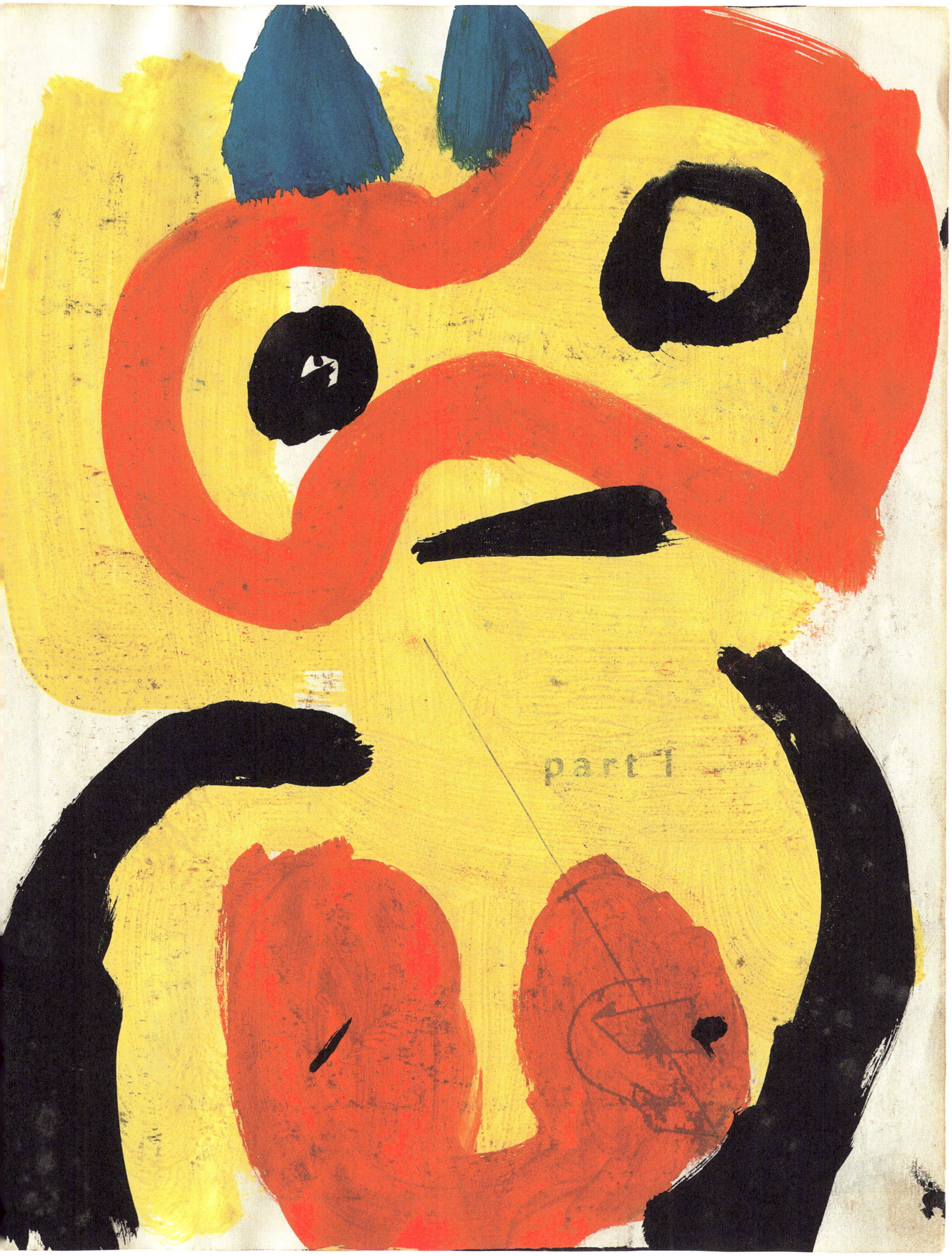
part 1

Evaluation of Psychopathological Art

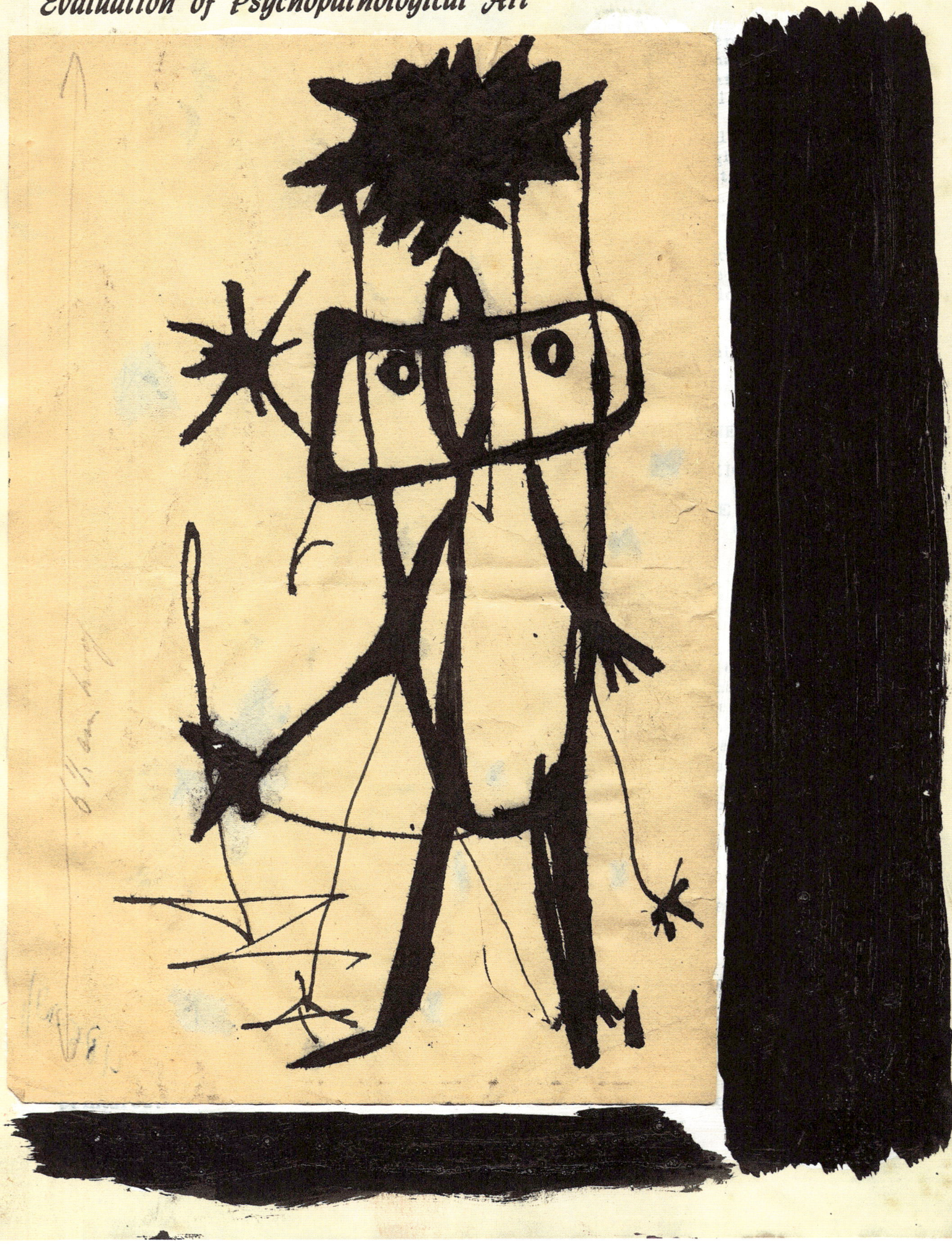

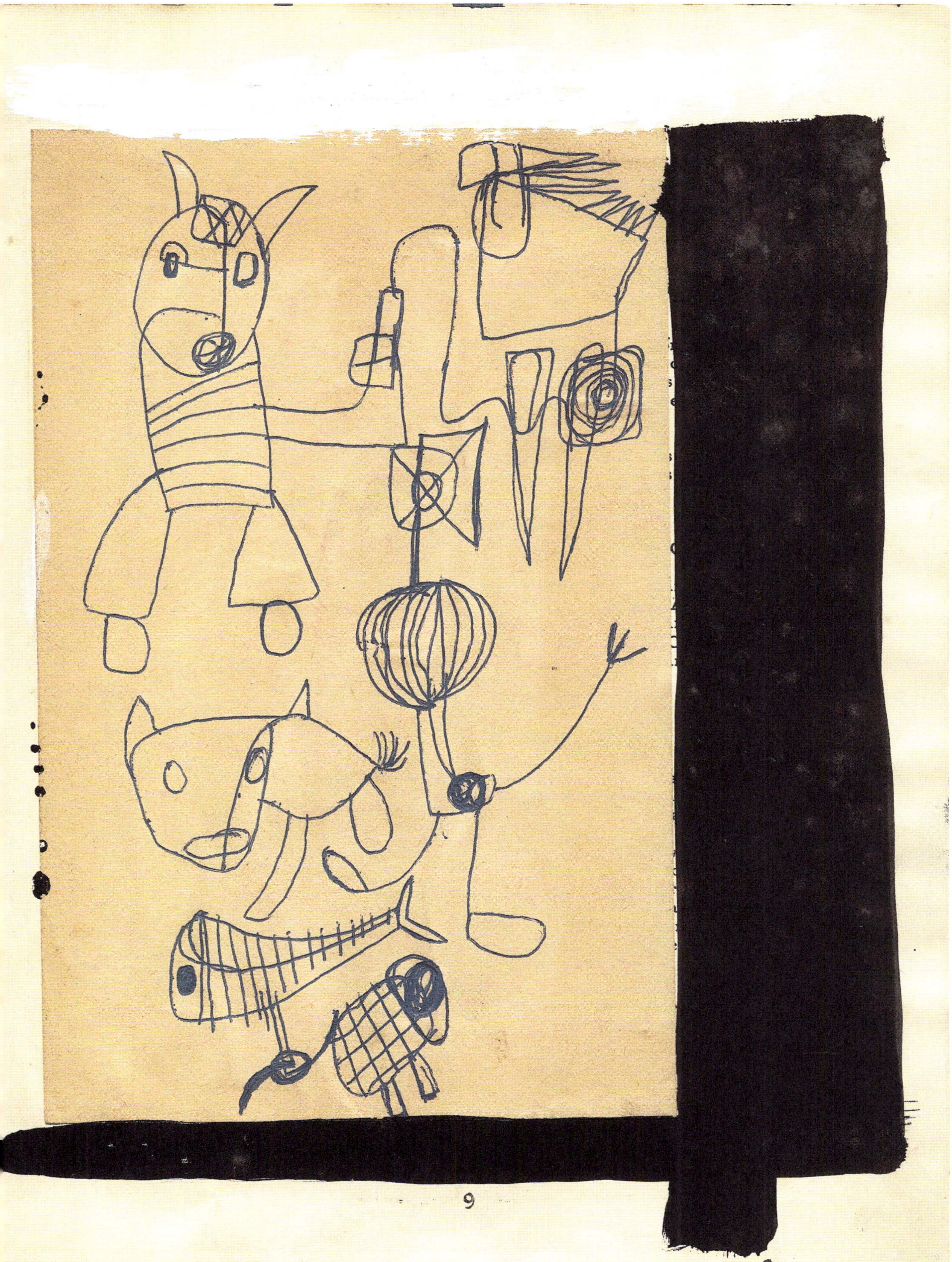

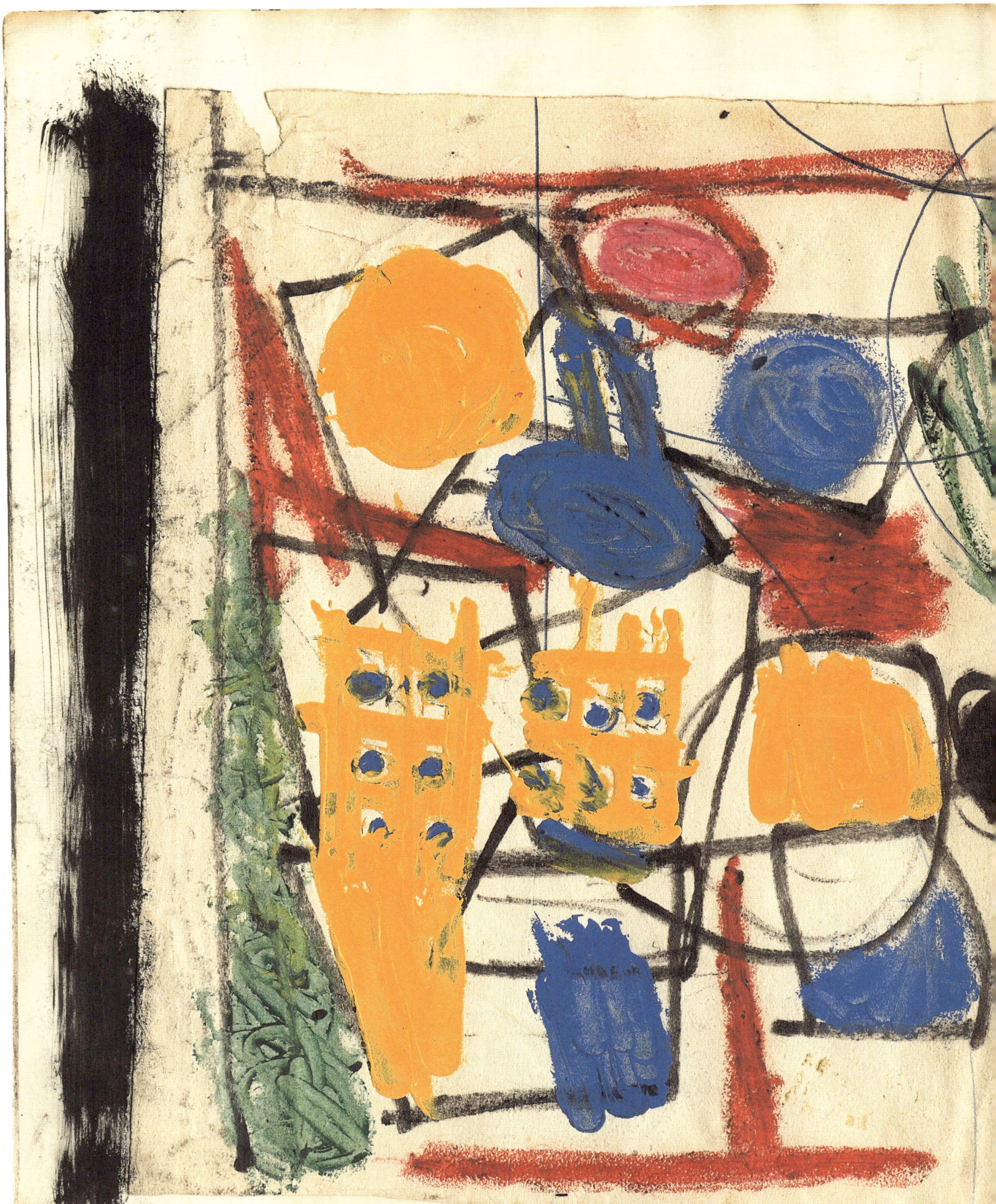
10

11

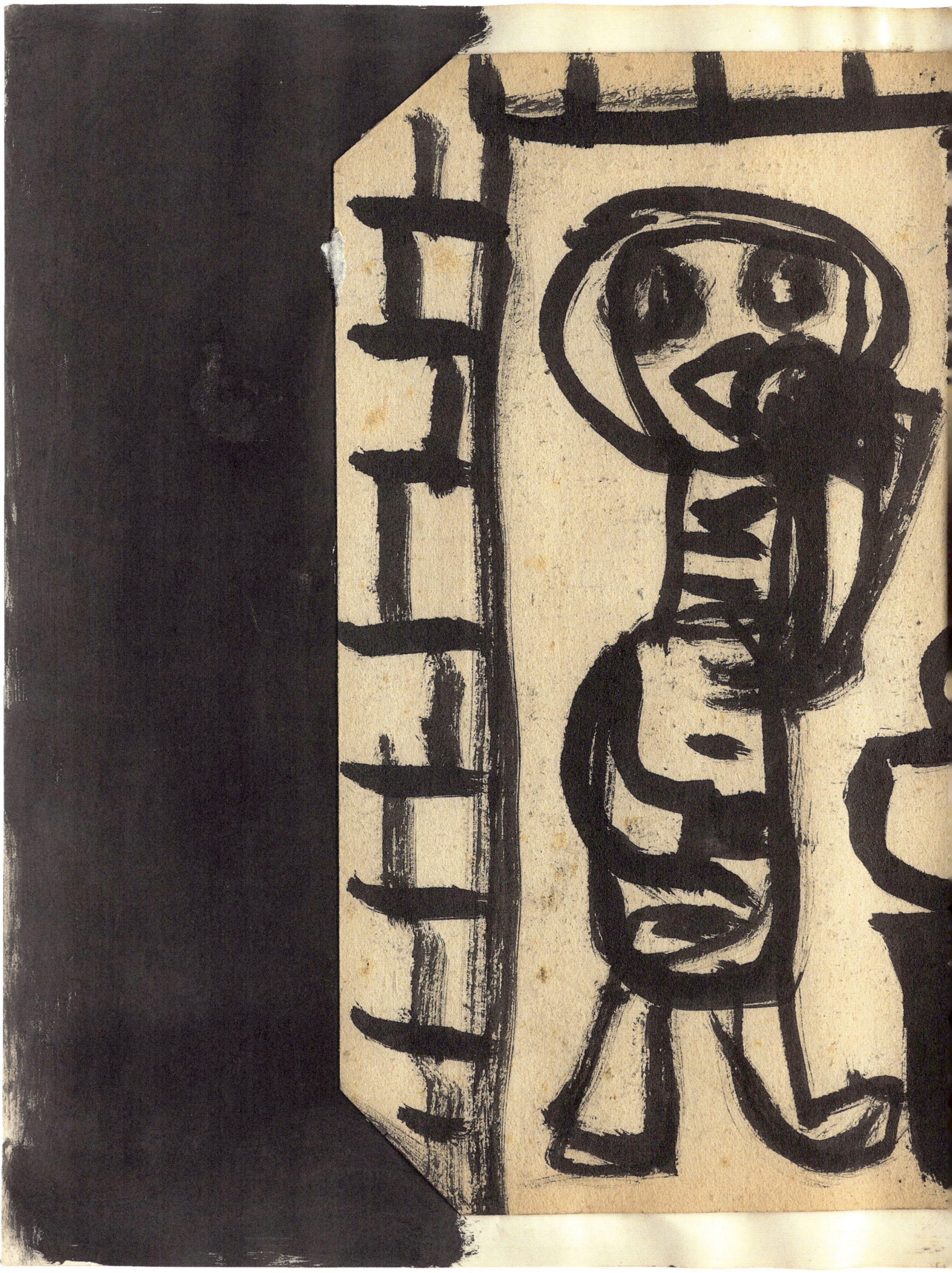

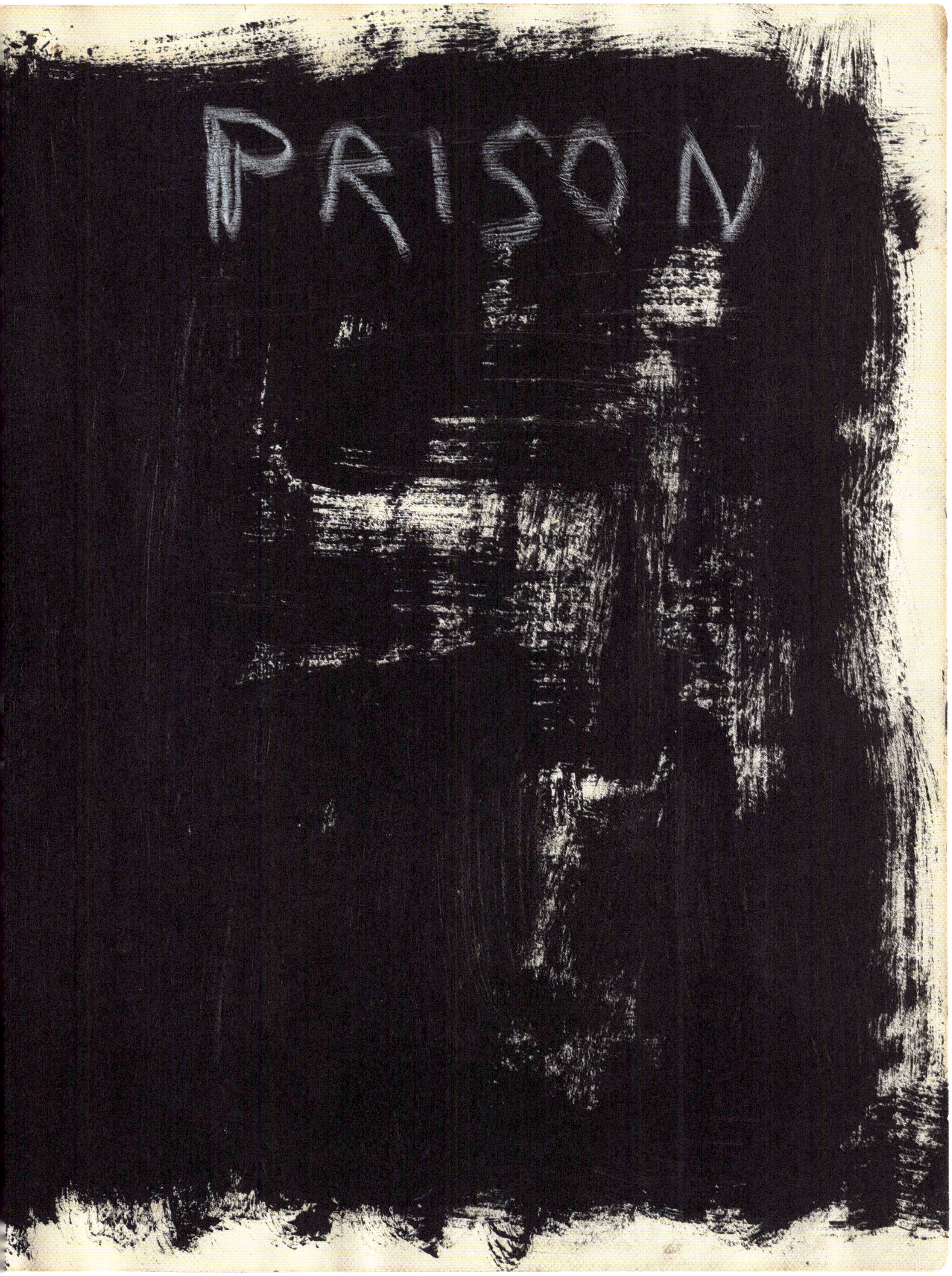
PRISON

Forme-Première Partie

5.
"Landscape with Trees" Huile

Malade:
Schizophrène, manque d'expression de pensées.

Traits caractéristiques:
Lignes droites, pas d'efforts de variations.

6.
"Landscape with Trees" Huile

Malade:
Schizophrène, pénurie d'expression de pensées, ton émotif monotone et vide.

Traits caractéristiques:
Lignes droites sans efforts de variations.

7.
"Tree" Huile

Malade:
Maniaque, e

Traits carac
Lignes
branches

Forma-Parte 1

5.
"Landscape with Trees" Pittura a olio

Malato:
Schizofrenico, pocchezza d'idee nel contenuto.

Caratteristiche:
Linee diritte, nullo tentativo di variazione.

6.
"Landscape with Trees" Pittura

Malato:
Schizofrenico, pocchezza
nel contenuto, il tono em
insípido e vacuo.

Caratteristiche:
Linee diritte, nullo te
variazione.

7.

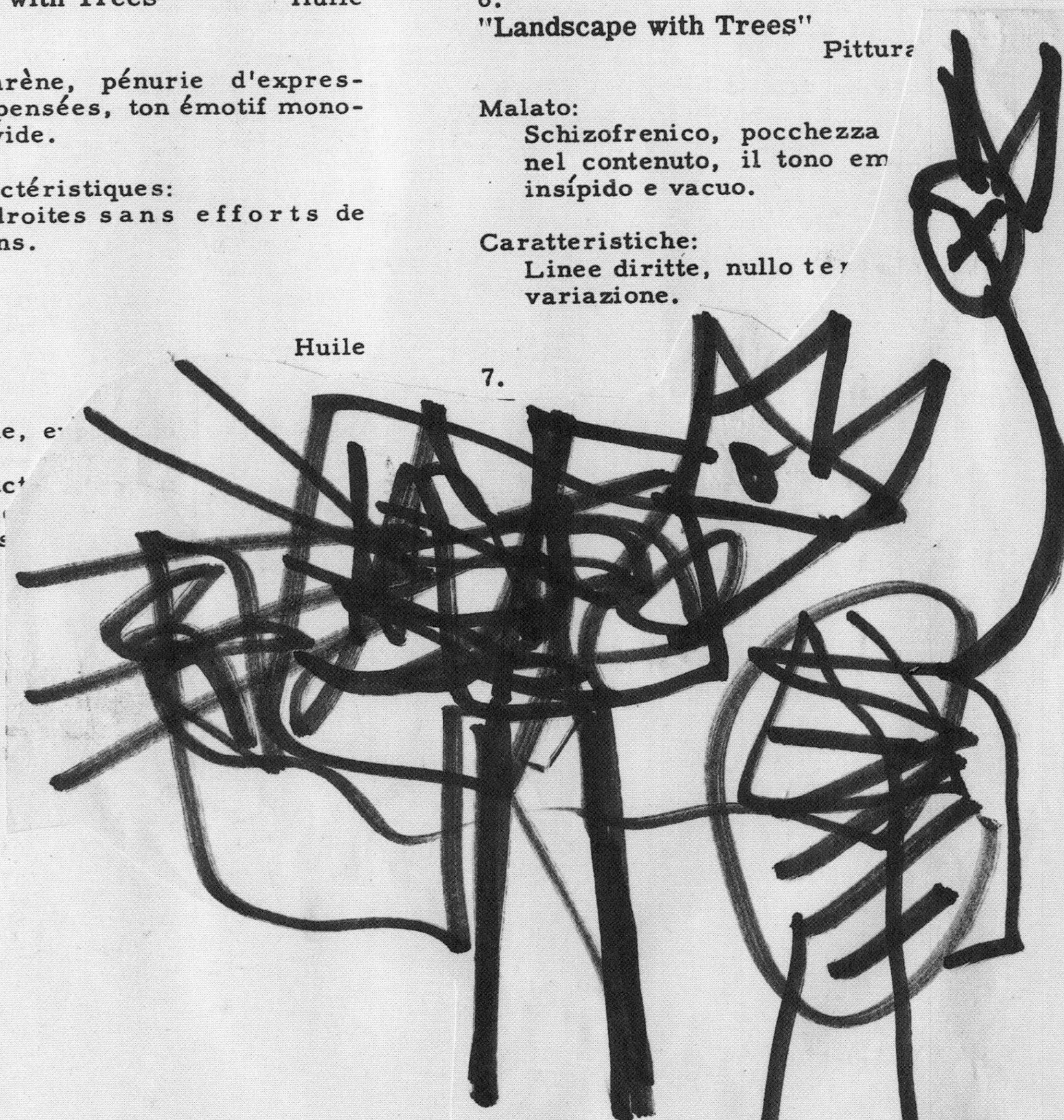

Form - Part 1

5.
Landscape with Trees Oil

Patient:
Schizophrenic, paucity of thought content.

Characteristics:
Straight lines, no attempts at variations.

6.
Landscape with Trees Oil

Patient:
Schizophrenic, paucity of thought content, flat and empty emotional tone.

Characteristics:
Straight lines with no attempts at variations.

7.
Tree Oil

Pa

Ch

Forma-Parte 1

5.
"Landscape with Trees" Al óleo

Paciente:
Esquizofrénico, pobreza de contenido intelectual

Características:
Líneas rectas, sin atentar variaciones.

6.
"Landscape with Trees" Al óleo

Paciente:
Esquizofrénico, pobreza de contenido intelectual, tono emocional superficial y sin sentido.

Características:
Líneas rectas sin atentar variaciones.

7
Al óleo

ndioso.

abundancia

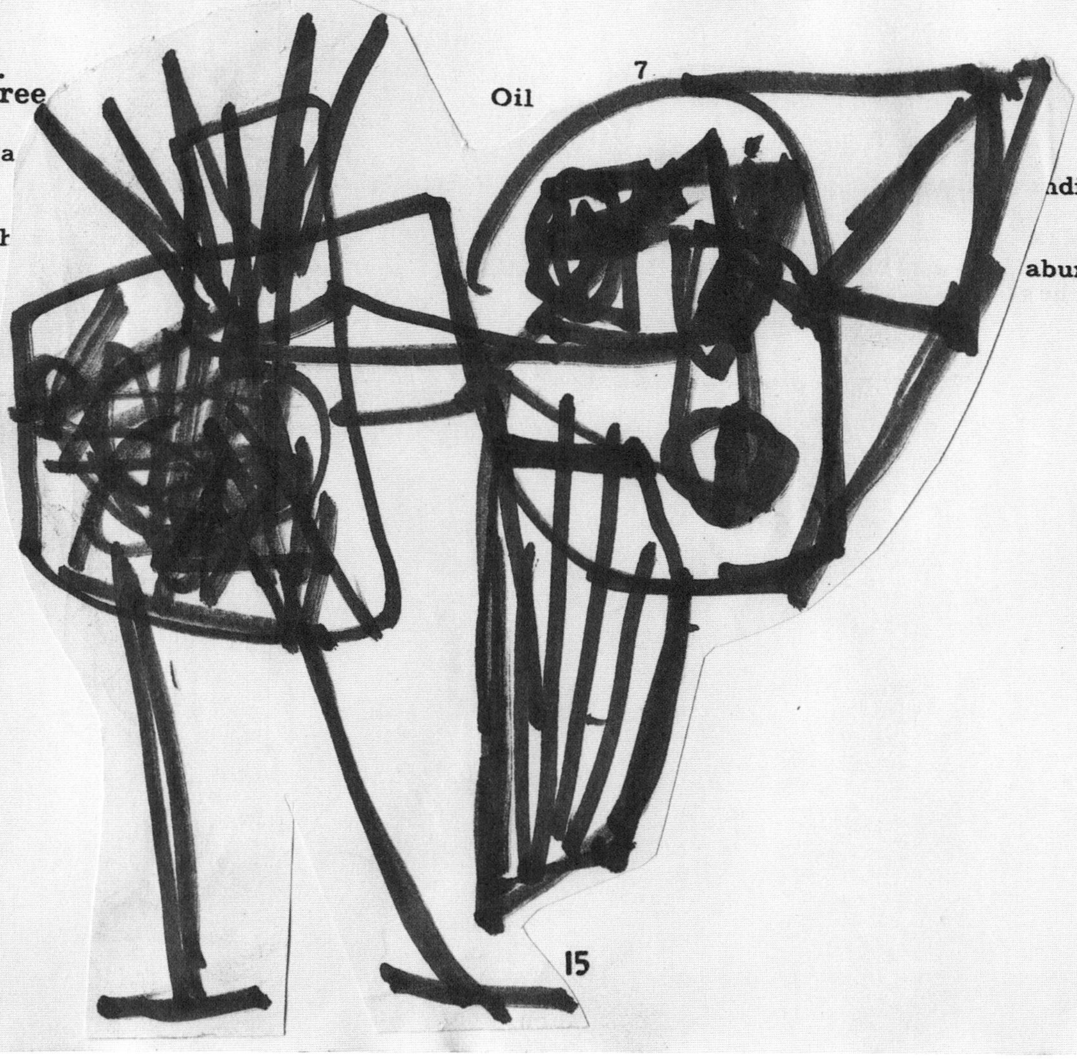

Forme-S

8.
"Cat" … a a olio

Malade:
Etudian … Schizo-
(de bonn … realità,
caractè

Traits cara
Allonge

9.
"Lovers" … a a olio

Malade:
Etudian … Schizo-
(de b … realtà,
chimér

Traits car
Allonge

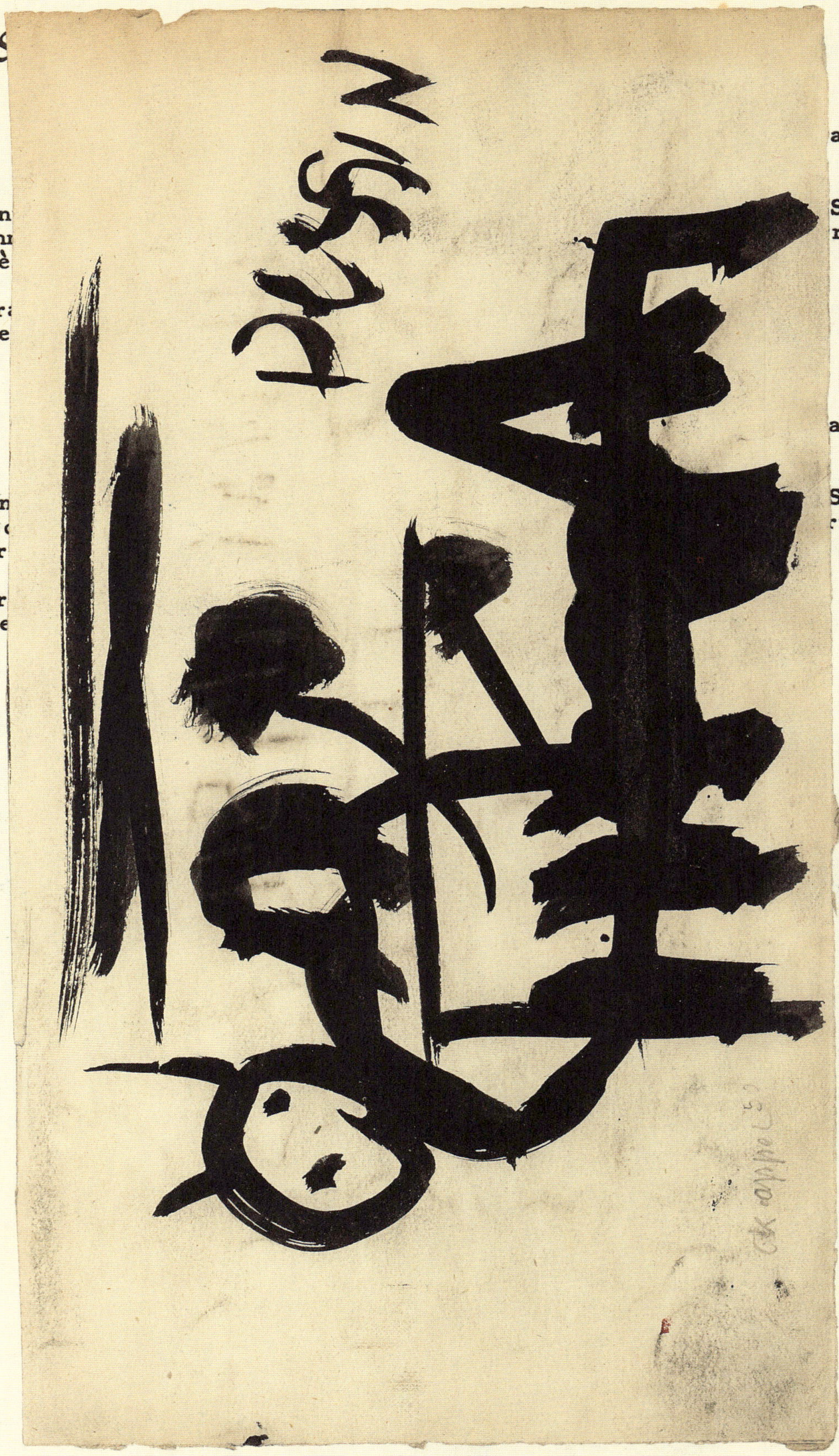

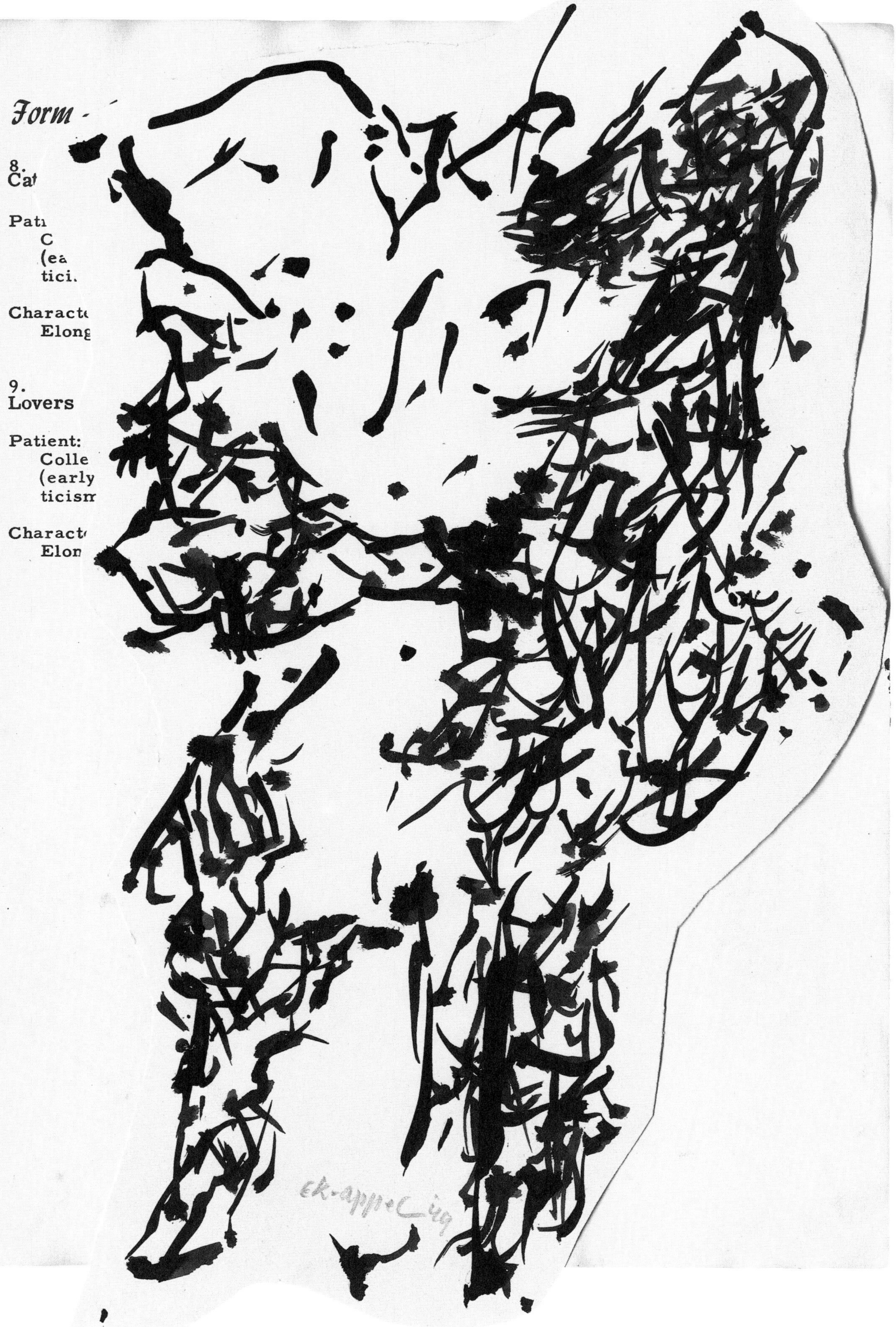
Form -
8.
Ca
Pat
C
(ea
tici.
Charact
Elong
9.
Lovers
Patient:
Colle
(early
ticism
Charact
Elon

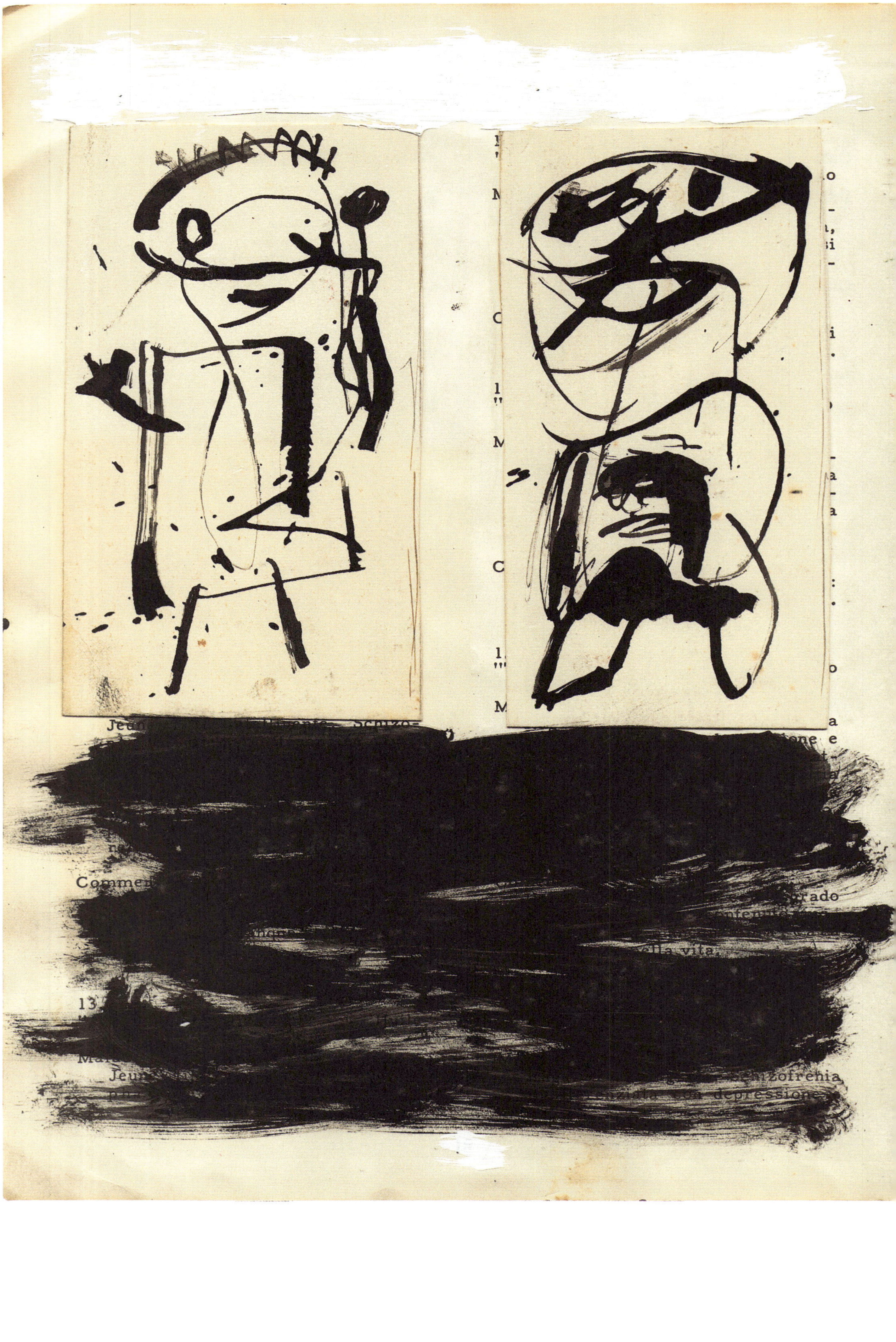

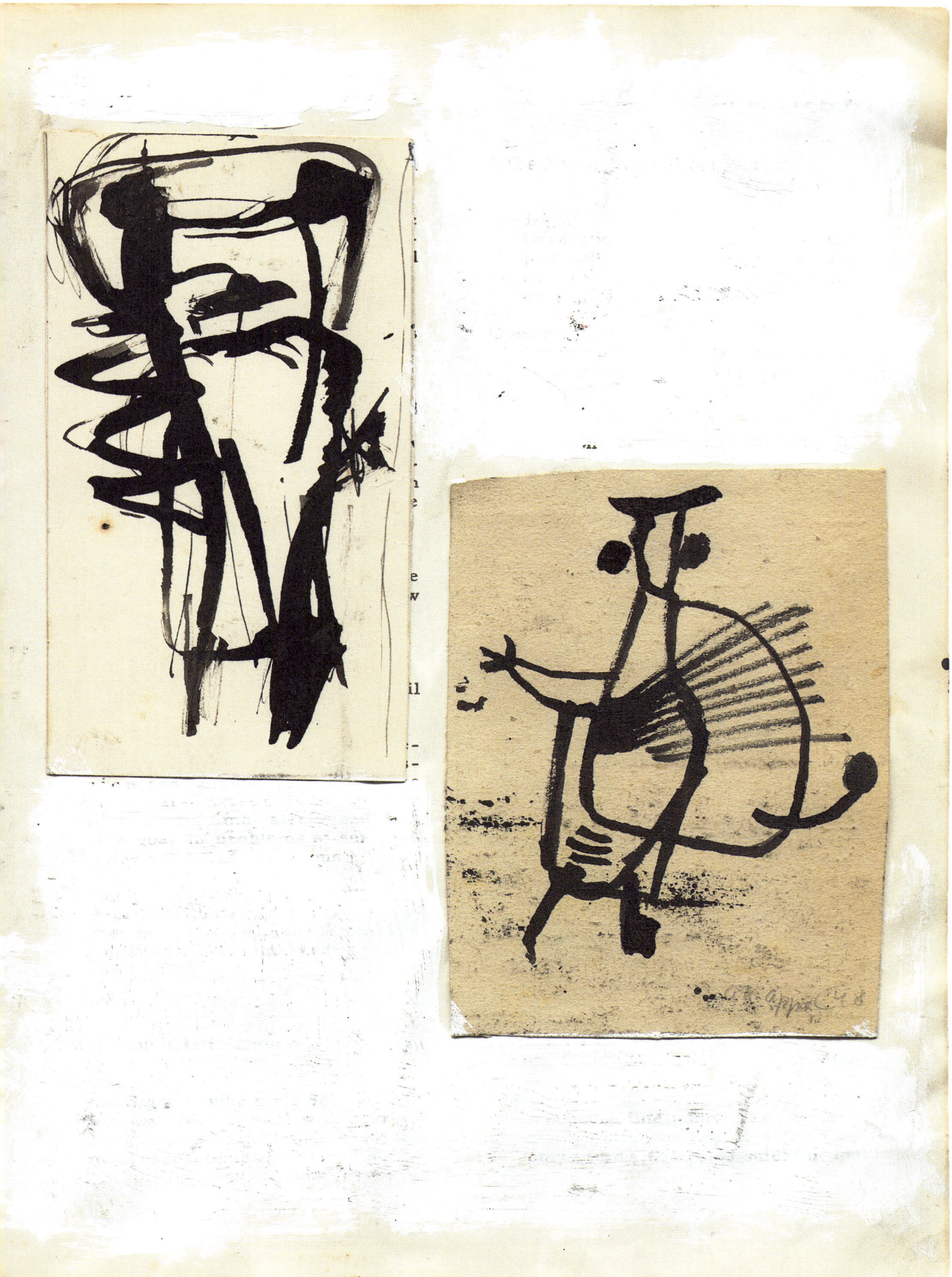

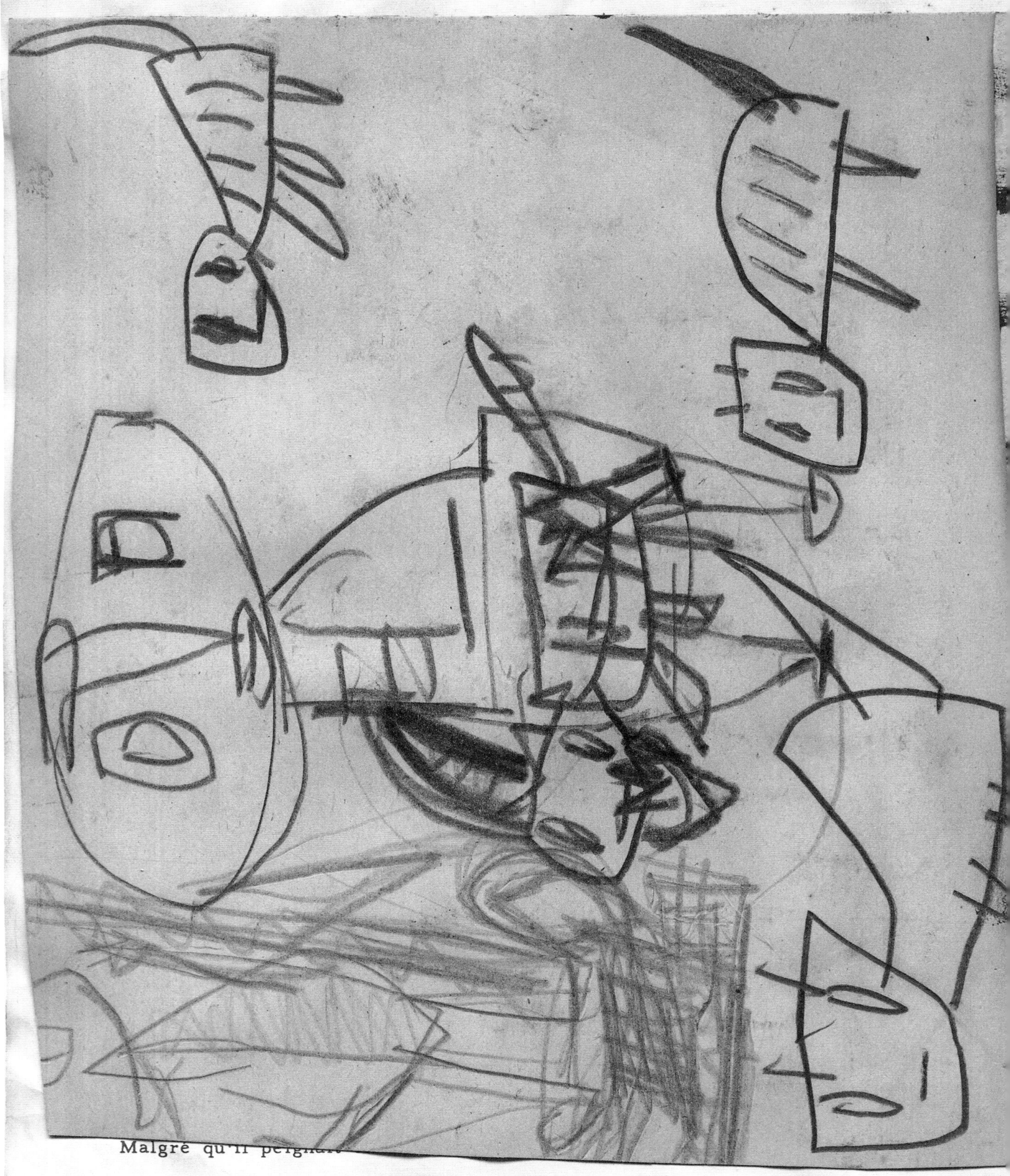

Malgré qu'il peigna

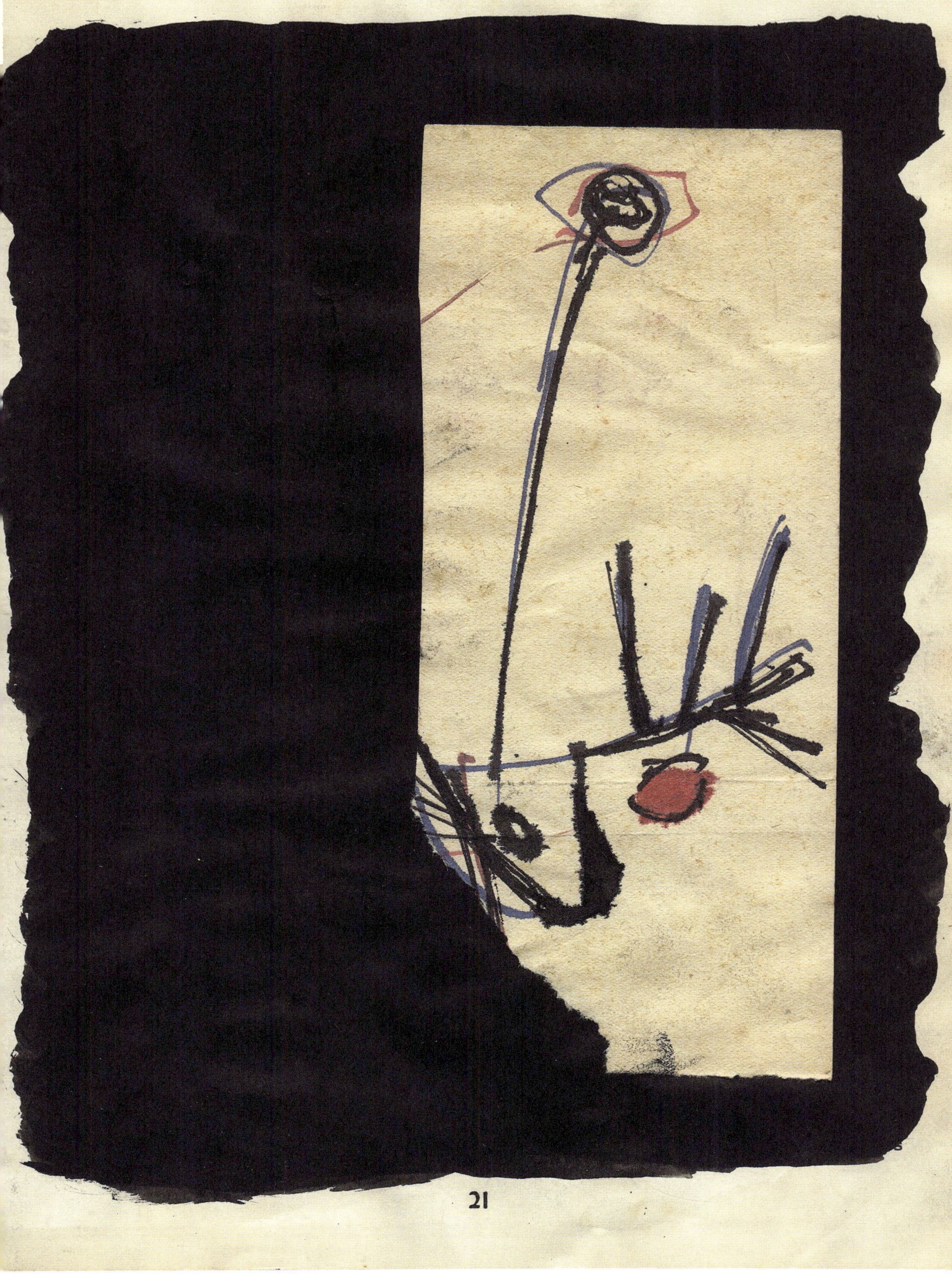

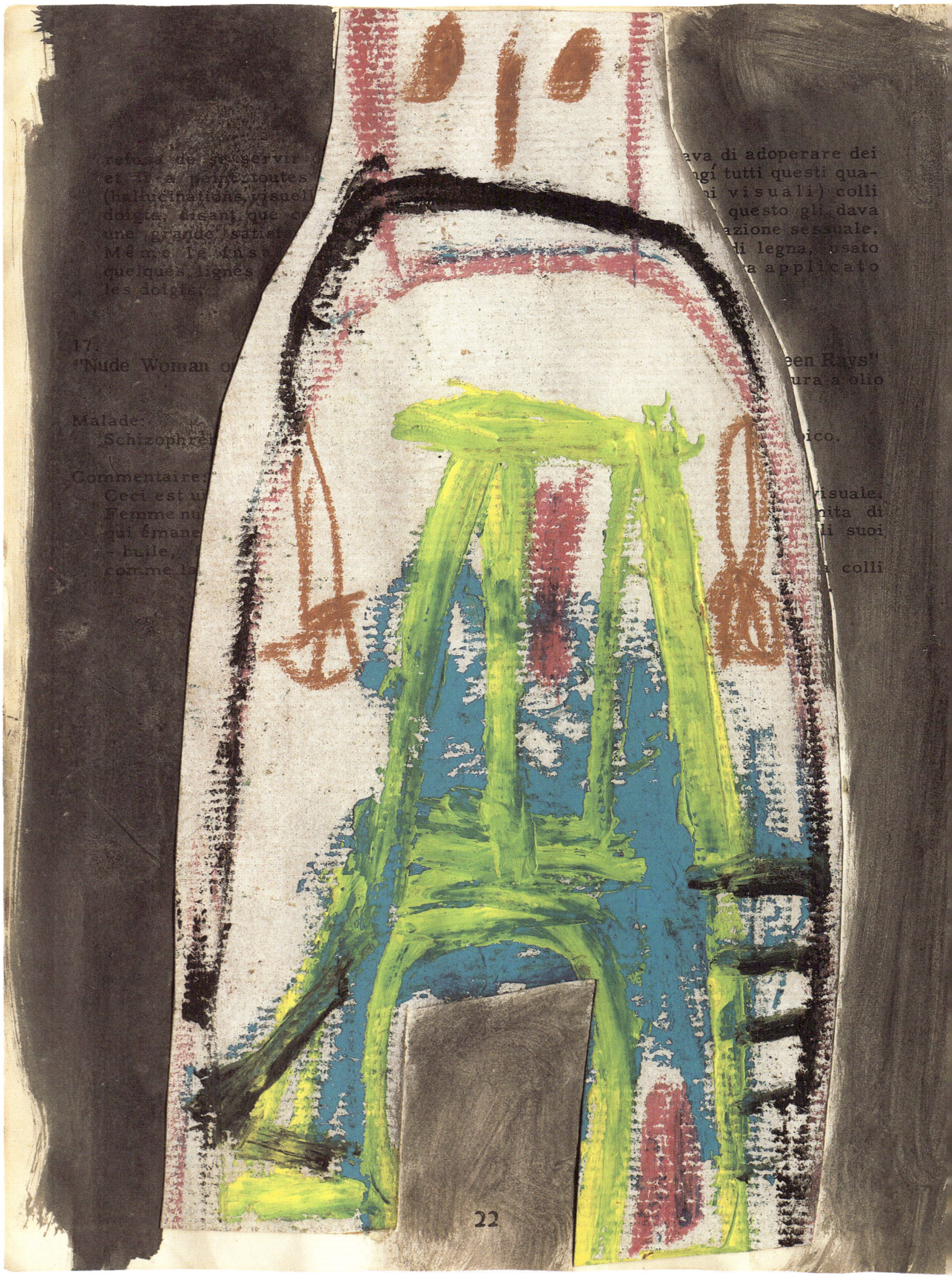

ava di adoperare dei
tutti questi qua-
visuali) colli
questo gli dava
azione sessuale.
di legna, usato
a applicato
les doigts.
17:
"Nude Woman
een Rays"
ura a olio
Malade:
Commentaire
visuale.
colli
22

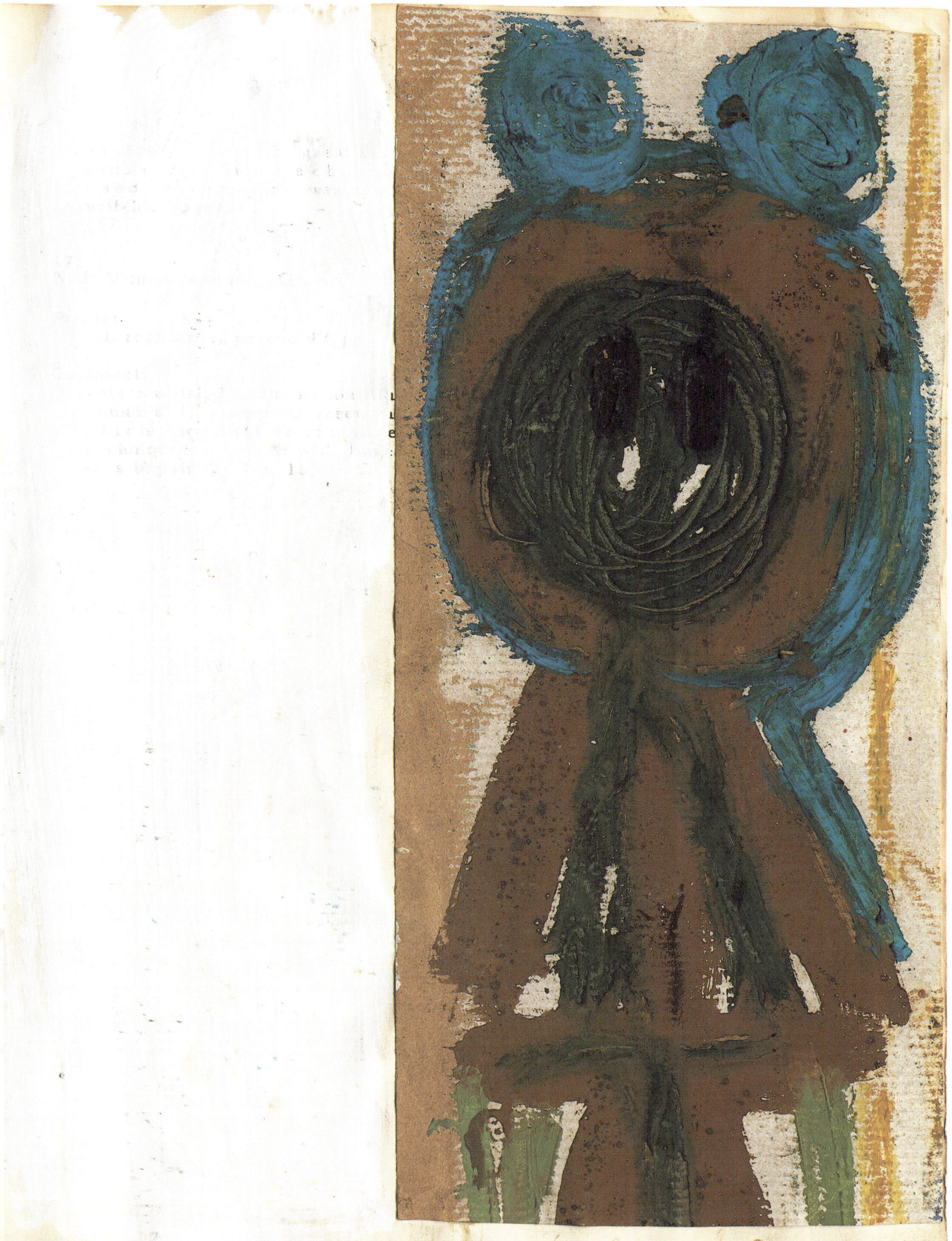

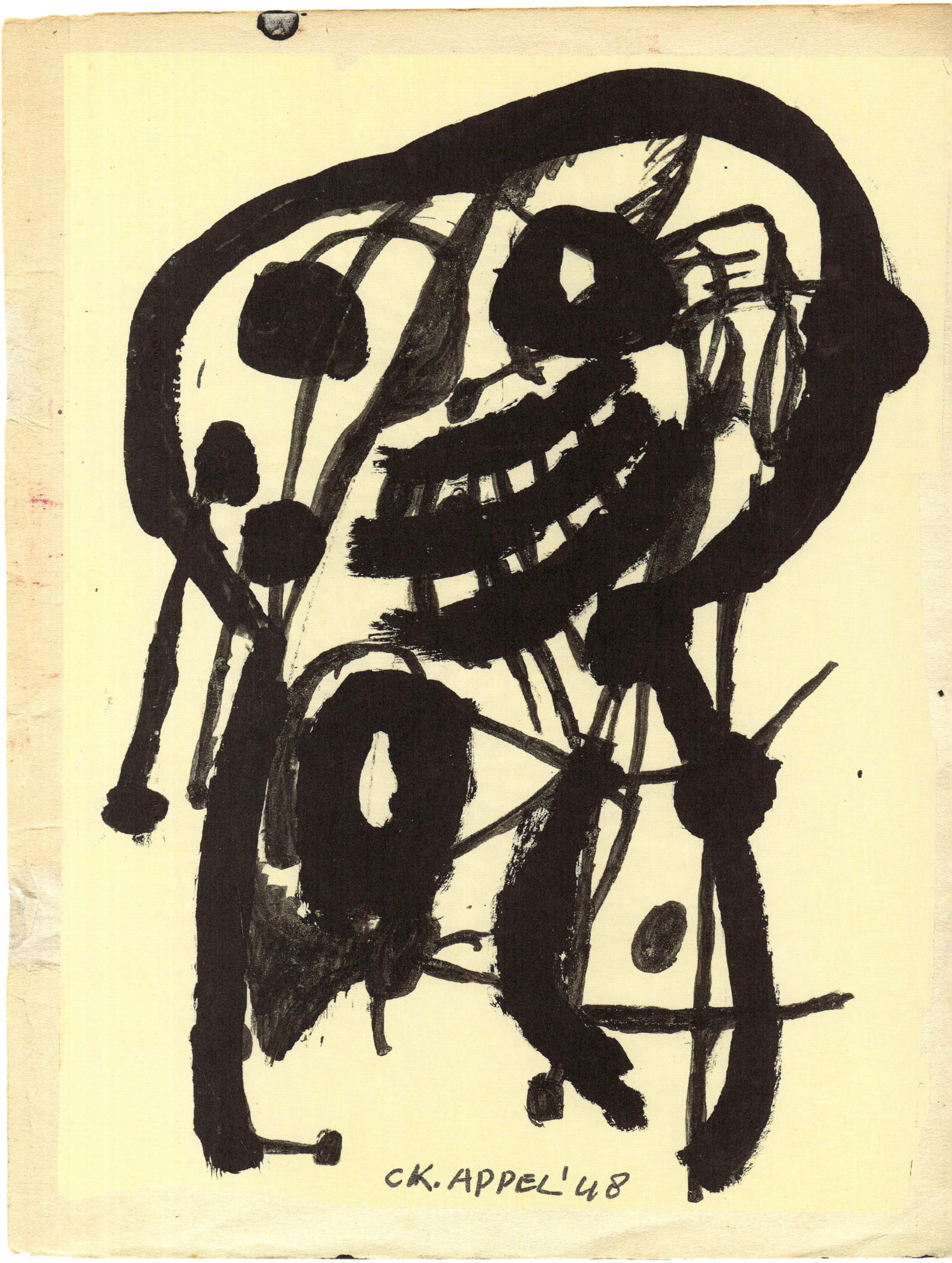
CK. APPEL '48

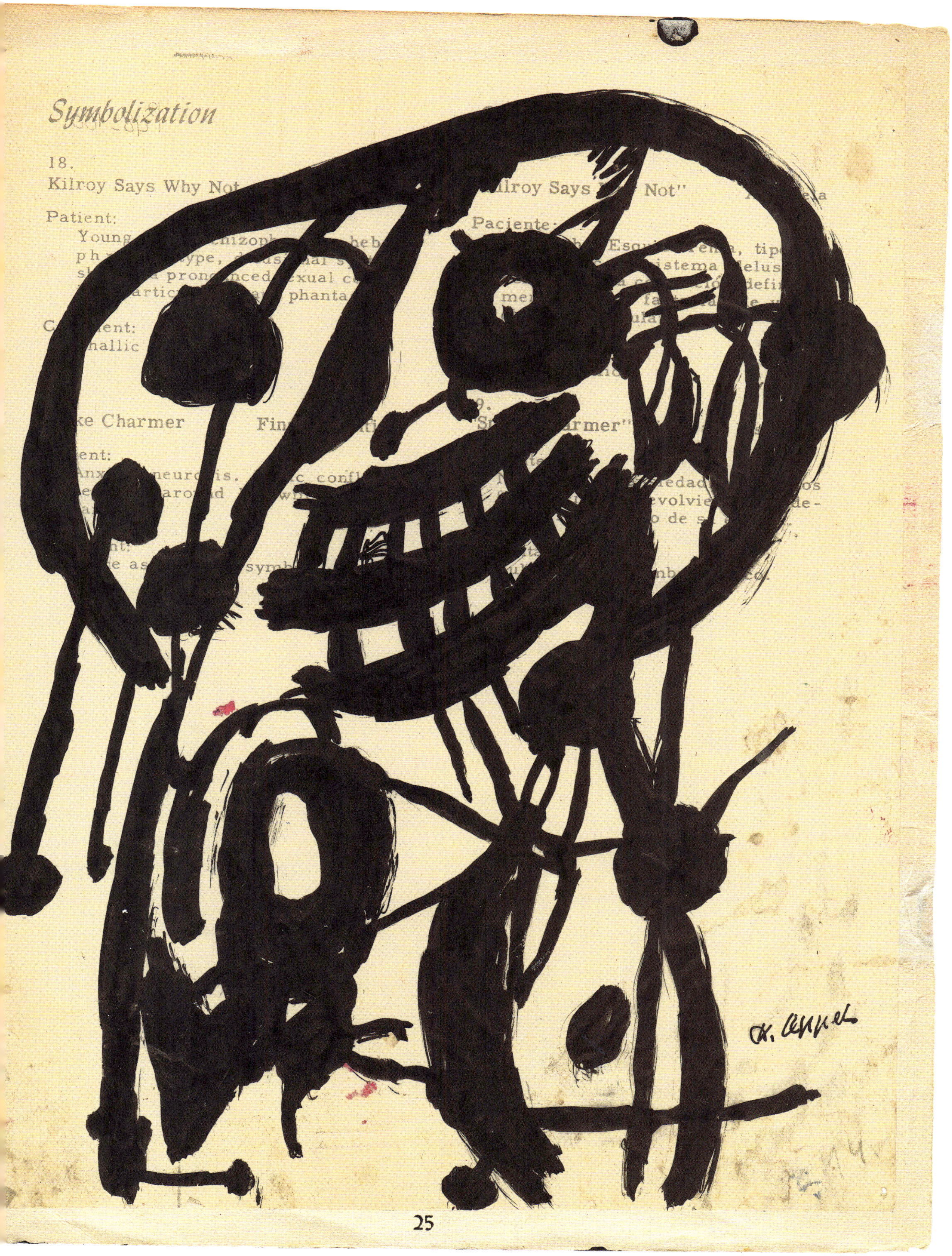
Symbolization
18.
Kilroy Says Why Not
Patient:
Paciente:
25

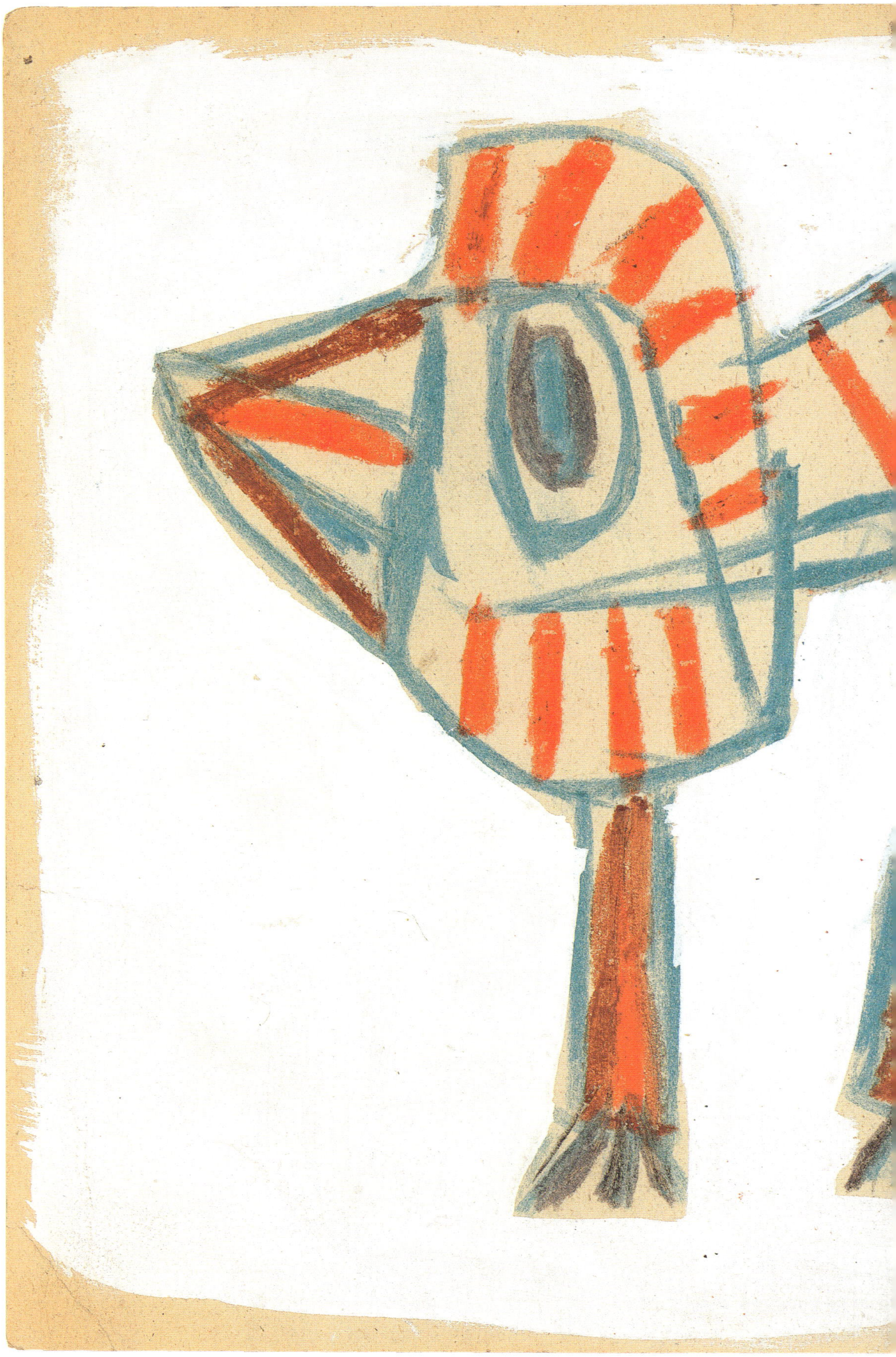

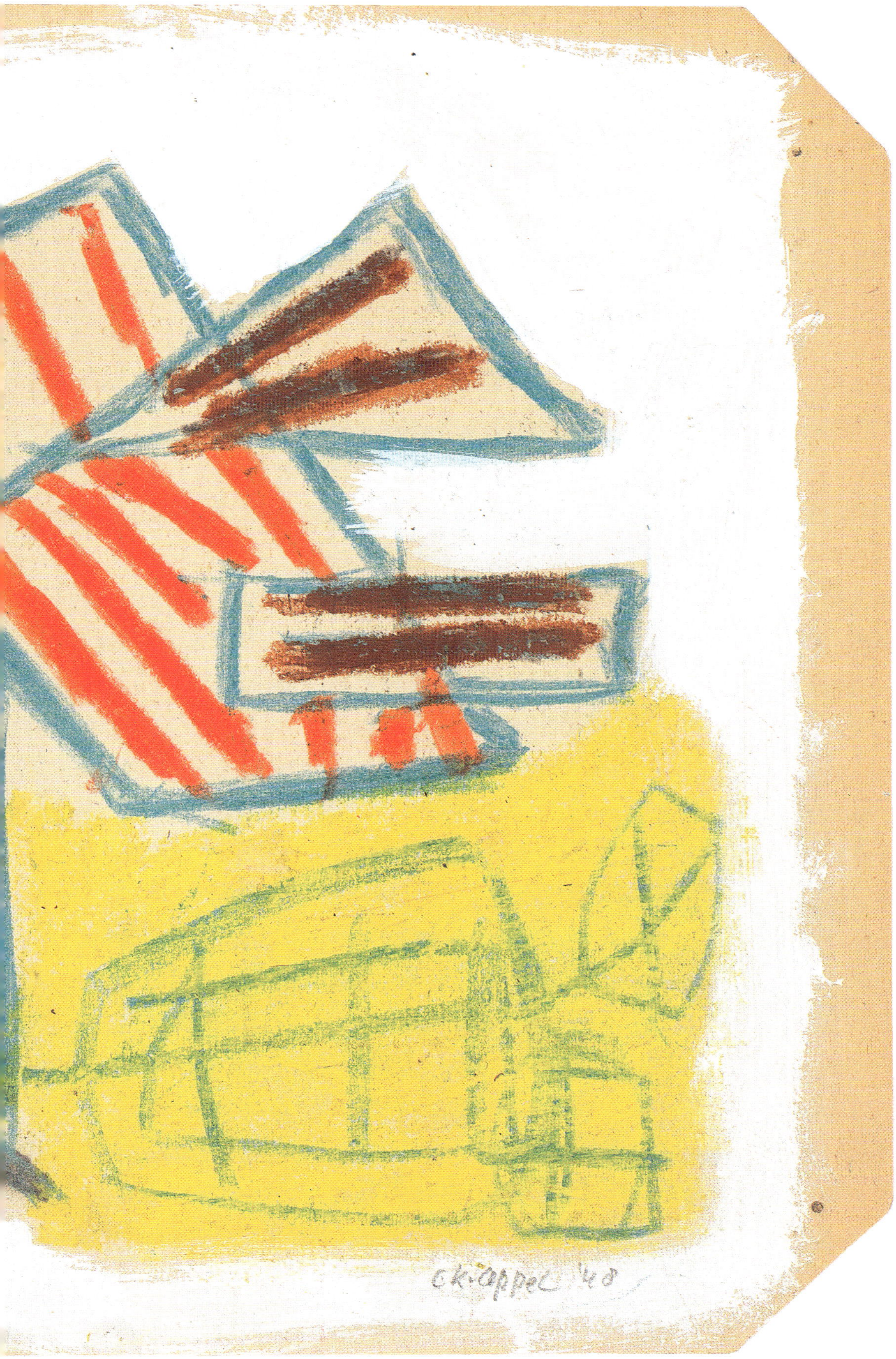
ck appel '48

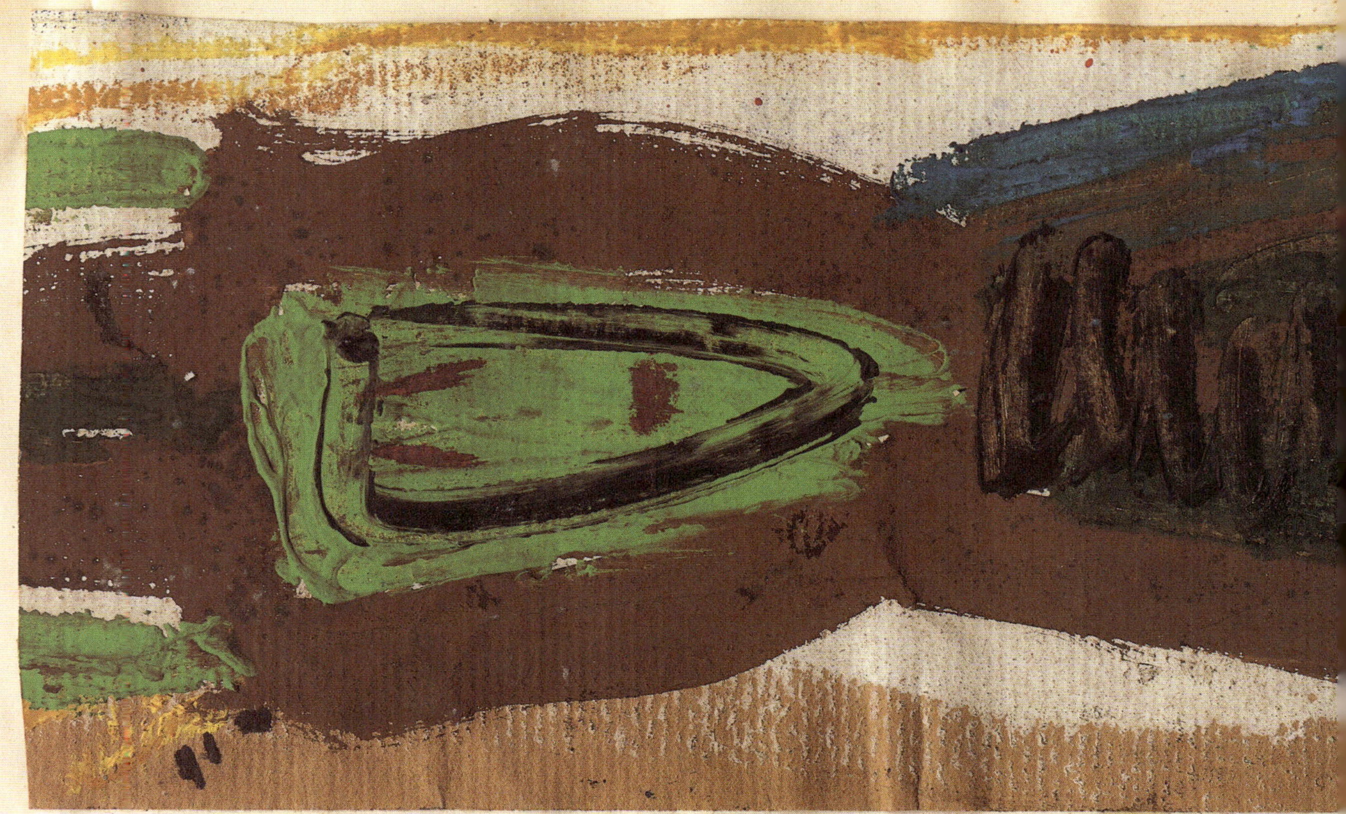

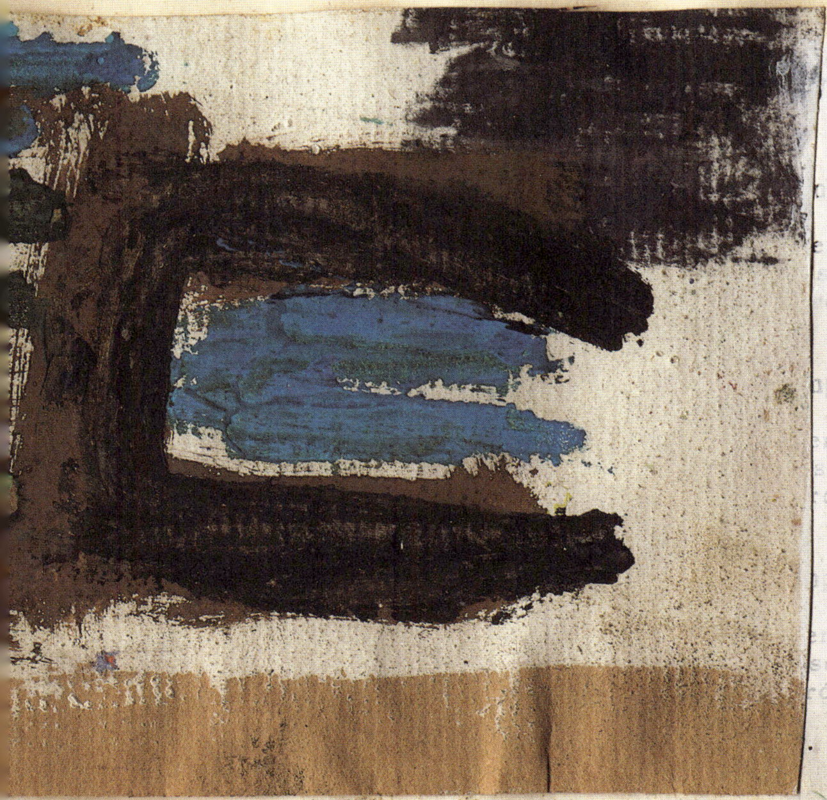

...aración

...posició... ...l óleo

...ente:
...squizofr...ico, ...ipo ...anoide,
...ónico. ...re...no

...position ...l óleo

...ente:
...squizofrénico ...po paranoide,
...ónico De...eis...o.

...posi...on" ...Al óleo

...ente
...squizofrénico, ...ipo paranoide,
...ónico. Dereismo.

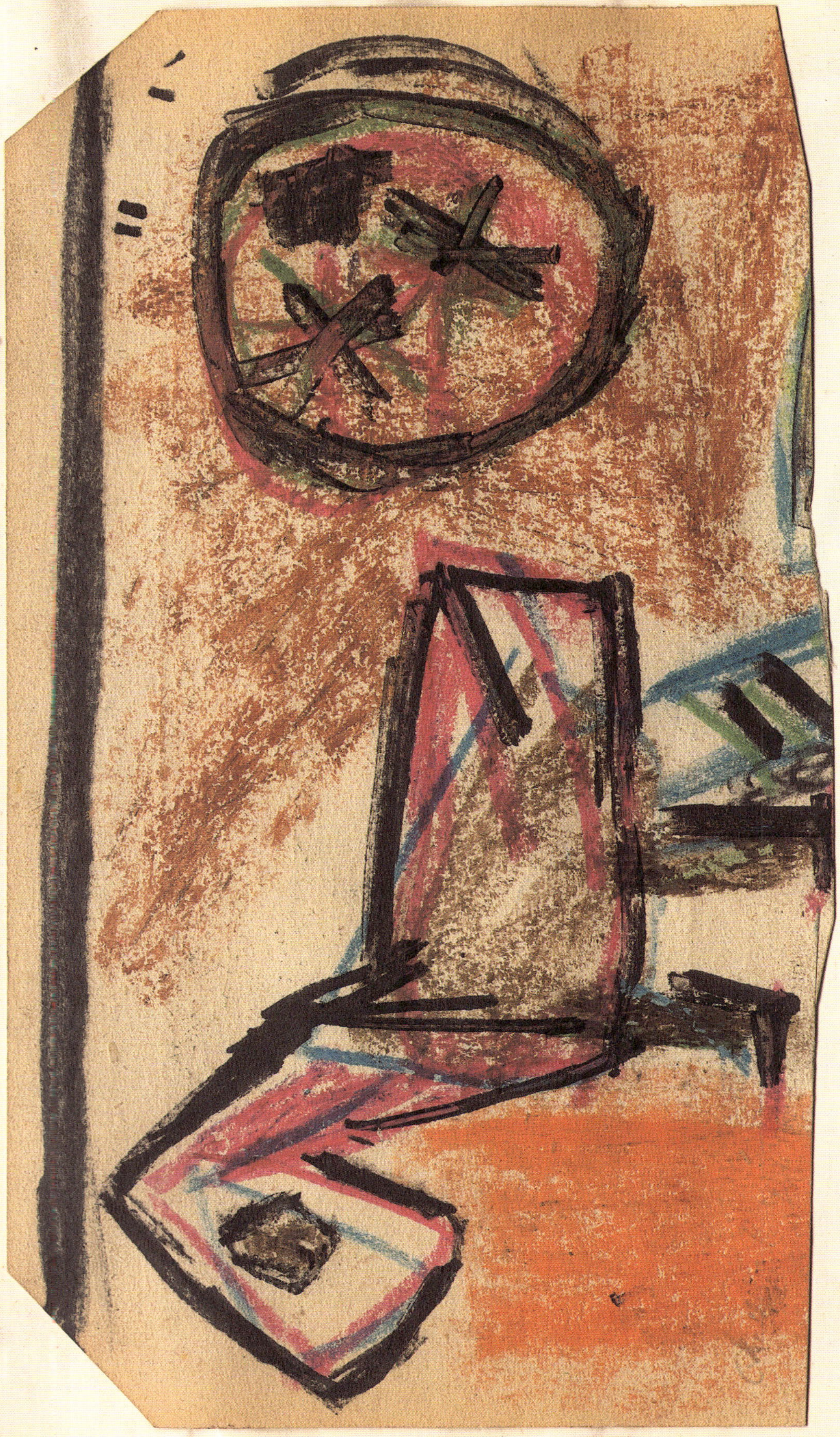

part 2

23. Dock

Diagnostic: Schizophrénie, type paranoide.

Diagnosi: Schizofrenia, tipo paranoido.

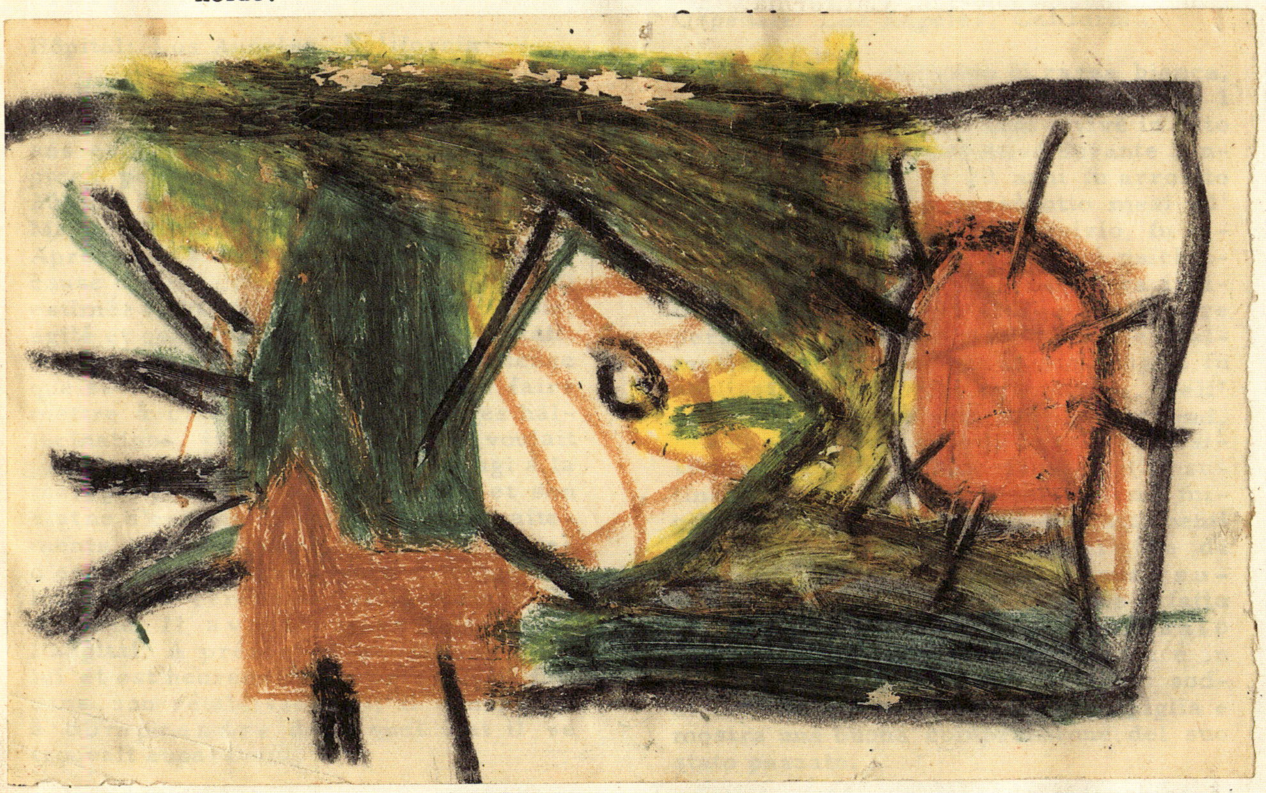

Depuis les premières semaines à la classe d'art, le malade a montré beaucoup de talent en peignant à l'aquarelle, malgré qu'il était agité et inquiet, ne pouvant pas finir les peintures qu'il avait commencées. La première peinture qu'il compléta a été montrée à l'exposition nationale d'arts des vétérans, et il a reçu le second prix. Avec cet encouragement son intérêt à la peinture augmenta, et il devint plus sûr de sa technique. Depuis qu'il est sorti de l'hôpital, le malade va a un institut d'art avancé, et il produit de très belles pièces d'art.

Dalle prime settimane, quando era assegnato al corso di pittura, il paziente dimostrava una notevole destrezza nella tecnica all'acquarello, benchè era inquieto ad ansioso, non in grado di finire nessuna delle pitture comminciate. Il primo quadro, il quale completò, fu ammesso in un'esposizione nazionale di pittura di Veterani di Guerra e ricevì il secondo premio. Questo incoraggiamento aumentò suo interesse nella pittura e sua tecnica divenì più sicura. Dal tempo quando partì dall'Ospedale, il paziente ha seguito un corso avanzato in una scuola di pittura ed è stato straordinariamente produttivo sul punto di vista dell'arte.

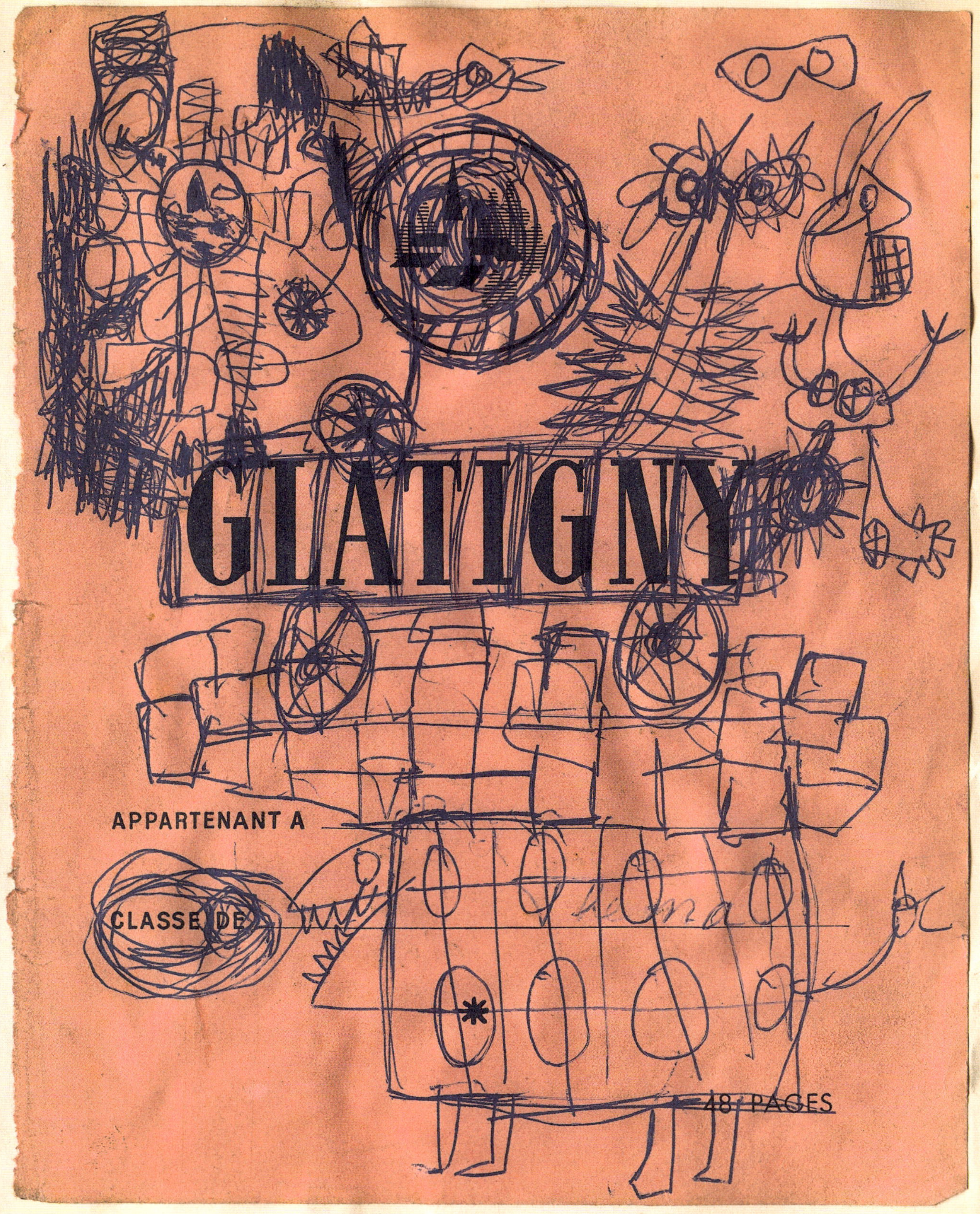
GLATIGNY
APPARTENANT A
CLASSE DE
48 PAGES

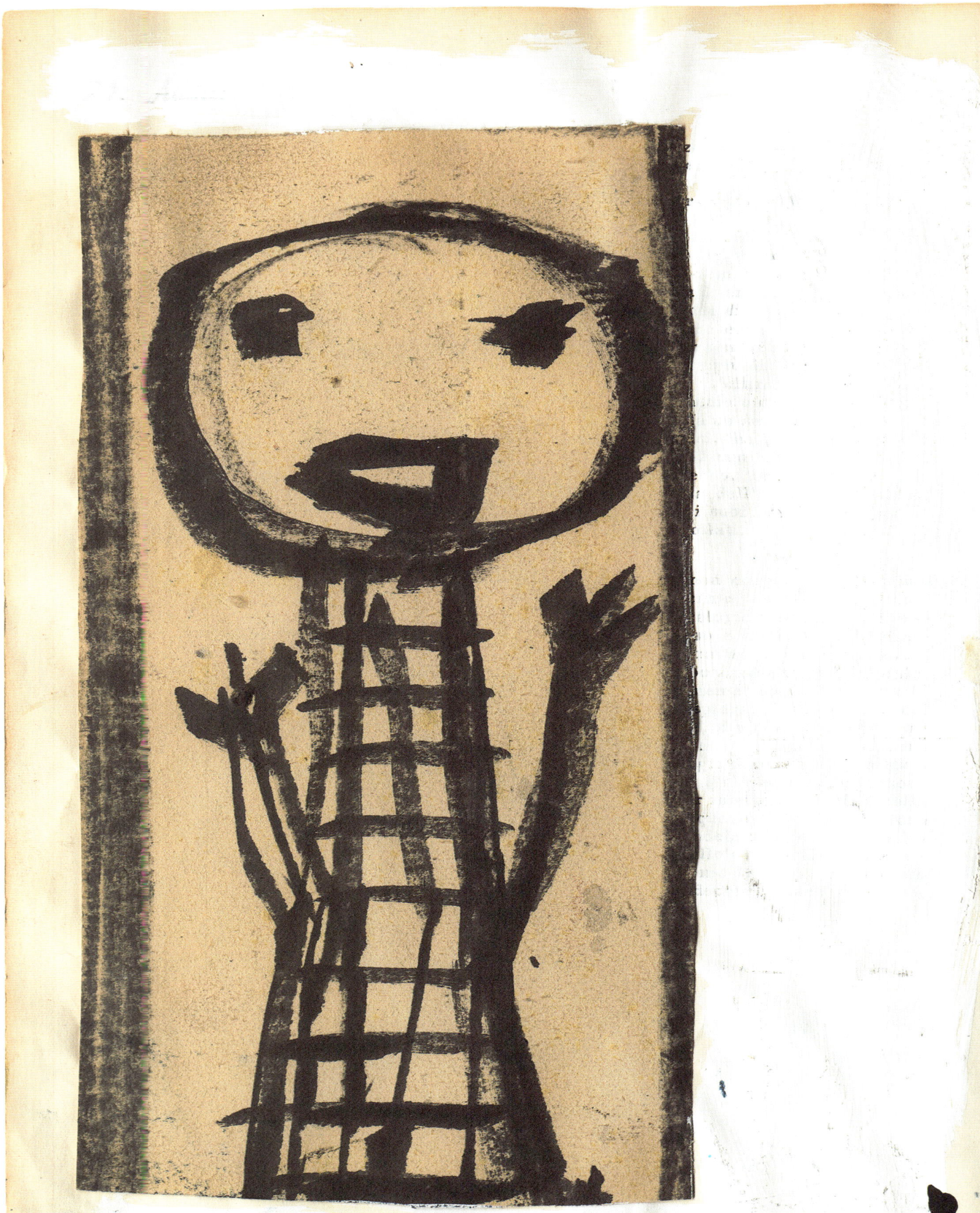

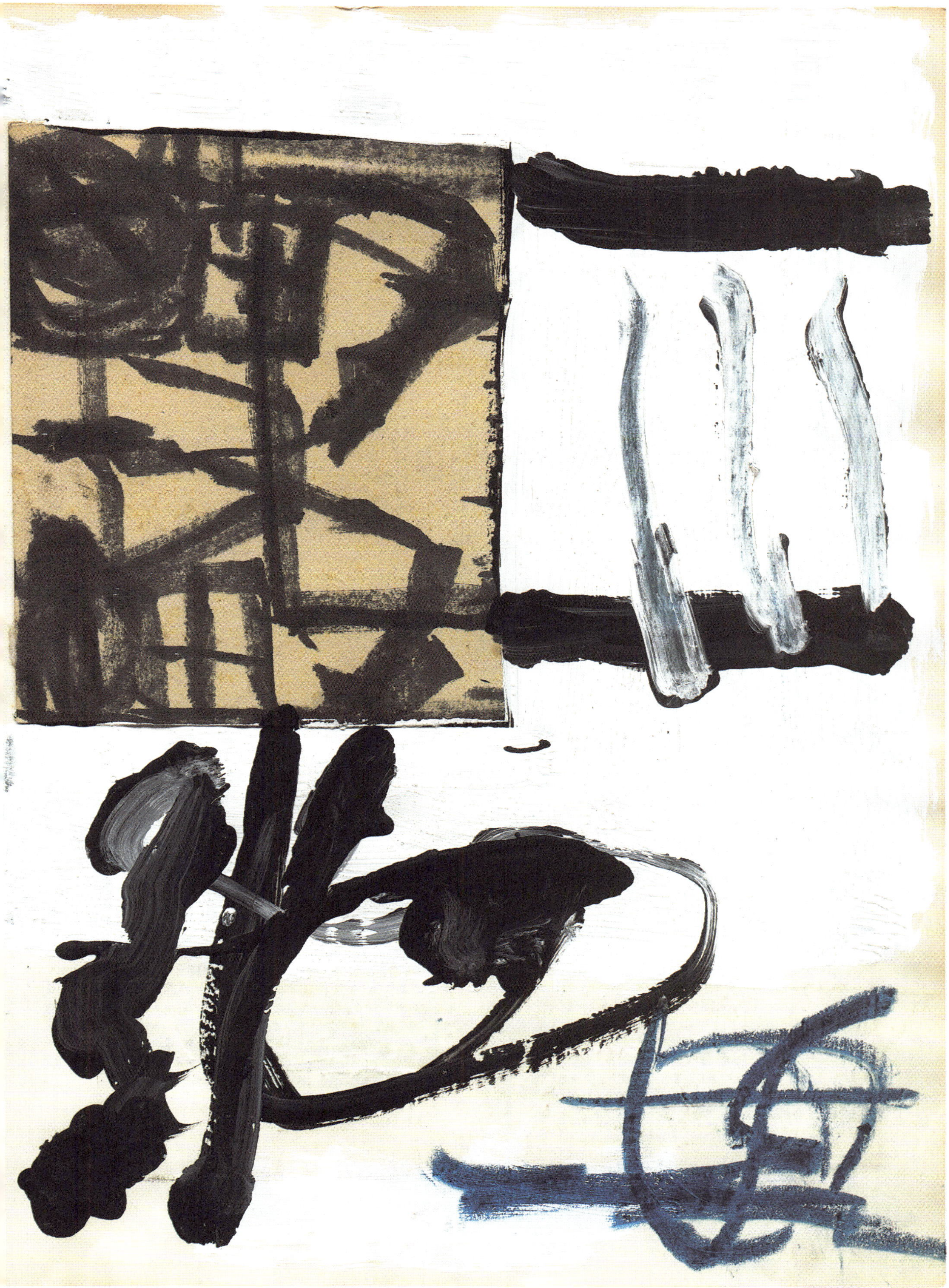

25. *Deer*

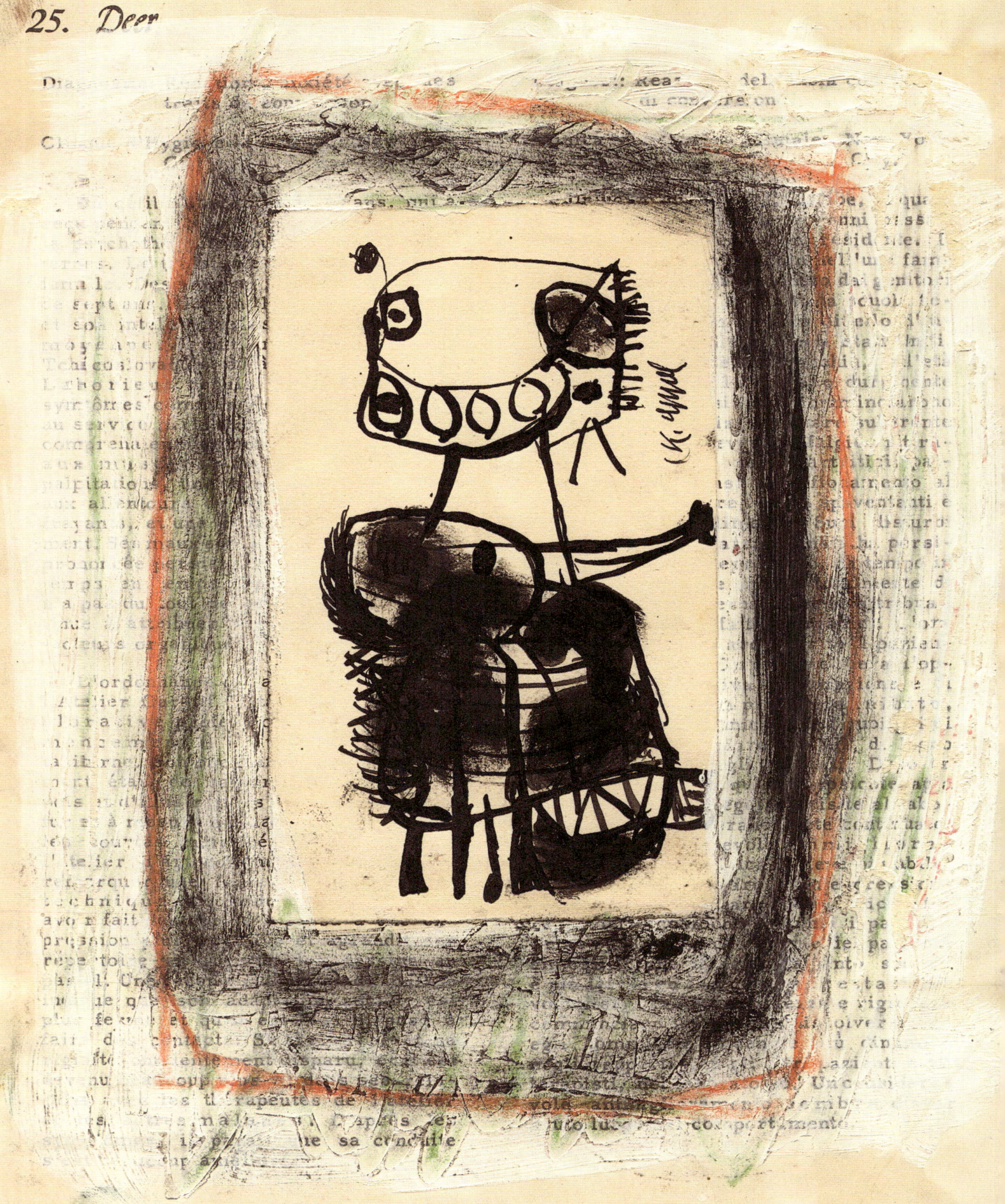

25. Deer

26. 100% Parastructive

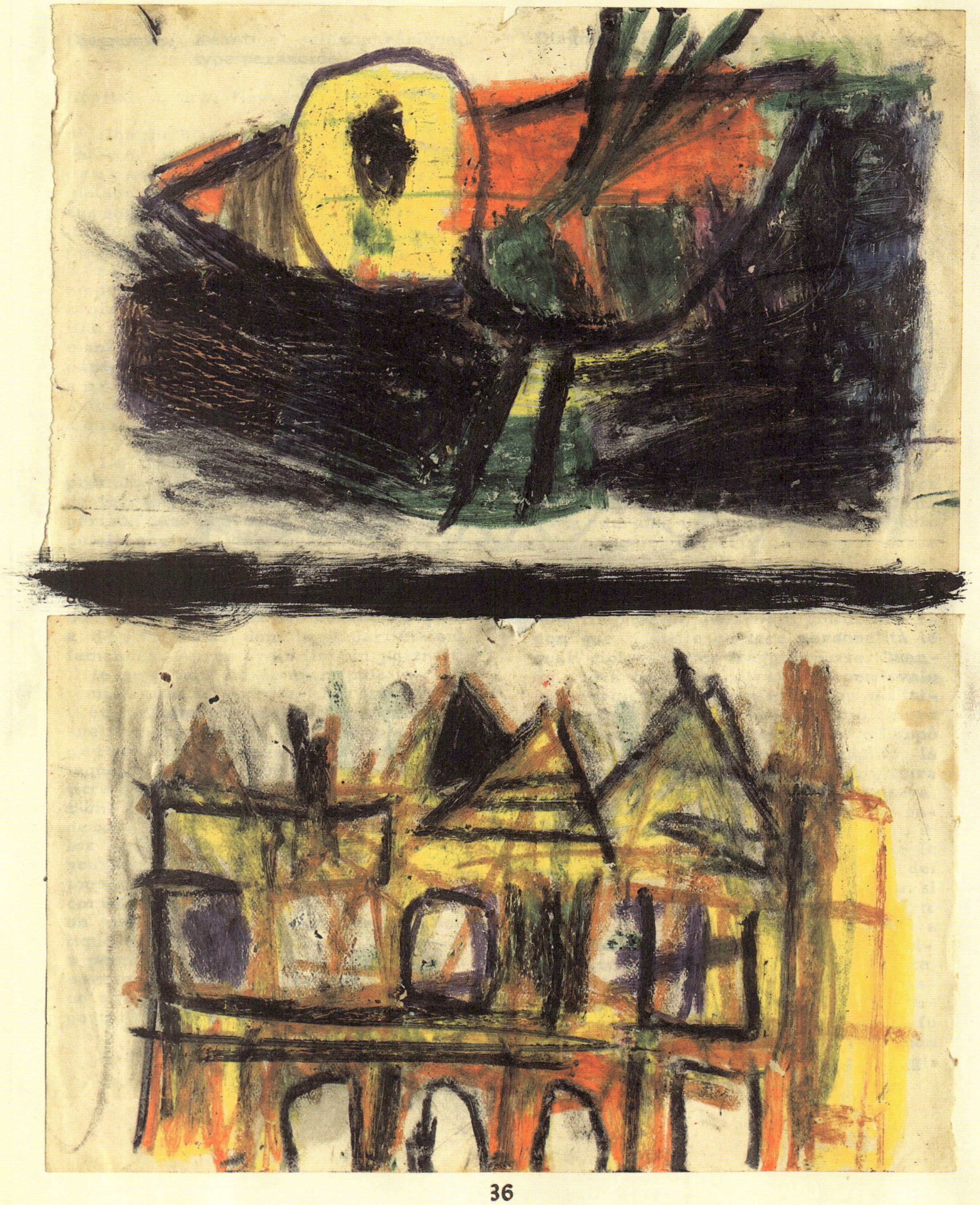

26. 100% Parastructive

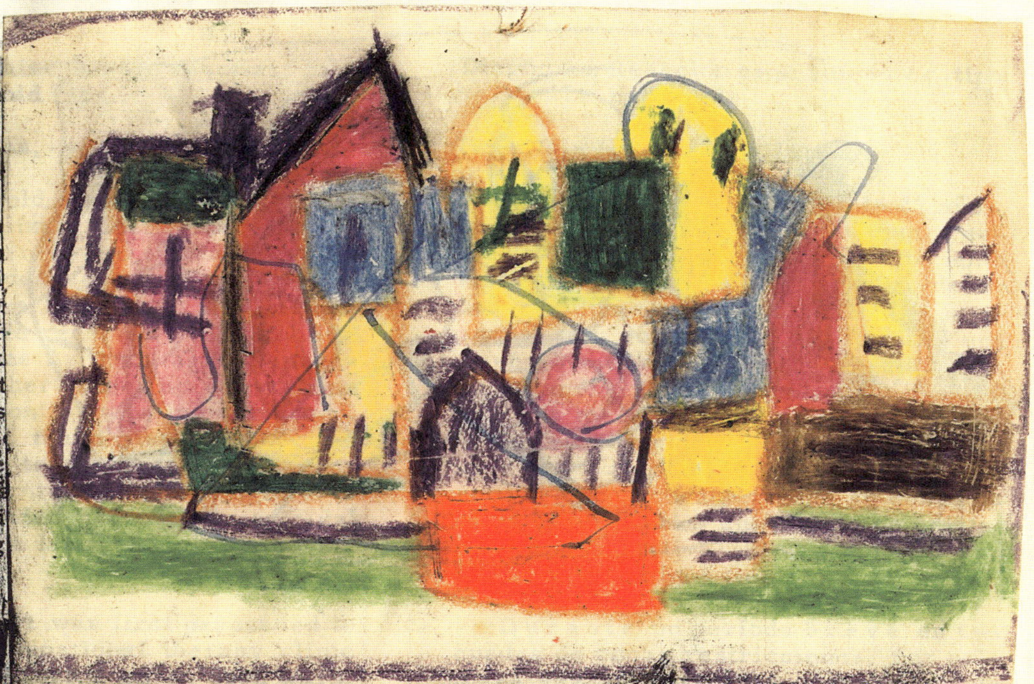

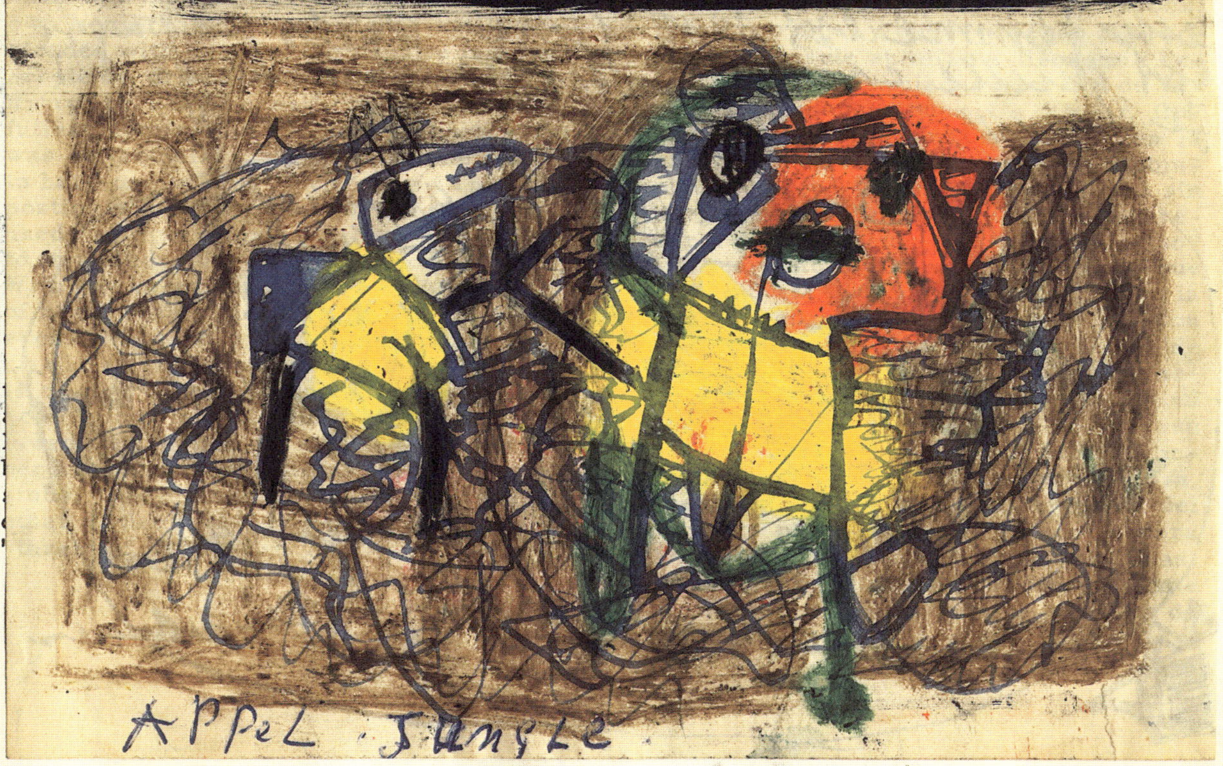

27. *Sunflowers*

Diagnostic: Schizophrénie, type catatonique

Hôpital: Los Angeles, California

Le malade est un homme célibataire, âgé de 23 ans, et enfant unique. Sa mère, à laquelle il était dévoué, mourut quand le malade avait neuf ans. Son père s'est remarié, mais le malade n'aimait pas sa belle-mère, et, ne pouvant pas s'adapter à l'entourage familial, quitta la maison paternelle à l'age de seize ans. Son père autoritaire se moquait du premier intêret à l'art que le malade manifestait pendant sa jeunesse, et l'encouragea à devenir un mécanicien. Plus tard, le malade s'engagea dans la marine militaire et prit part aux combats au Pacifique du Sud pendant la seconde guerre générale. Après trois ans de service, il fut libéré par les médicins de la Marine et déclaré 50% invalidé à cause de son aliénation mentale. Il alla à l'école d'art, mais il avait beaucoup de difficulté de s'adapter à la vie civile, et finalement on dû l'hospitaliser à cause de sa suractivité et de ses hallucinations. On lui donna 18 traitements d'électrochoc à l'hôpital, d'où il sortit après neuf mois.

Le malade passait une grande partie de son temps à peindre pendant son séjour à l'hôpital, souvent des journées entières. Des le commencement il manifesta beaucoup d'habileté naturelle, et sur la base des ouvrages accomplis pendant qu'il était sous traitement il fut admis à un institut d'art peu de temps après sa sortie de l'hôpital. Il a été à l'école d'art pendant les trois dernières années; une partie de ses ouvrages a été exposée aux musées locaux, et il reçut des acclamations. Une de ses peintures a été achetée récemment par un critique d'art réputé.

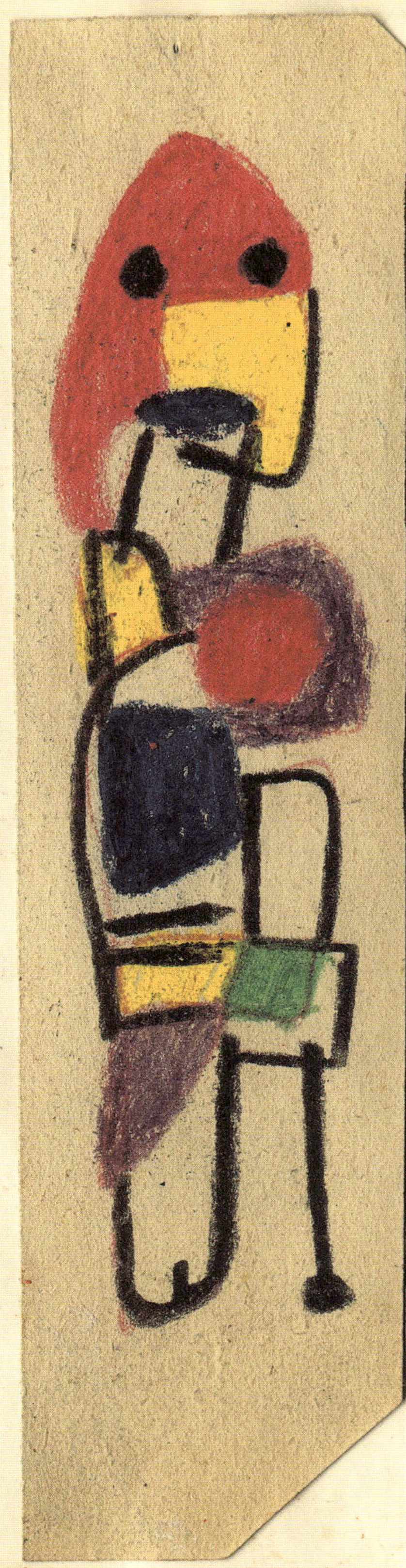

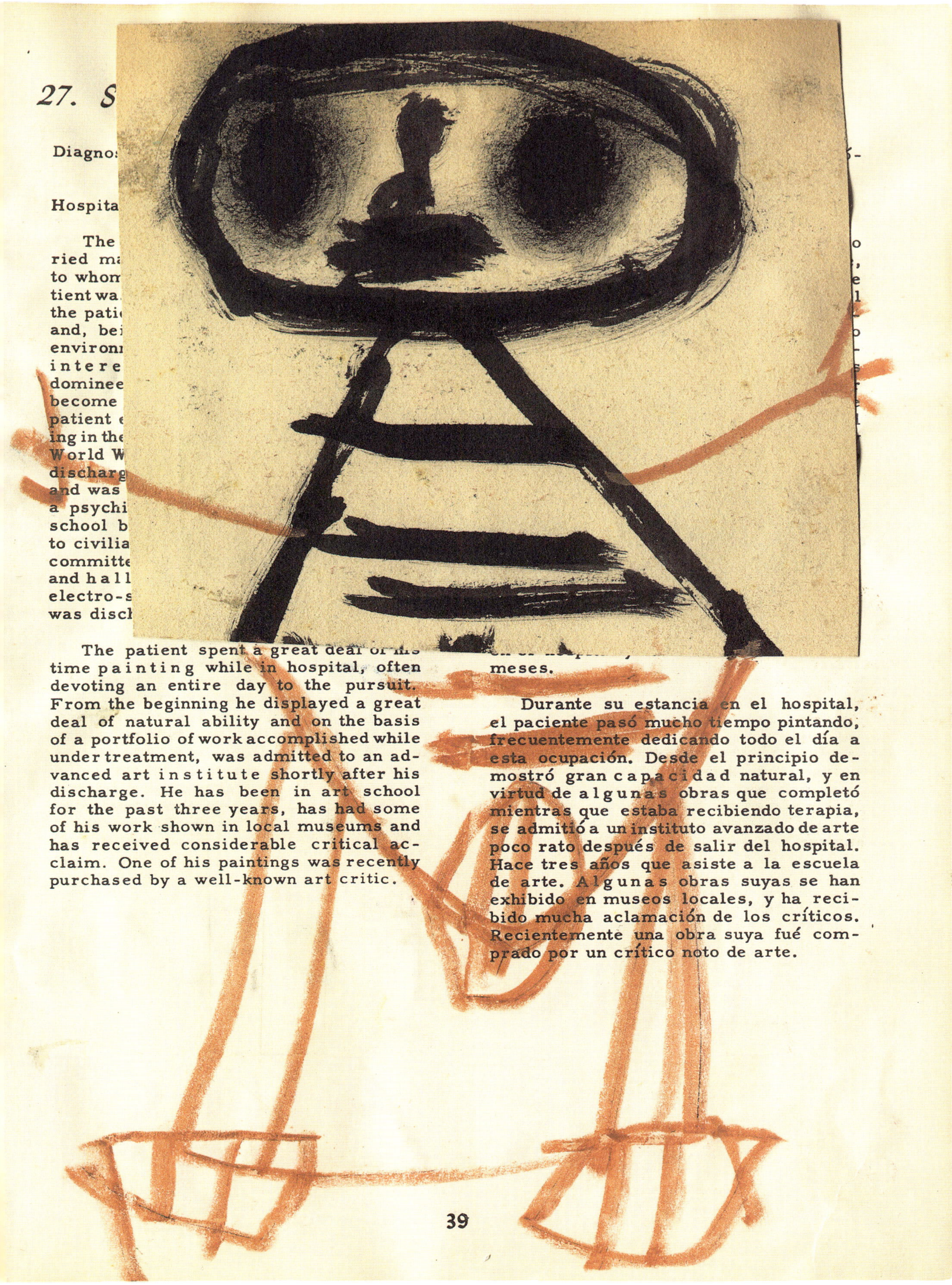
27. S
Diagno
Hospita
The
ried ma
to whom
tient wa
the pati
and, bei
environ
intere
dominee
become
patient
ing in the
World W
discharg
and was
a psychi
school b
to civilia
committe
and hall
electro-s
was disch
The patient spent a great deal of his time painting while in hospital, often devoting an entire day to the pursuit. From the beginning he displayed a great deal of natural ability and on the basis of a portfolio of work accomplished while under treatment, was admitted to an advanced art institute shortly after his discharge. He has been in art school for the past three years, has had some of his work shown in local museums and has received considerable critical acclaim. One of his paintings was recently purchased by a well-known art critic.
meses.
Durante su estancia en el hospital, el paciente pasó mucho tiempo pintando, frecuentemente dedicando todo el día a esta ocupación. Desde el principio demostró gran capacidad natural, y en virtud de algunas obras que completó mientras que estaba recibiendo terapia, se admitió a un instituto avanzado de arte poco rato después de salir del hospital. Hace tres años que asiste a la escuela de arte. Algunas obras suyas se han exhibido en museos locales, y ha recibido mucha aclamación de los críticos. Recientemente una obra suya fué comprado por un crítico noto de arte.
39

28. *Abstraction*

Diag… …ronica,

Hôpi…

H… …di razza qui, … …po sette ren… …e la te- mala… …madre lorsc… …a 5 anni était… …, sfor- été é… …igna in- et sa… …nessuna et m… …evero e viol… …i vio- jama… …micizie duré… …marcati sess… …nde bi- sité… …guito ad de co… …n'ansia et de… …e, dif- affai… …ità, de- tenti… …all'ad- et de…

L… …labora- d'art… …i mesi. jami… …dipinto, l'ais… …pittura a

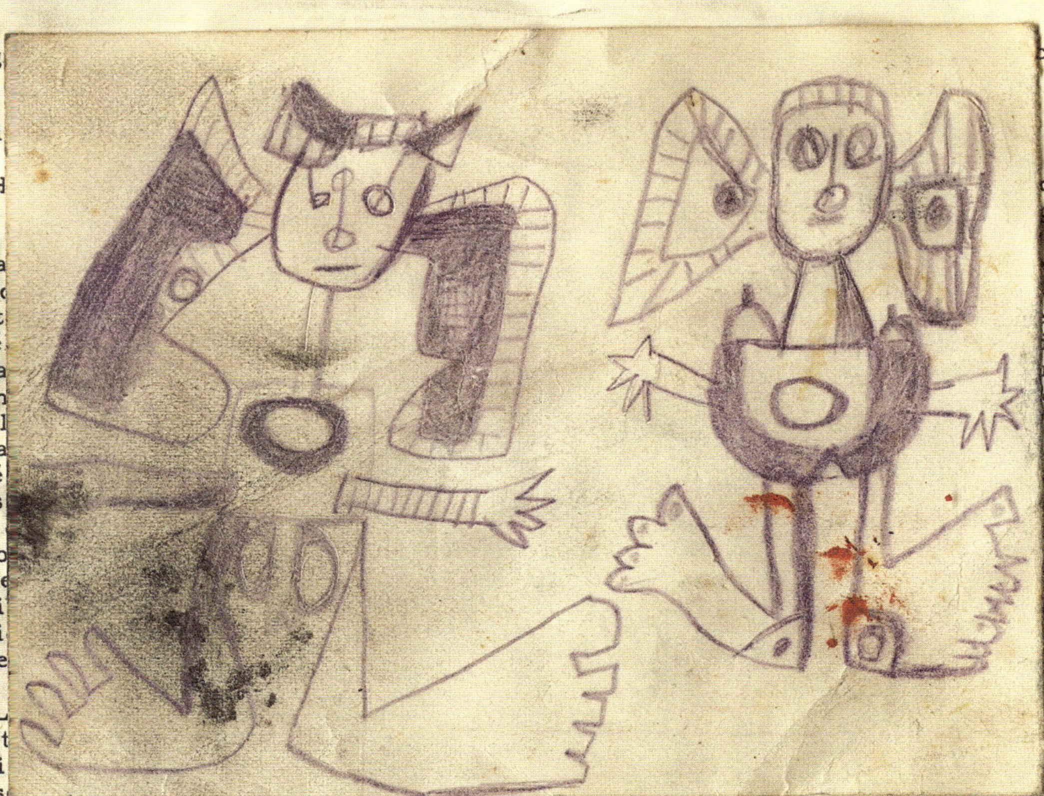

doigts pour la première fois, jusqu'à ce qu'il développa ce genre de peinture en une activité compulsive. Après il choisit l'huile. Tout en maintenant sa prudente technique compulsive, son ouvrage devint de plus en plus symbolique. Cette traduction de matière de conflit sur la toile coincidait avec une amélioration clinique, et le malade fut renvoyé pour recevoir la psychothérapie comme un malade externe.

diti, imbarazzavalo e rendevalo incerto, finchè egli non lo sviluppò in un'attività coattiva. Allora passò alla pittura a olio. Benchè egli conservò questa tecnica accurata e coattiva, suo lavoro diveni sempre più simbolico. Tale trasferimento del materiale di conflitto sulla tela coincideva con miglioramento clinico ed il malato fu rilasciato per ricevere la psicoterapia come un paziente esterno.

UR FORM
UR ANGST

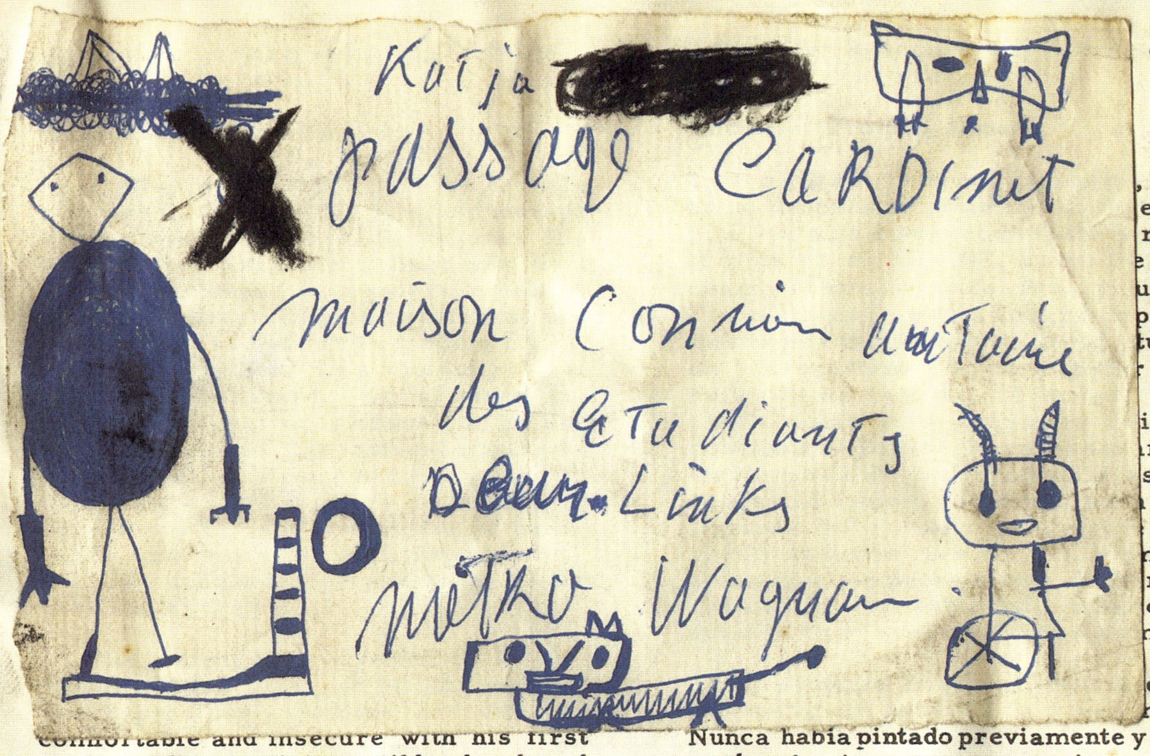

comfortable and insecure with his first medium, fingerpaints, until he developed this into a compulsive activity. He then changed to oils. While maintaining his careful, compulsive technique, his work became increasingly s y m b o l i c . This translation of conflictual material to the canvas coincided with clinical improvement and the patient was discharged to receive psychotherapy as an outpatient.

cróni-

, de 37
el hos-
recibió
murió
u niñez
por una
tuosa y
en un
El pa-
imos o
rcada-
s y una
éxito.
desa-
nas de
recon-
ento y
nen.

de arte
meses. Nunca había pintado previamente y estaba incómodo y inseguro en su primer medio, el pintar a los dedos, hasta que desarrollo ésta en una activadad compulsiva. Luego cambió al pintar al óleo. Aunque mantenía su técnica compulsiva y cuidadosa, sus obras se ponían cada vez más simbólicas. Esta traducción al lienzo de materia que engendraba conflictos coincidió con mejoramiento c l í n i c o , y el paciente se hizo enfermo de fuera y recibió psicoterapia en el hospital.

U R

29. *Napoleon*

Diagnostic: Réaction schizophrénique, type paranoide.

Hôpital: Lyons, New Jersey.

Cette peinture est l'ouvrage du même malade dont le tableau "100% Parastructive" est montré ailleurs à l'exposition.

Diagnosi: Reazione schizofrenica, tipo paranoido.

Ospedale: Lyons, New Jersey.

Questo quadro è il lavoro del medesimo malato di cui il "100% Parastructive" e mostrato in un'altro luogo dell'esposizione.

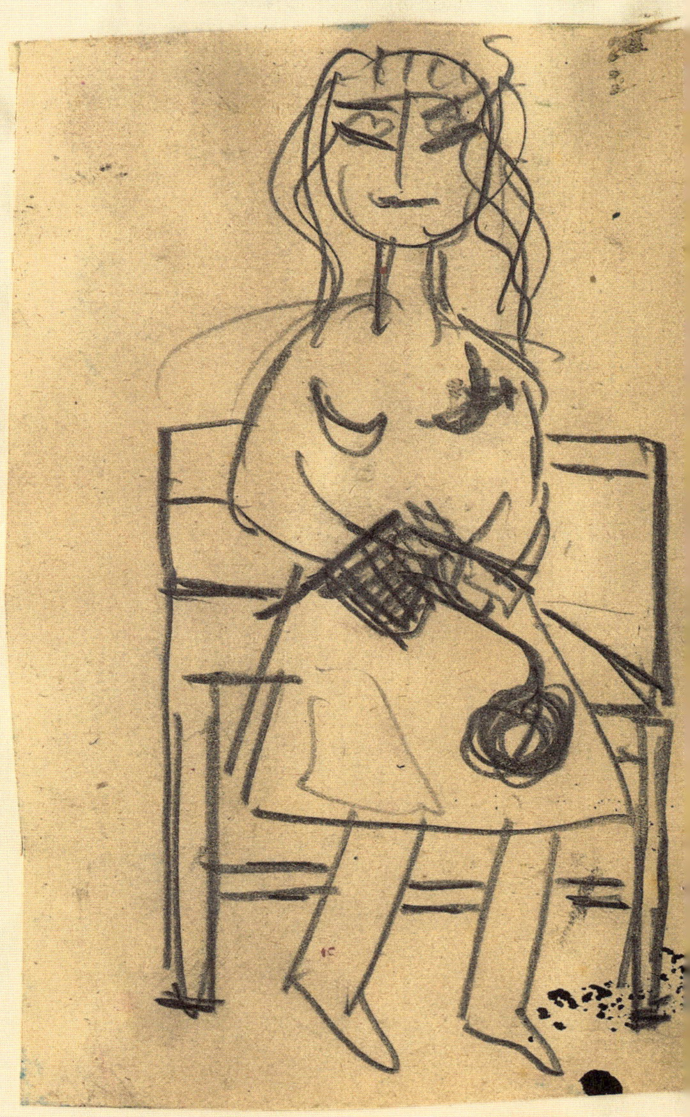

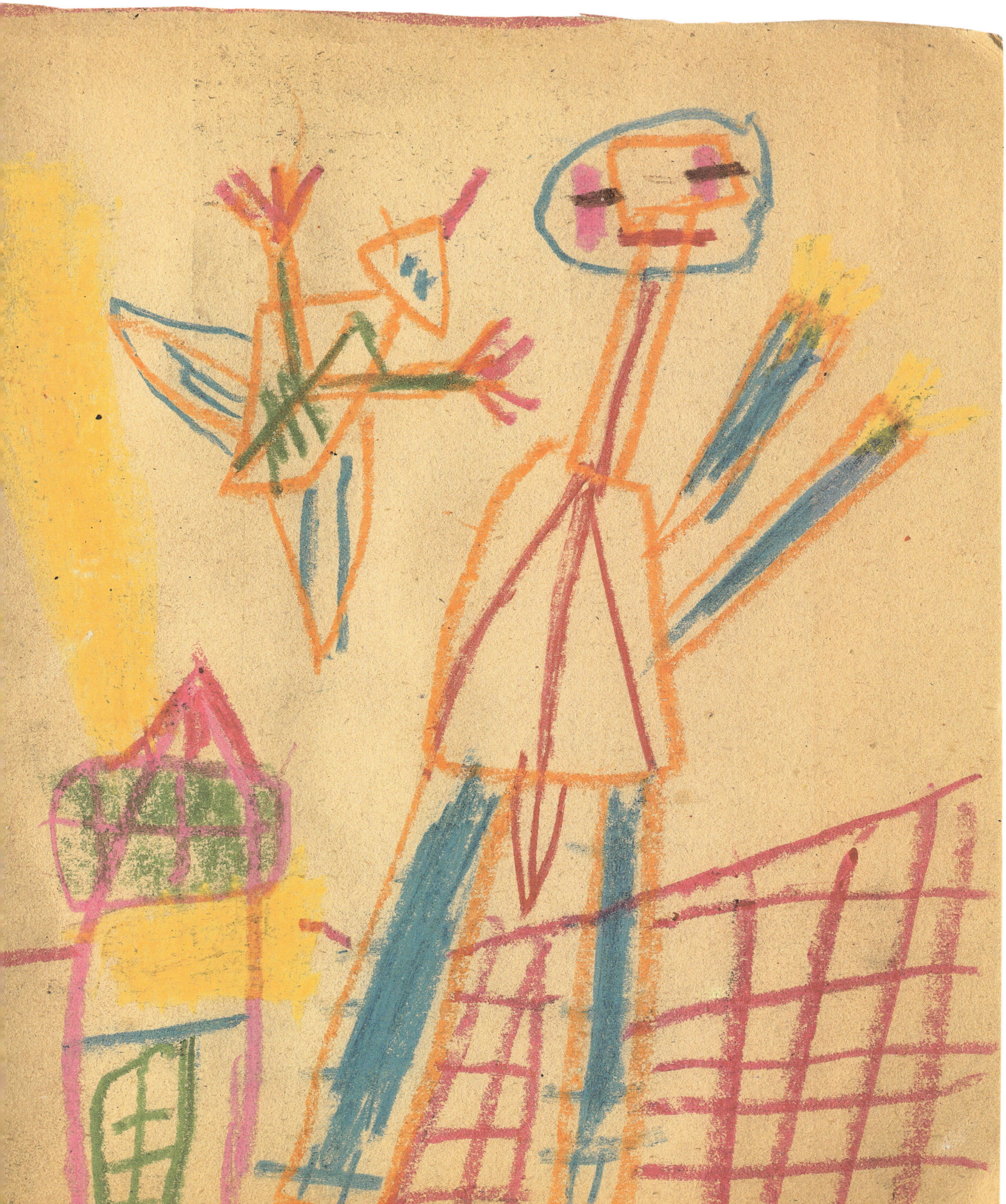

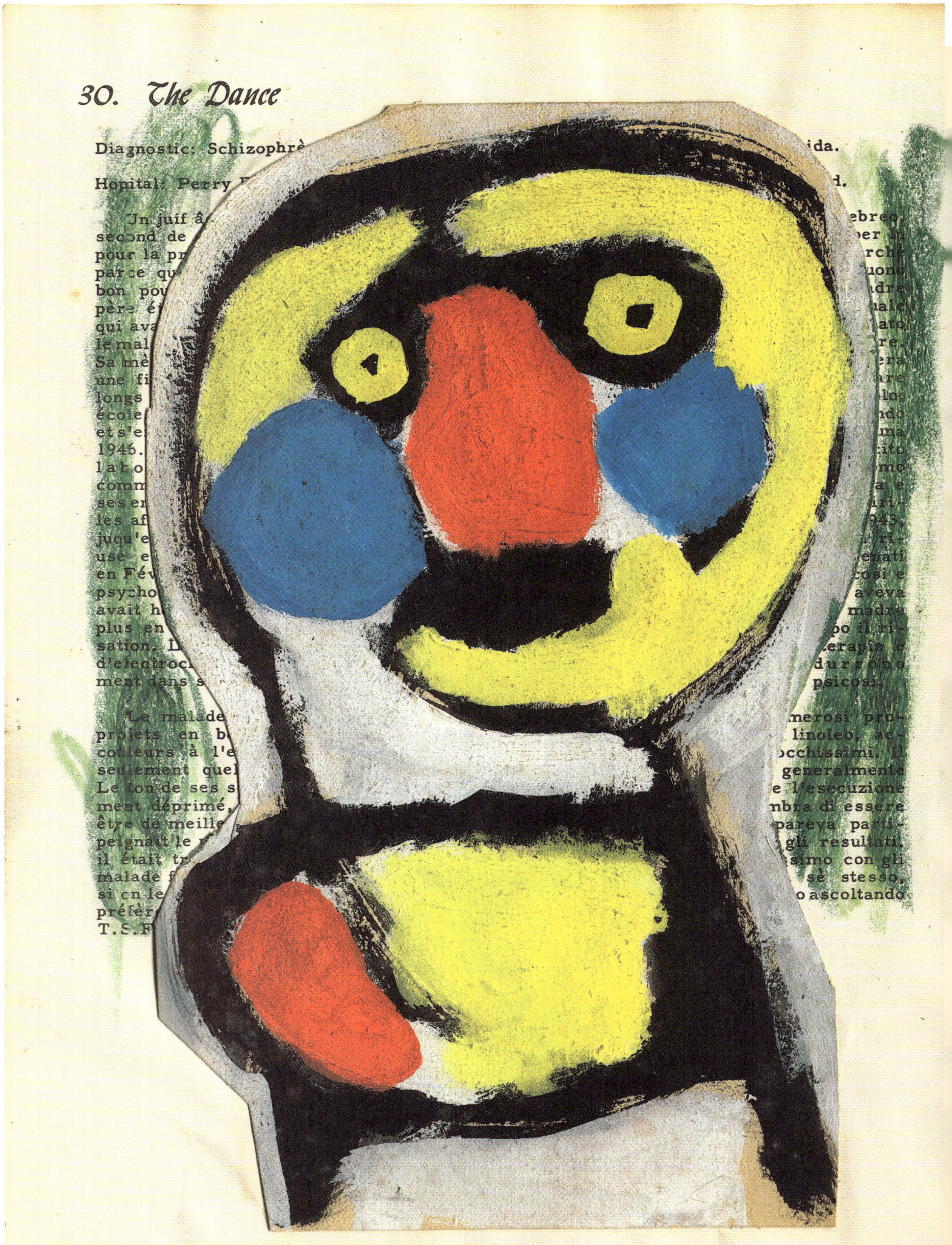
30. The Dance
Diagnostic: Schizophrè
Hopital: Perry

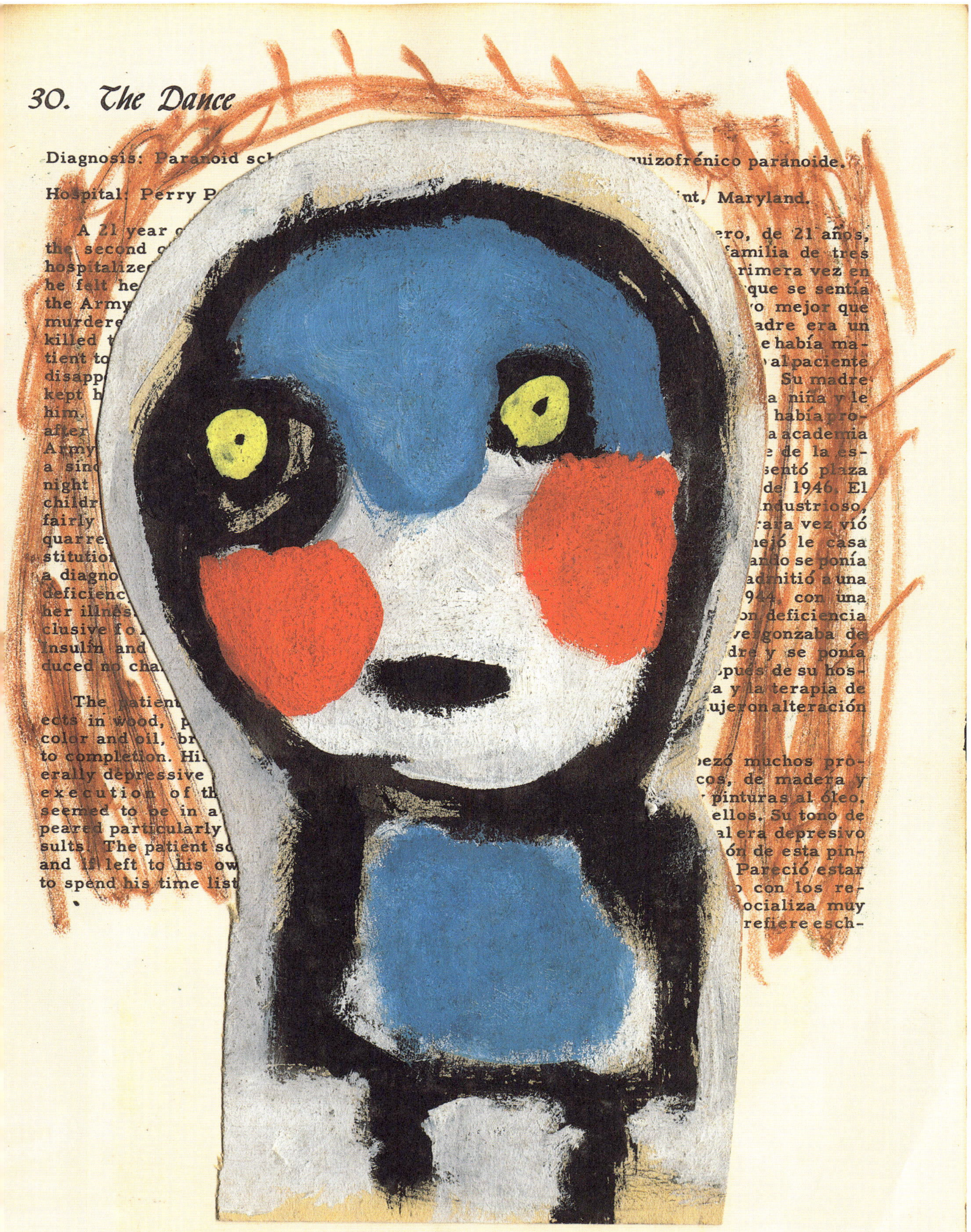
30. The Dance
Diagnosis: Paranoid sch
quizofrénico paranoide.
Hospital: Perry P
int, Maryland.
A 21 year
ero, de 21 años,
familia de tres
rimera vez en
que se sentía
o mejor que
adre era un
e había ma-
al paciente
Su madre
a niña y le
había pro-
a academia
e de la es-
sentó plaza
de 1946. El
industrioso,
rara vez vió
nejó le casa
ando se ponía
admitió a una
1944 con una
on deficiencia
vergonzaba de
dre y se ponía
spués de su hos-
a y la terapia de
ujeron alteración
The patient
ects in wood,
color and oil,
to completion.
erally depressive
execution of th
seemed to be in a
peared particularly
sults. The patient sc
and if left to his ow
to spend his time list
ezó muchos pro-
cos, de madera y
pinturas al óleo.
ellos. Su tono de
al era depresivo
ón de esta pin-
Pareció estar
o con los re-
ocializa muy
refiere esch-
45

31. *Composition*

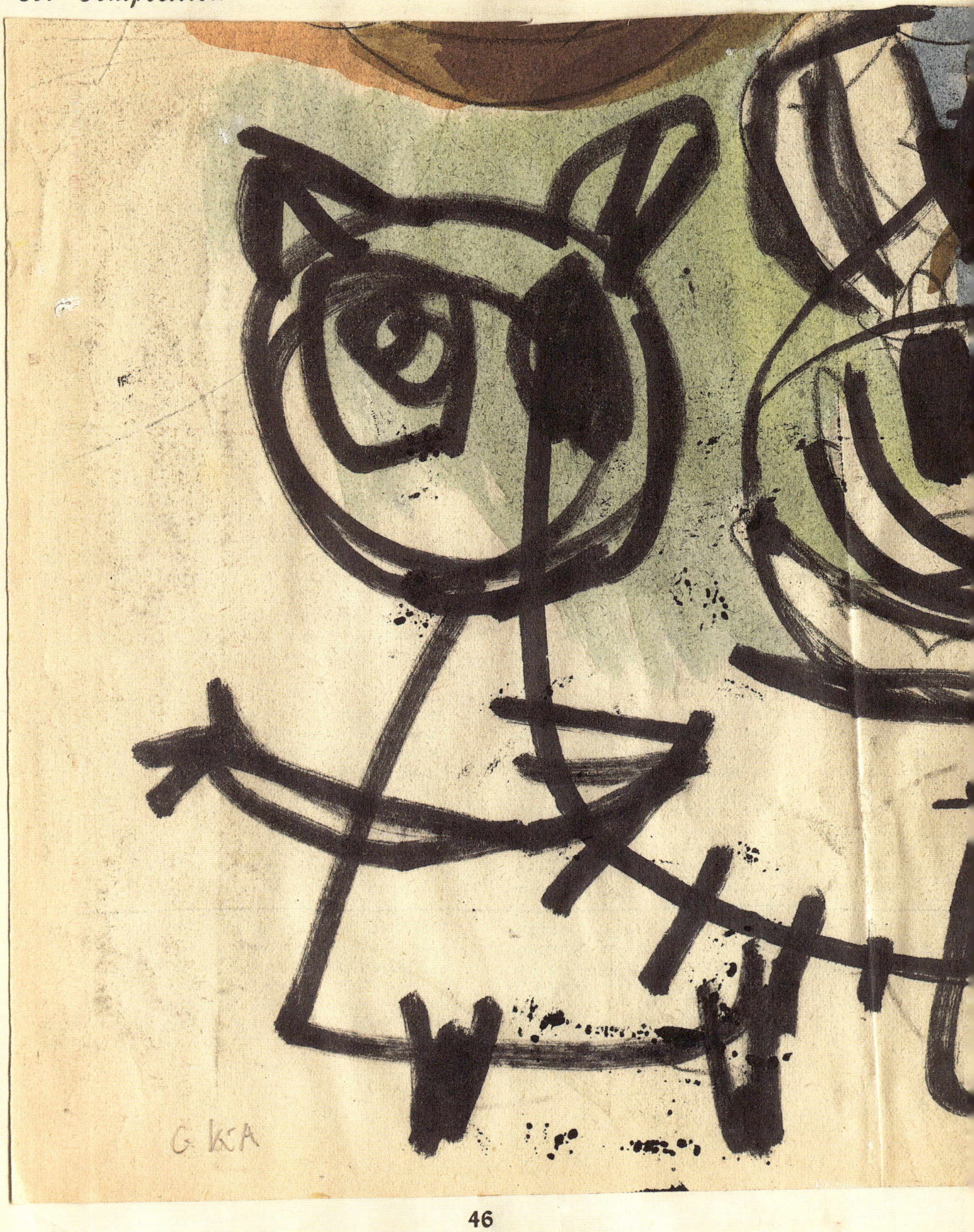

31. *Composition*

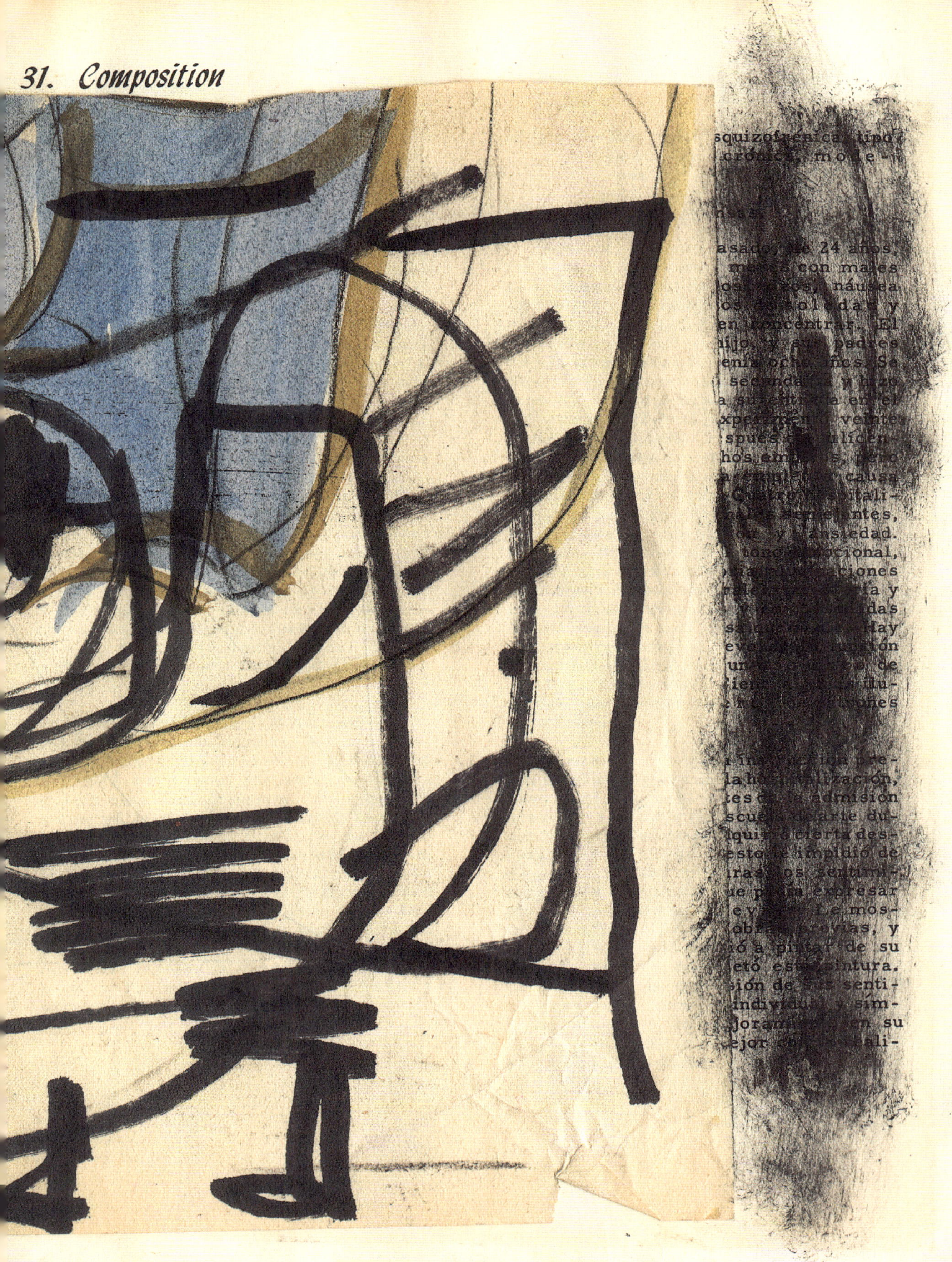

32. Hand

Diagnostic: Schizophrénie, type paranoide

Hôpital: Los Angeles, California.

Cette peinture est l'ouvrage du même malade dont le "Skull" est montré ailleurs à l'exposition.

Diagnosi: Schizofrenia tipo paranoido.

Ospedale: Los Angeles, California.

Questro quadro era dipinto dal medesimo paziente, che dipingi il "Skull" mostrato ad un'altro luogo dell'esposizione.

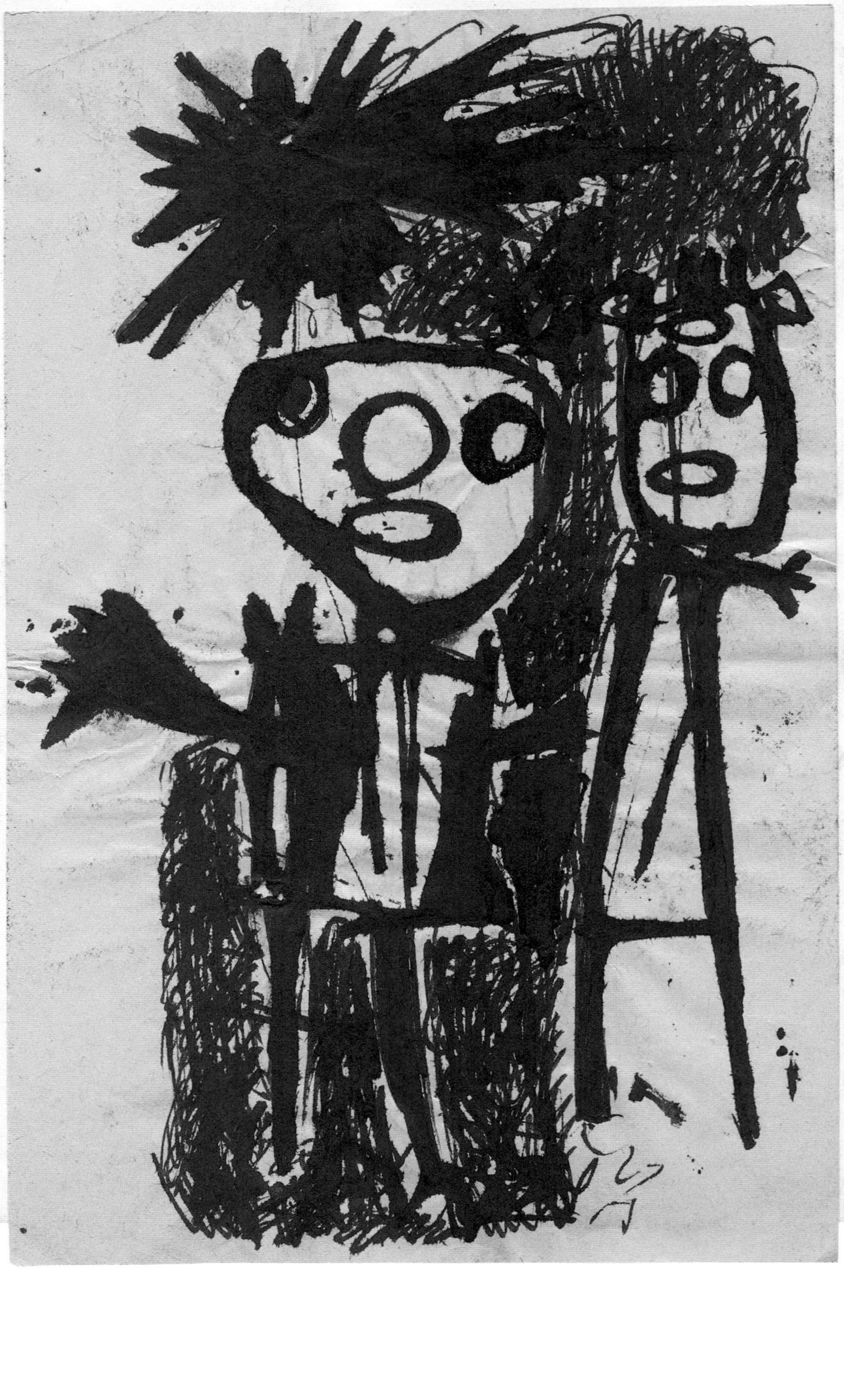

32. *Hand*

Diagnosis: Schizophrenia, paranoid type.

Hospital: Los Angeles, California.

This painting is the work of the same patient whose "Skull" is displayed elsewhere in the exhibit.

Diagnosis: Esquizofrenia, tipo paranoide.

Hospital: Los Angeles, California.

Esta pintura es la obra del mismo paciente cuya pintura "Skull" se exhibe en cualquiera otra parte de la exposición.

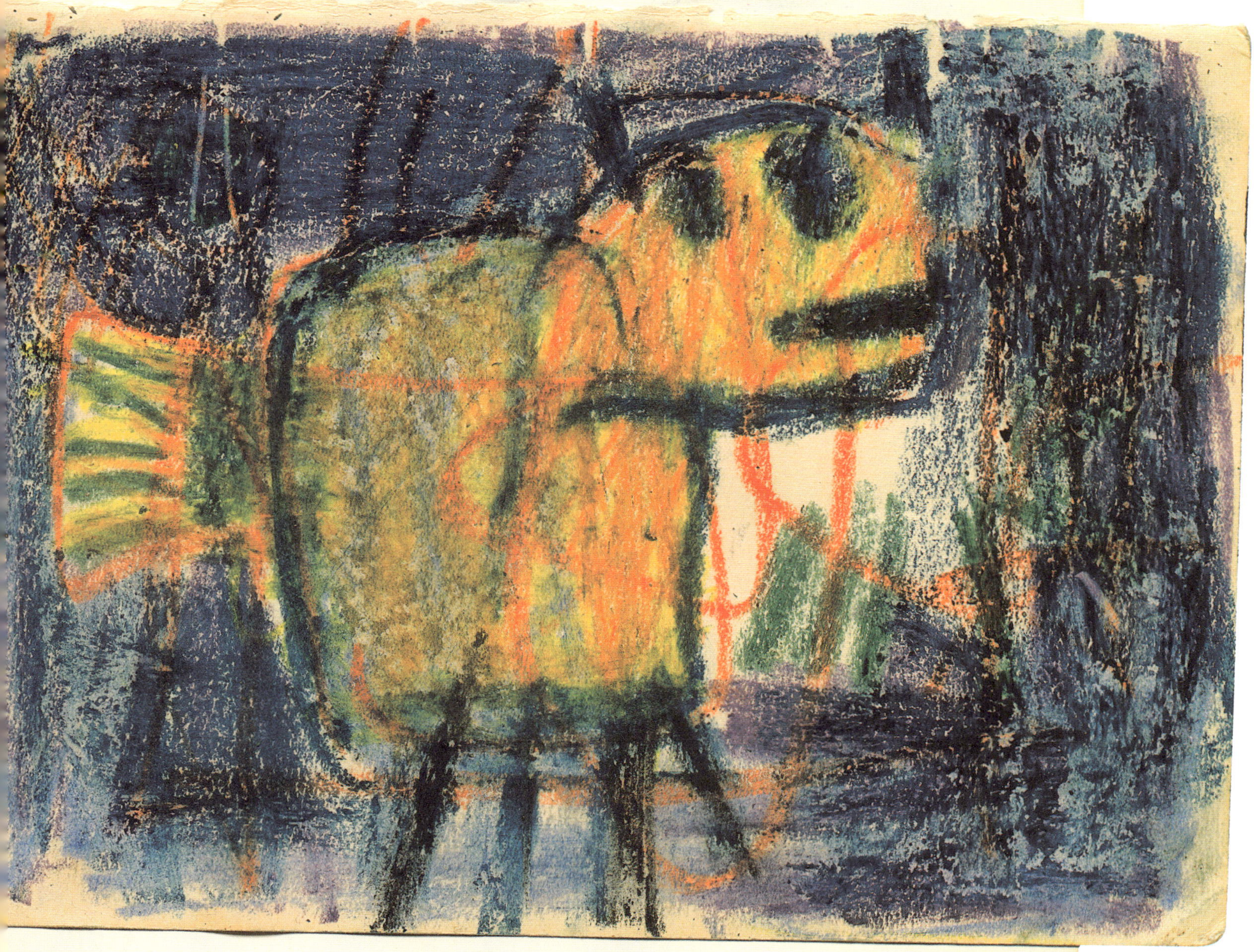

33. *Man and Wife*

Diagnostic: Réaction schizophrénique, type paranoide.

Hôpital: Topeka, Kansas

Homme blanc, âgé de 31 ans, célibataire, à l'hôpital depuis trois ans. Il est l'enfant unique d'une famille riche. Son père mourut lorsque le malade avait trois ans, et la mère est instable et neurasthenique. Sa vie au domicile paternel a été malheureuse. Il était un enfant obéissant, efféminé, isolé, qui devint plus tard très désobéissant et un garçon délinquant qui, à l'âge de 15 ans, fut déclaré sur les en-têtes des journaux "le plus jeune faux-monnayeur du pays". Il menait la vie d'un vagabond alcoolique, paresseux et débauché. Plus tard il fut emprisonné pour vol, lorsque sa mère refusa de l'envoyer à un asile d'aliénés, et en prison il contracta une psychose aigue. Il avait de grandioses illusions, une confusion de sa propre identité et une affection de pensée. Il exprimait des intentions d'homicide contre sa mère.

Le malade s'est enrôlé à l'atelier pendant qu'il était encore considéré comme un psychopathe dangereux. Il accueillit cette occasion avec plaisir et montra du talent créateur. Ses premières peintures exprimaient ses conflits et le dérangeaient tellement qu'il changea son style en le faisant "glacé" et compulsif. Peu a peu il paraissait se preter au milieu tolerant de l'atelier et peignait de nouveau avec expression, produisant le tableau "Man and Wife". Il l'a discuté avec son psychiatre et a obtenu un aperçu partiel de ses illusions qu'il reconnait maintenant comme étant des fantaisies. Il a été transféré à une salle d'hôpital mi-ouverte.

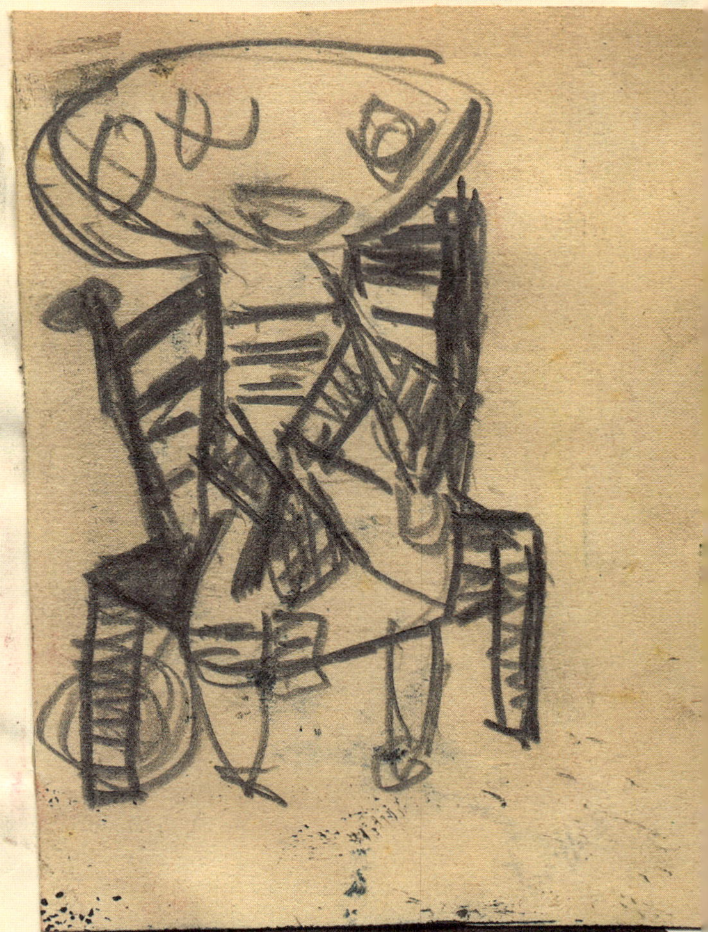

[redacted]

33. *Man and Wife*

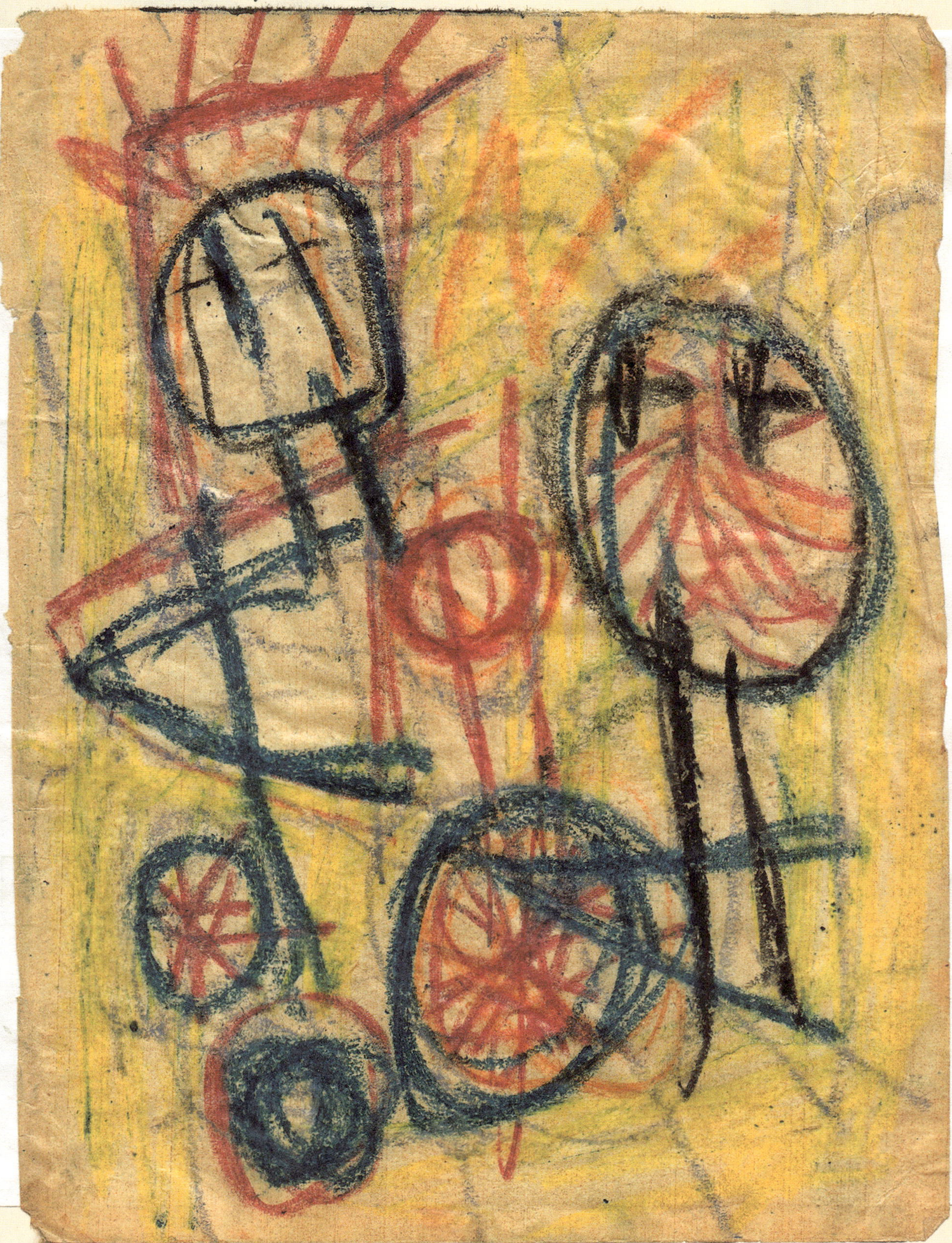

34. U.S.A.

Diagnostic: Personalité psychopathique avec sexualité pathologique; uranisme; alcoolisme chronique.

[redacted]

34. U.S.A.

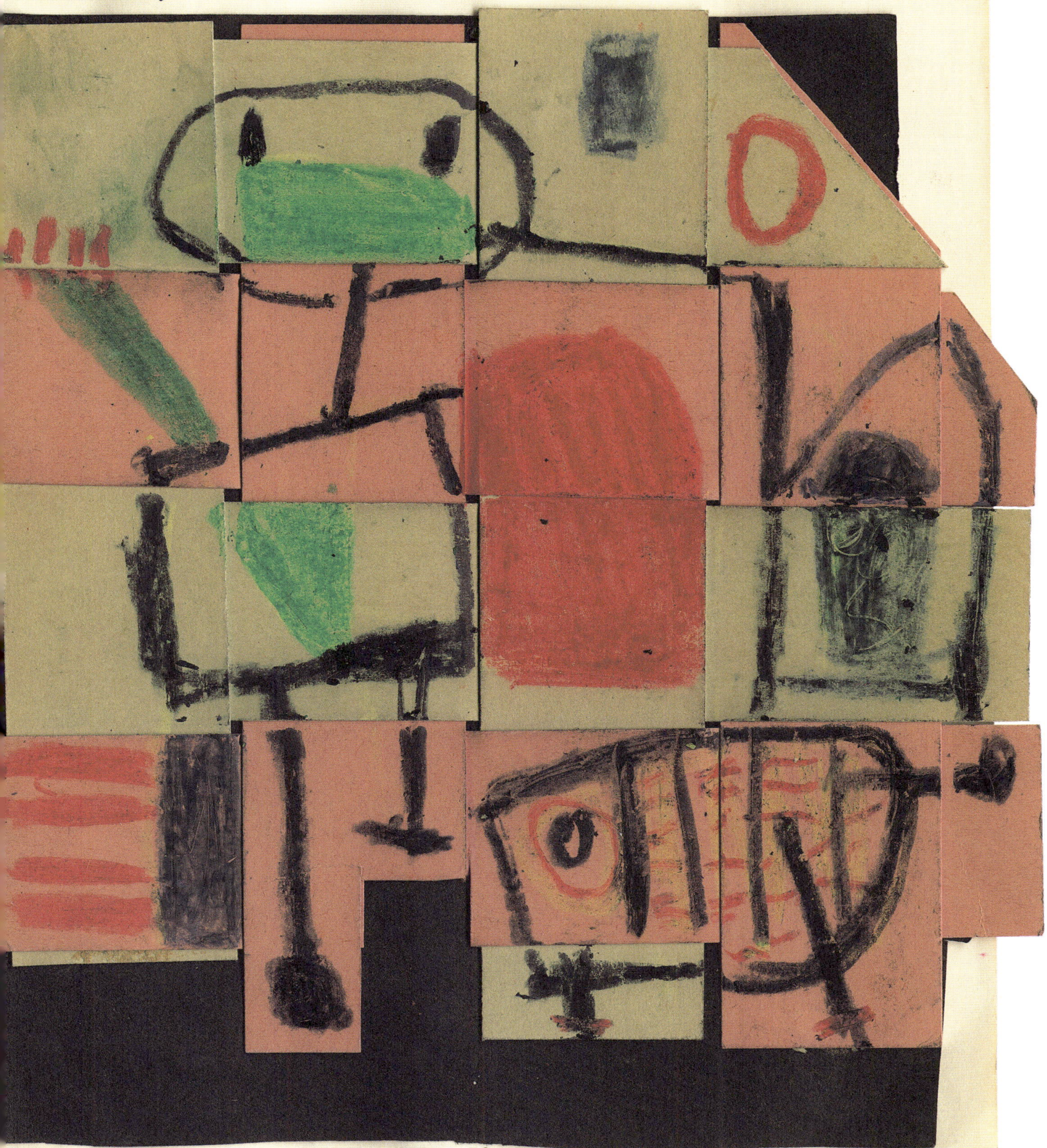

35. *Flowers*

Diagnostic: Personnalité schizoide avec des tendances paranoïdes.

Diagnosi: Personalità schizoida con tendenze paranoide.

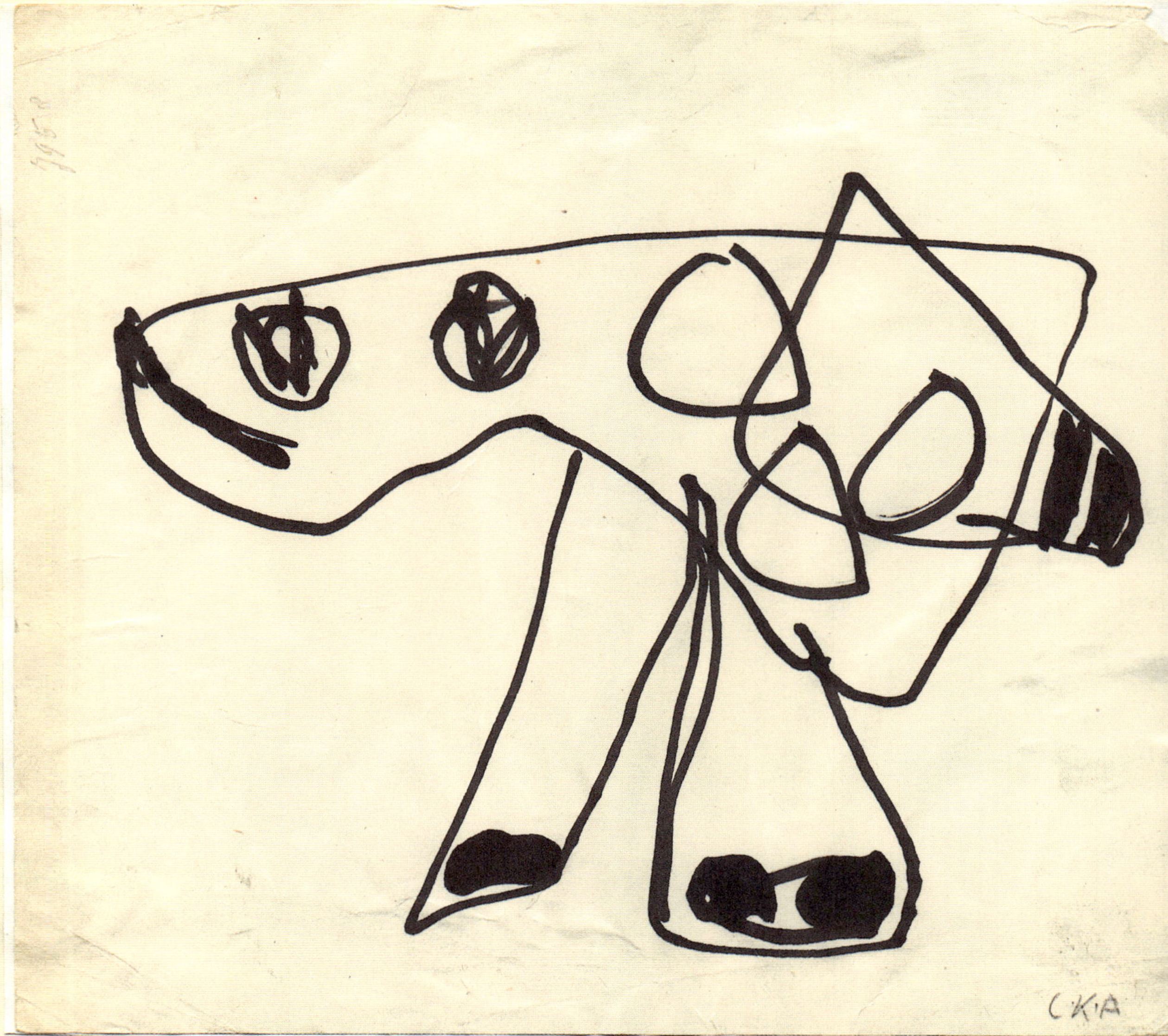

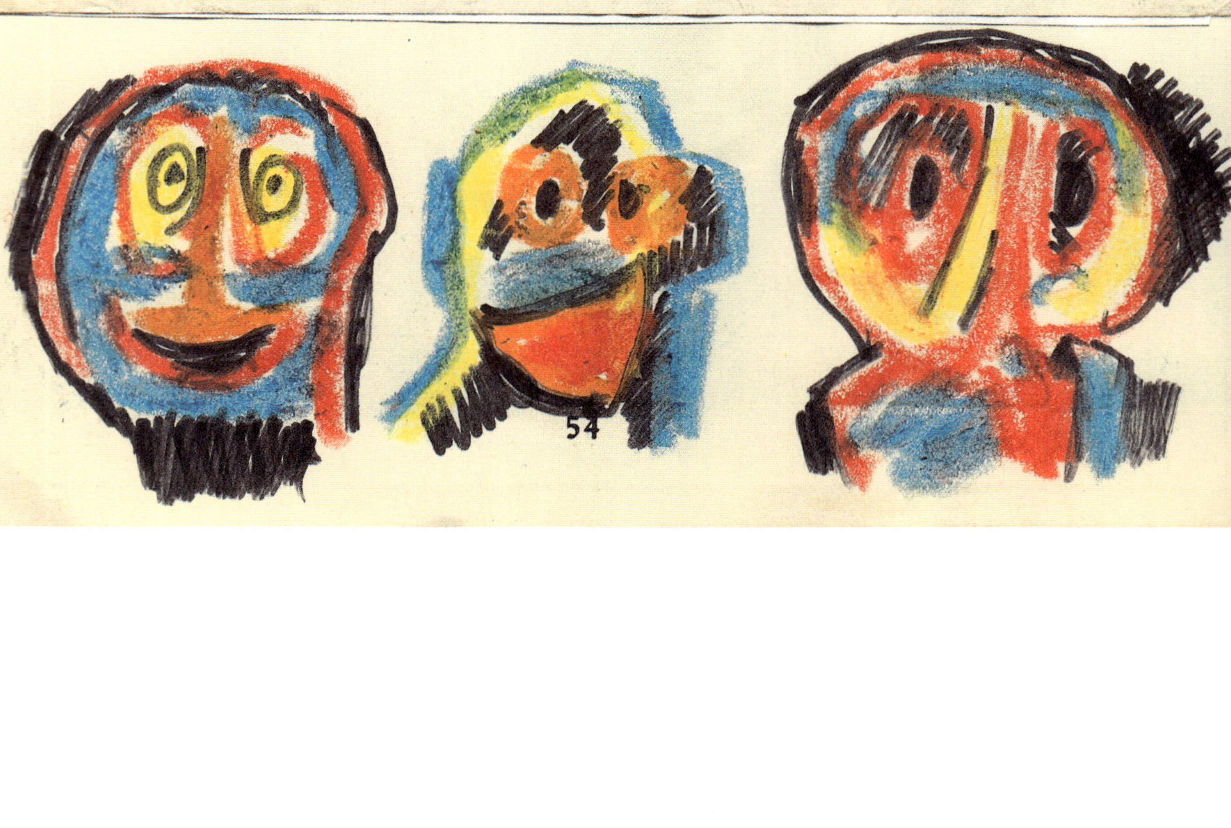

35. *Flowers*

Diagnosis: Schizoid personality with paranoid trends.

Diagnosis: Personalidad esquizoide con tendencias paranoides.

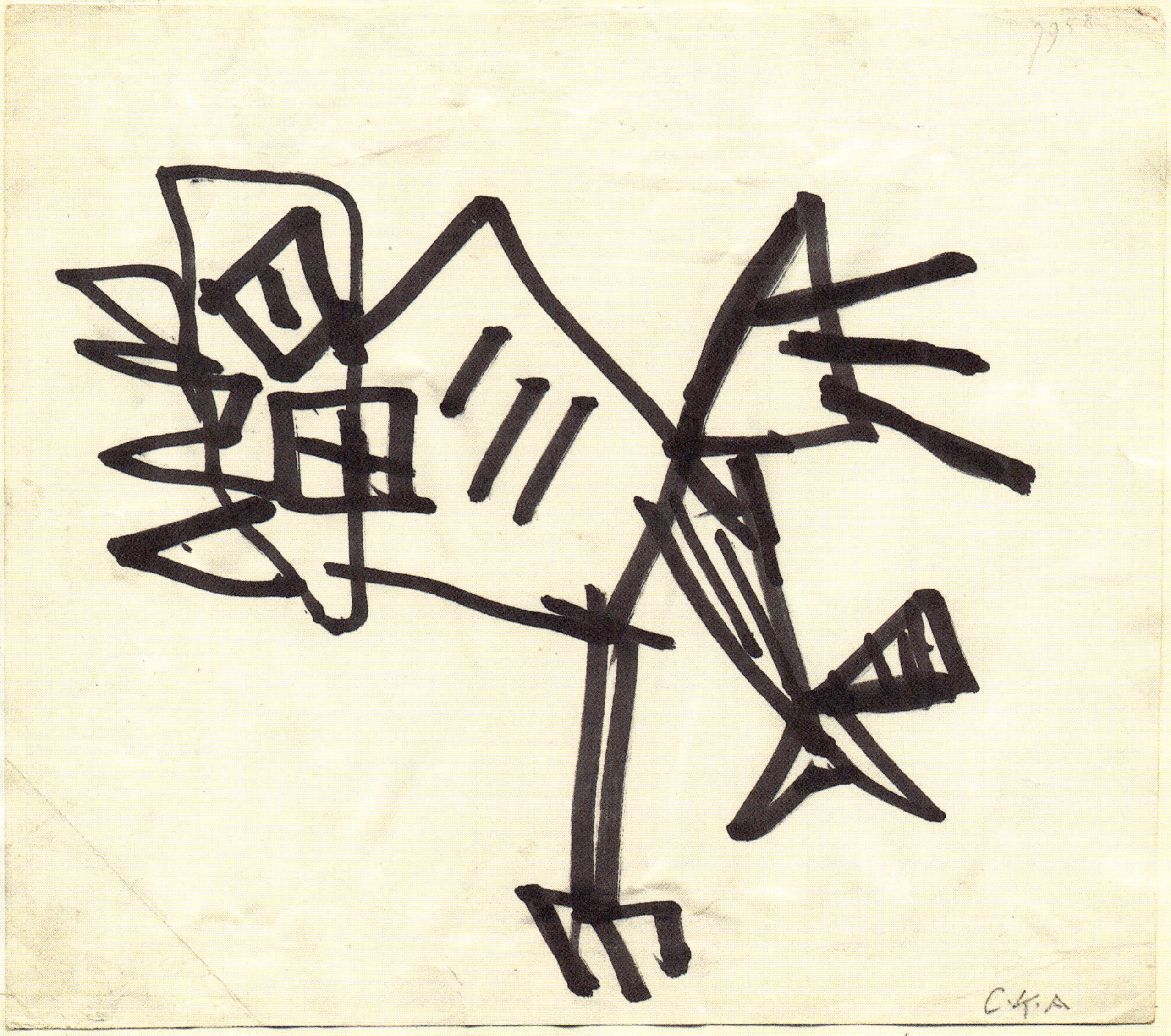

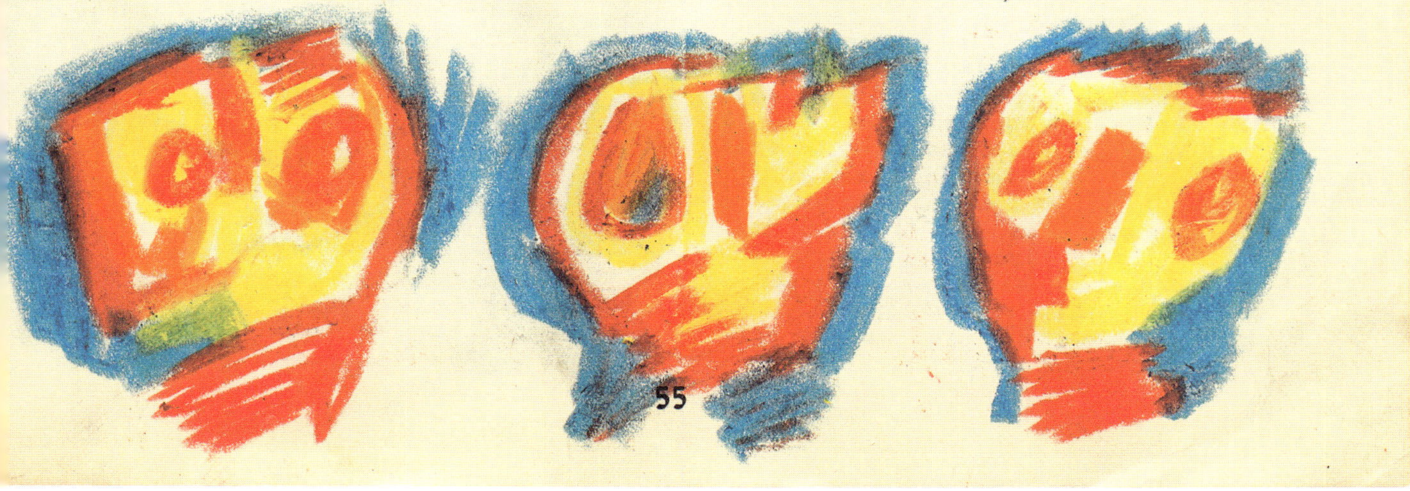

36. *Composition*

Diagnostic: Schizophrénie, type paranoide.

Clinique d'Hygiène Mentale: New York City.

Homme blanc, âgé de 44 ans, célibataire, qui était hospitalisé pendant quatre mois en 1946. Sa mère mourut quand il était très jeune, et le malade ainsi que ses quatre frères et soeurs ont passé leur enfance et adolescence dans des hospices et maisons d'adoption. Il a finit l'école primaire et a un quotient d'intelligence de 83. Il a été marchand forain, marin et gardien jusqu'au moment de son enrôlement dans le service militaire. Des crises d'hostilité alternent avec une conduite conciliante. Il a une impulsion sexuelle formidable, homosexuelle aussi bien qu'hétérosexuelle, avec peu de choix apparent d'objet. Il ne manifeste pas d'illusions ou hallucinations, mais il se considère un des plus grands artistes du monde.

Le malade a été envoyé à l'Atelier Curatif pour la thérapie pendant une visite d'essai d'un hôpital national. Il a montré du développement technique rapide malgré qu'il était très retiré, taciturne et sensible à la critique. Son habillement et sa conduite donnaient l'impression d'un grand artiste; il donnait des titres exotiques à ses ouvrages; il était prêt à passer par plusieurs soi-disantes "périodes" et affirmait qu'il avait inventé de nouvelles techniques d'art. Il croyait que la peinture lui offrait un langage par lequel il pouvait exprimer ses sentiments concernant les épreuves traumatiques, et bientôt il s'associait facilement à ses ouvrages, établissant un rôle confessionnel pour son maître d'art. Il n'a commencé que récemment à peindre à l'huile et à montrer une technique mure. La sexualité de ses premiers tableaux est devenue maintenant plus symbolique, mieux dissimulée et plus artistique. Avec quelques rechutes cycliques, il a de plus en plus accepté les manières d'expression conventionnelles, il est mieux maîtrisé, et se prépare pour un vrai publique. L'adaptation générale continue sur une base

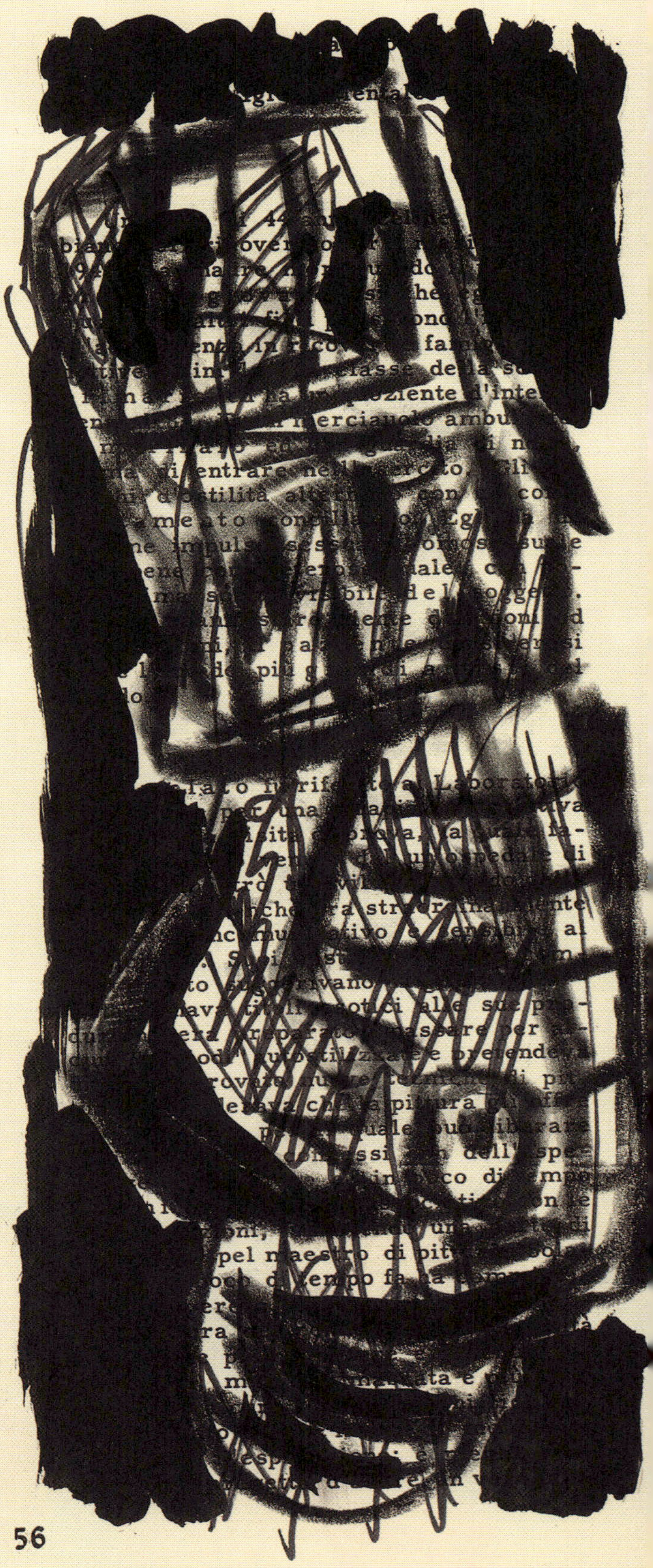

36. *Composition*

Diagnosis: Schizophrenia, paranoid type.

Mental Hygiene Clinic: New York City.

A 44 year old, unmarried, white male who was hospitalized for four months in 1946. His mother died when he was very young and he and four siblings spend their childhood and adolescence in institutions and foster homes. He completed the sixth grade of school and has an I.Q. of 83. He had been an itinerant peddler, a seaman and a watchman until his enlistment in the military service. Outbursts of hostility alternate with conciliatory behavior. He has a tremendous sexual drive, both homosexual and hetersexual, with little apparent choice of object. He manifests no delusions or hallucinations, but considers himself one of the world's greatest artists.

The patient was referred to the Curative Workshop for supportive therapy while on trial visit from a state hospital. He displayed rapid technical development in spite of being unusually withdrawn, uncommunicative and sensitive to criticism. His dress and conduct suggested the great artist; he assigned exotic titles to his productions; was prepared to pass through several self-styled "periods" and claimed the invention of new art techniques. Painting, he felt, offered him a language by which he could release his feelings over traumatic experiences and he soon became easily associative to his productions, establishing a confessional role for his art instructor. He has only recently begun to work in oils and to show a mature brush technique. The sexuality of his early pictures has now become more symbolic, better disguised and more artistic. With some cyclical retrogressions, he has increasingly accepted conventional ways of expression, is better controlled and plans for a real audience. Total adjustment continues on a precarious level with some improvement in social adjustment and personal hygiene. Shyness and withdrawal are less evident, and the patient has been able to reestablish a continued, though tenuous psychotherapeutic relationship.

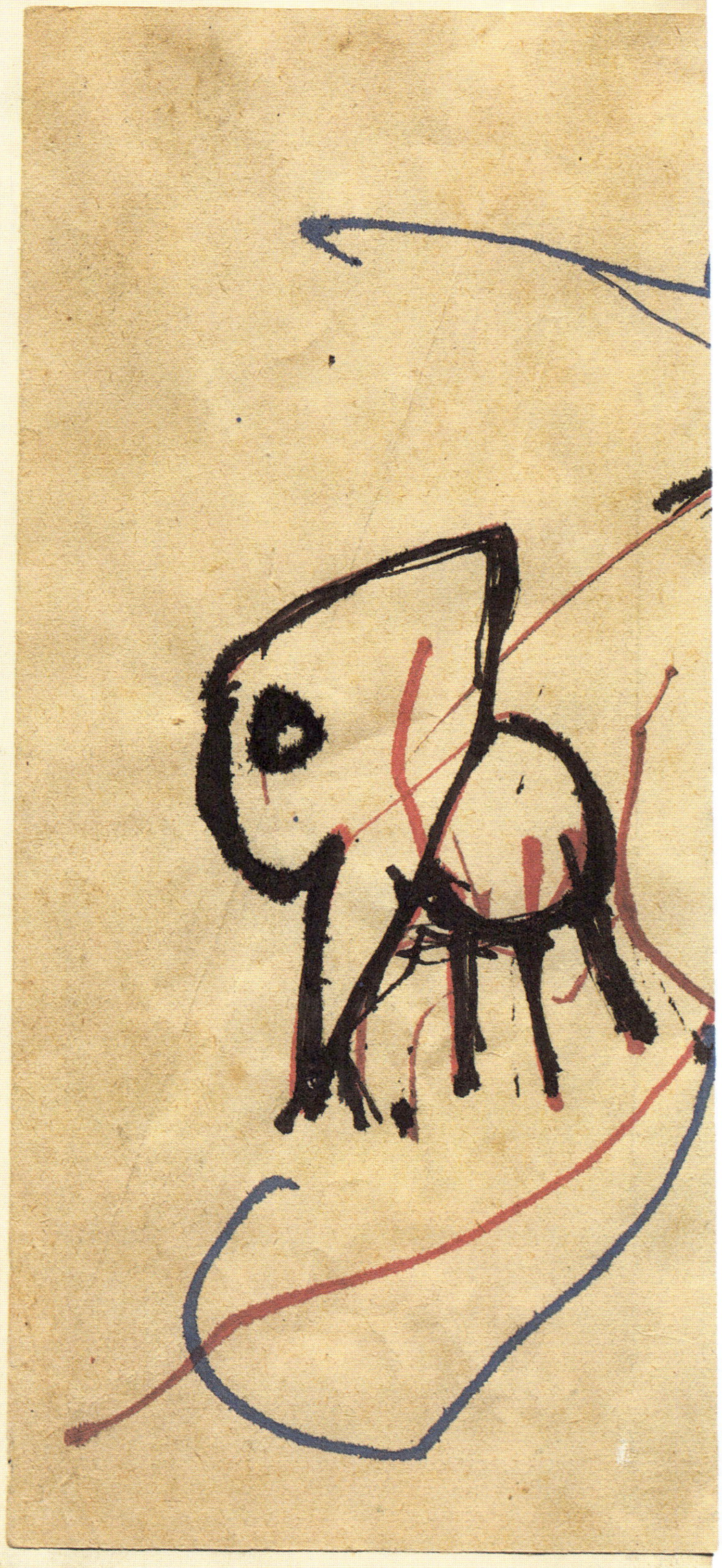

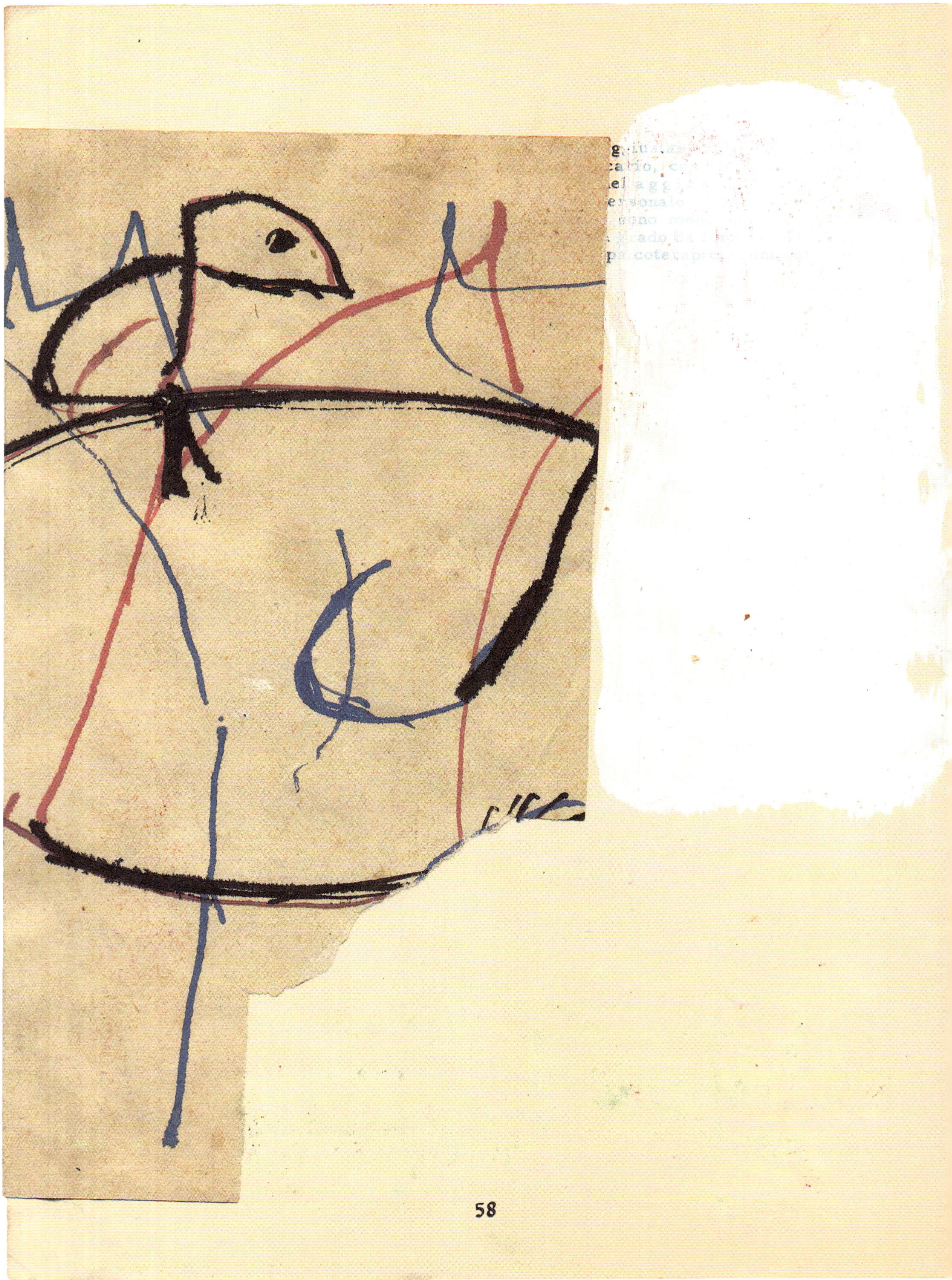
58

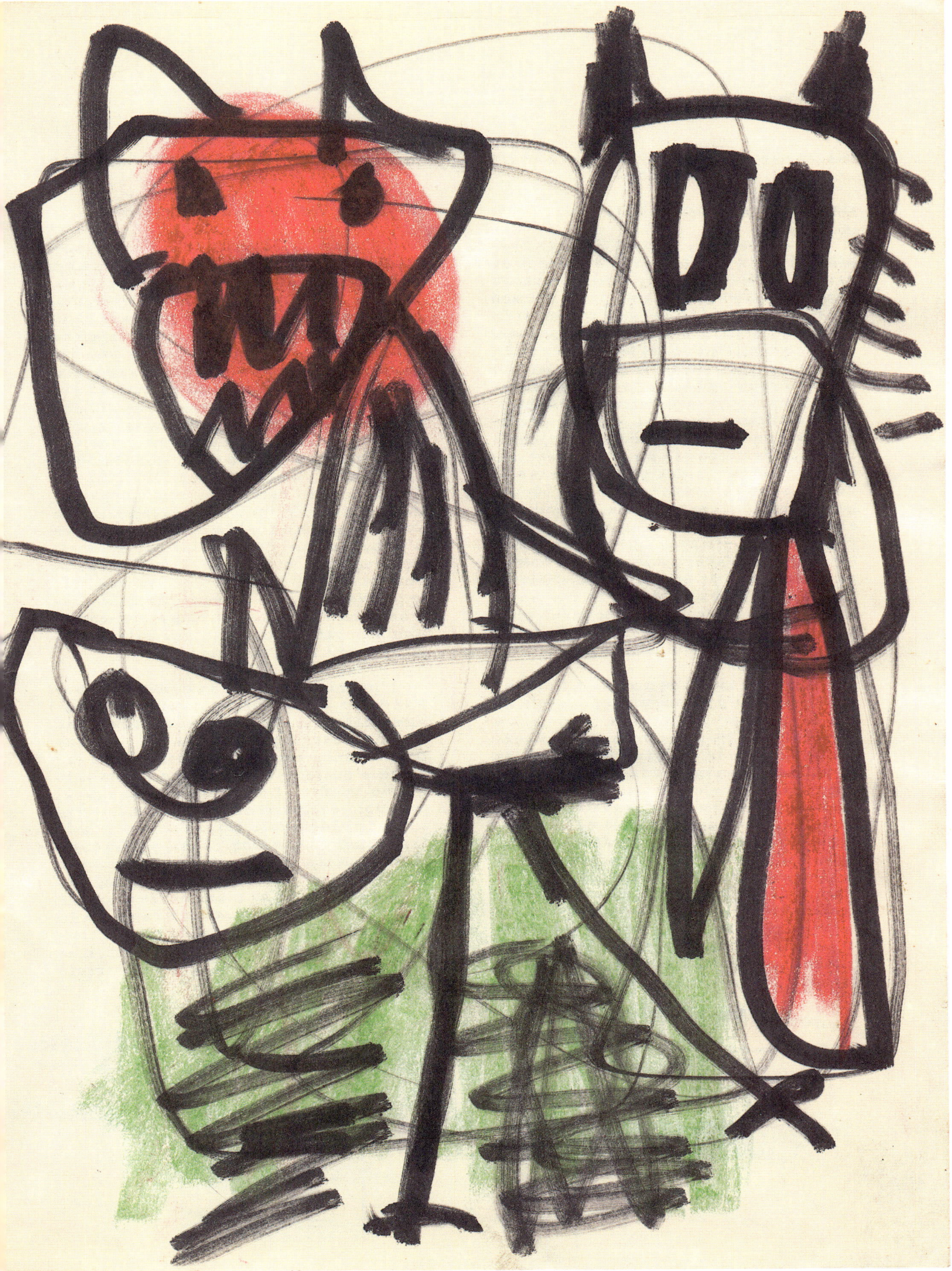

37. *Curtain*

Diagnostic: Perversion Sexuelle avec un état d'anxiété.

Hôpital: Perry Point, Maryland

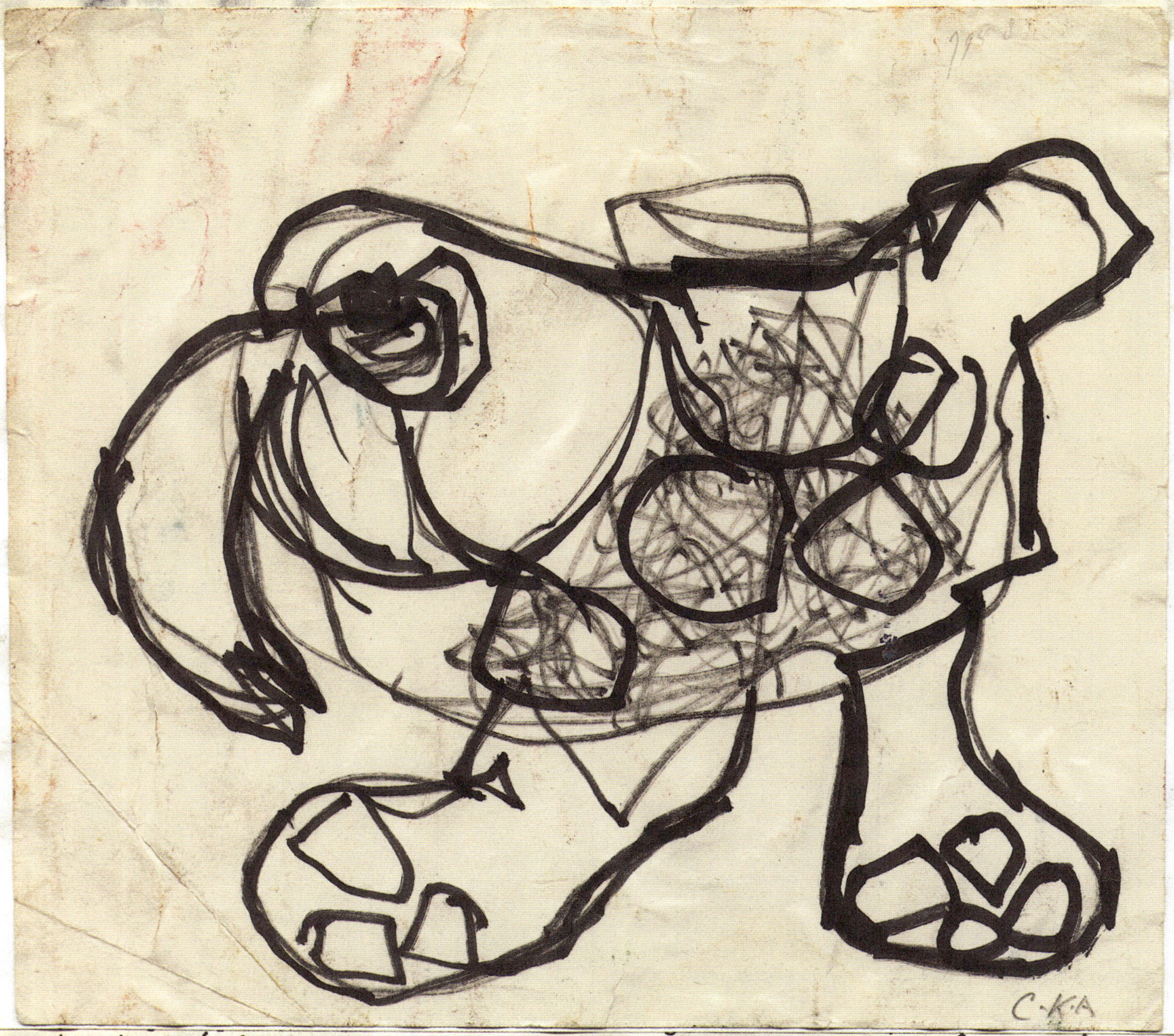

vie qui est née de nouveau.

Diagnosi: Perversione sessuale con stato d'ansia.

Ospedale: Perry Point, Maryland.

come la vita rinata.

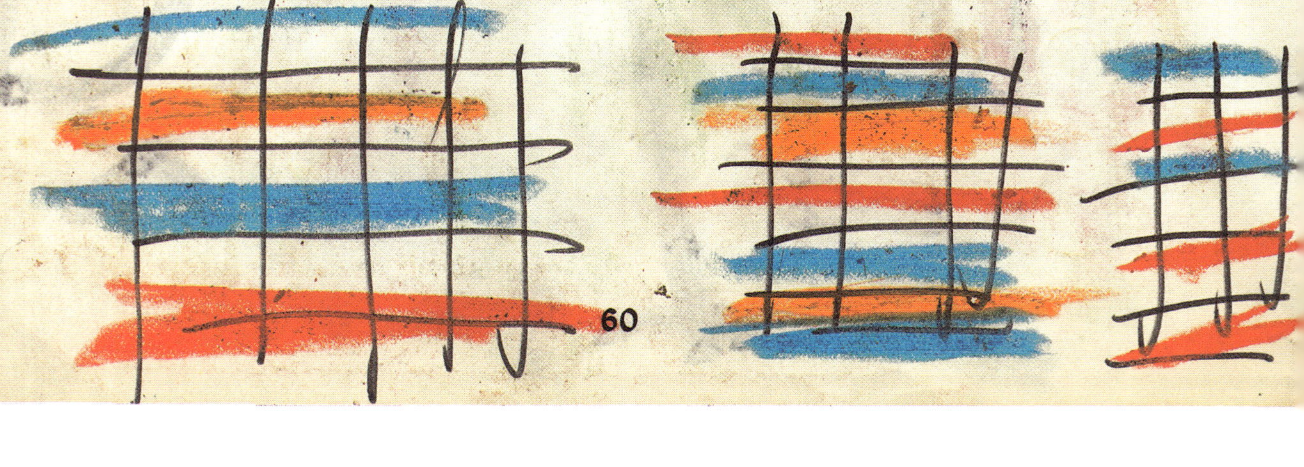

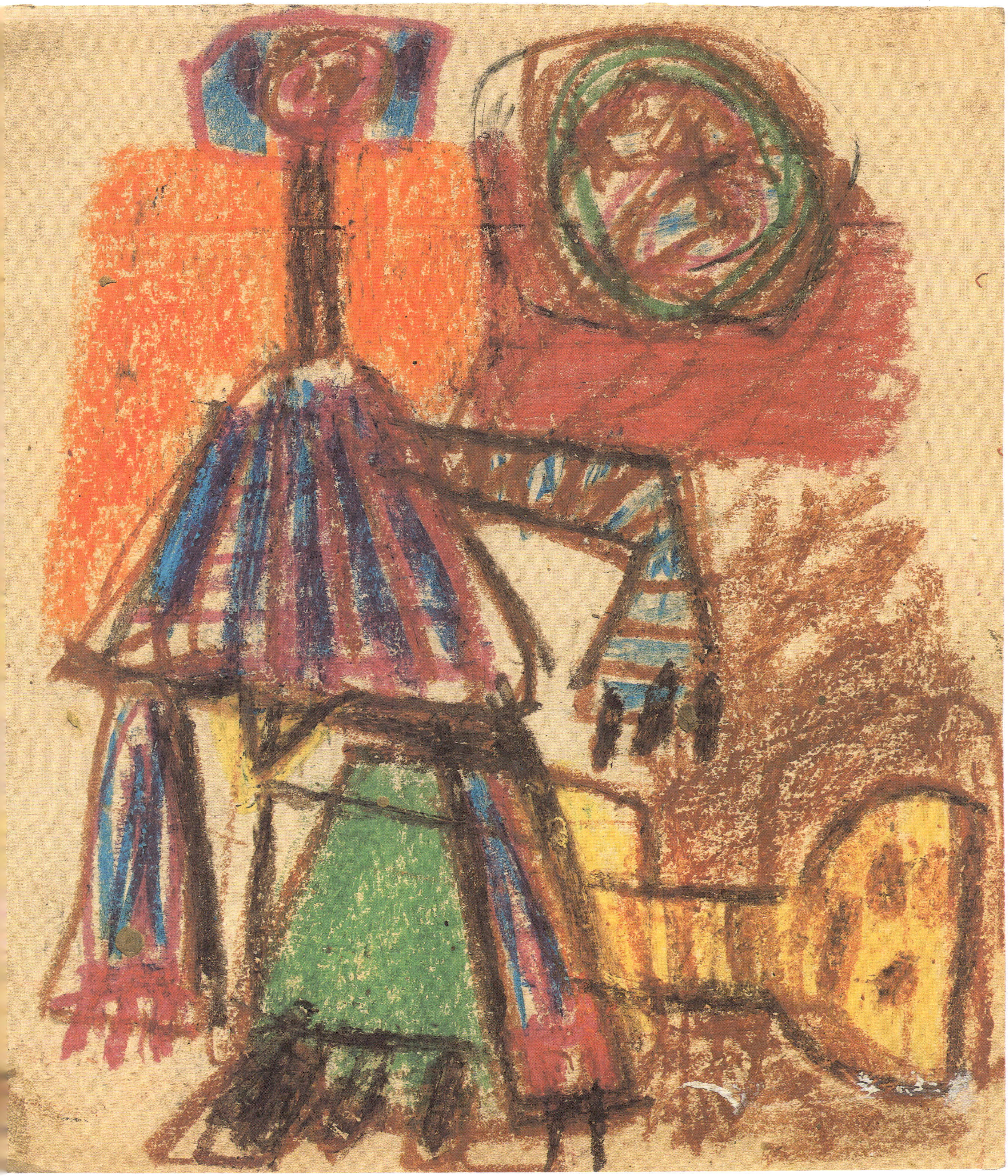

38. U

Diagnos

Clinique

Un
été soig
par la p
durant
mort à
Sa mère
ose et
trovers
tait ma
Enrôlé
croyait
religi
maladie
premièr
était la
de son
Il fut
hospit
mois en
d'établi
perso
tendance
est part
faute su
son défa

Ce m
courte
qu'il re
quitta s
un prog
nelle. D
travaille
de la pa
lui était
autres n
attitude

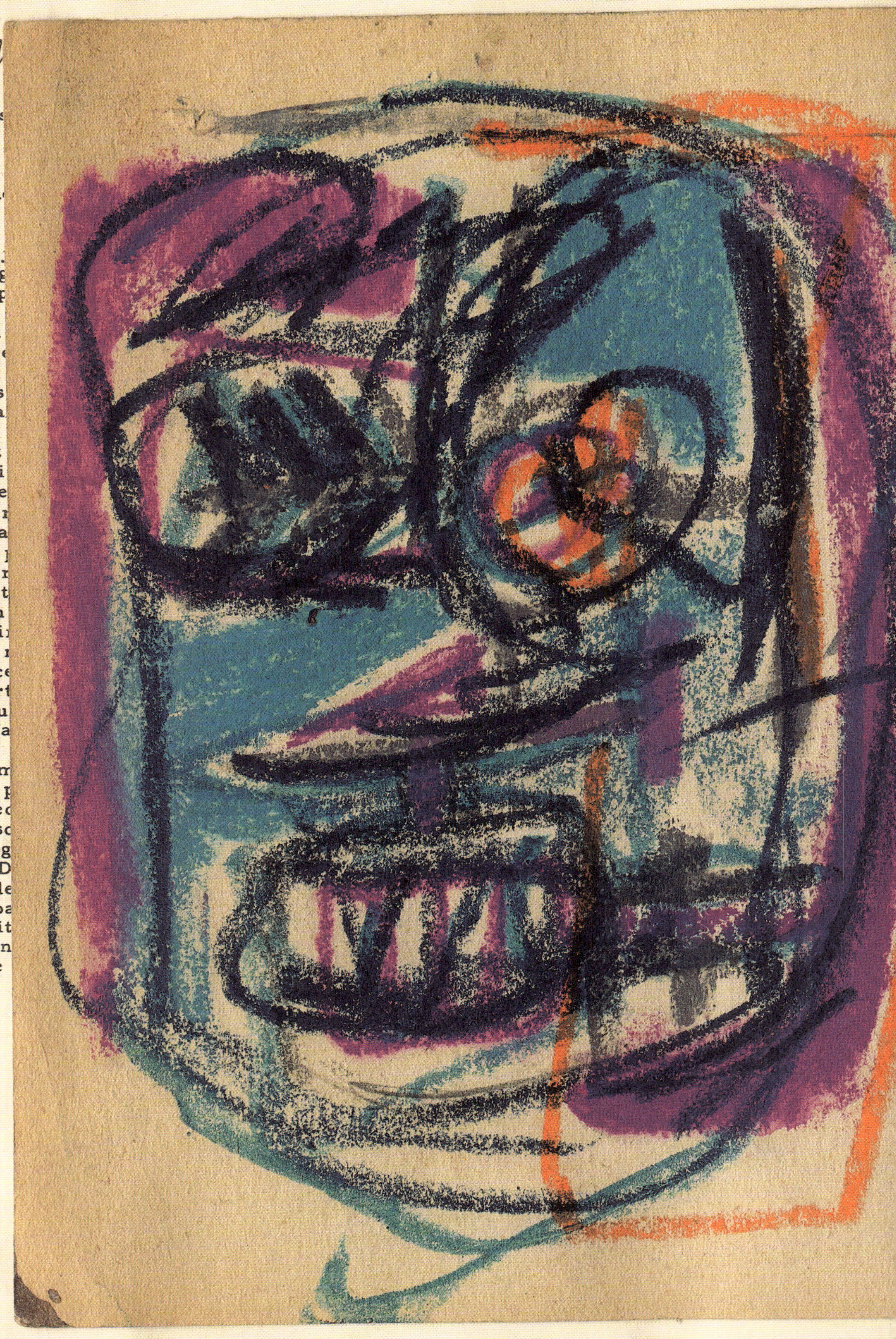

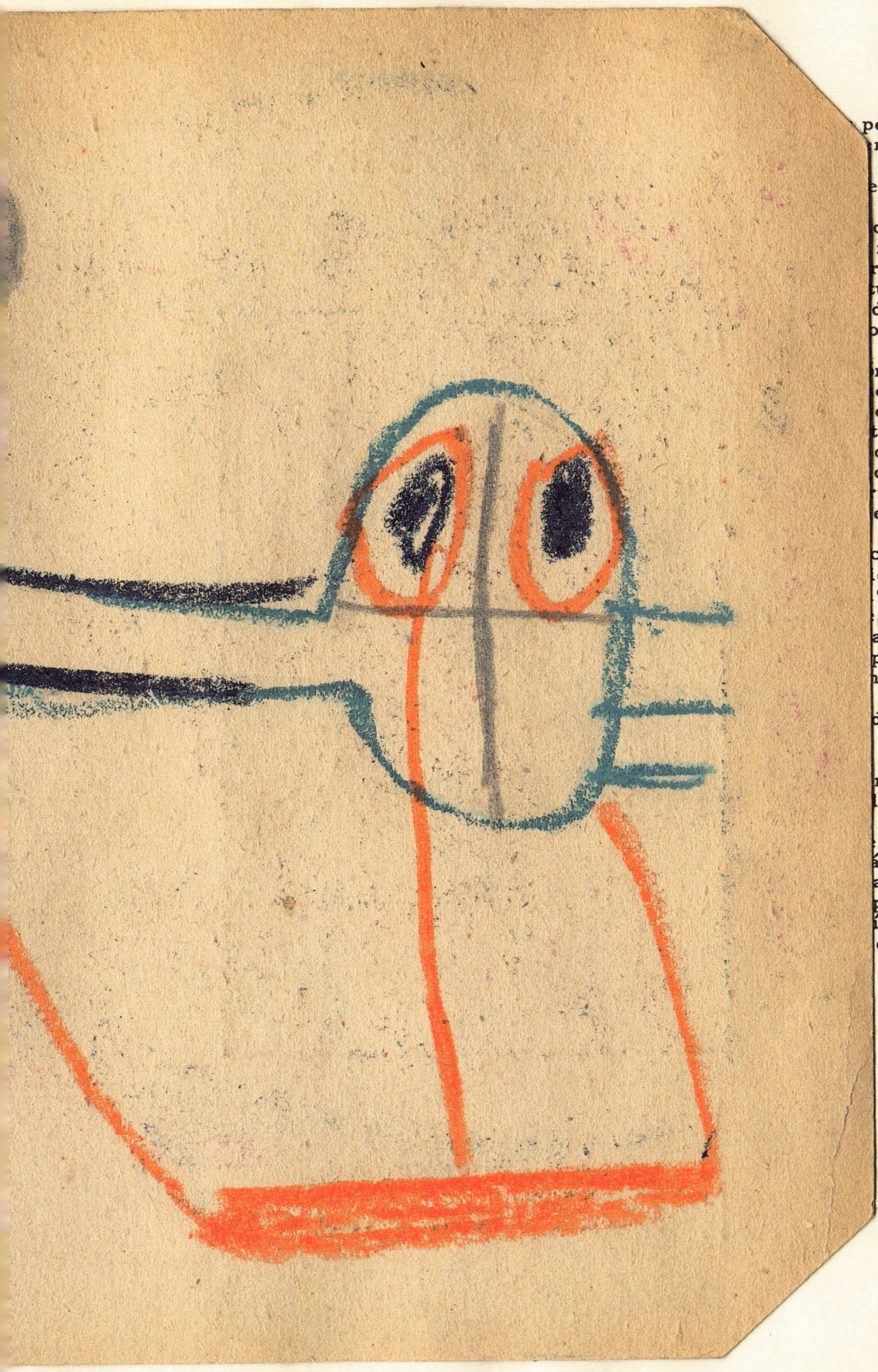

personalidad
misión.

ew York City.

de 33 años,
individual y
rante el año
tuberculosis
dre vive to-
osclerosis y
ha demos-
n y la adap-
ela y en sus
ervicio mi-
tía ser la
oso. Des-
d grave con
rimera hos-
el resultado
militar sin
cia absoluta
ó a hospi-
949. El pa-
establecer y
ales, y re-
portarse de
e una parte
a los pari-
de su mala

más que un
e arte mi-
psicotera-
empezar un
áctica. Du-
abajar solo
peuta. Que
ía inferirse
quieta y no

39. *Trio*

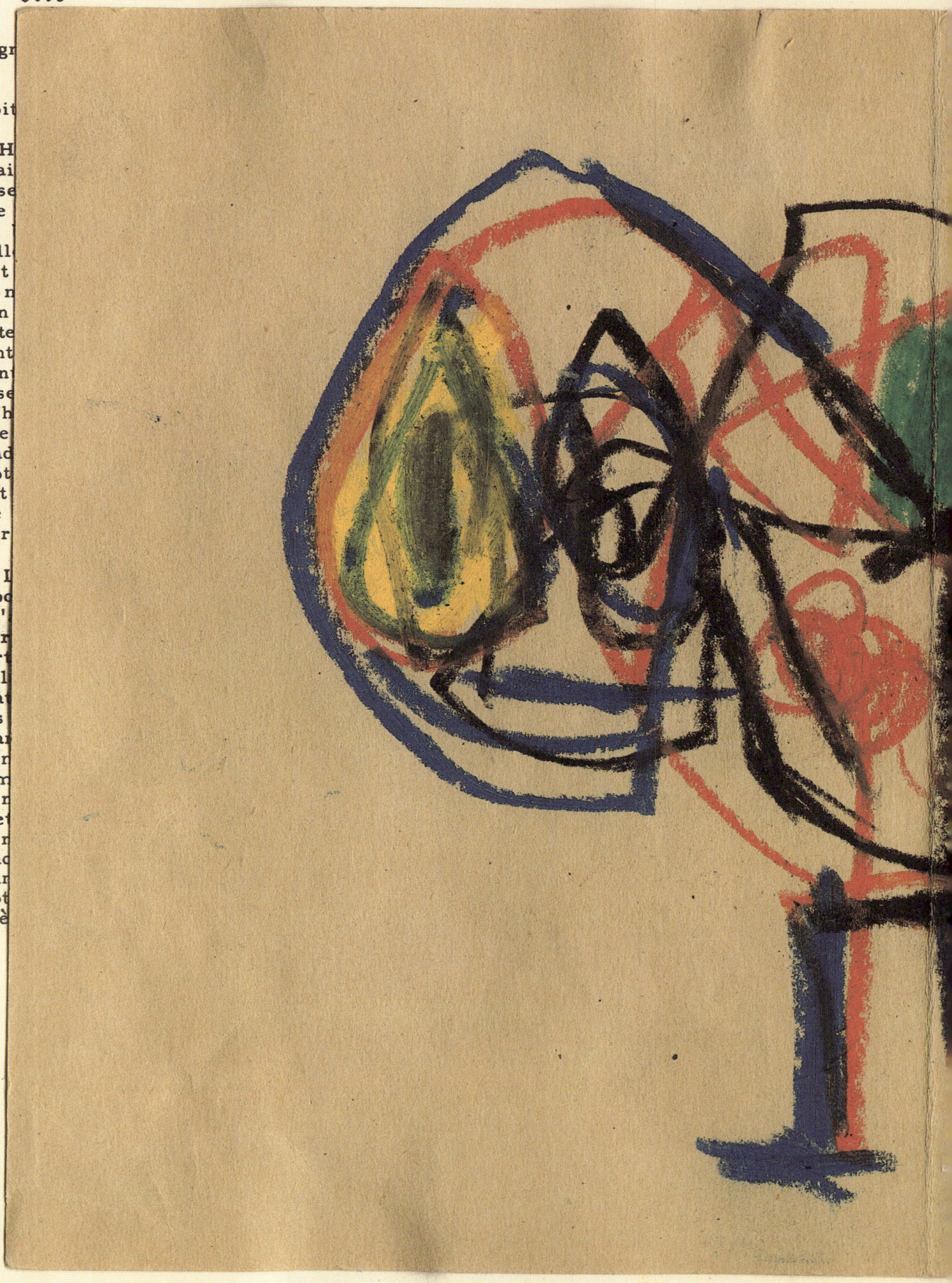

Diagr

Hôpit

H
batai
de se
cise
son
d'all
part
tion
sen
suite
s'int
men
et se
a l'h
idée
grad
quot
test
une
mor

L
sopo
à l'
four
pert
mal
L'a
ces
gra
mêr
l'im
sen
gre
men
amo
pein
mot
thè

39. Trio

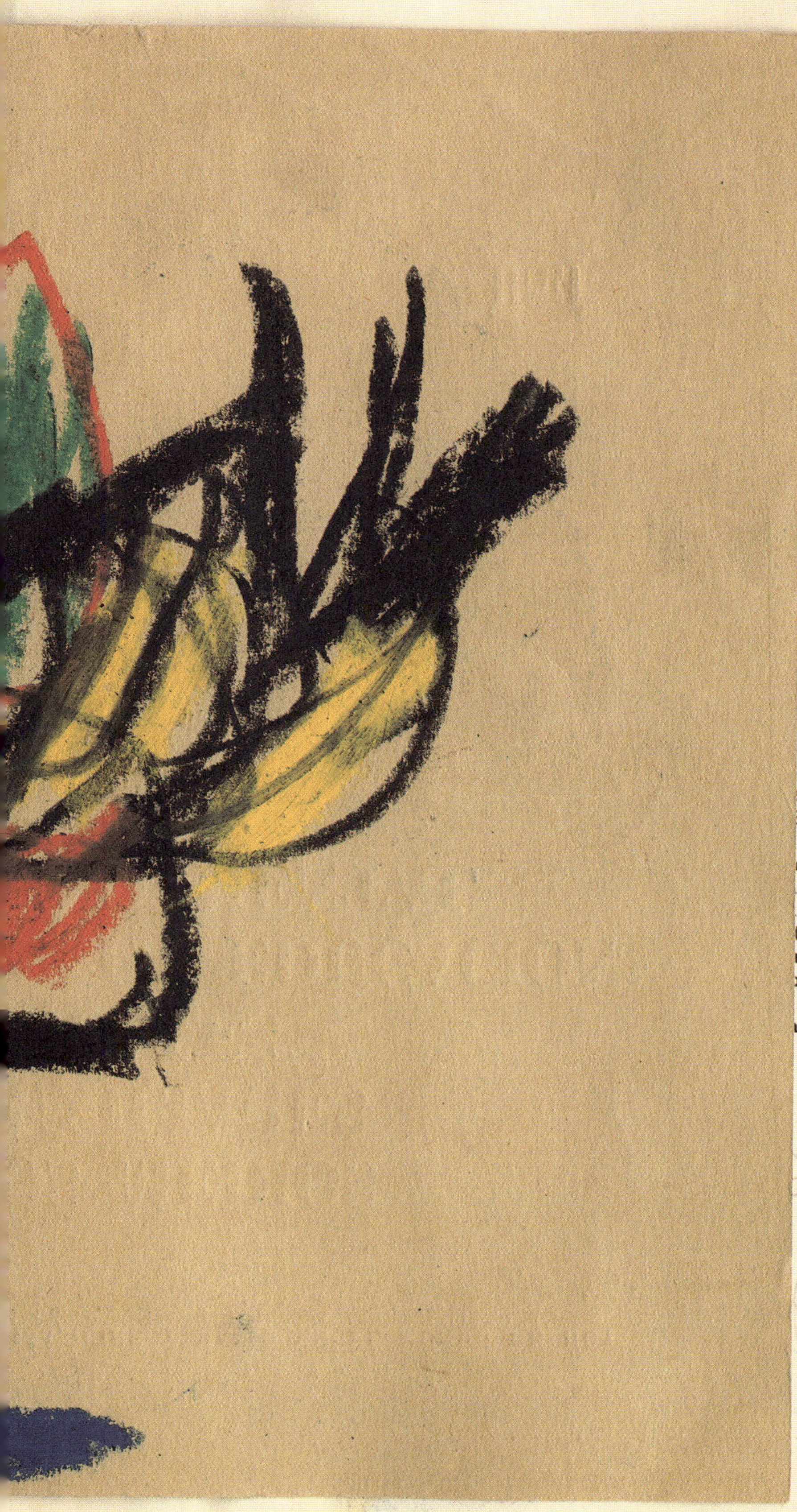

reacción esquizofrénica,
ipo paranoide.

peka, Kansas.

blanco, soltero, de 25 años,
pital después de 16 meses.
storia distinta de la pri-
severa durante la infancia
na rígida de la eliminación
res inhibidos y convencion-
iente llegó a ser un joven
diente y afeminado. Después
o de servicio en el ejército,
náticamente de un movimi-
paz mundial, se puso hiper-
mostró el comportamiento
Cuando se admitió, estaba
so, grandioso y ilusivo. Se
n instituto de arte recono-
cociente de inteligencia de
es psicológicos evidenciaron
lidad premorbosa, obsesiva
a y que se pone intelectual.

nte demostró una reacción
la insulinoterapia de coma.
estudio de arte para las
nes sustitutivas que esto le
después de la pérdida de sus
ómanas y como medio de
ión y reintegración. Esto
ejoramientos en todos estos
El paciente pintó con gran
cia y destreza técnica. El
ó que hubiera perdido el
erza creadora presentes en
s y sintió la pérdida. Pero,
te, no había una diminución
ncia creadora, aunque el
ostró un cambio de motivos
enojados a temas líricos y
te dibujados.

40. Portrait

Diagnostic: Réaction schizophrénique, type non classé, grave.

Clinique d'Hygiène Mentale: New York City.

Un nègre âgé de 27 ans, célibataire, présentement sans travail. Le père était trop indulgent et la mère négligeante. Les parents se séparaient à plusieurs reprises. Le malade bégaye depuis sa jeune enfance, désavoue toute aventure hétérosexuelle et homosexuelle, et dit qu'il a quitté l'école secondaire pendant le septième semestre, à l'âge de 18 ans. Il a eu deux emplois de courte durée avant de s'enrôler dans l'Armée, où il fut hospitalisé presque immédiatement et congédié avec le diagnostic de schizophrénie. Il est insociable, paresseux, mal peigné, et grimace et sourit sans raison apparente. Sa conversation est souvent non pertinente et incohérente. Il a des hallucinations auditives récurrentes, avec un trait paranoide. Sa pensée est désorganisée et affective, et ses facultés volitives affaiblies. Il élabore beaucoup de fantaisies et a un défaut dans sa perception de la réalité.

Ce malade a été envoyé à l'Atelier Curatif pour la thérapie. Il n'a pas compris les instructions, et il était difficile de trouver des projets assez élémentaires pour qu'il puisse les exécuter avec succès. Il est resté docile, modérément confus et vague, gesticulant et monologant; fréquemment il s'endort pendant qu'il travaille à un projet. Auparavant retiré et parlant très peu aux autres malades, maintenant il leur répond ainsi qu'aux thérapeutes lorsqu'on lui adresse la parole. L'ouvrage, qui était au commencement de qualité inferieure accompli rapidement et incorrectement, est fait maintenant à une allure plus modérée. Graduellement il s'est habitué à travailler principalement à l'atelier d'art, où il passe beaucoup de temps à copier des caricature, ajoutant des couleurs éclatantes sans égard pour leur place dans le tableau. Parfois le malade accomplit maintenant quelques ouvrages de talent, la plupart en couleur à l'eau, indépendamment du materiel copié. Dans ces cas-la ses tableaux présentent une logique artistique et un developpement

Diagnosi: Reazione schizofrenica, tipo non classificato, acuta.

Clinica dell'Igiene Mentale: New York City.

Un negro di 27 anni, celibe, presentemente disoccupato. Il padre era stato troppo indulgente, la madre negligente. I genitori erano stati separati a più riprese. Il paziente ha tartagliato dalla sua bassa infanzia; nega qualunque esperienze od eterosessuali od omosessuali e dice, che aveva abbandonato la scuola all'età de 18 anni, quando era nella 4 a classe. Fu impiegato brevemente due volte prima di entrare nell'esercito, dove fu ricoverato quasi subito, poi rilasciato con diagnosi di schizofrenia. L'ammalato è insocievole, letargico, trascurato in riguardo alla sua apparenza; smorfie e sorride senza raggione apparente. La sua conversazione è spesso irrelevante ed incoerente. Vi erano ricorrenti allucinazioni auditorie con contenuto paranoido. Il modo di pensare è disorganizzato ed affettivo e le facultà conative sono sminuite. Vi è molto d'elaborazione di fantasie ed un difetto nella sua percezione della realtà.

Questo paziente fu riferito al Laboratorio Curativo per una terapia appoggiativa. Non capì le direzioni, sì ch'era difficile di trovare progetti abbastanza simplici, progetti che possa compire con successo. Il paziente è rimasto docile, un po' confuso e rimosso; gesticola e parla a sè stesso e frequentemente addormentasi lavorando ad un progetto. Mentre precedentemente ritiravasi, parlando di rado cogli altri ammalati, risponde ora quando essi, o gli terapisti, gli parlavano. Il suo lavoro insoddisfacente, era compito da prima presto e senza esatezza; ora è fatto ad un passo più moderato. Venì, gradualmente, a lavorare sopratutto nel laboratorio di pittura dove passa molto di tempo, copiando caricature, addendo dei colori vivaci senza riguardo al loro luogo nel quadro. Al presente il paziente dà talvolta, di rado, dei lavori sporadici mostrandi il talento, per il più degli acquarelli, independentemente del materiale copiato. Allora le sue pitture mos-

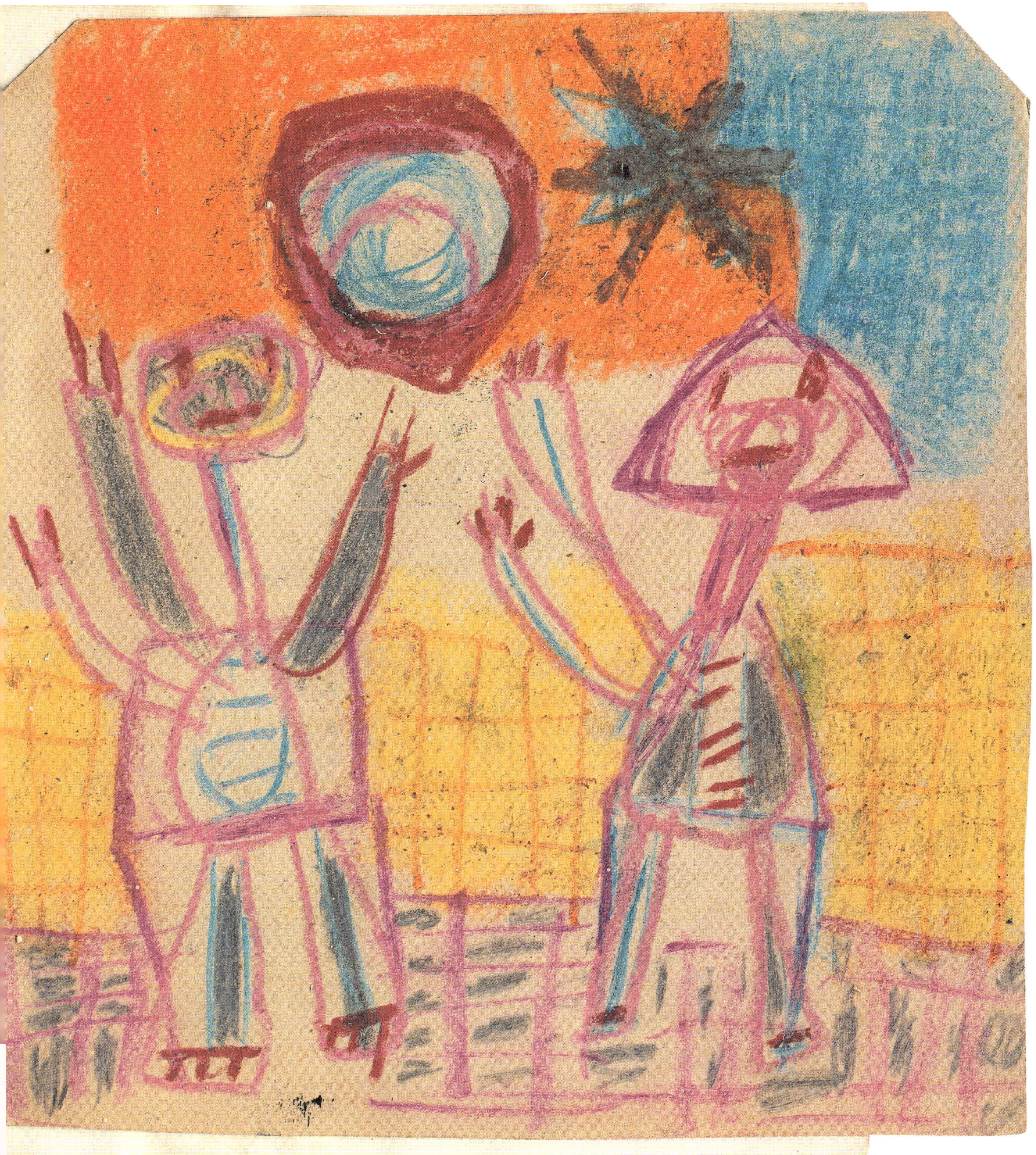

dramatique authentique du sujet. Le rapport n'a pas beaucoup changé, et il n'y a pas eu d'amélioration sensible dans son intégration de personnalité.

trano una logica artistica ed un autentico sviluppo dramatico del soggetto. Il rapporto non ha cambiato in nessun modo significativo e non vi era nulla di miglioramento apprezabile nell'integrazione della sua personalità.

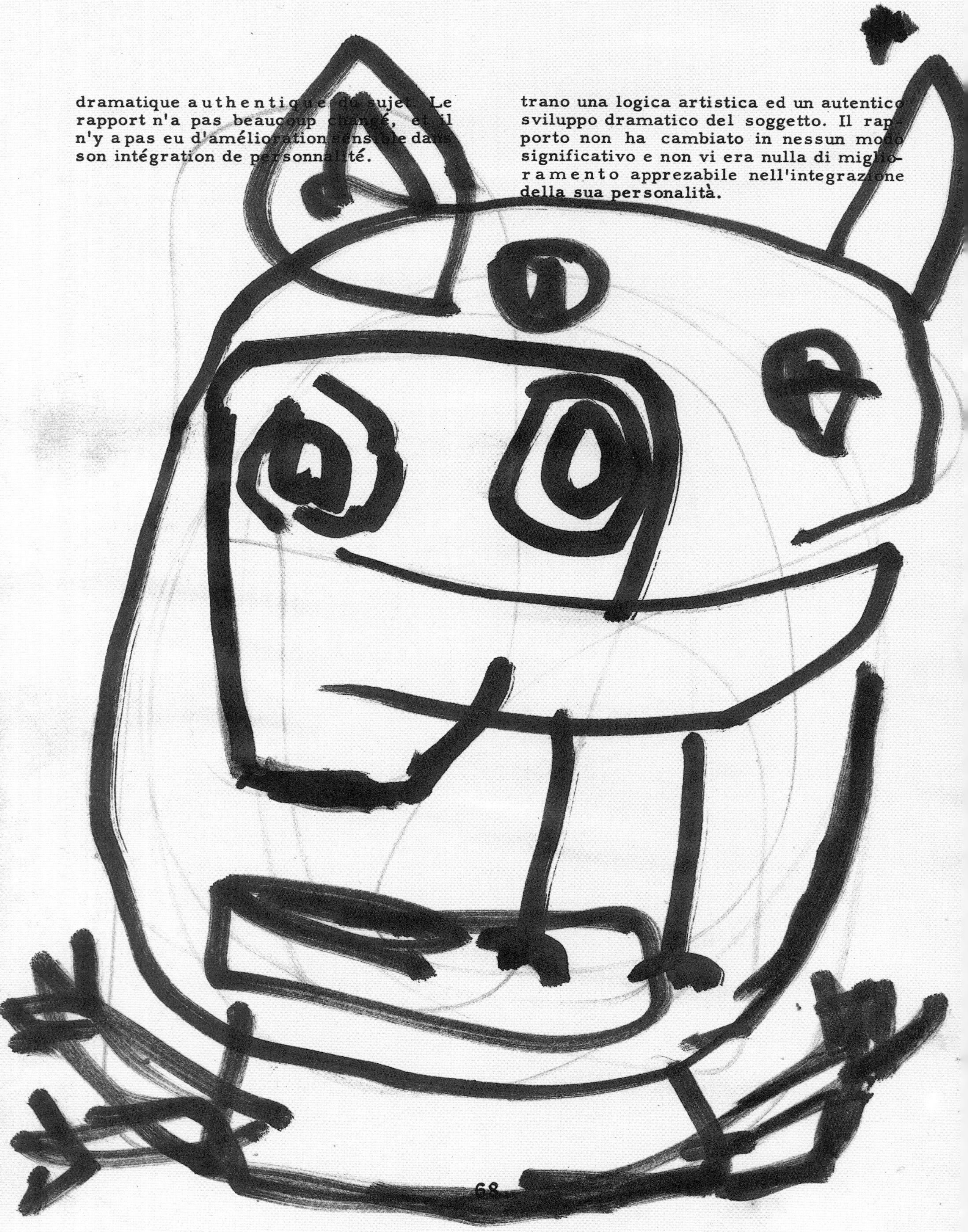

tales ocasiones sus pinturas demuestran la lógica artística y el desarrollo auténtico y dramático del tema. La concordancia no se ha cambiado significativamente, y no ha habido mejoramiento notable de la integración de su personalidad.

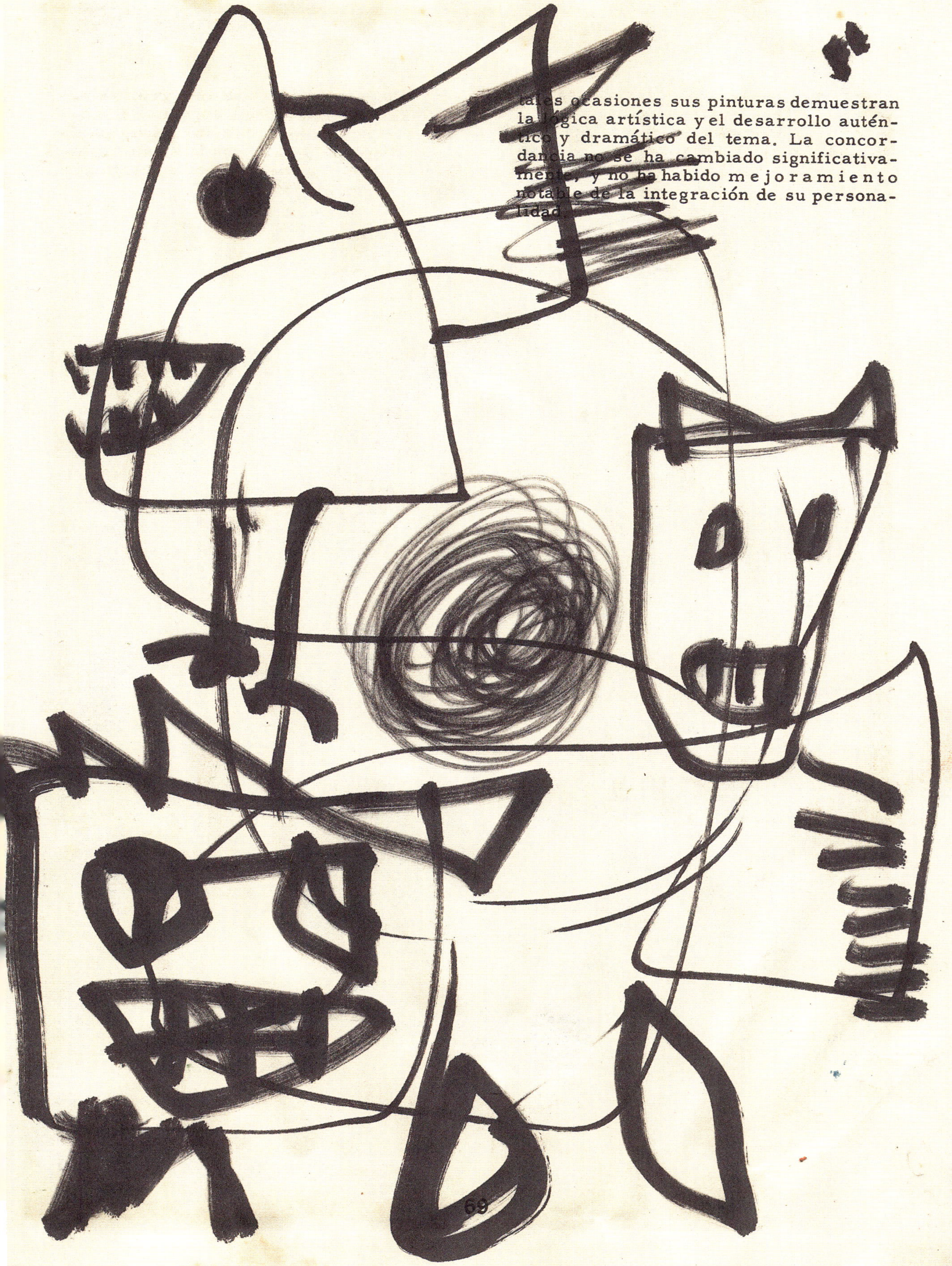

41. Hel

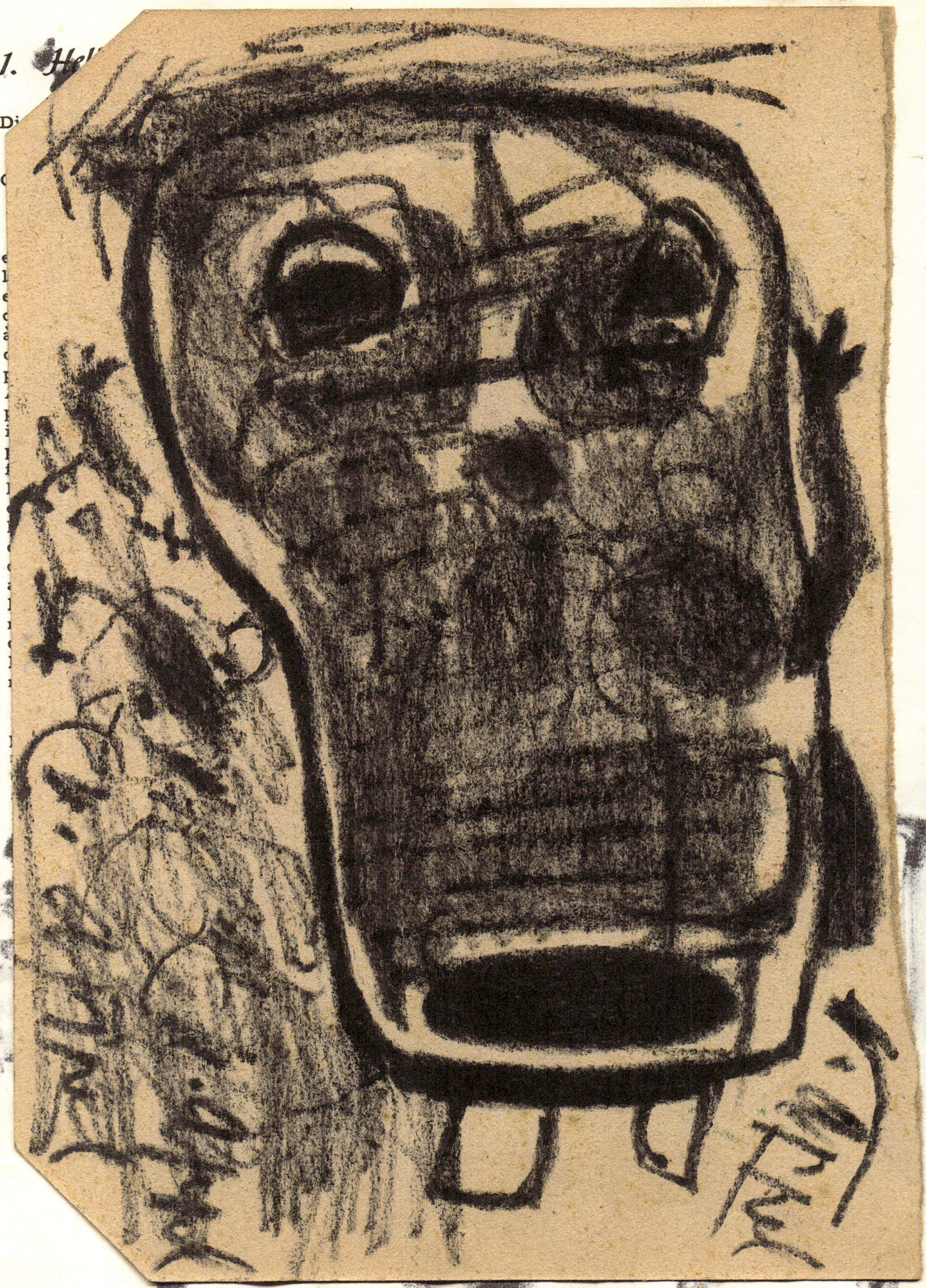

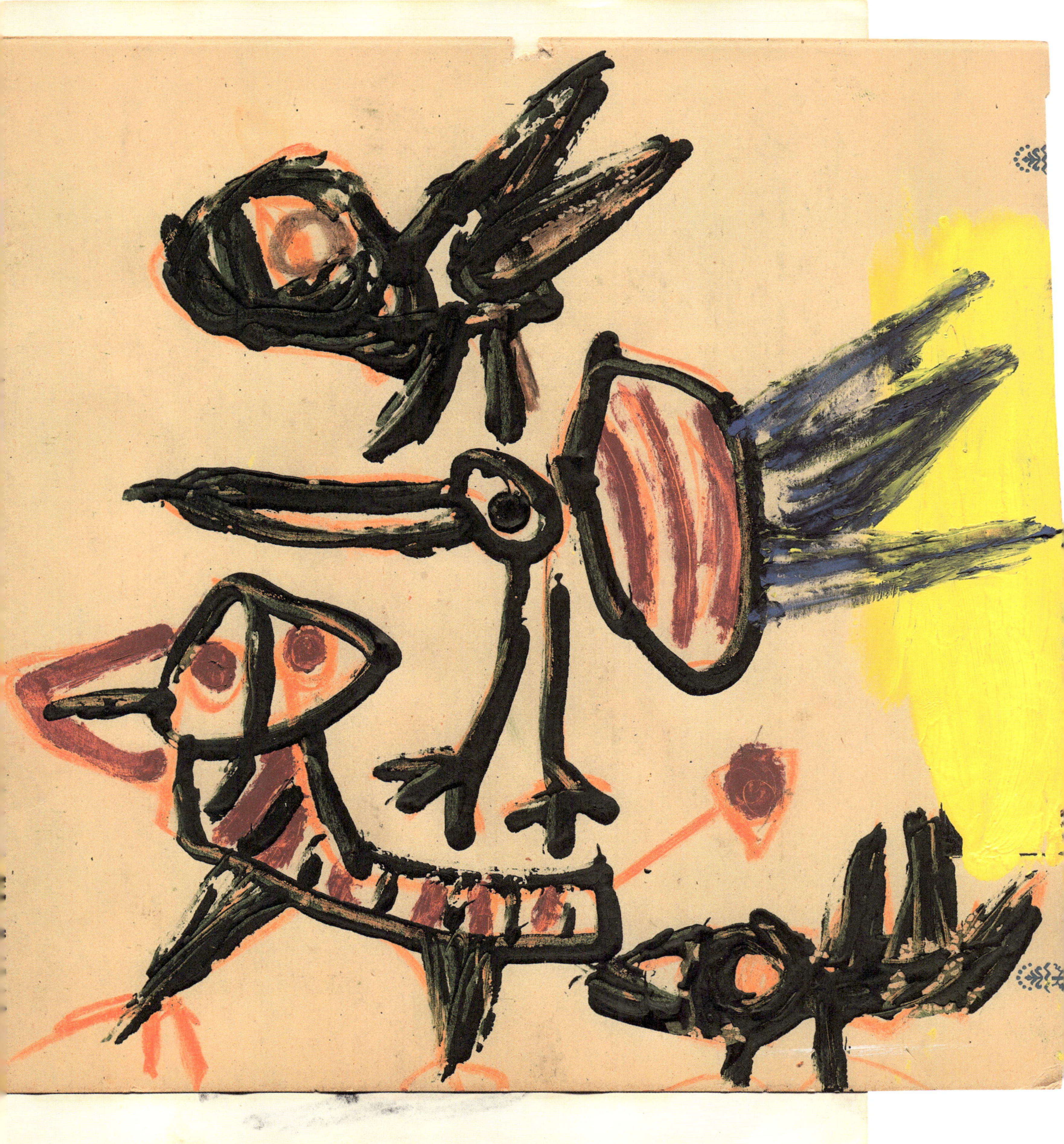

42. *Lost and Gone*

Diagnostic: Réaction schizophrénique, type paranoide.

Hôpital: Lyons, New Jersey.

Cette peinture est l'ouvrage du même malade dont le tableau "100% Parastructive" est montré ailleurs à l'exposition.

Diagnosi: Reazione schizofrenica, tipo paranoido.

Ospedale: Lyons, New Jersey.

Questa pittura è un lavoro del paziente di cui il "100% Parastructive" è mostrato in un'altro luogo dell'esposizione.

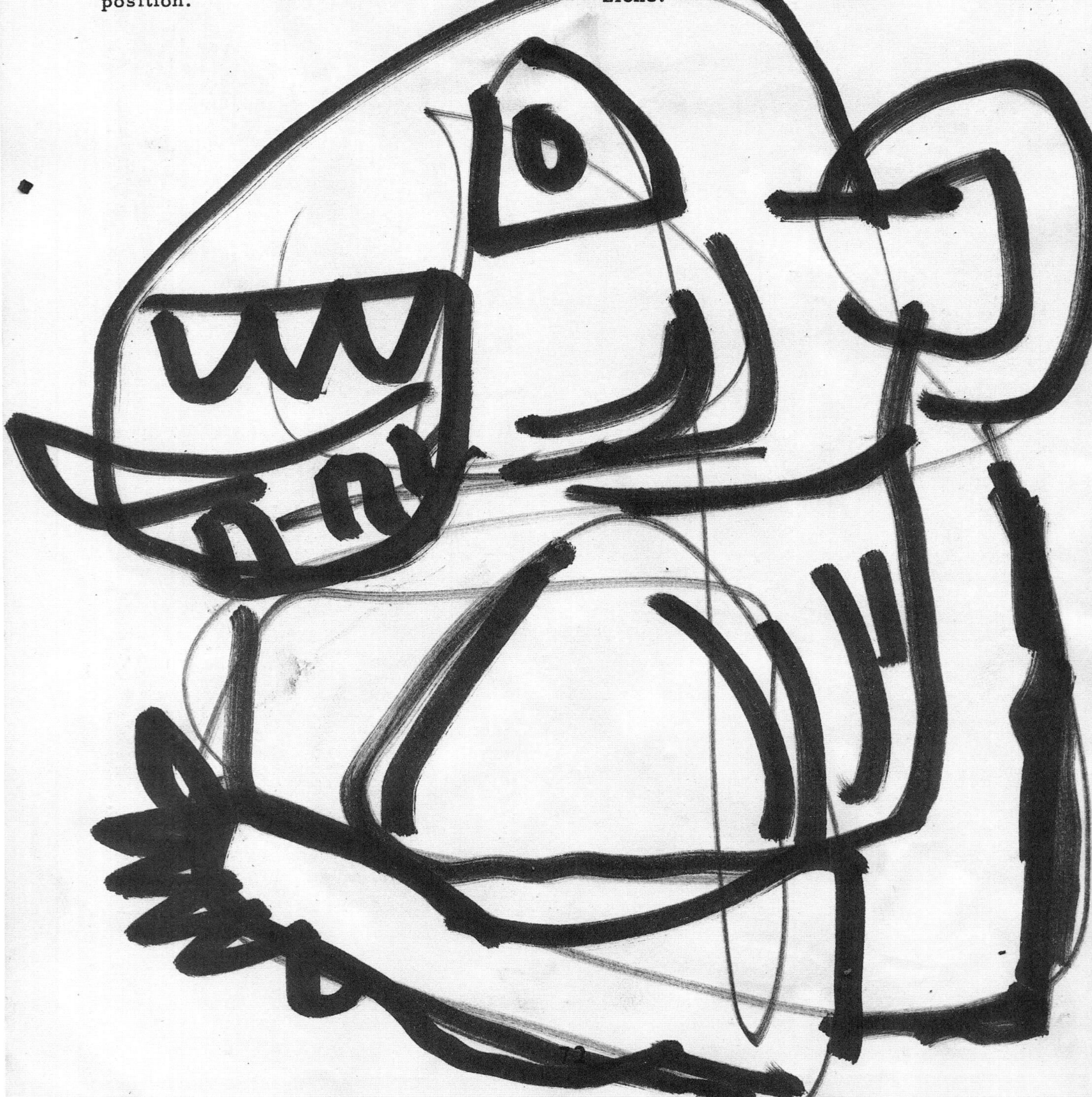

42. *Lost and Gone*

Diagnosis: Schizophrenic reaction, paranoid type.

Hospital: Lyons, New Jersey.

This painting is the work of the same patient whose "100% Parastructive" is displayed elsewhere in the exhibit.

Diagnosis: Reacción esquizofrénica, tipo paranoide.

Hospital: Lyons, New Jersey.

Esta pintura es la obra del mismo paciente cuya pintura "100% Parastructive" se exhibe en cualquiera otra parte de la exposición.

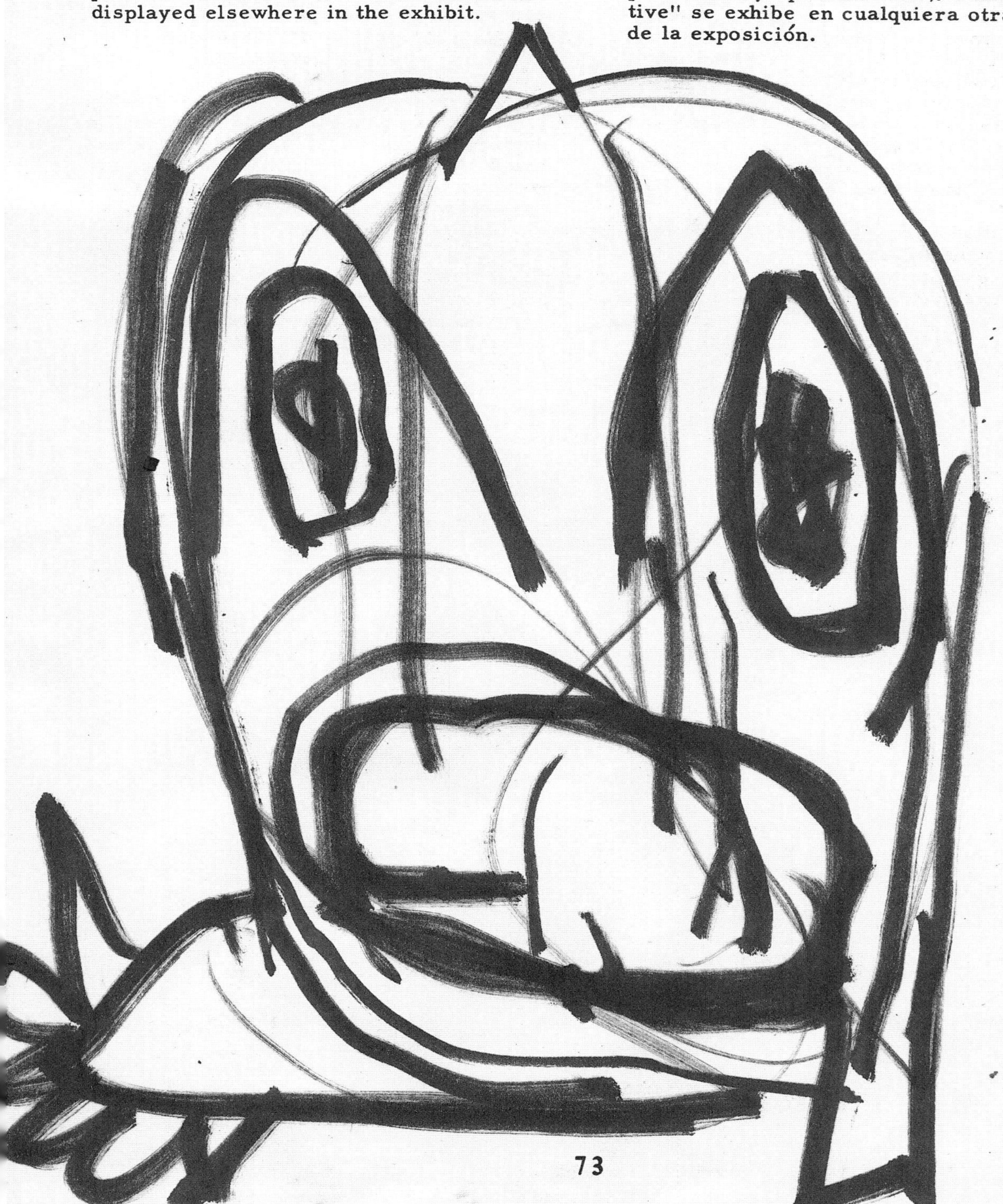

43. *Mother*

Diagnostic: Réaction schizophrénique, type mixte.

Hôpital: Los Angeles, California.

Un homme blanc, âgé de 20 ans, célibataire. Le malade refuse de fréquenter les autres malades et s'occupe constamment de son ouvrage d'art, dont il a beaucoup d'illusions grandioses. Il ne s'est pas amélioré par le traitement, et il fut envoyé chez lui pour une visite d'essai sur la demande de ses parents. Pendant qu'il était à l'hôpital, le malade a peint un grand nombre de tableaux, tous avec presque le même sujet.

Diagnosi: Reazione schizofrenica, tipo mischiato.

Ospedale: Los Angeles, California.

Un'uomo di 20 anni, celibe, di razza bianca. Il paziente si rifiuta d'associare con gli altri pazienti, è constantemente preoccupato per lavori di natura artistica, in riguardo per gli quali ha delle numerose delusioni di grandezza. Non mostrò un miglioramento in corso del trattamento e fu inviato alla sua casa, in seguito alla domanda dei genitori. Durante il suo soggiorno all'ospedale, dipingì un gran numero di quadri, tutti i quali trattavano più

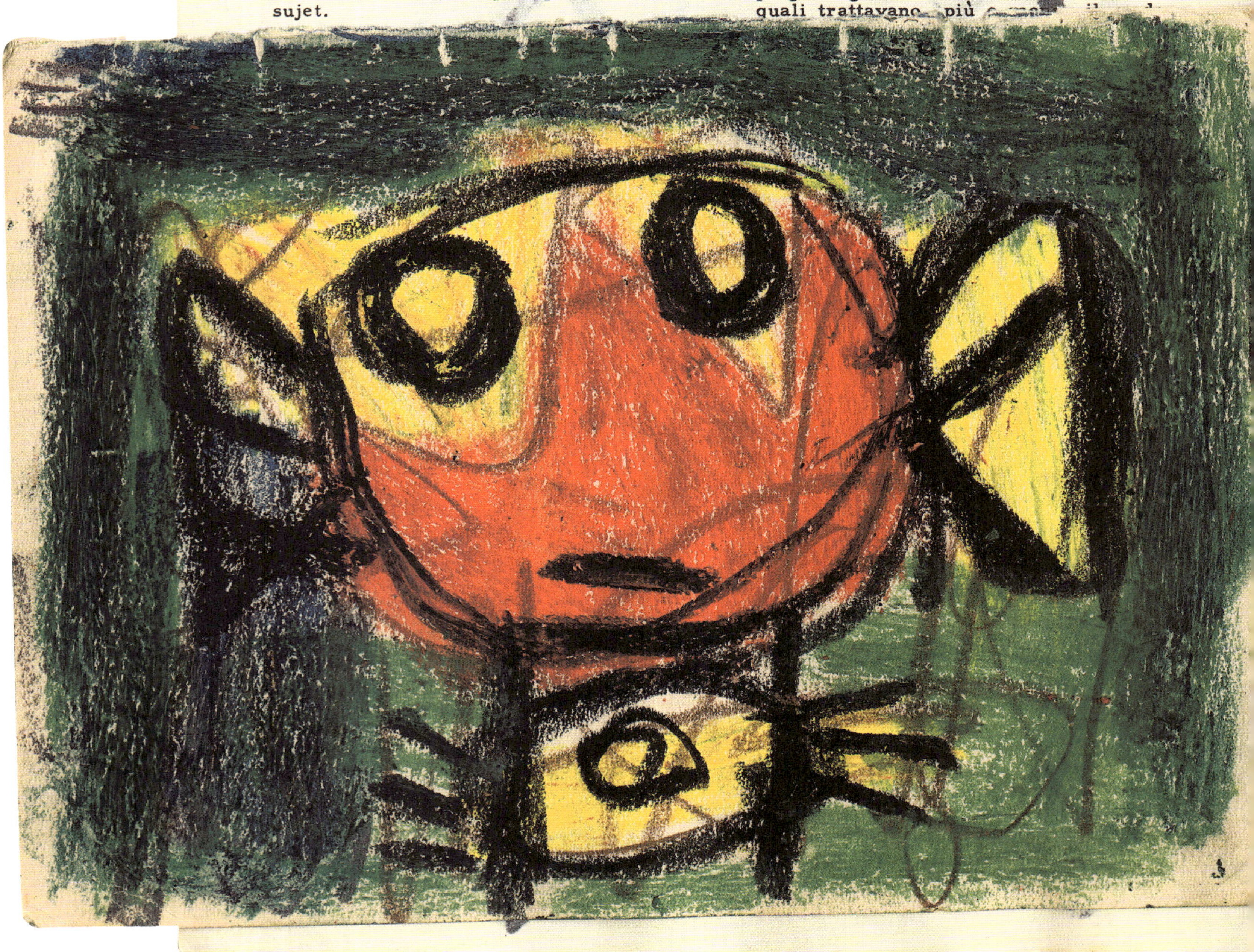

43. *Mother*

Diagnosis: Schizophrenic reaction, mixed type.

Hospital: Los Angeles, California.

Age 20, single, white male. Patient refuses to associate with other patients and is constantly preoccupied in art work concerning which he has numerous grandiose delusions. He did not improve under treatment and was sent home on a trial visit at the solicitation of his parents. While in hospital, the patient painted a great number of canvases, all of them dealing with much the same subject matter.

The patient's behavior, attitudes and technical
change du
ance in th
his painti
gest stero

Diagnosis: Reacción esquizofrénica, tipo mixto.

Hospital: Los Angeles, California.

Hombre, blanco, soltero, de 20 años. El paciente se niega a asociarse con los otros pacientes, y constantemente está preocupado en obras de arte respecto a que tiene numerosas ilusiones grandiosas. No se mejoró por tratamiento, y se envió a casa para una visita de prueba a petición de sus padres. Durante su hospitalización completó numerosas pinturas, todas de las cuales trataron de asuntos semejantes.

El comportamiento, las actitudes y la destreza técnica del paciente no sufrió
nte el tiempo que
un el contenido de
niforme que pareció

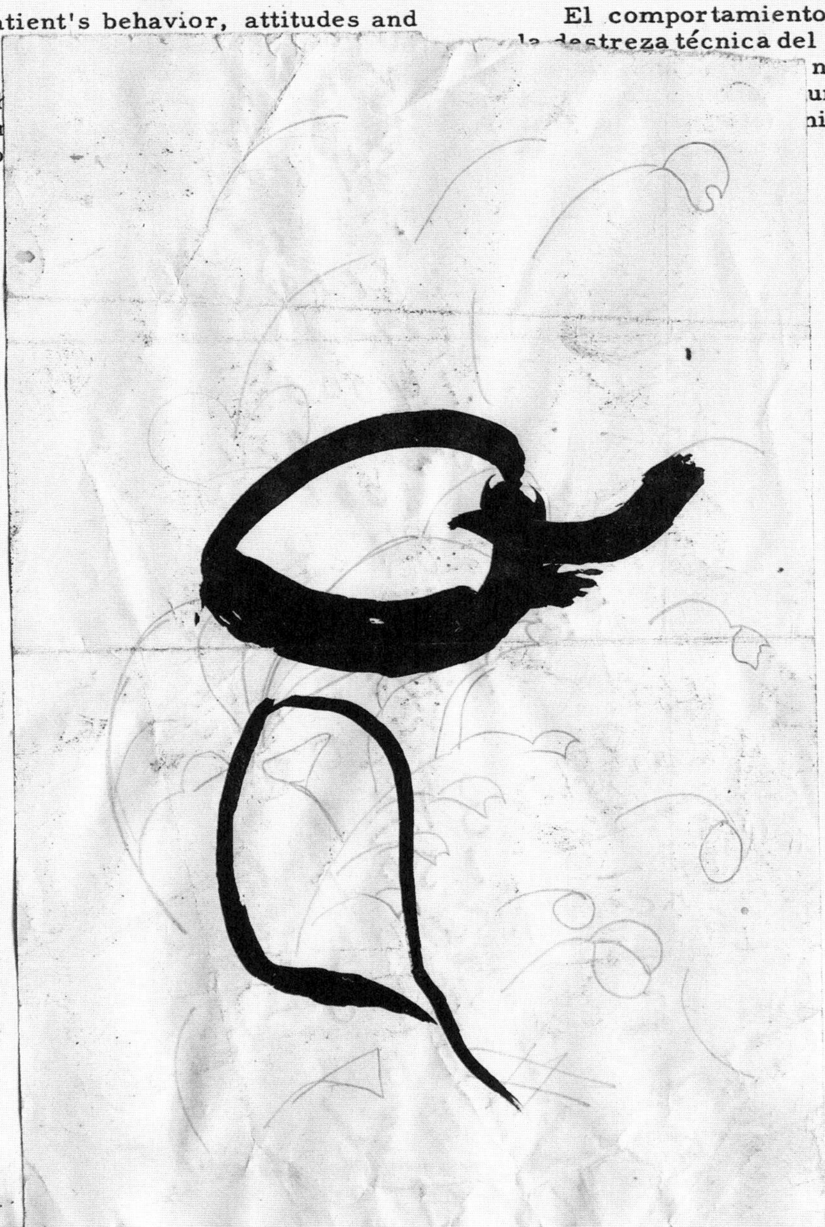

44. *Grapes*

Diagnostic: Psychonévros
iété chez un
schizoide.

Hôpital: Topeka, Kansas.

Homme blanc, âgé de
bataire, sorti de l'hôpital
Histoire d'adoption à l'
Un enfant turbulent qui
gâté, mais qui avait peu
Mouvements de mauvaise
bas âge. Un jeune homme
de nombreuses affectatio
l'école militaire et comme
de collège, mais qui était
son travail. Il développa
de grande richesse fastu
querelles avec sa mère.
l'hôpital à cause de nervos
de concentrer son attentio
folie, et des sentiments
observé. Quotient d'intelli

Lorsqu'il entra à l'ate
avait une apparence haga
et craintive. Au comme
voulait pas travailler, ma
il fit un croquis, duquel il
première peinture. Celle-
son conflit, présentant un
de piano avec des ombres
chevauchantes au-dessu
elles étaient celles d'obs
visibles. Comme la théra
gressait, il peignait des
agressives et de la matie
d'une profondeur psycholo
sante qui était employé
thérapie individuelle. Sa c
ployer ces perspicacités
par une amélioration clin
parence changea, el
sociable. Il compléta ave
visite d'essai de trois mo
voyé guéri.

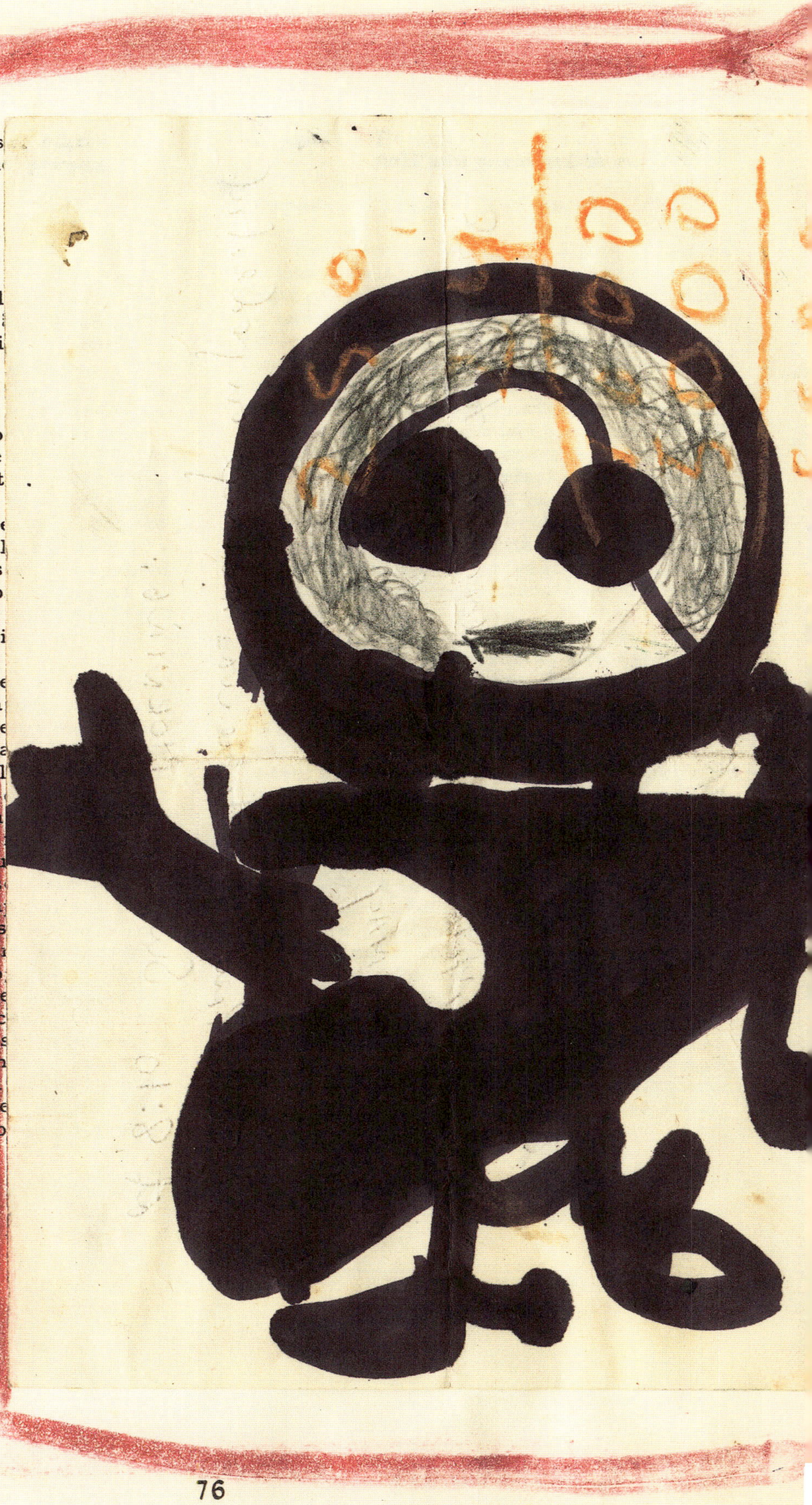

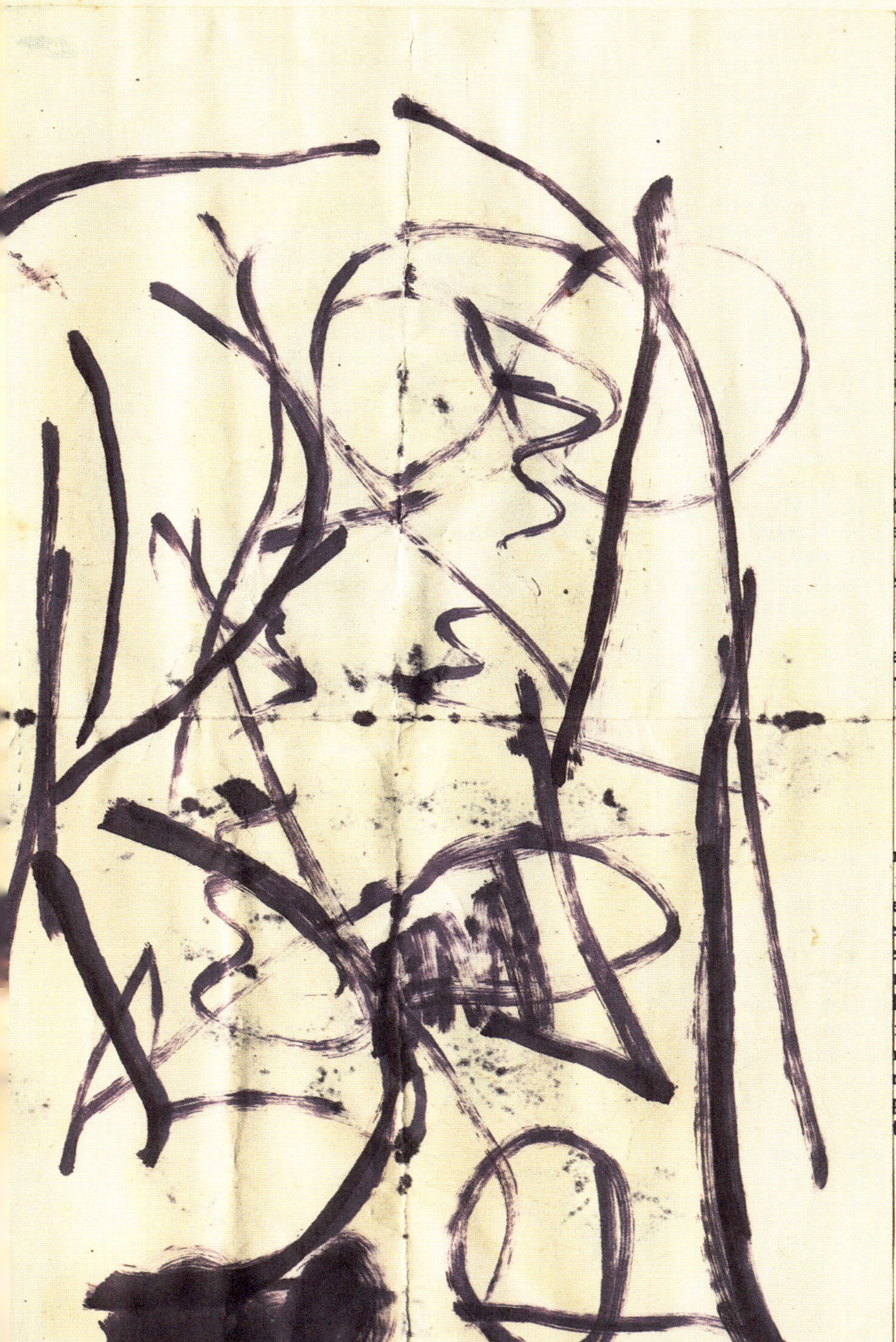

iconeurosis, estado de an-
edad en una personalidad
quizoide.

eka, Kansas.

lanco, soltero, de 19 años,
tal después de un año. His-
pción a la edad de un mes.
al ajuste, se mimó y se le
ió, pero no recibió mucha
ra. Accesos de cólera du-
ncia. Un joven afeminado
ectaciones, asistió a una
r y se matriculó en el co-
, pero estuvo perezoso en
Descubrió fantasías de la
tentosa y grande. Tenía
tas petulantes con su ma-
ió a causa de nervosidad,
reconcentrarse, temores
, y una sensación vaga de
espiaba. Cociente de in-
l.

arse en el estudio de arte,
resentó un aspecto trasno-
o y atormentado. Al prin-
a pintar, pero en fin pro-
de que pintó su primera
simbolica de su conflicto,
teclado grande de piano
amenazantes que se sola-
ros, como si de veladores
medida que progresaba le
e arte, por medio de sus
exteriorizaba de fantasías
materia que la engendraba
ra de una creciente pene-
lógica, lo que se usaba en
ndividual. Su capacidad de
aprensión se evidenció por
nto clínico. Mudó de apa-
puso más sociable. Acabó
to una visita de prueba de
salió del hospital.

45. *Skull*

Diagnostic: Schizophrénie, type paranoide.

Hôpital: Los Angeles, California.

Un homme blanc, âgé de 23 ans, célibataire, à l'hôpital depuis deux ans et demi. Il est l'aîné de deux enfants. Ses parents se sont divorcés lorsque le malade avait sept ans. Il resta avec sa mère qui l'éleva dans une ambiance sévère et très religieuse. Des hostilités contre les autoritées l'ont amené à plusieurs rencontres avec la police. Il était à la marine militaire pendant deux ans avant d'être libéré à cause de symptômes d'aliénation. De retour chez lui, il devint de plus en plus hostile envers sa mère, et fut mis a l'hôpital après l'avoir menacée de meurtre. Pendant son traitement ses idées de persécution diminuèrent.

Les premières peintures faites par le malade étaient des éclaboussures diffuses et des taches sans forme concrète. Pendant qu'il était dans la salle pour les fous furieux, une grande partie de ses ouvrages présentait un trouble émotif intense. Au fur et à mesure que son état s'améliorait, on pouvait remarquer sa tendance à symboliser ses idées. Le malade interprète le present tableau comme suit: "Le cerveau d'arachide dans le crâne est l'imperfection de l'homme. Comme il n'utilise pas ses yeux pour voir, les orbites sont saillants. Tous ces autres yeux sont ces maudits gendarmes." Des tendances paranoides sont évidentes dans le doigt accusateur. Des effets cathartiques se sont clairement manifestés à la suite de l'accomplissement de toutes ses peintures, et petit à petit le malade devint plus disposé à être guidé, plus influencable.

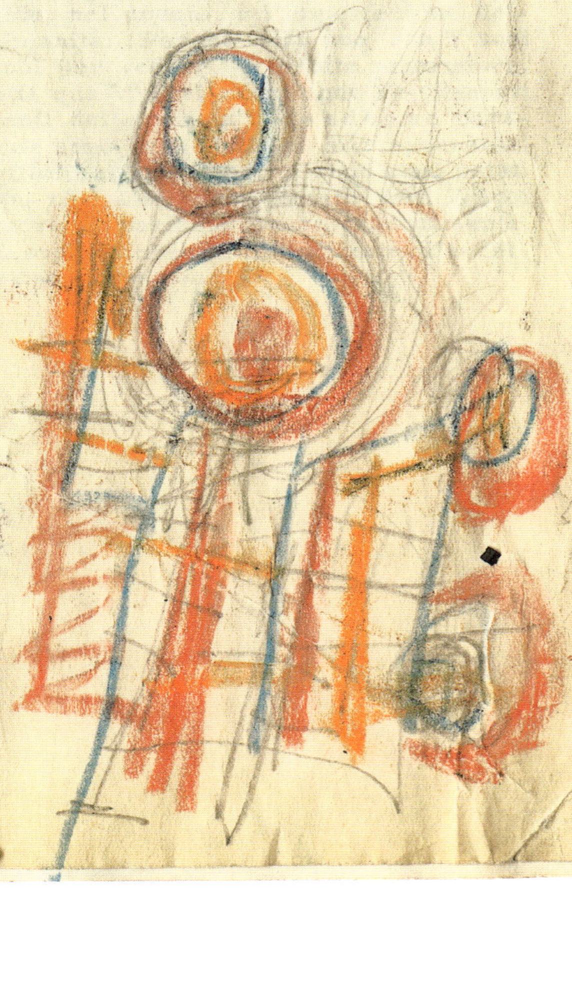

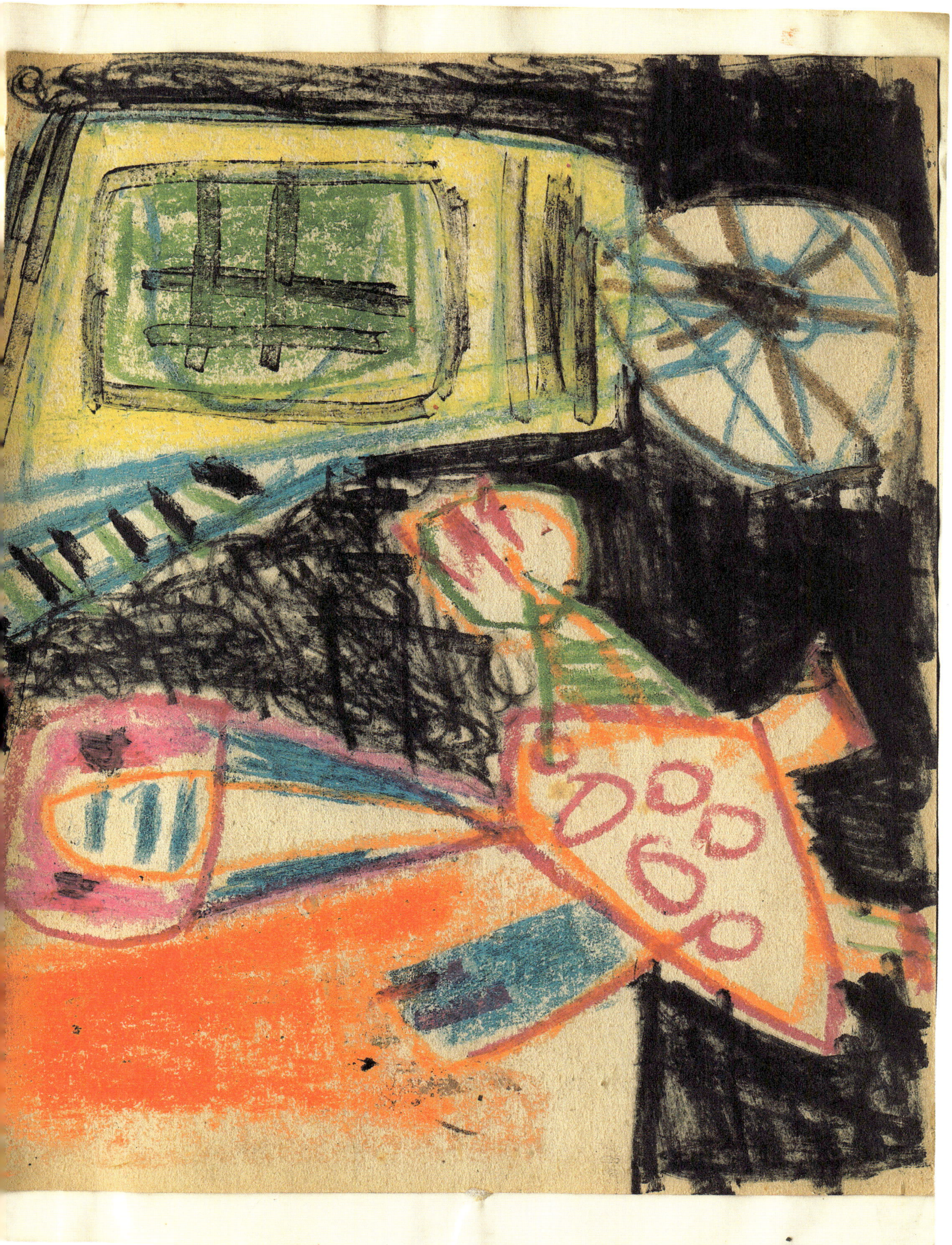

46. *Asleep*

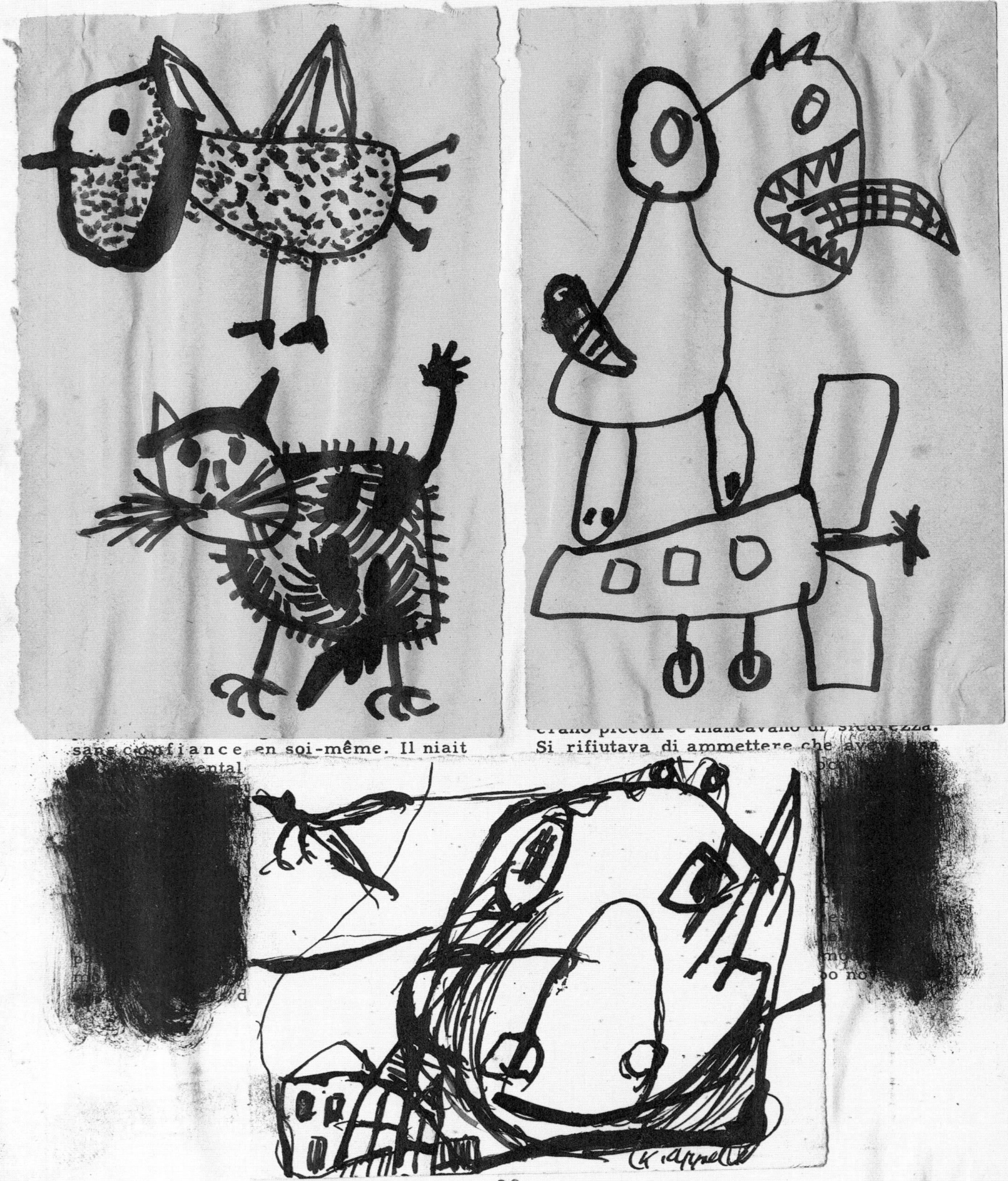
sans confiance en soi-même. Il niait
Si rifiutava di ammettere che
K. Appel

46. *Asleep*

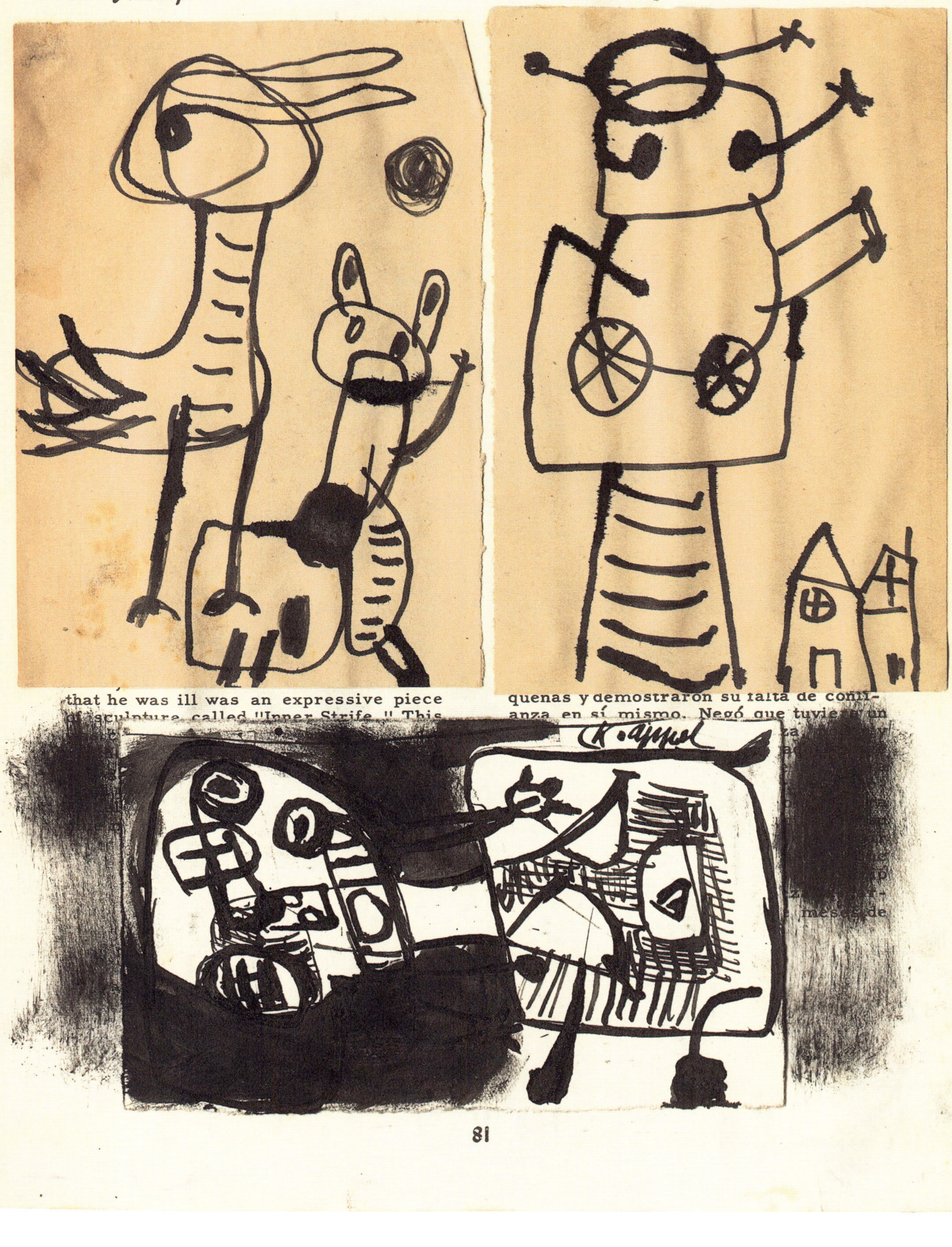
that he was ill was an expressive piece
quenas y demostraron su falta de confi-
K. Appel

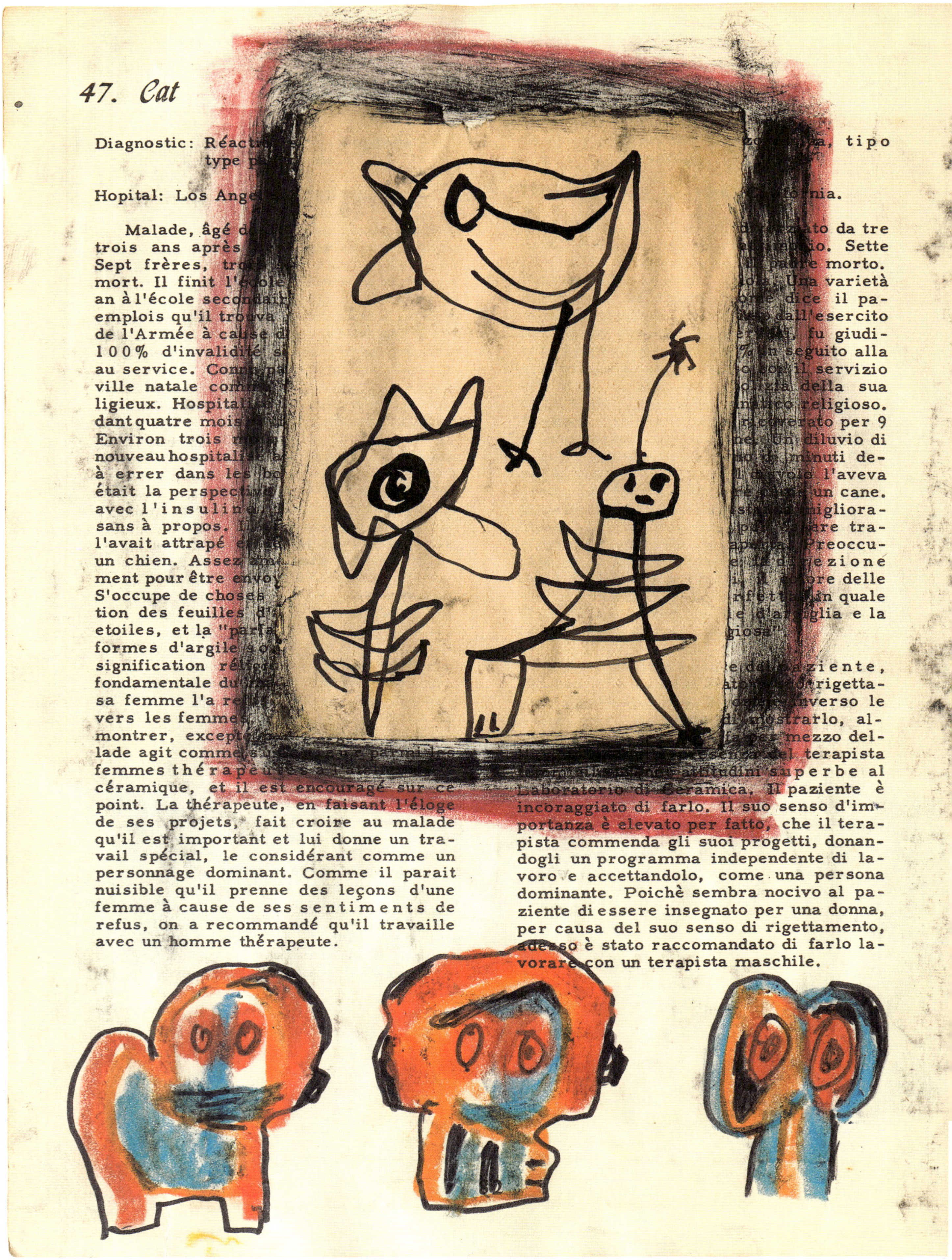
47. Cat
Diagnostic: Réacti
type p
, tipo
Hopital: Los Ange
fornia.
Malade, âgé d
trois ans après
Sept frères, tro
mort. Il finit l'école
an à l'école secondair
emplois qu'il trouva
de l'Armée à cause d
100% d'invalidité s
au service. Conn
ville natale com
ligieux. Hospital
dant quatre mois
Environ trois m
nouveau hospitali
à errer dans les bo
était la perspectiv
avec l'insuline
sans à propos.
l'avait attrapé
un chien. Assez
ment pour être envo
S'occupe de choses
tion des feuilles d
etoiles, et la "parl
formes d'argile
signification r
fondamentale du
sa femme l'a re
vers les femmes
montrer, except
lade agit comme
femmes thérapeu
céramique, et il est encouragé sur ce
point. La thérapeute, en faisant l'éloge
de ses projets, fait croire au malade
qu'il est important et lui donne un travail spécial, le considérant comme un
personnage dominant. Comme il parait
nuisible qu'il prenne des leçons d'une
femme à cause de ses sentiments de
refus, on a recommandé qu'il travaille
avec un homme thérapeute.
ato da tre
io. Sette
e morto.
Una varietà
dice il pa-
dall'esercito
fu giudi-
seguito alla
il servizio
della sua
religioso.
ricoverato per 9
Un diluvio di
minuti de-
l'aveva
un cane.
migliora-
re tra-
Preoccu-
zione
delle
quale
e la
iente,
rigetta-
verso le
mostrarlo, al-
mezzo del-
terapista
superbe al
Laboratorio di Ceramica. Il paziente è
incoraggiato di farlo. Il suo senso d'importanza è elevato per fatto, che il terapista commenda gli suoi progetti, donandogli un programma independente di lavoro e accettandolo, come una persona
dominante. Poichè sembra nocivo al paziente di essere insegnato per una donna,
per causa del suo senso di rigettamento,
adesso è stato raccomandato di farlo lavorare con un terapista maschile.

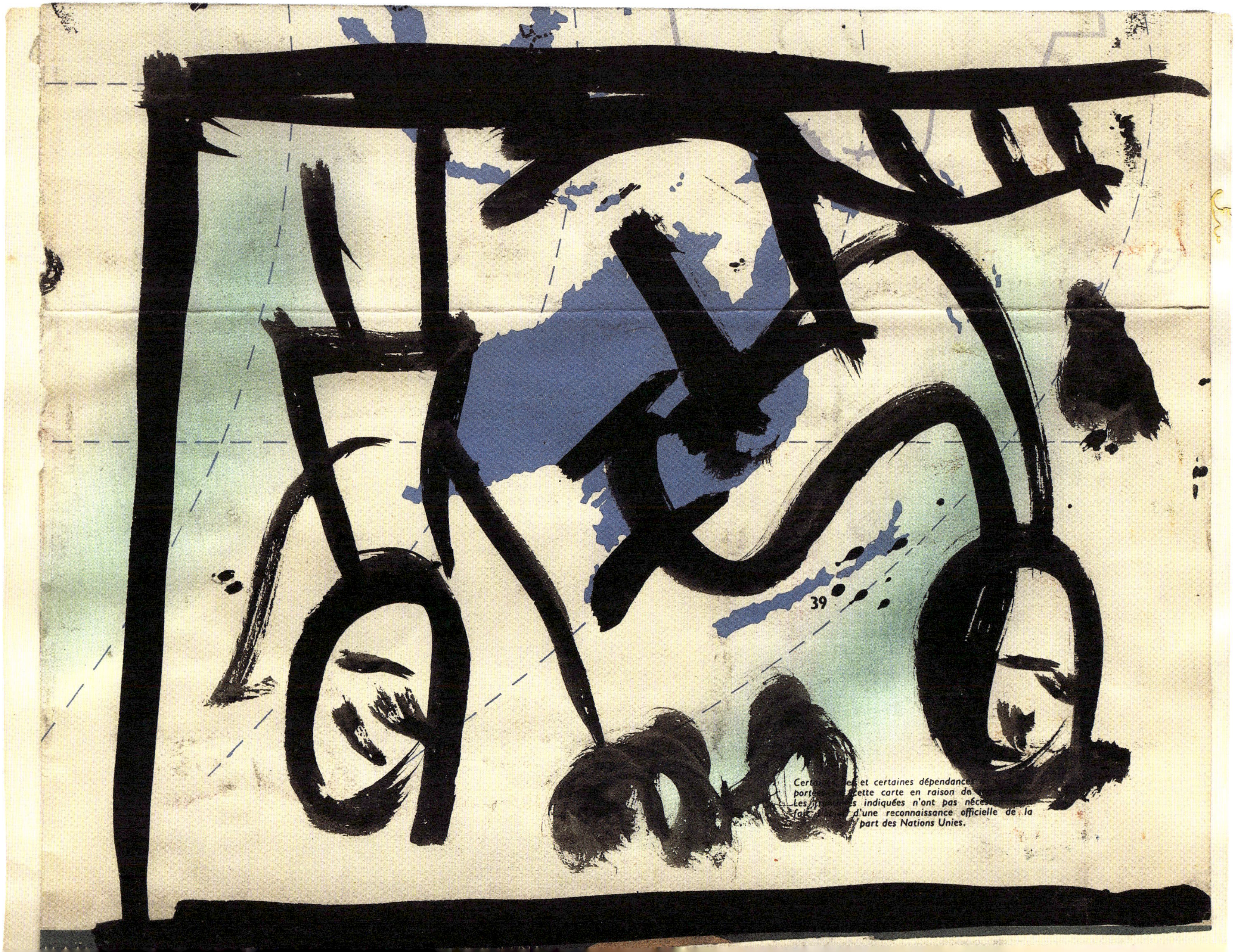
39
Certai... et certaines dépendances
portée... cette carte en raison de
Les ... indiquées n'ont pas néces...
... d'une reconnaissance officielle de la
part des Nations Unies.

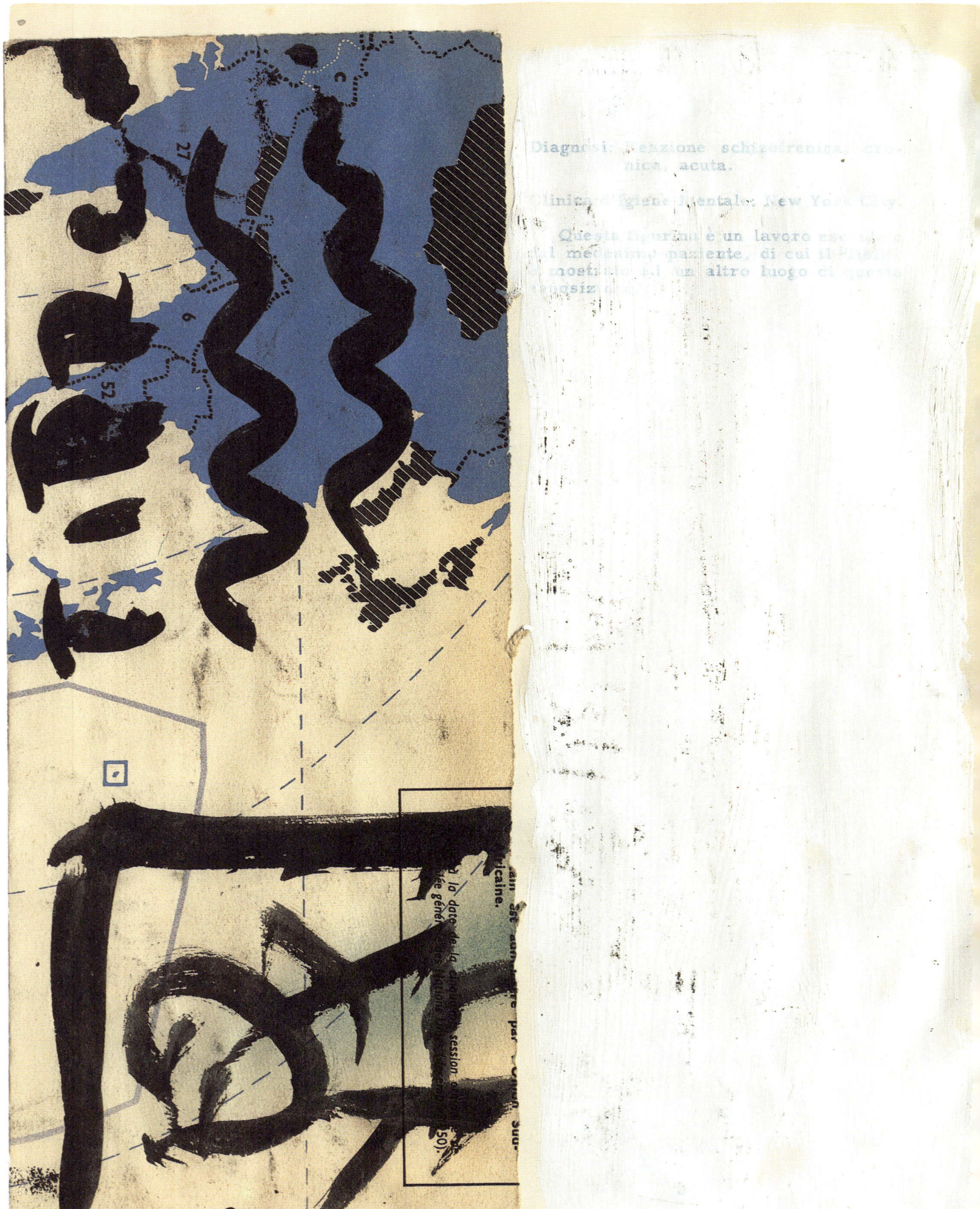

Diagn azione schi frenica
nica, acuta.
linica iene entale New Yor
Questa è un lavoro
al me ente, di cui il
mostr un altro luogo di

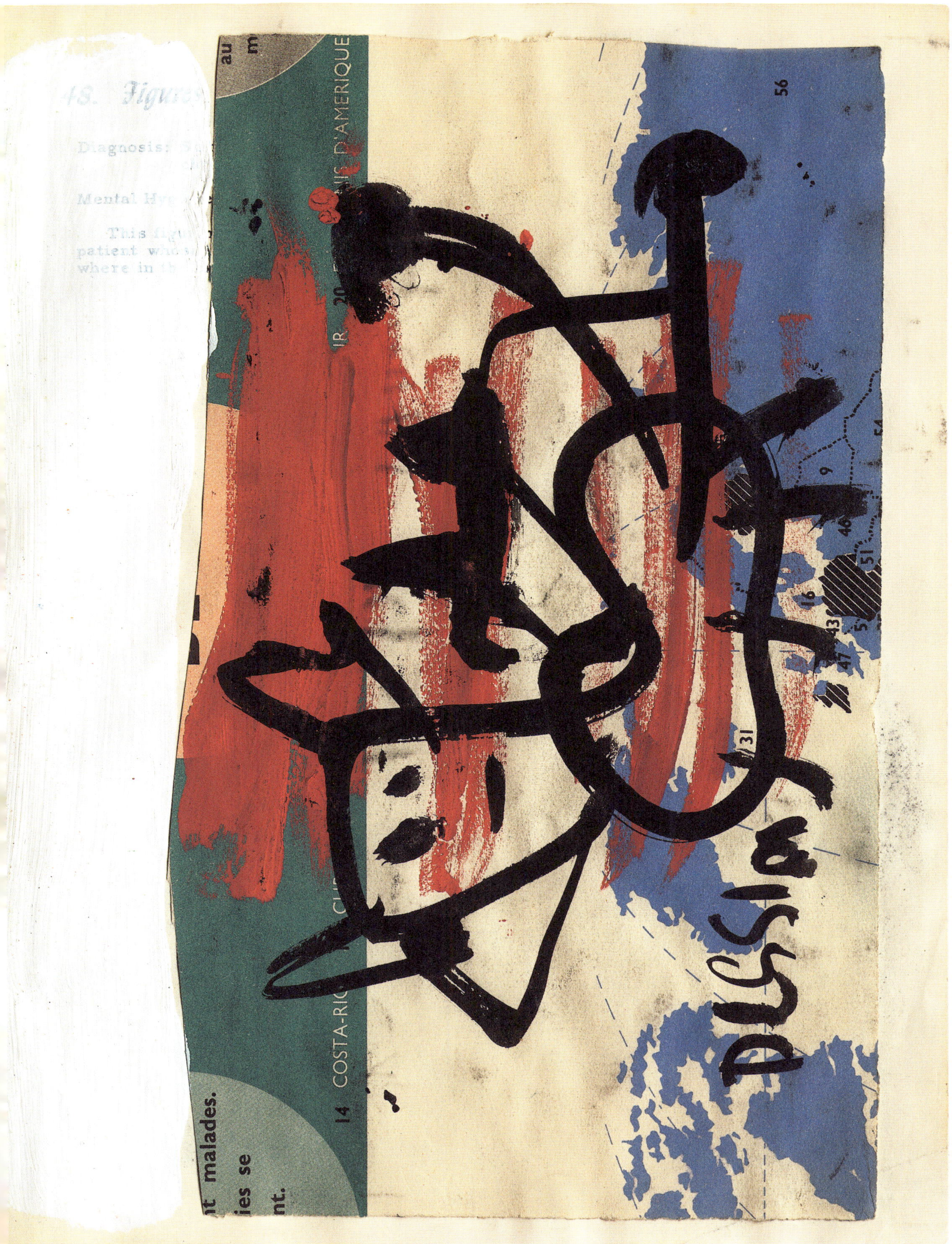

Diagnosis:
Mental Hy
COSTA-RIC
D'AMERIQUE
malades.
ies se
nt.

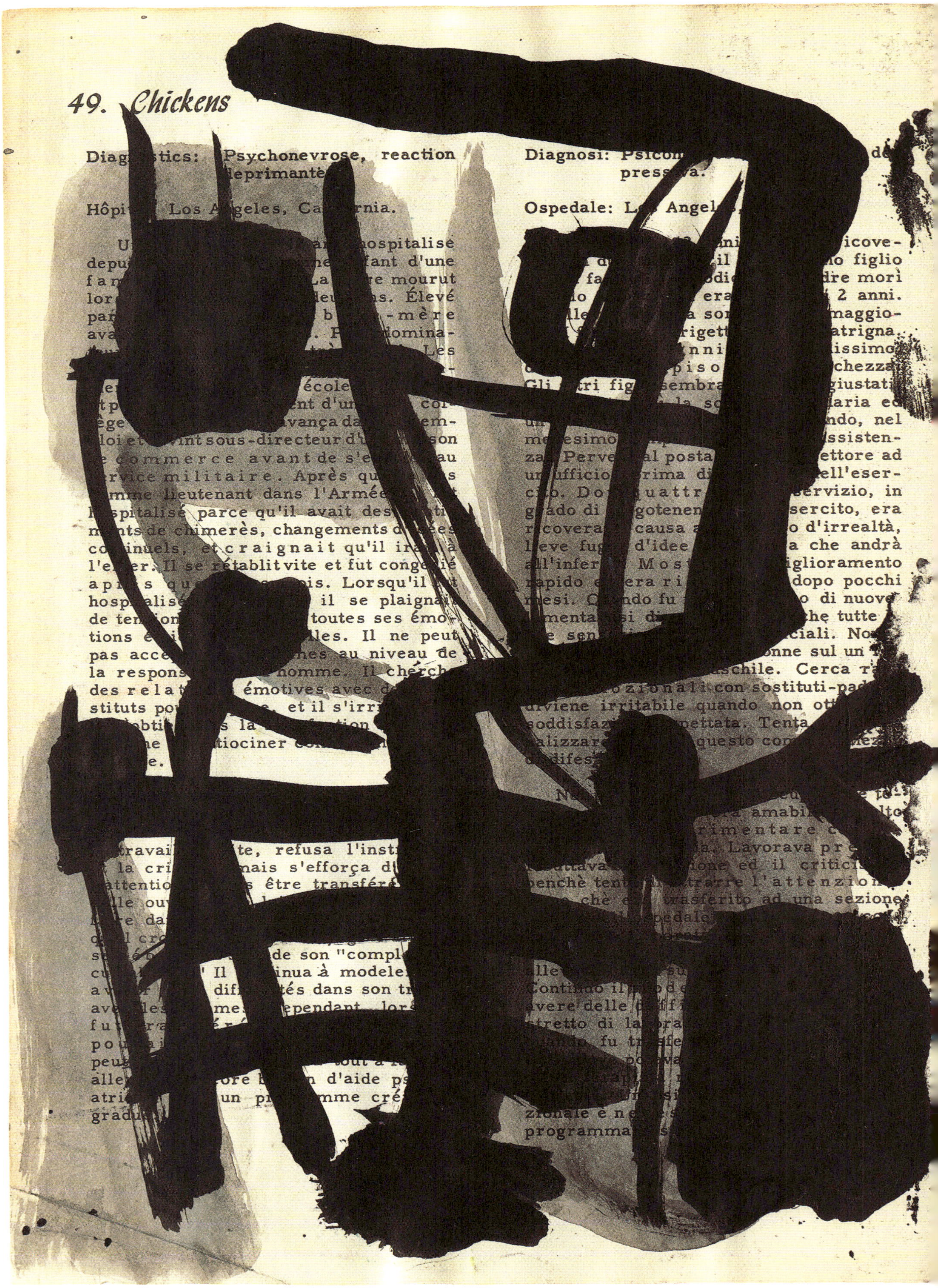

49. Chickens
Psychonevrose, reaction
Hôpit
Los Angeles, Ca
rnia.
Diagnosi:
Ospedale:

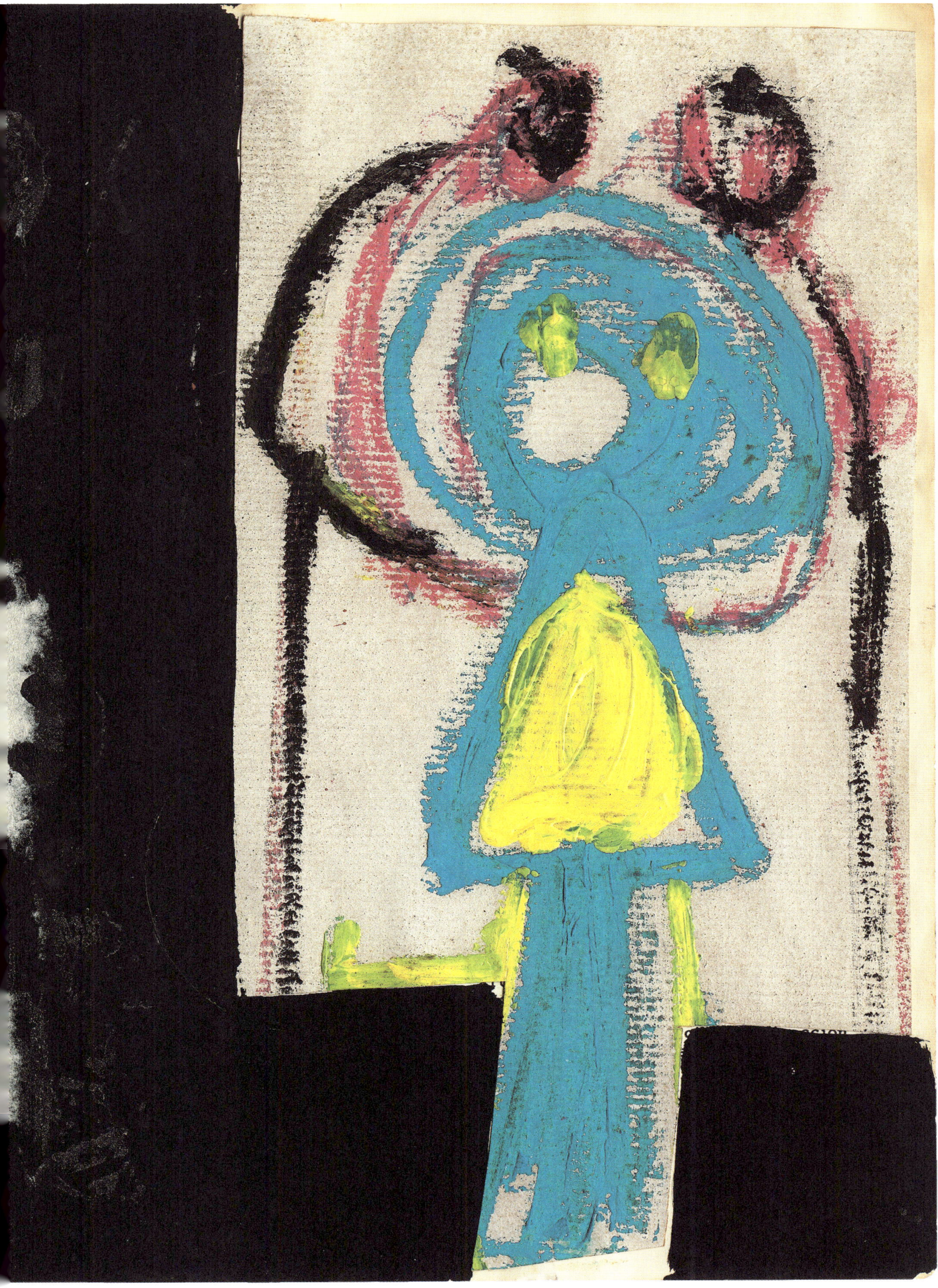

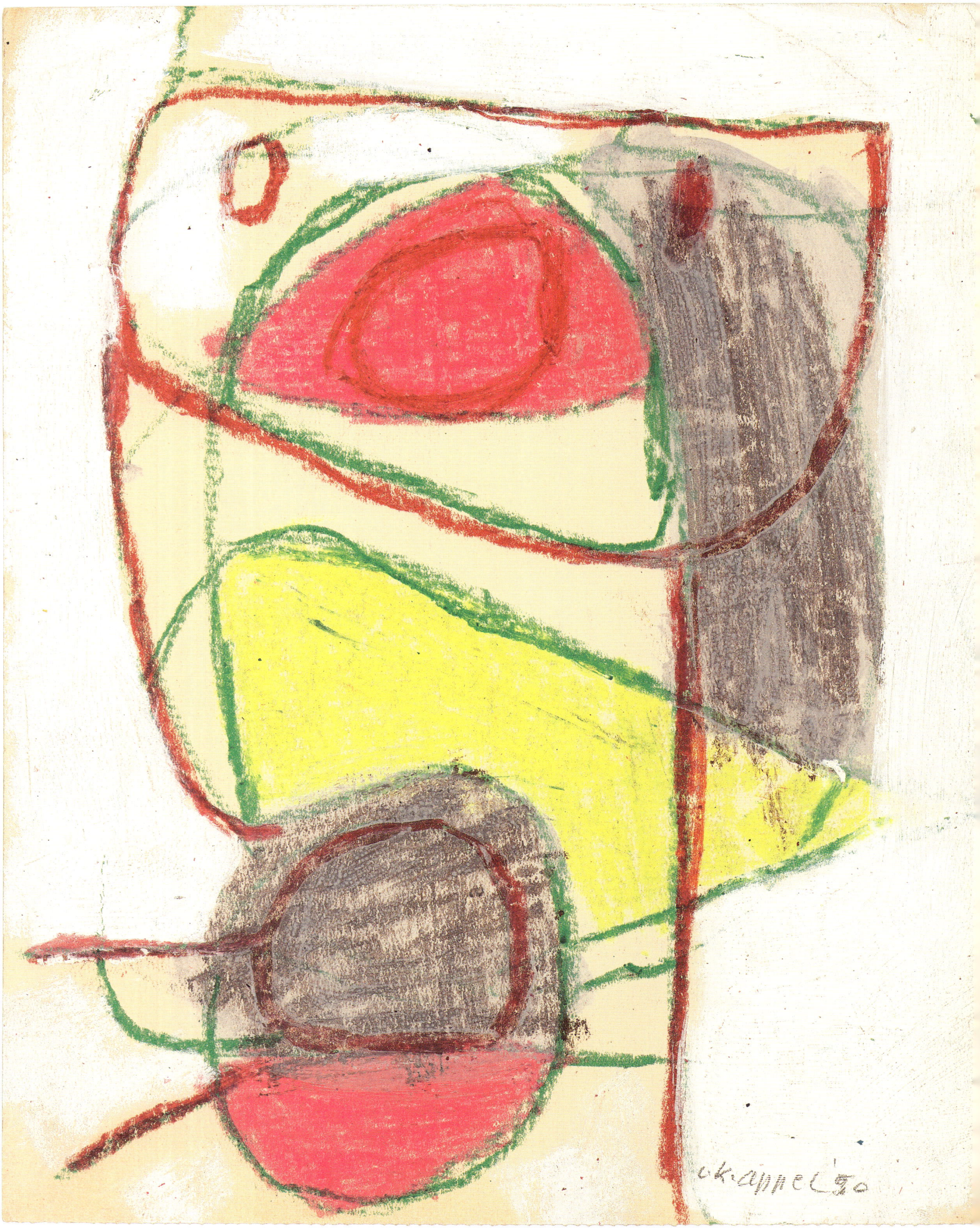

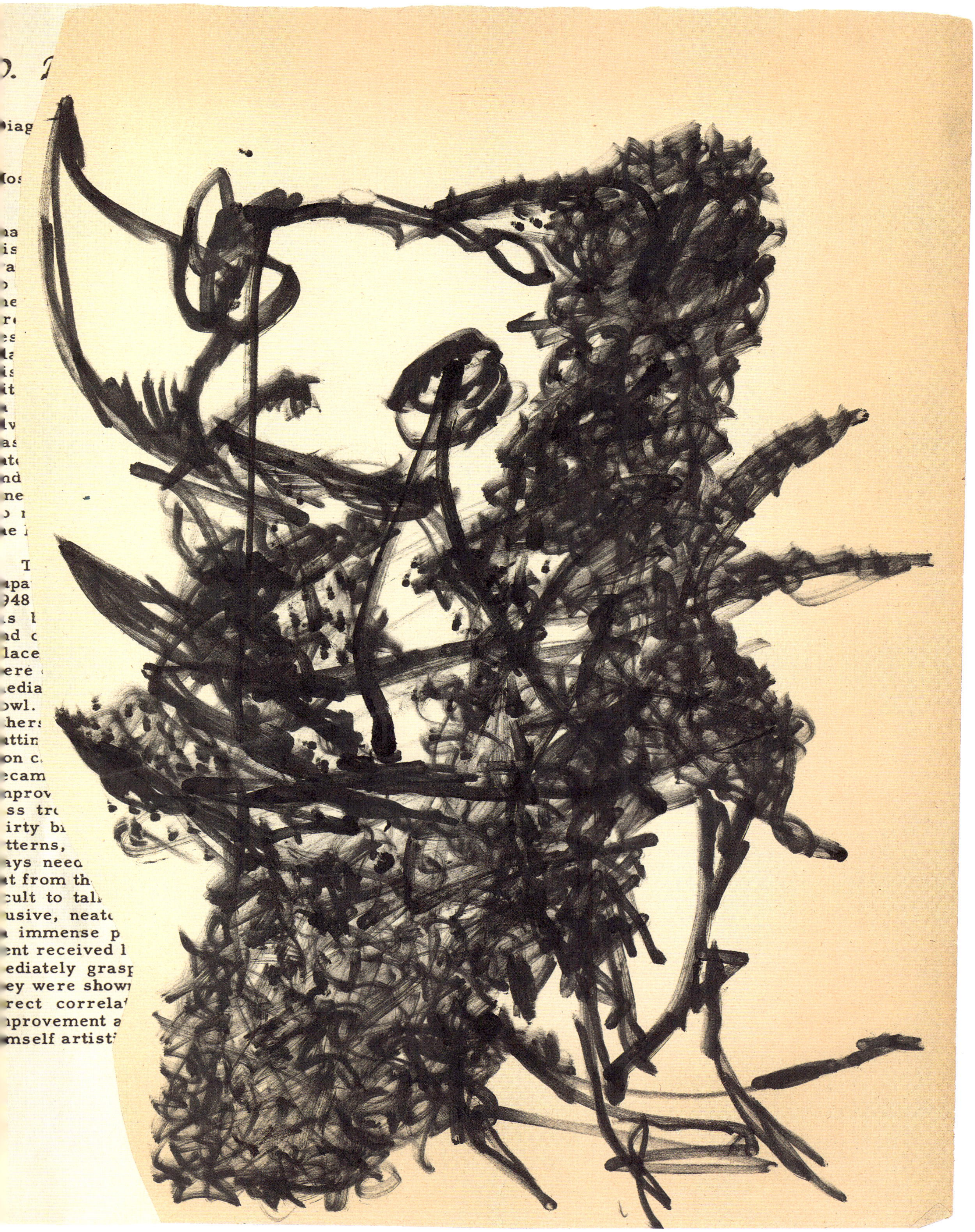

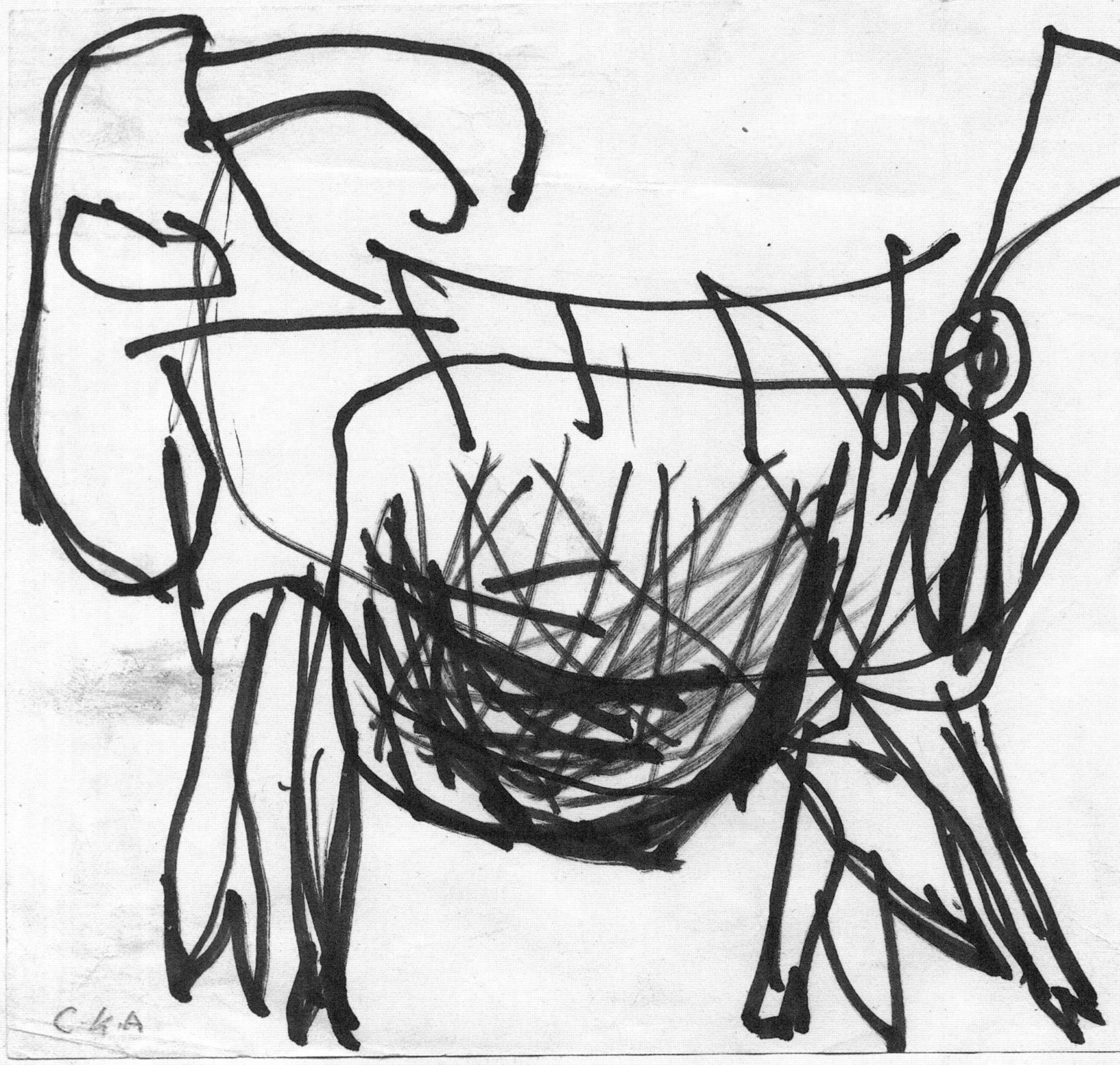
C.K.A

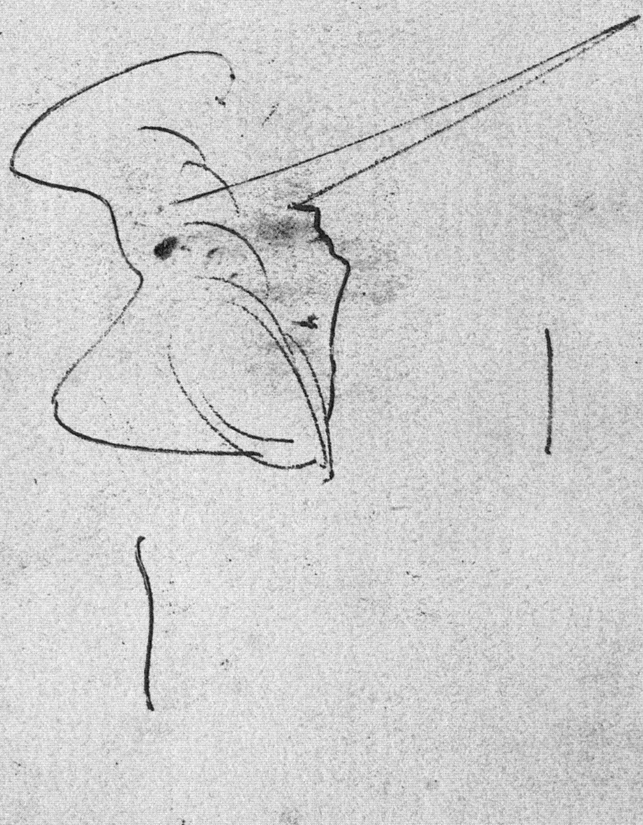

The following drawings
were done at the same time as the
"re-working" of the *Psychopathological art* brochure

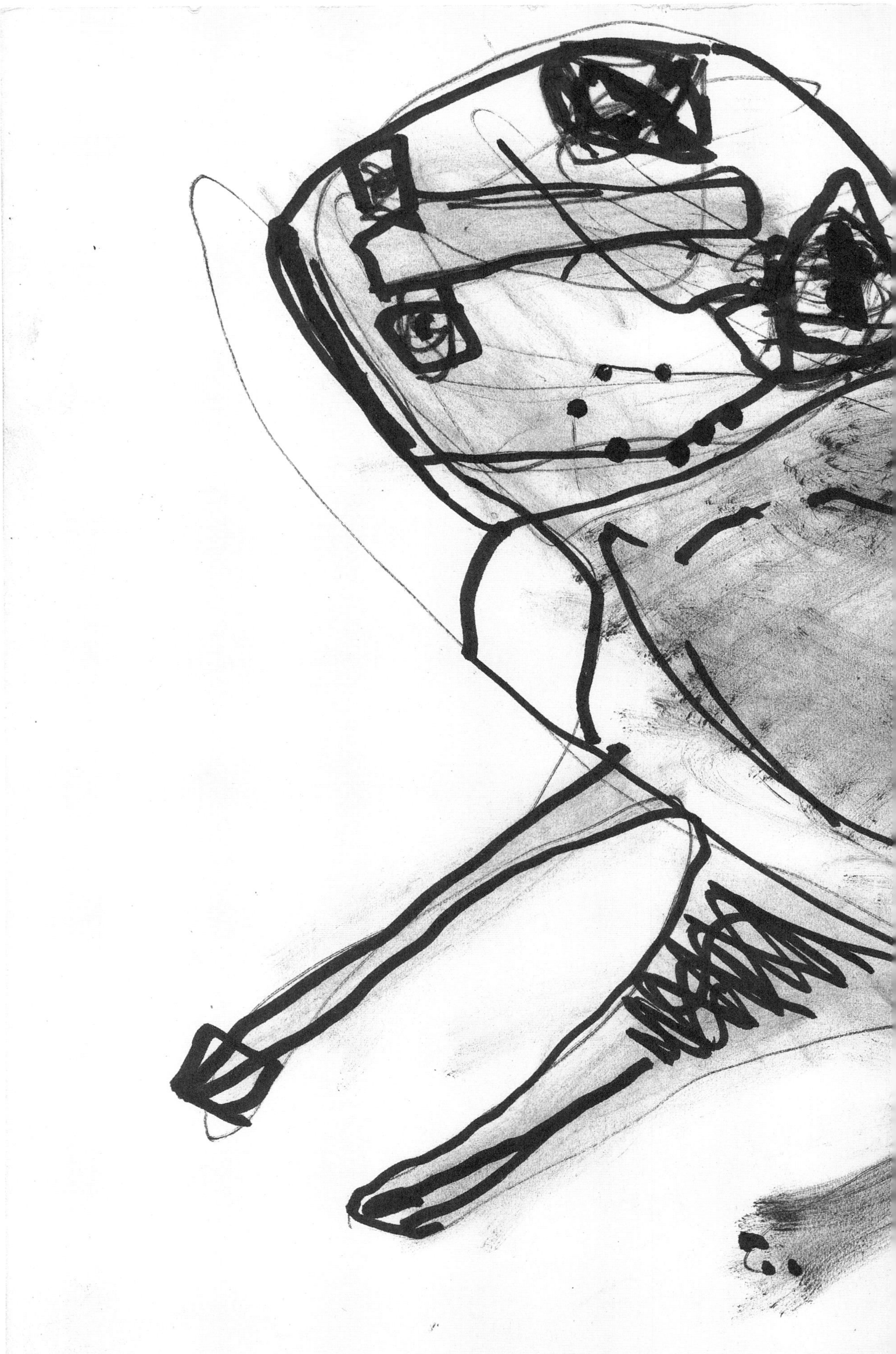

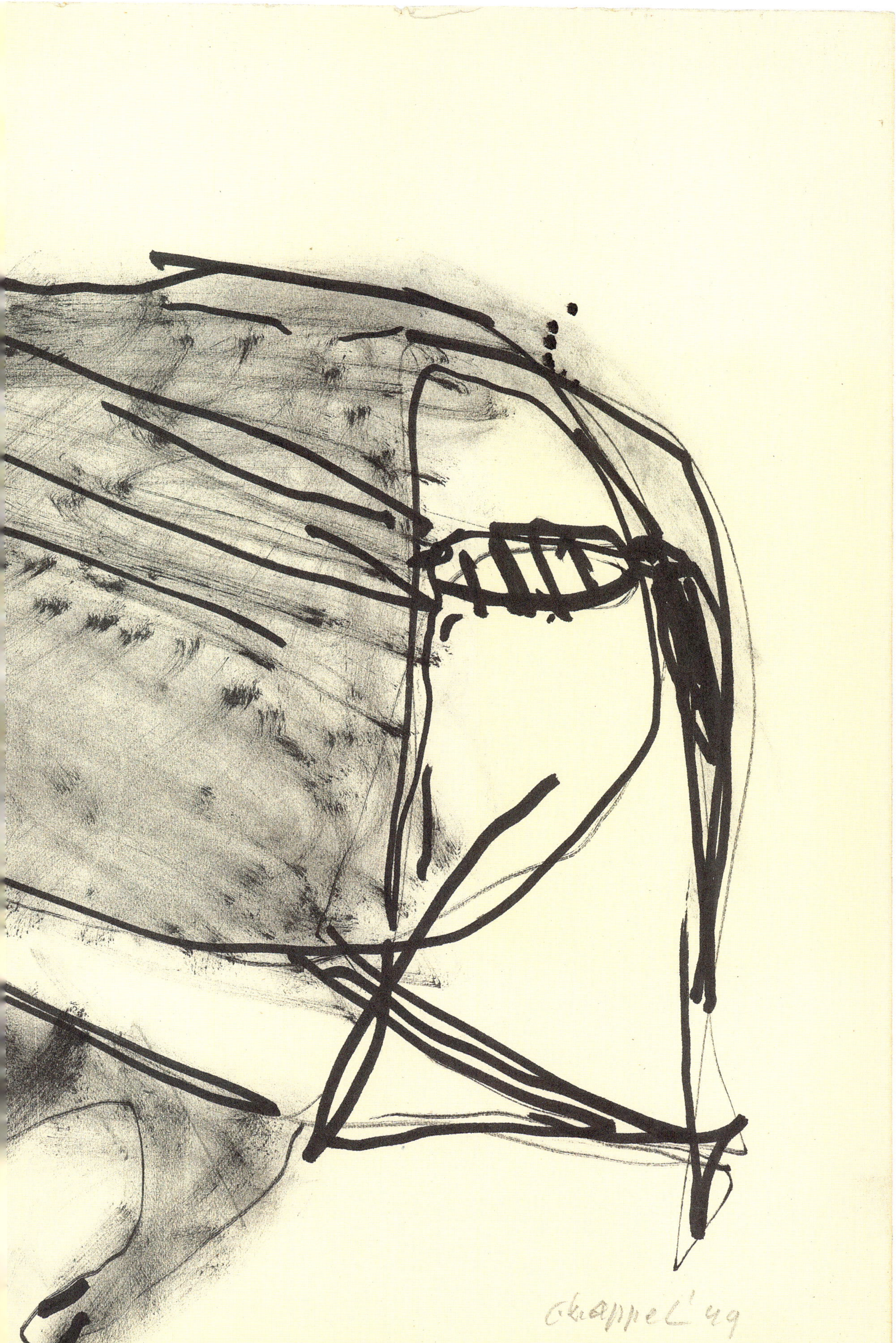
appel '49

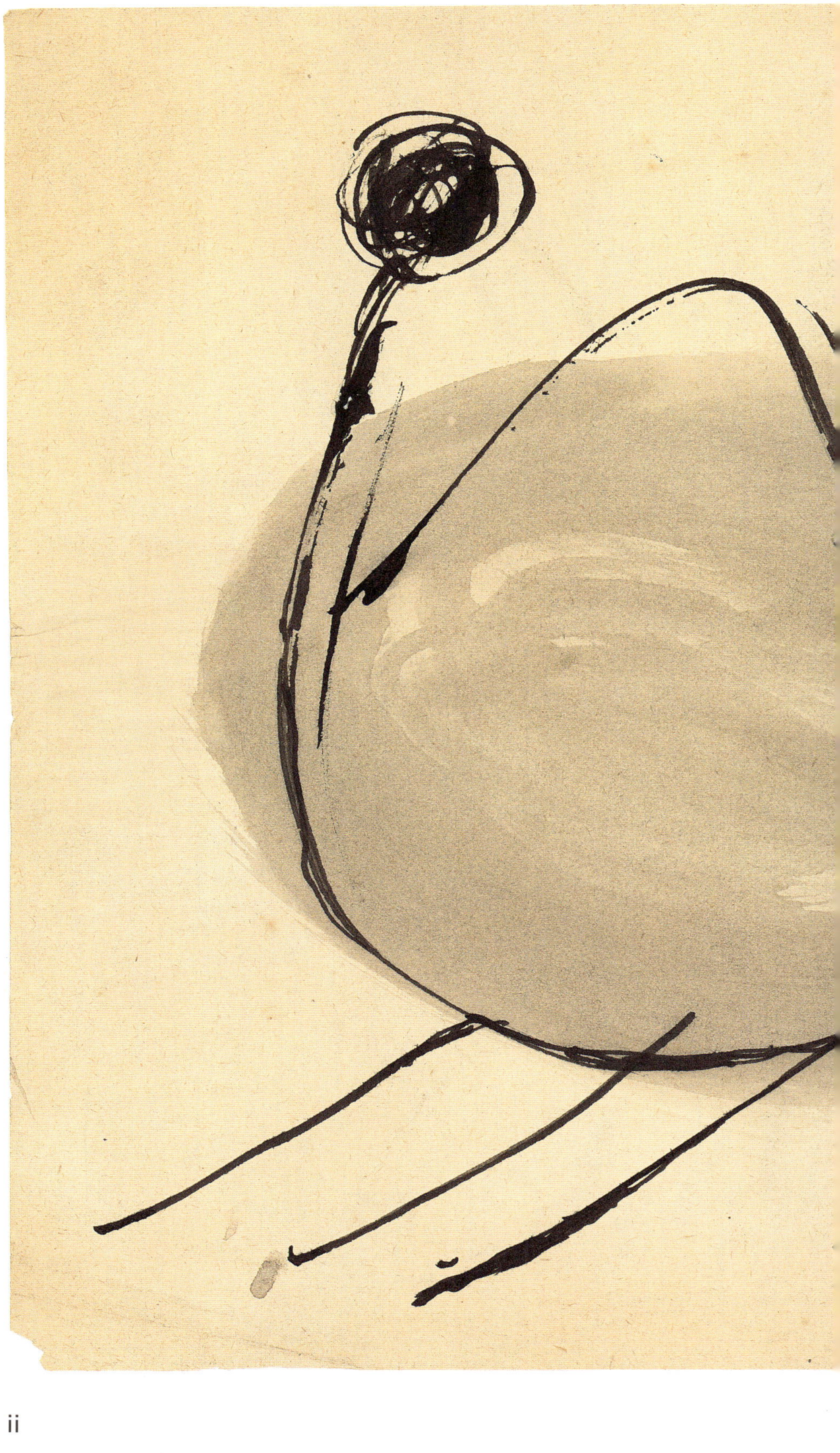

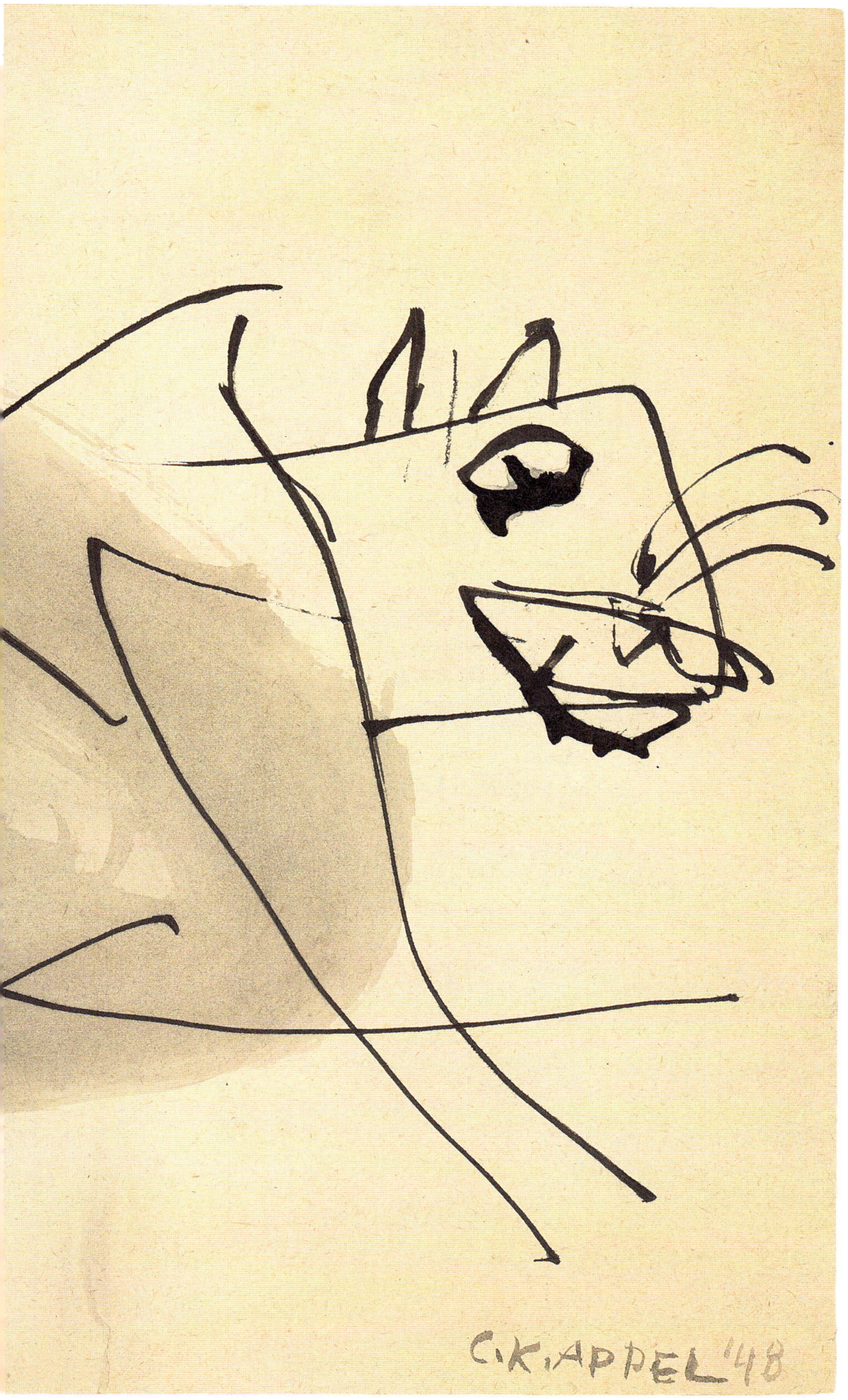
C.K.APPEL '48

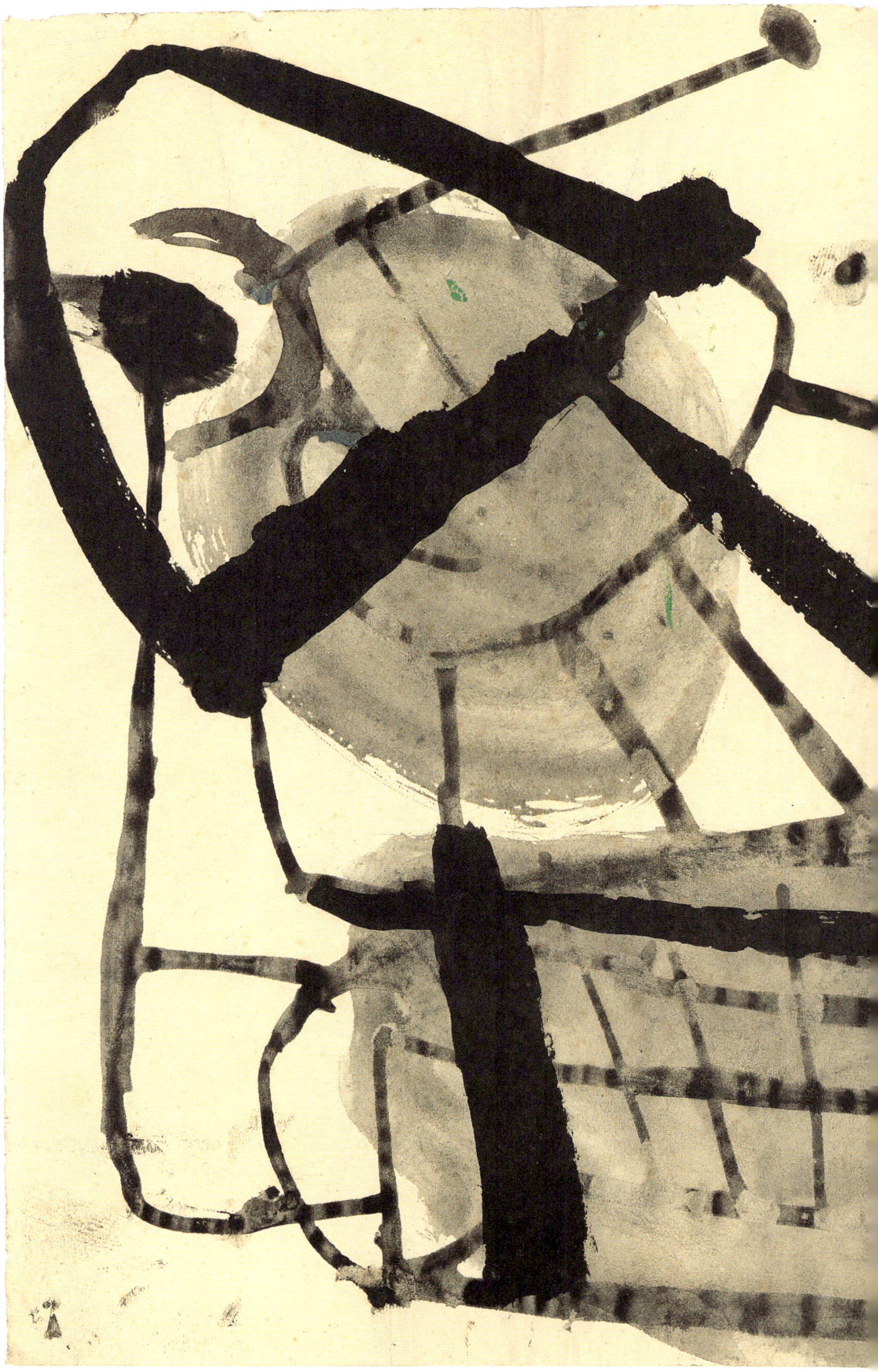

iii

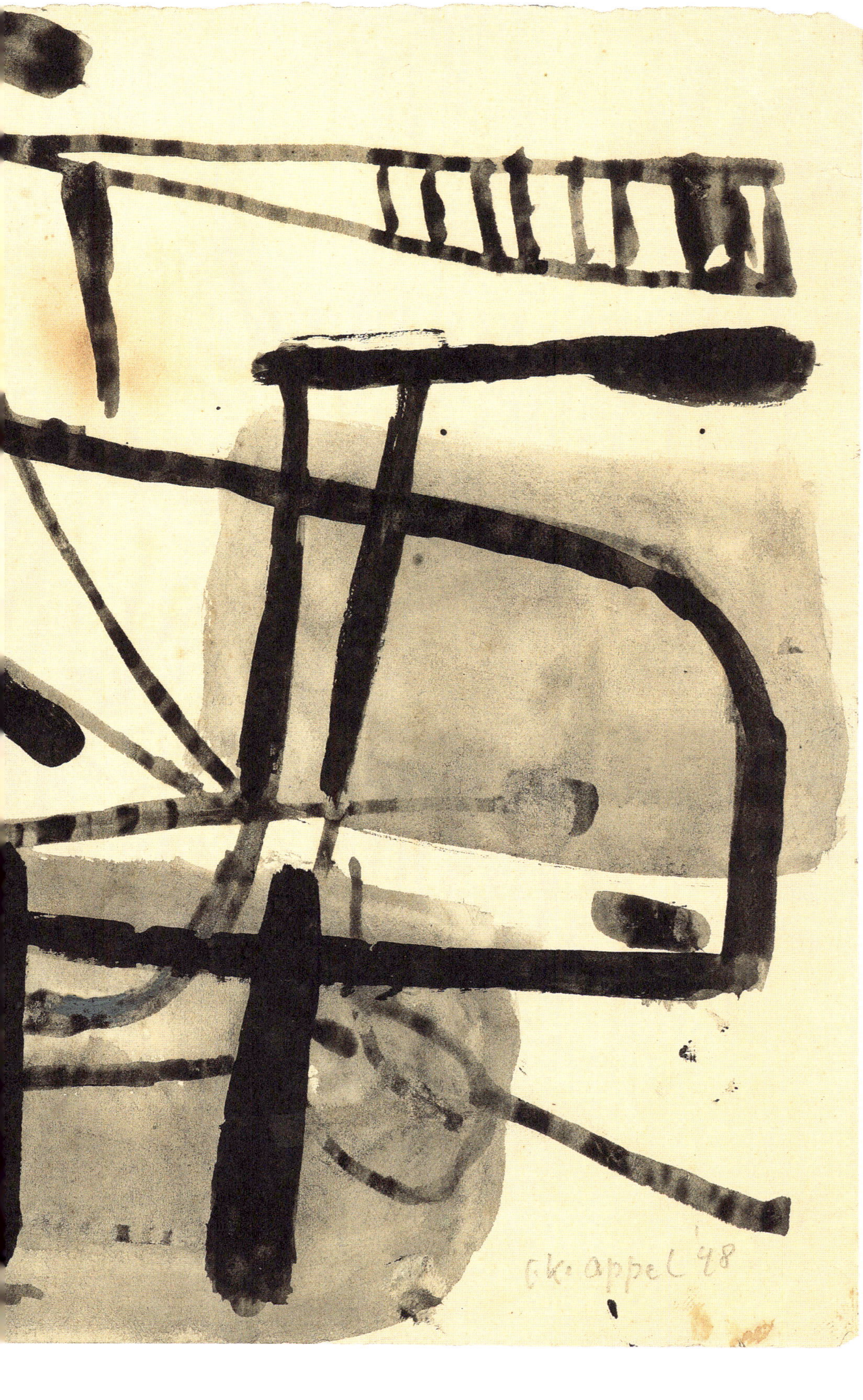
CK. appel '48

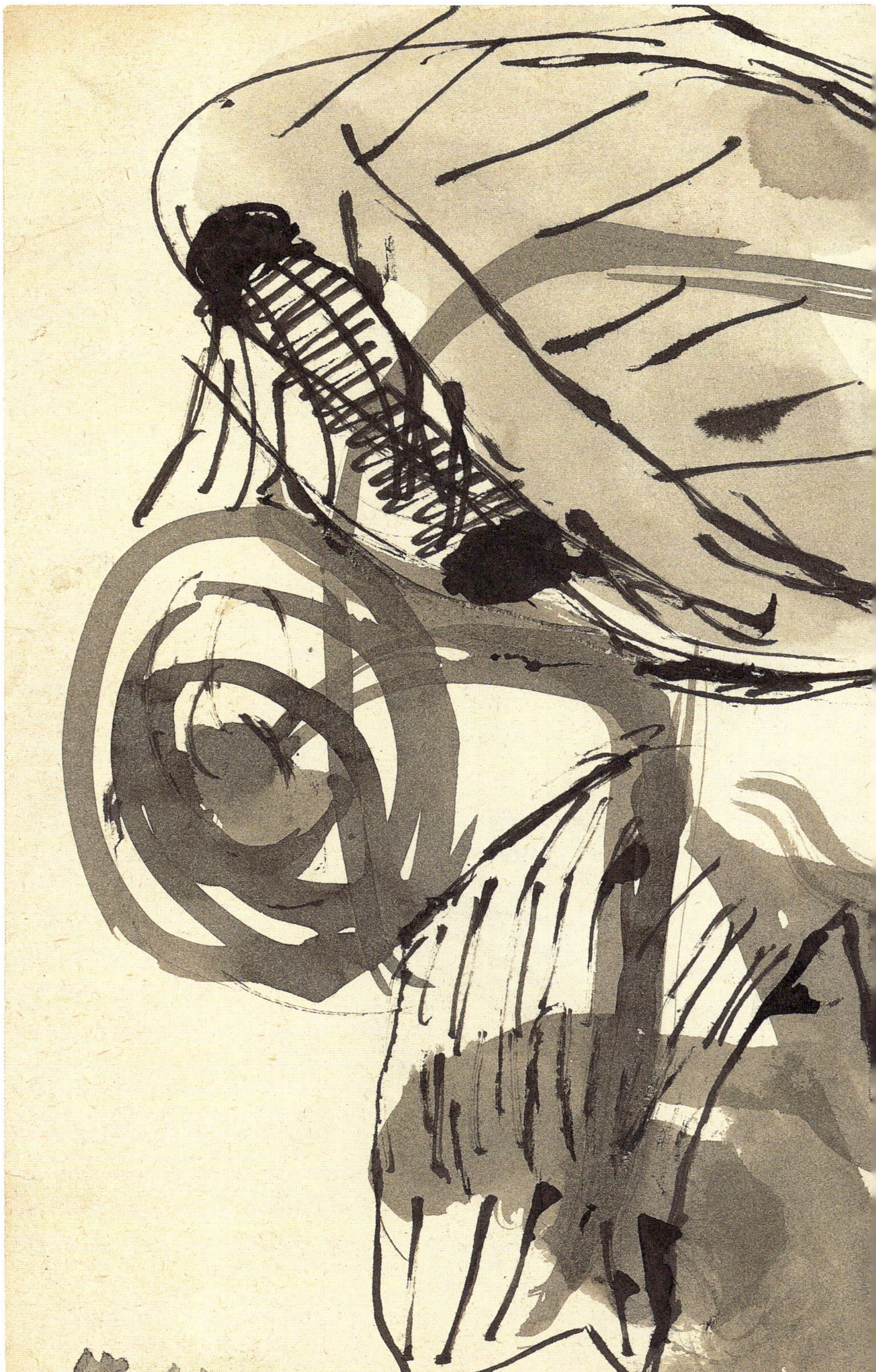

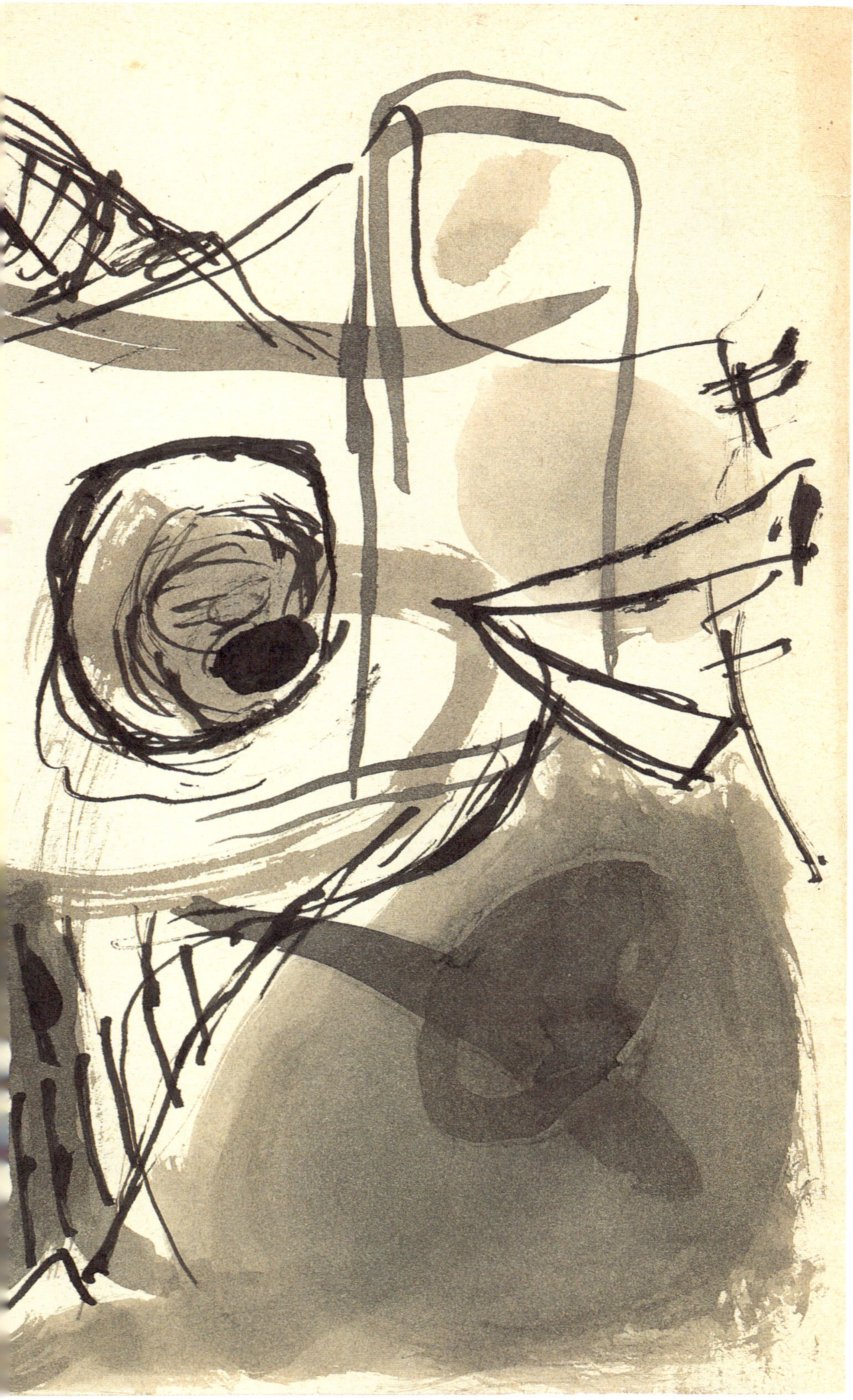

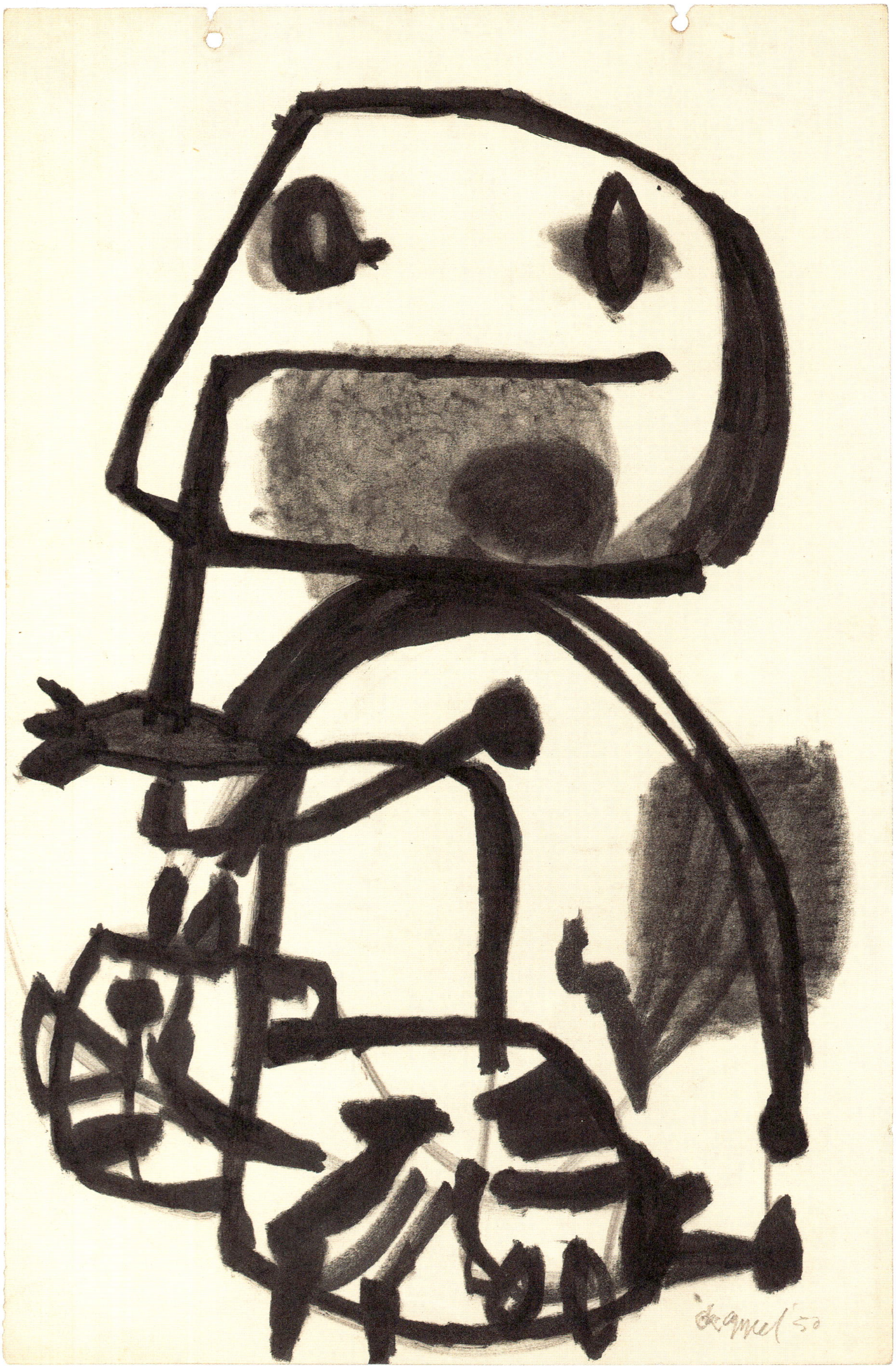

v

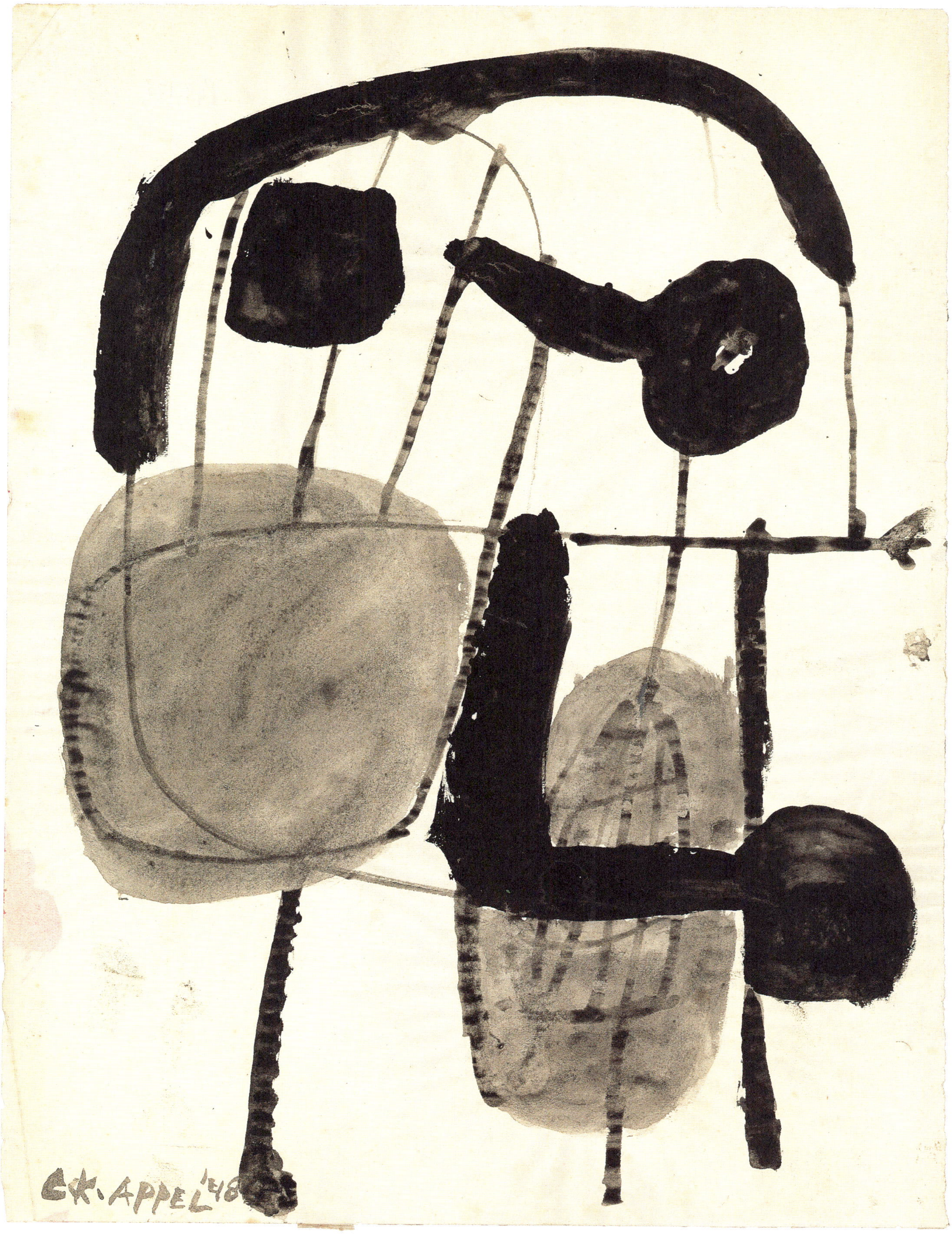
CK. APPEL '48

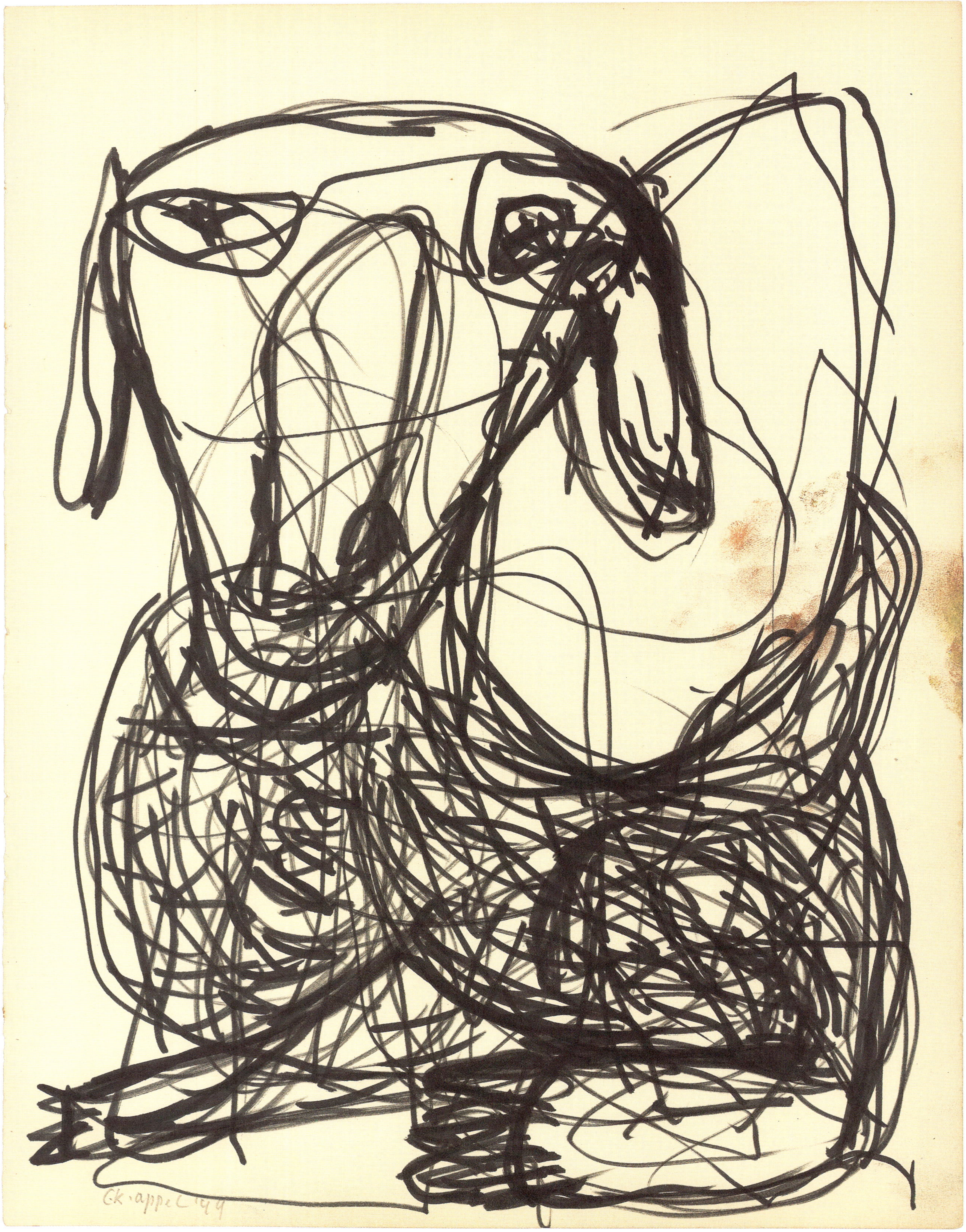
CK. appel '49

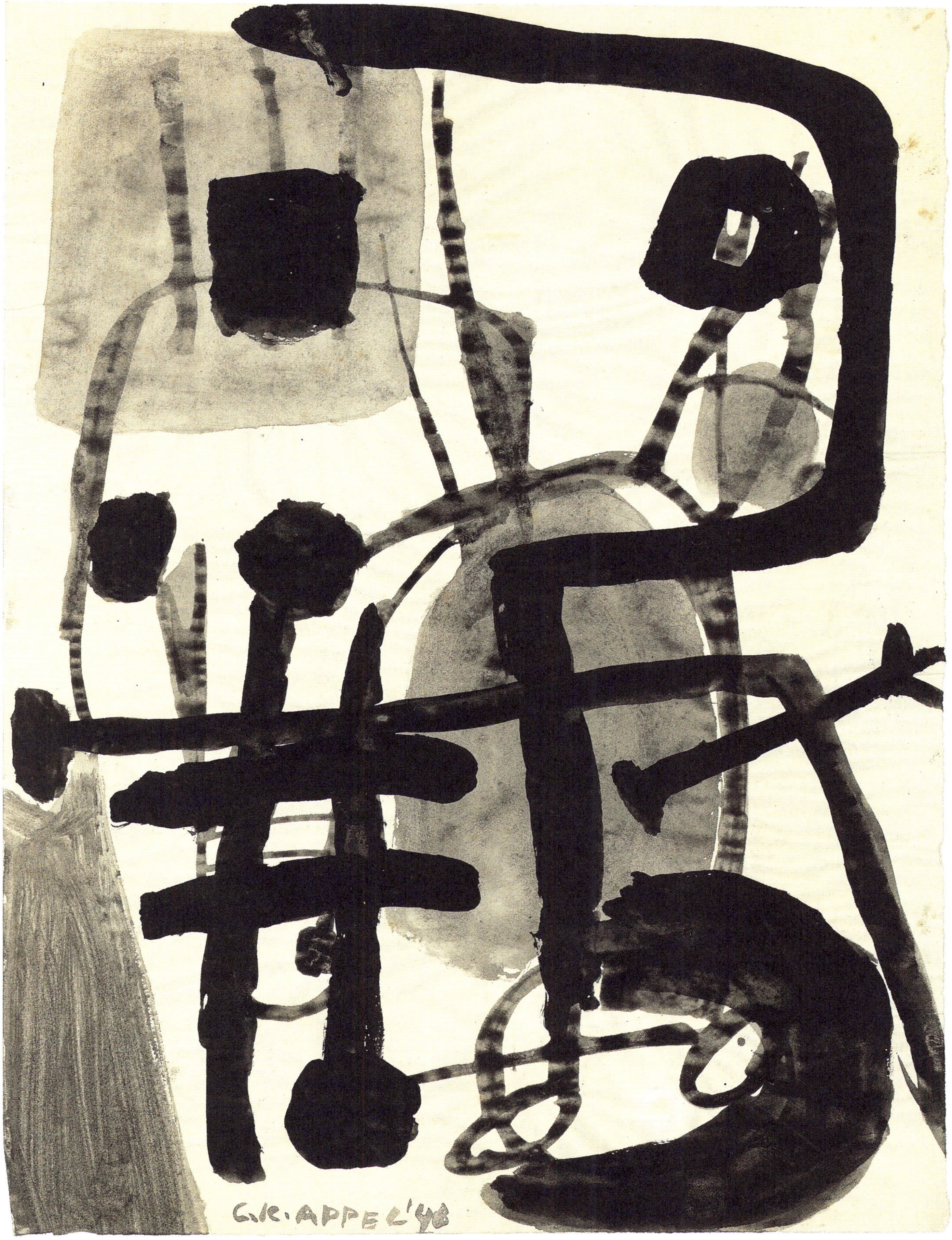
G.K. APPEL '48

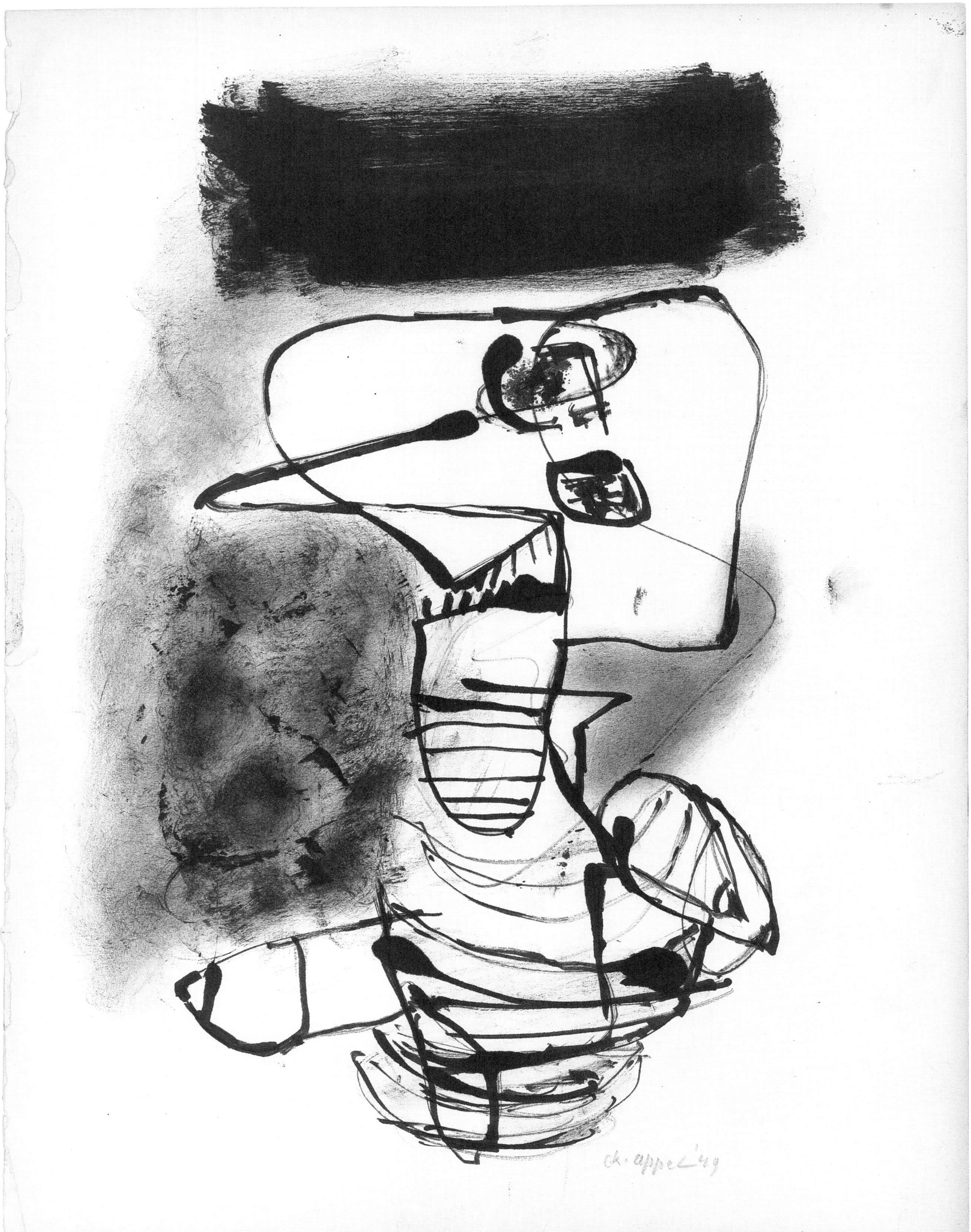
ch. appel '49

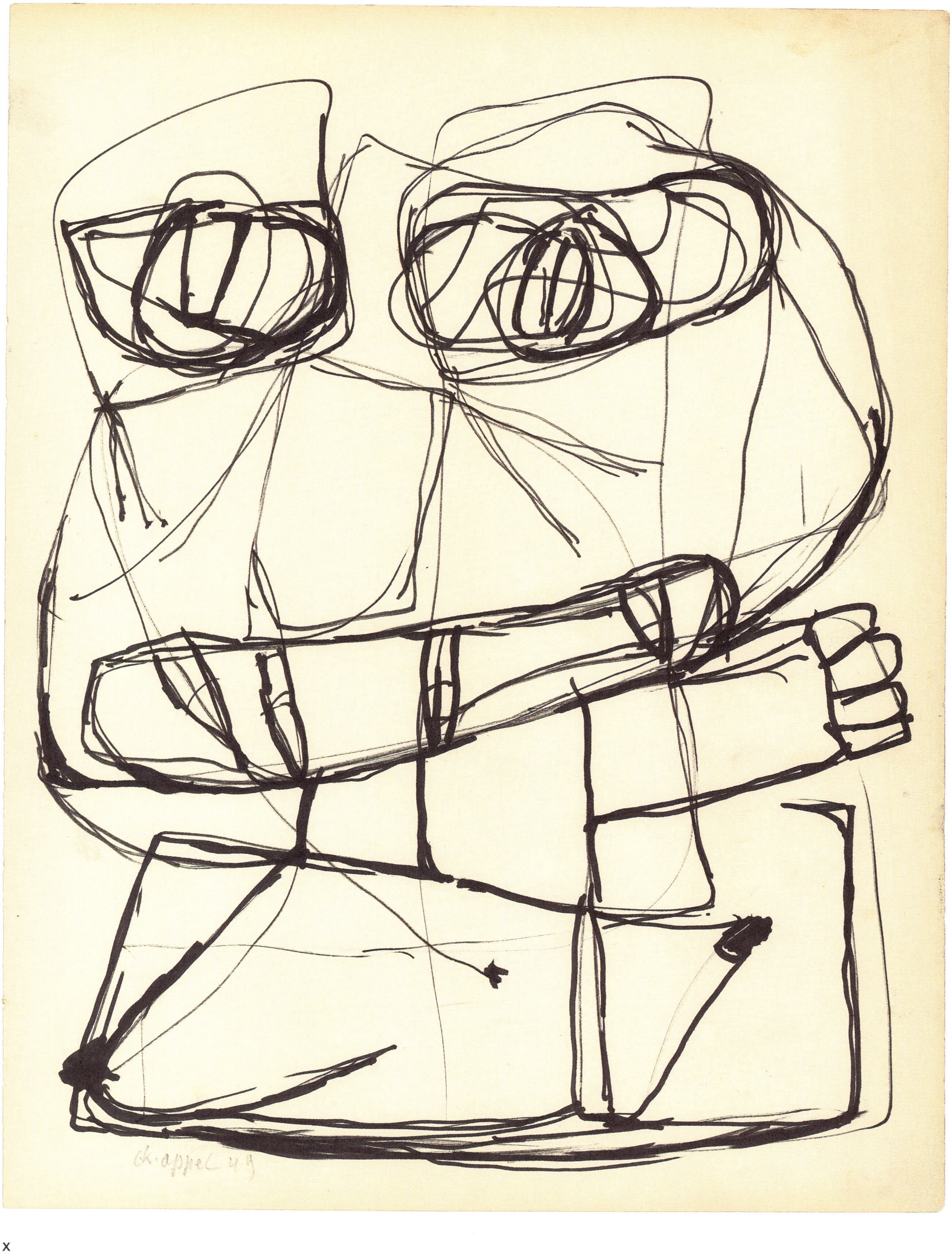

x

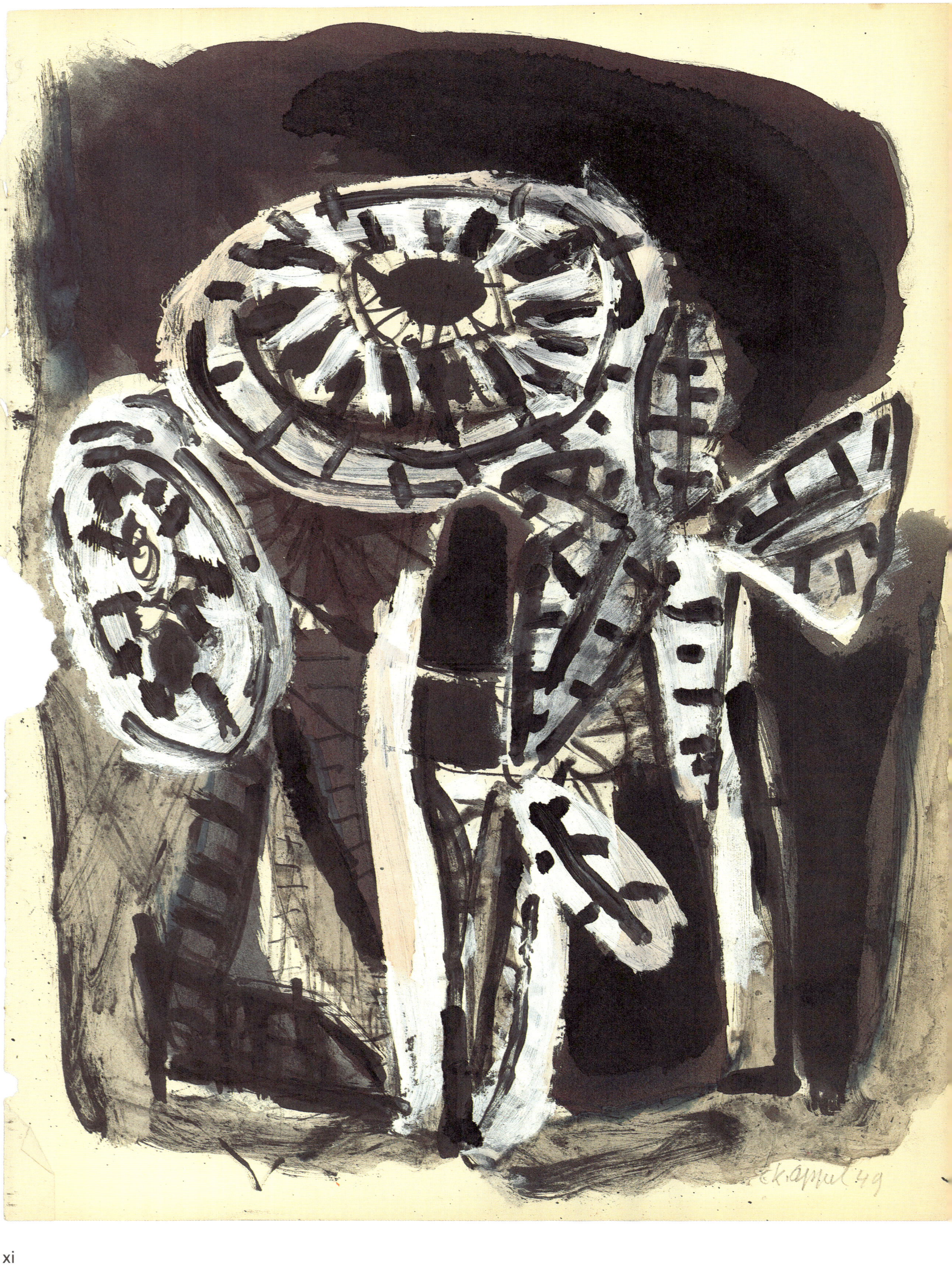

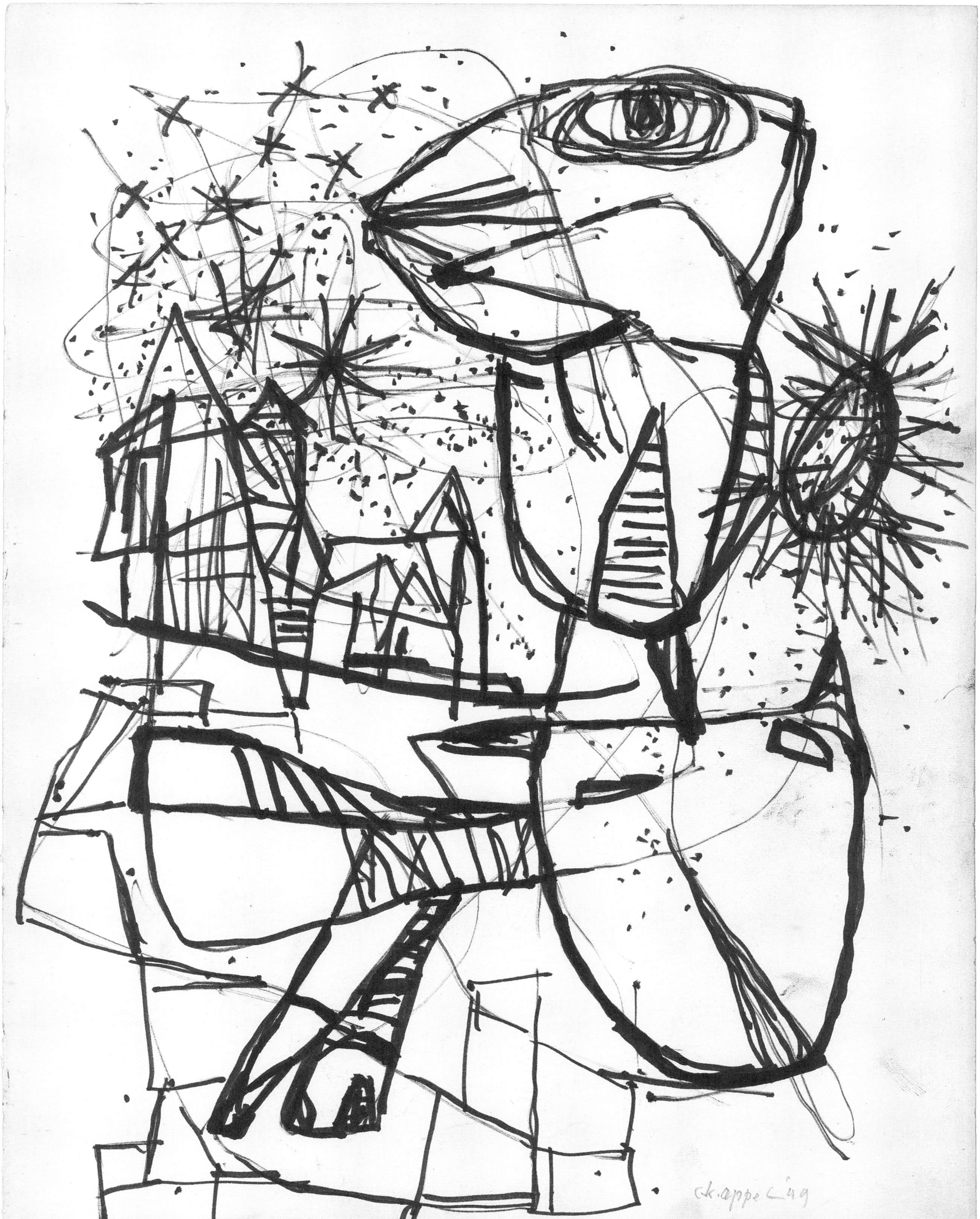

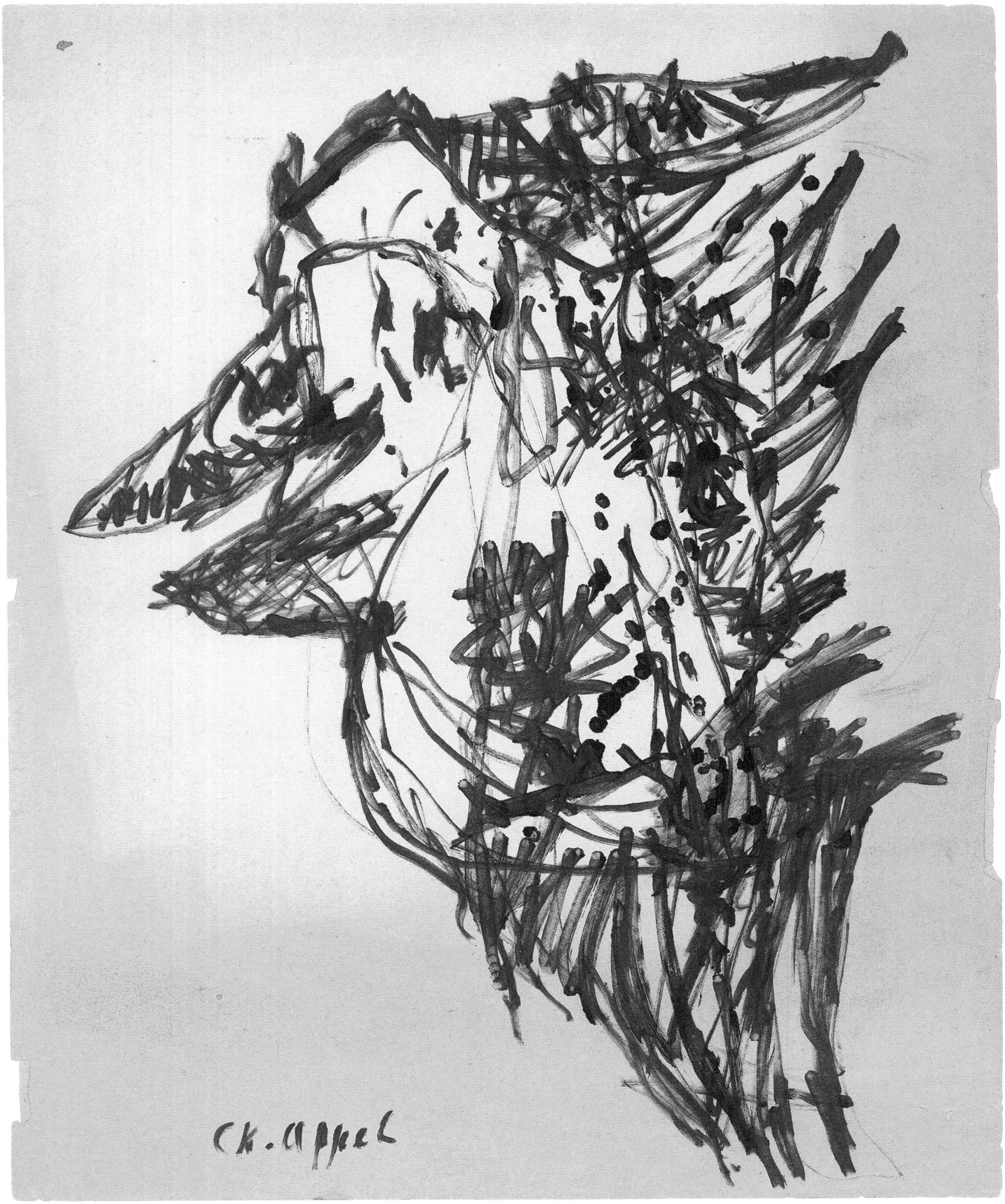
Ch. Appel

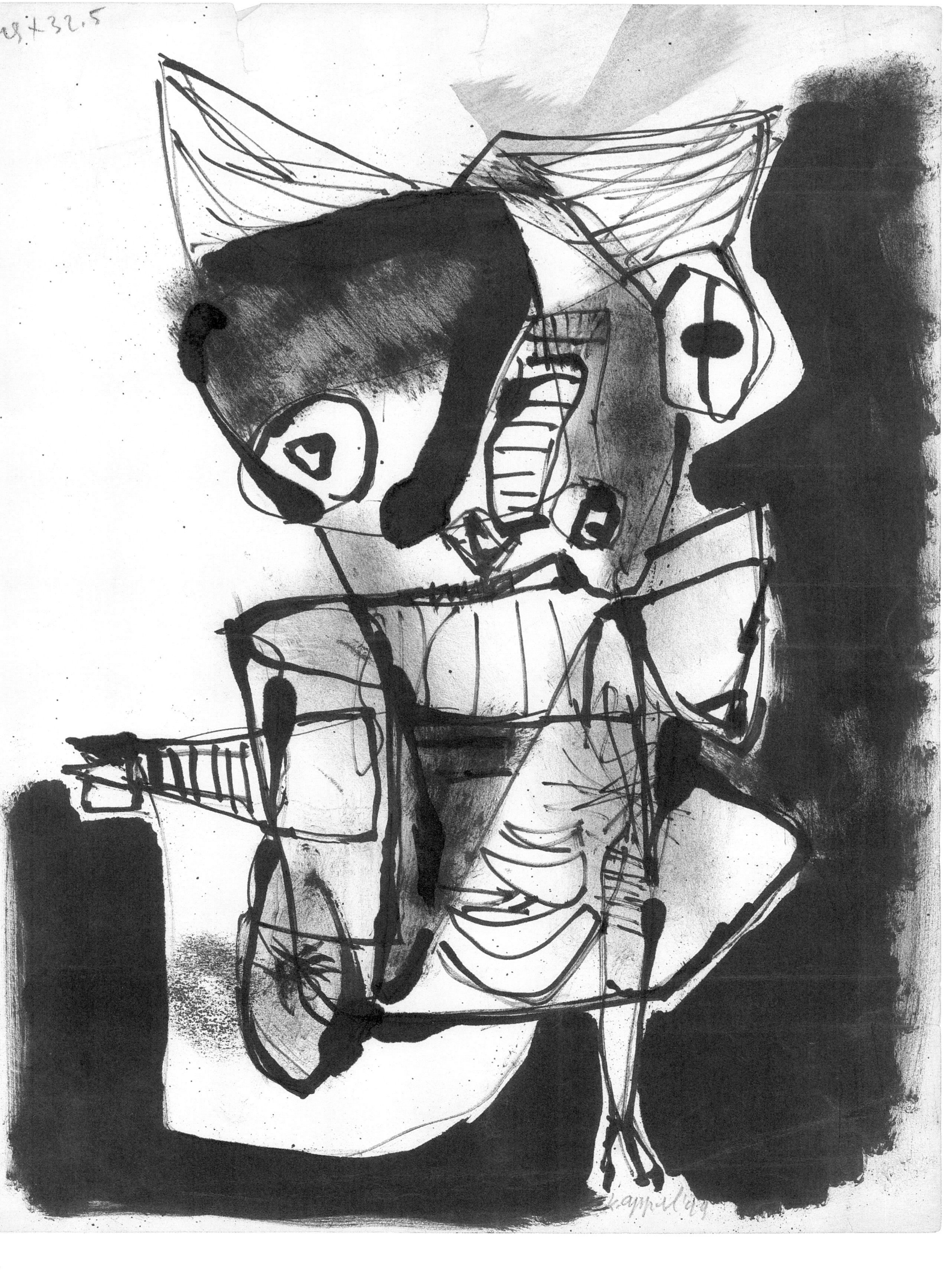
29x32,5

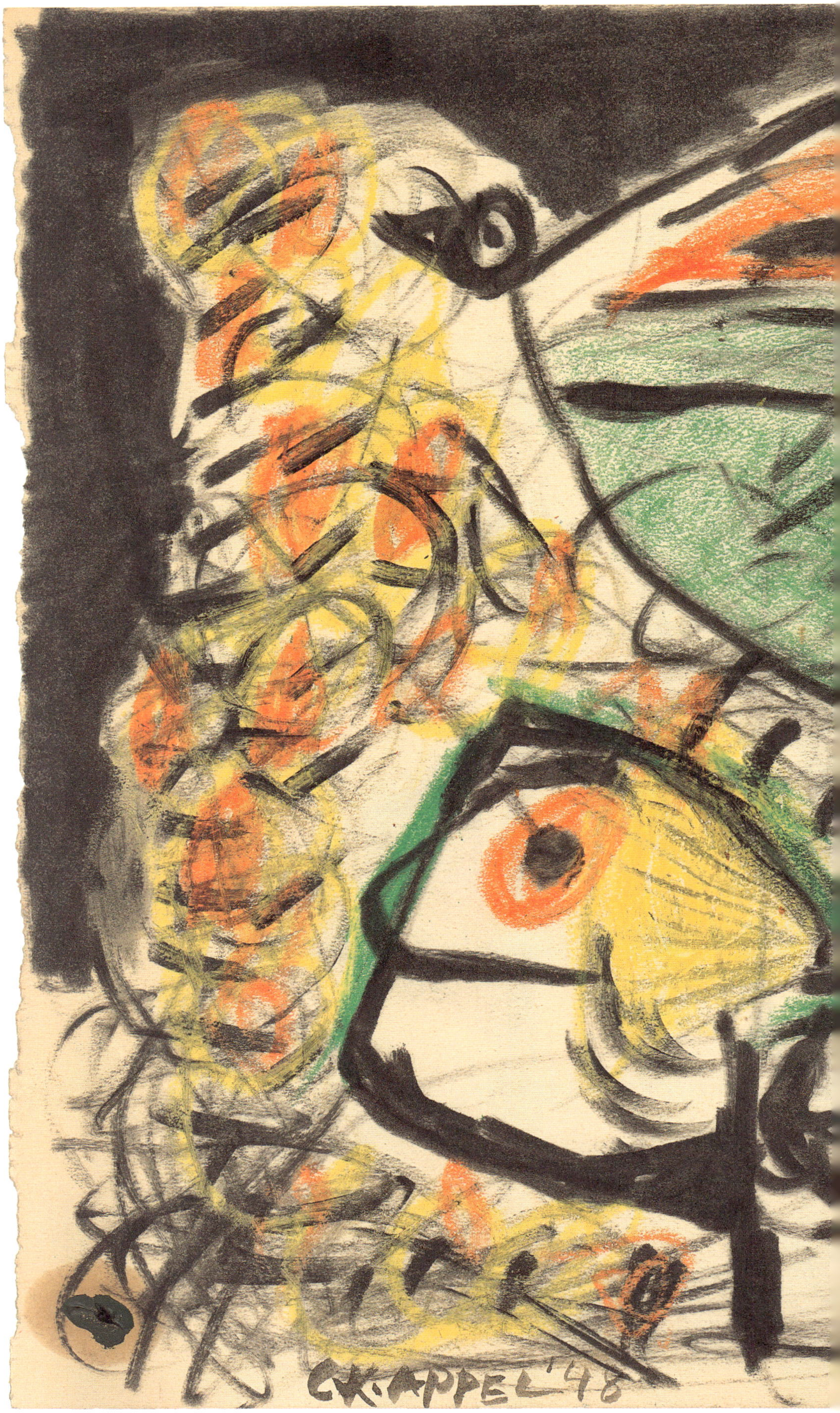
C.K. APPEL '48

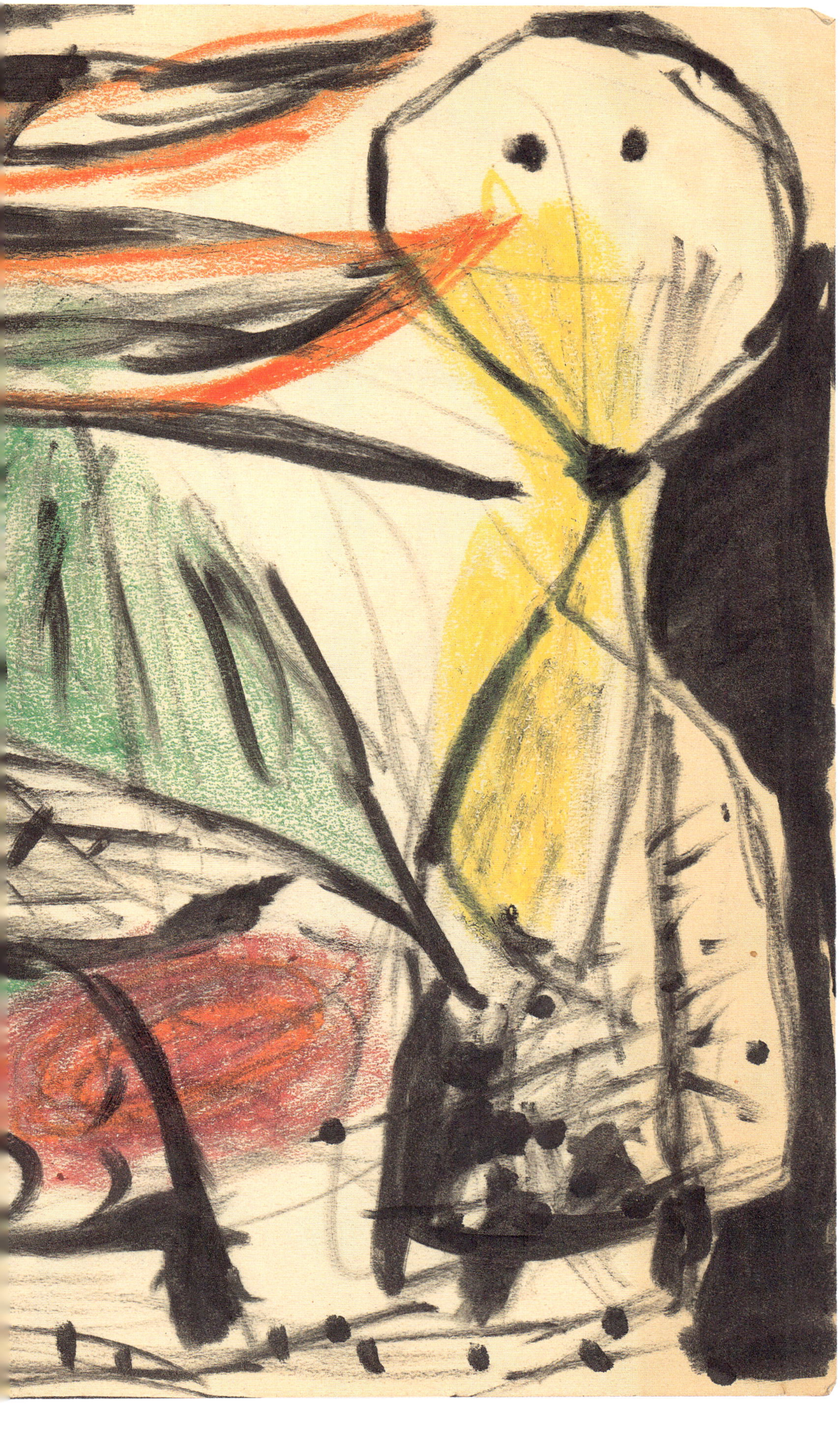

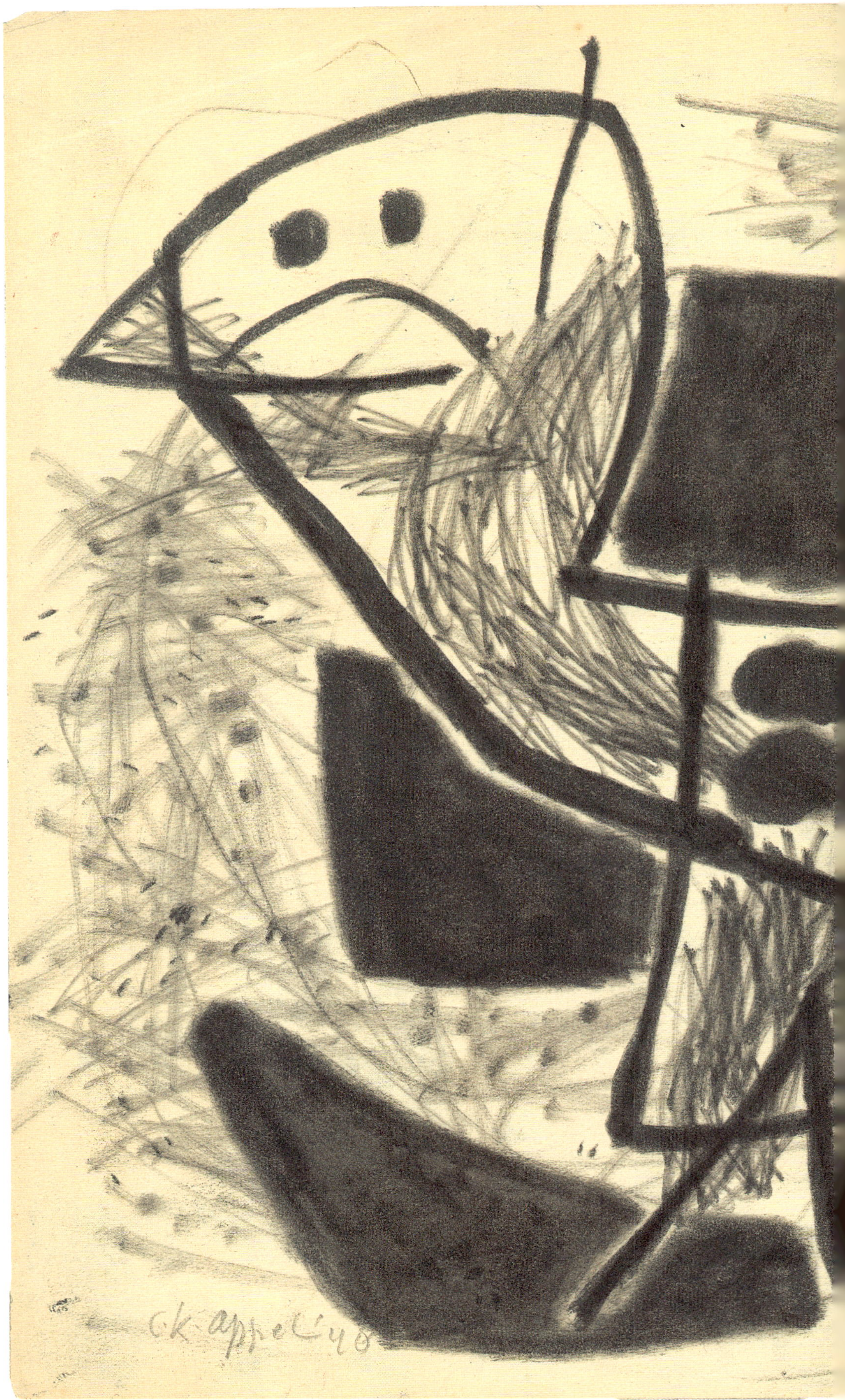
ck appel '48

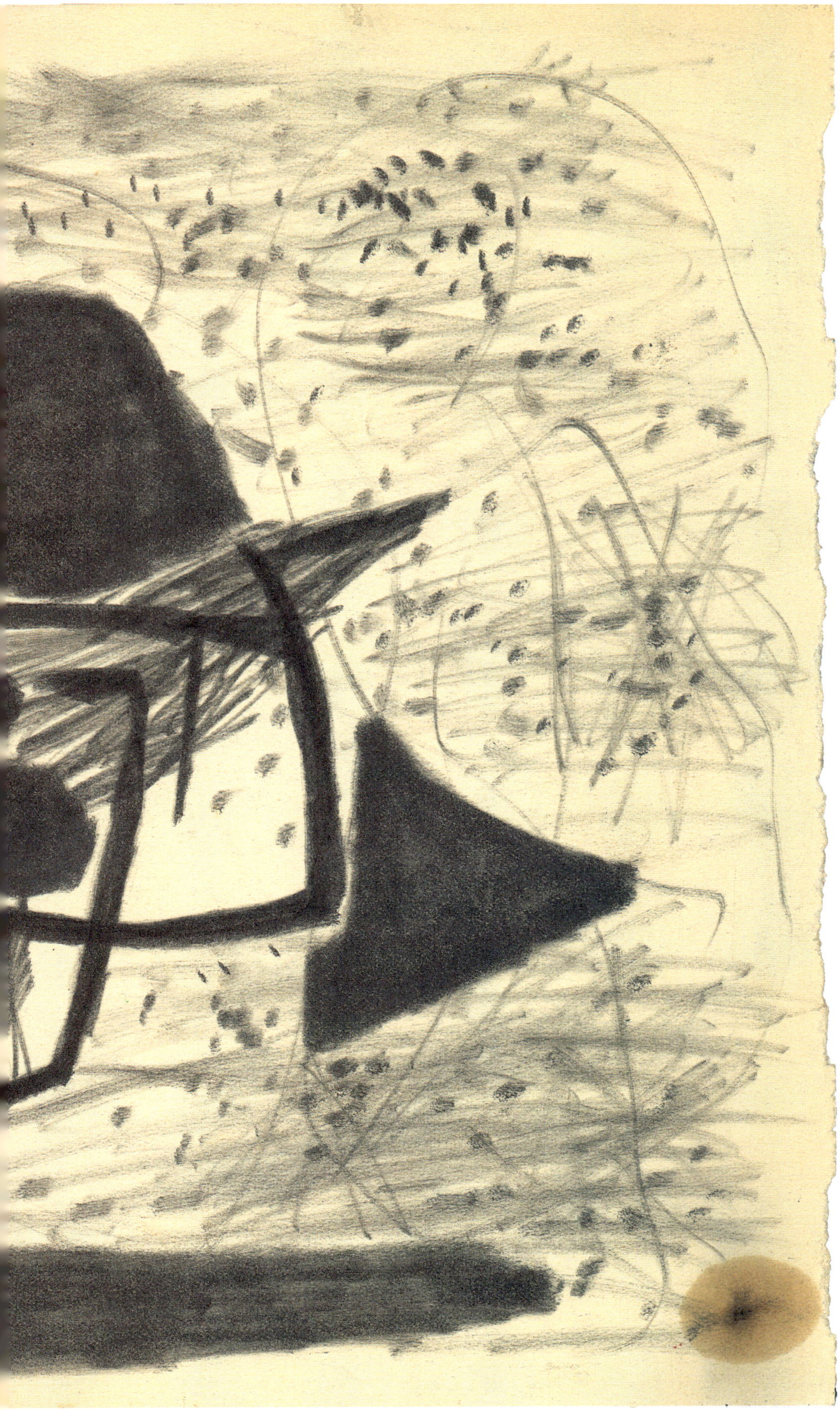

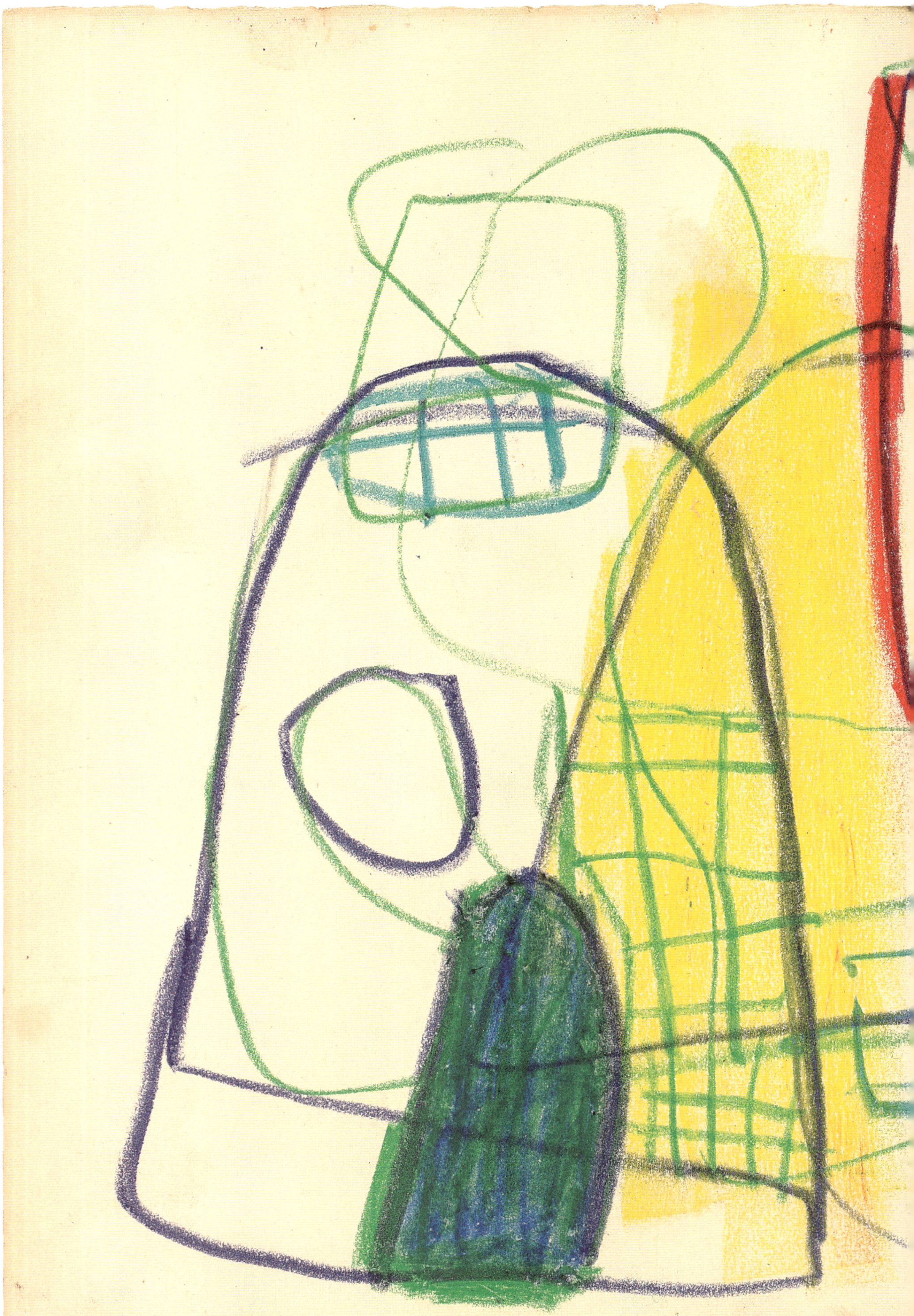

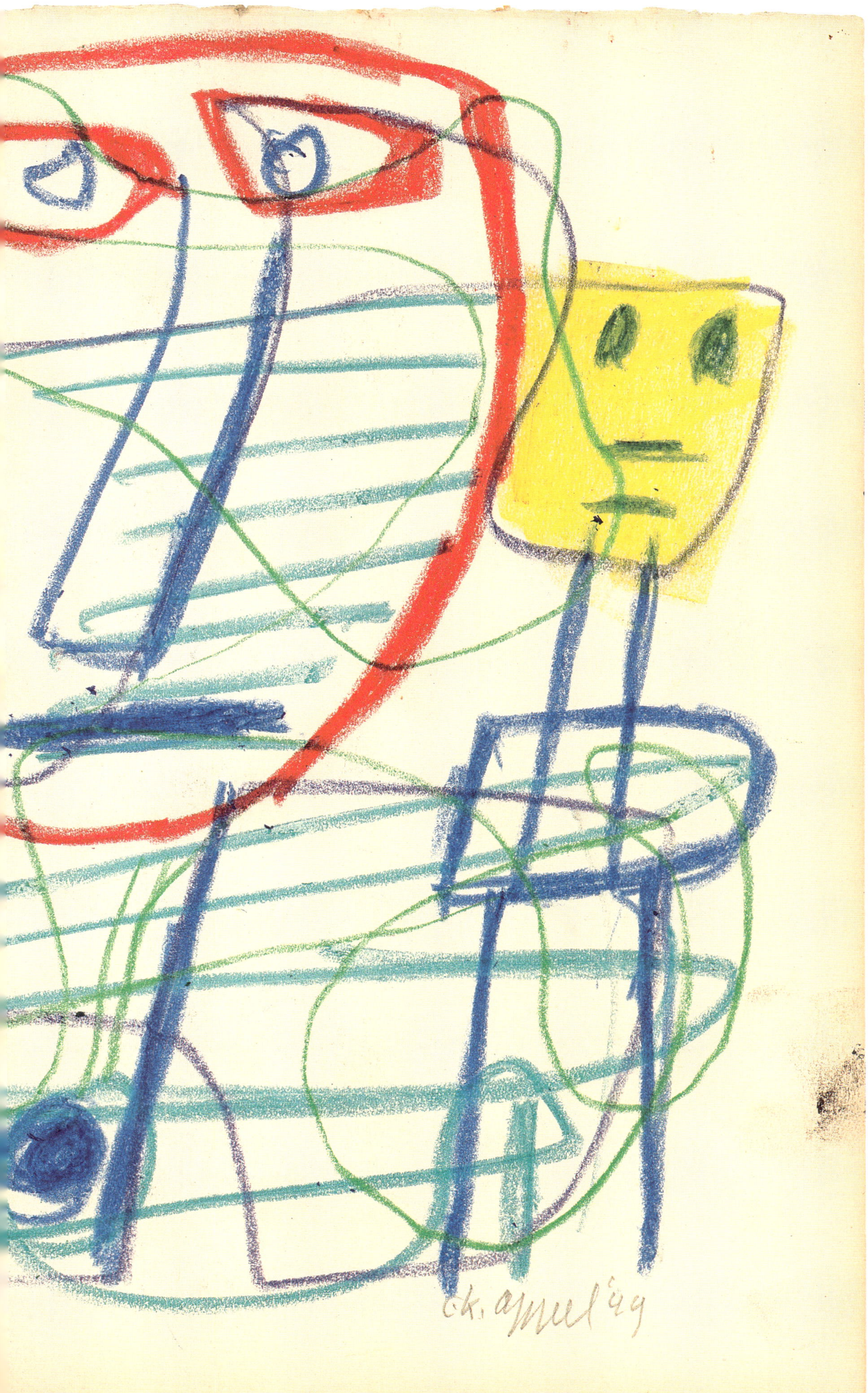

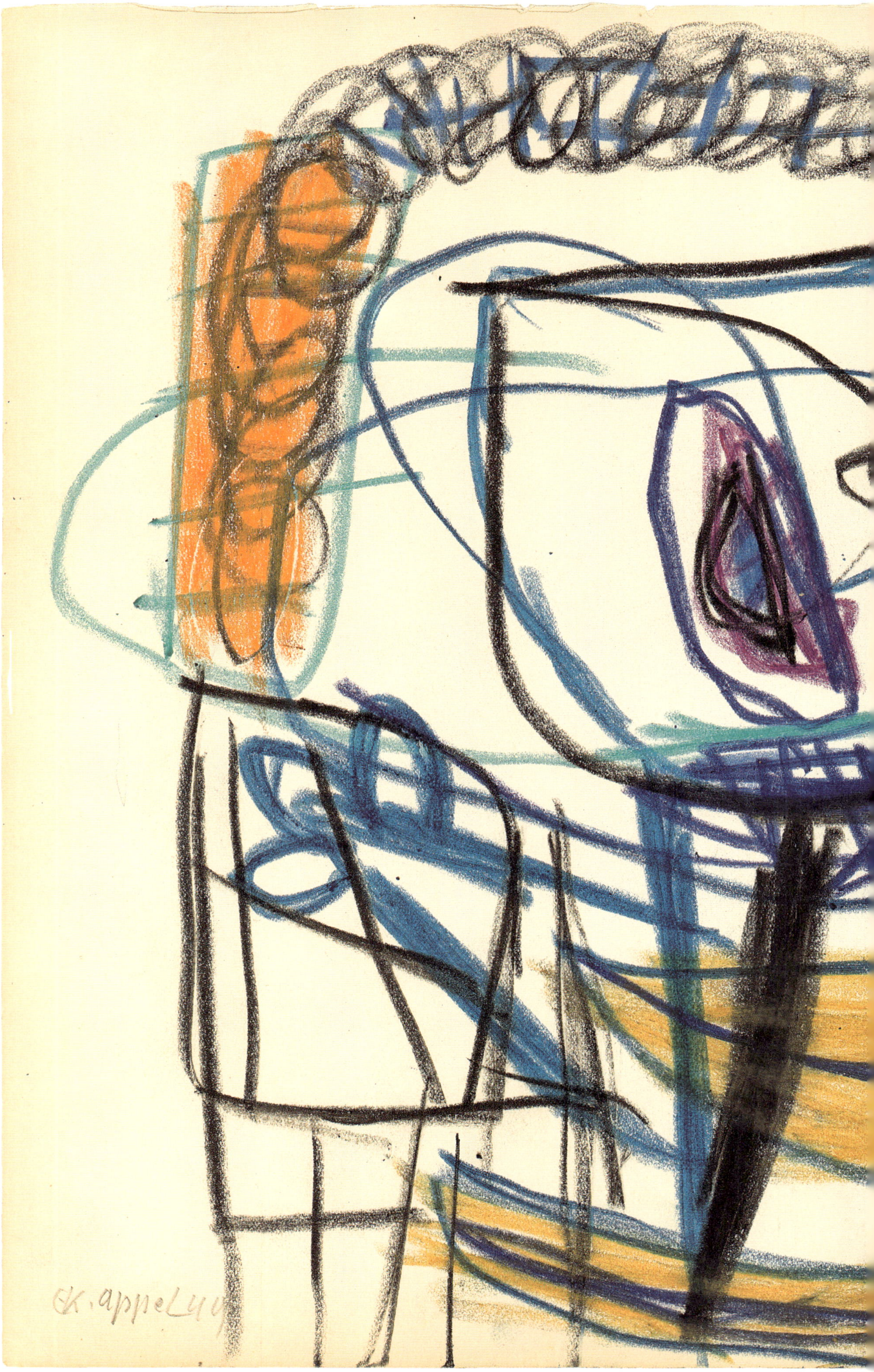

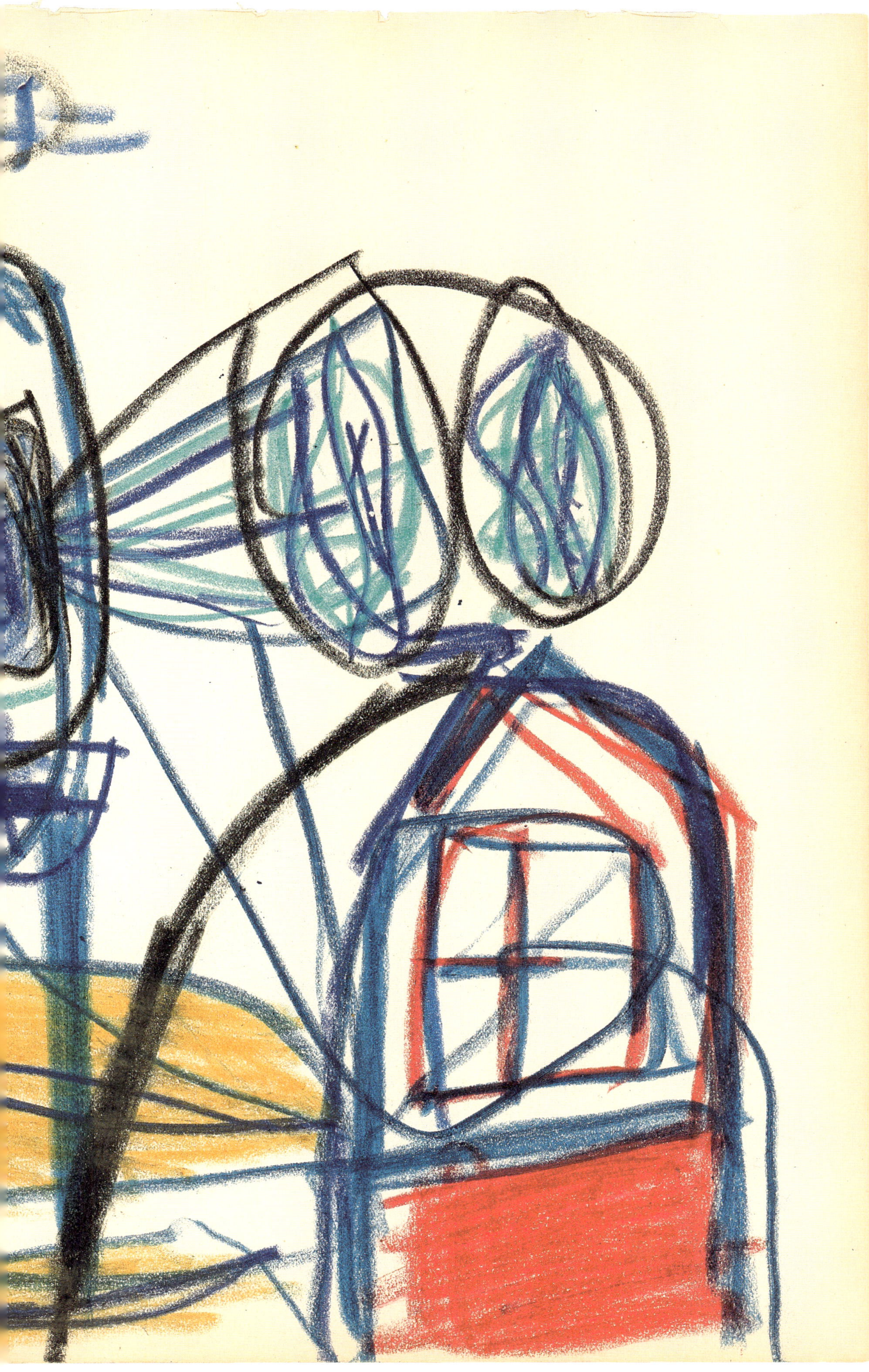

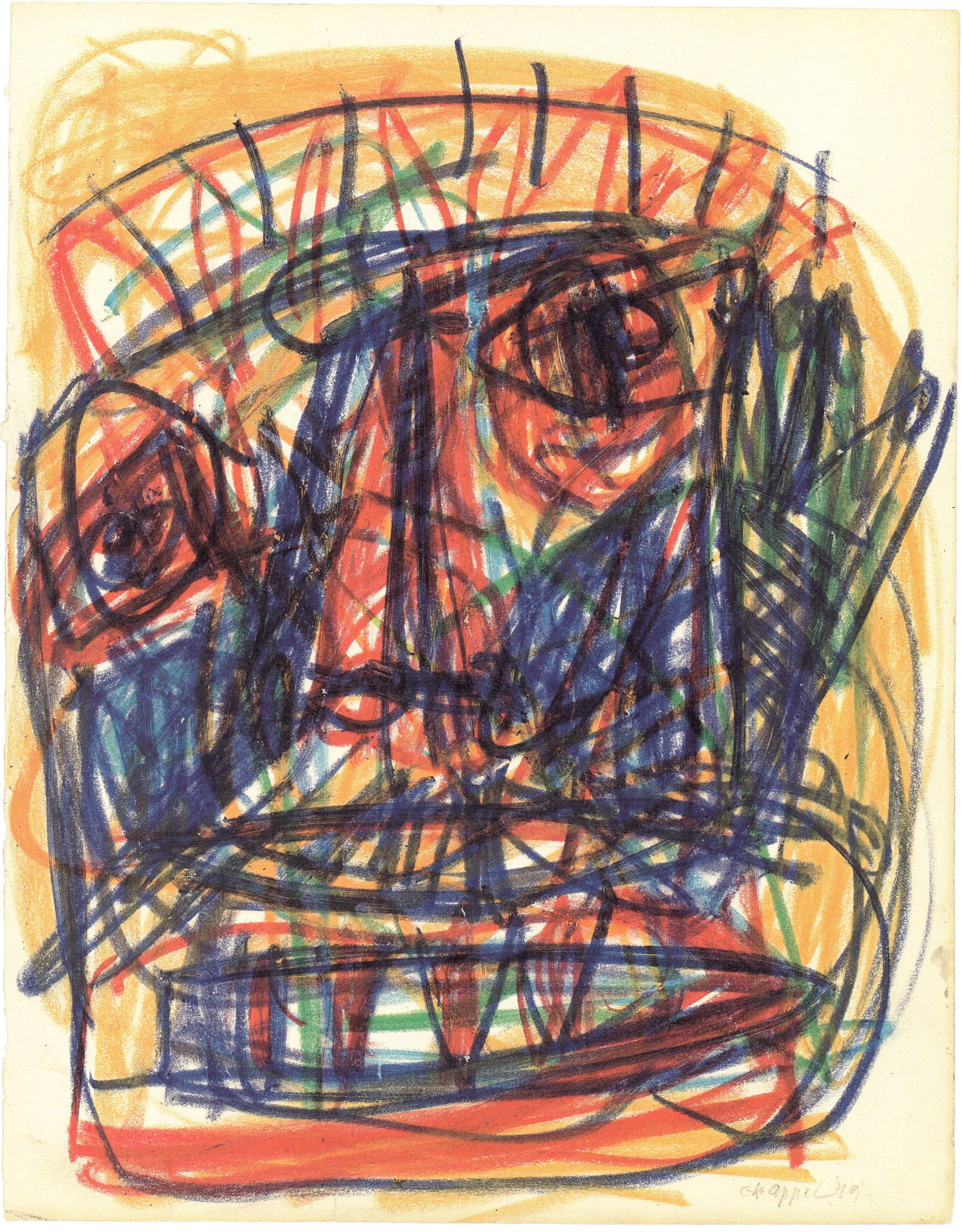

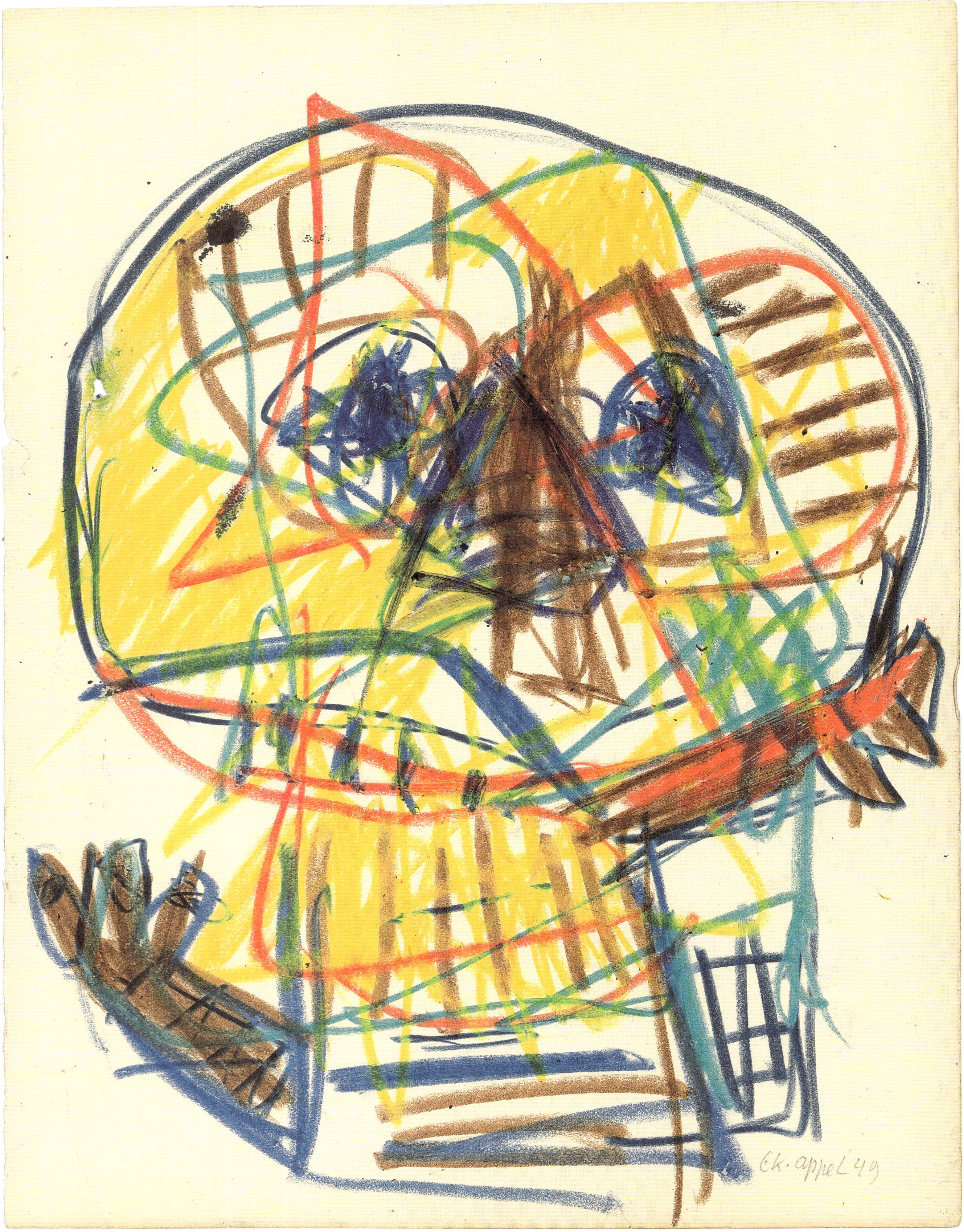
Ck. appel 49

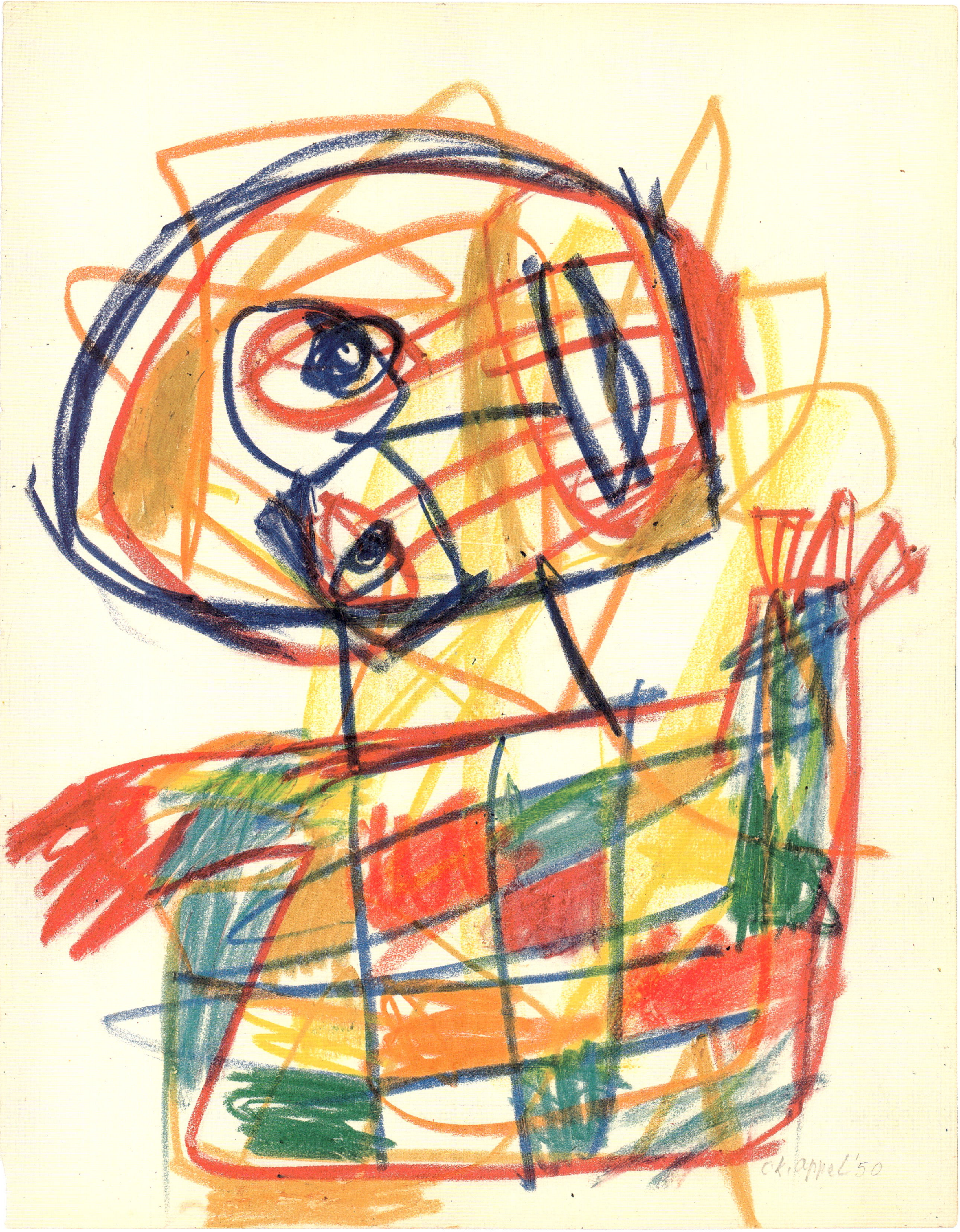

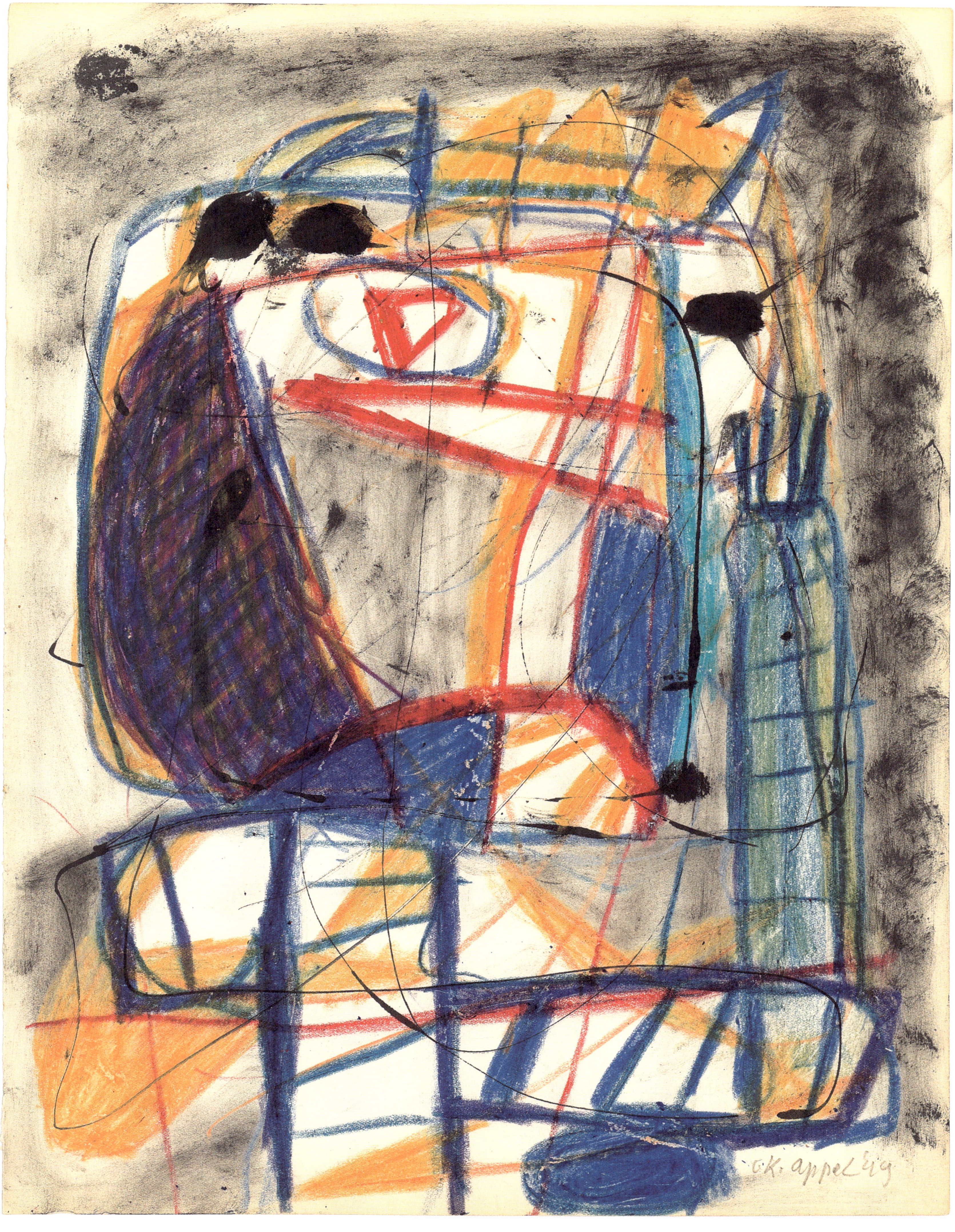

CK. appel '49

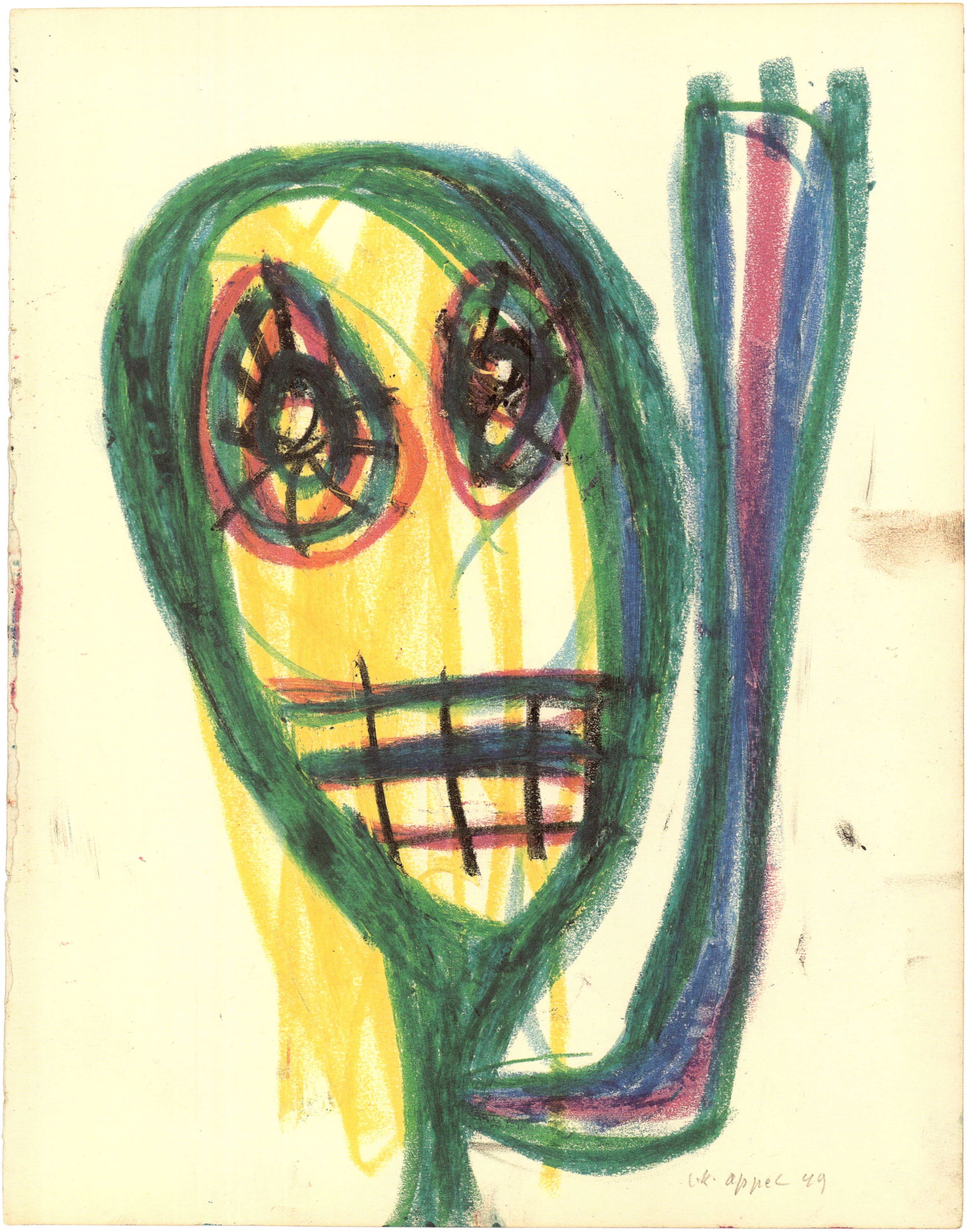

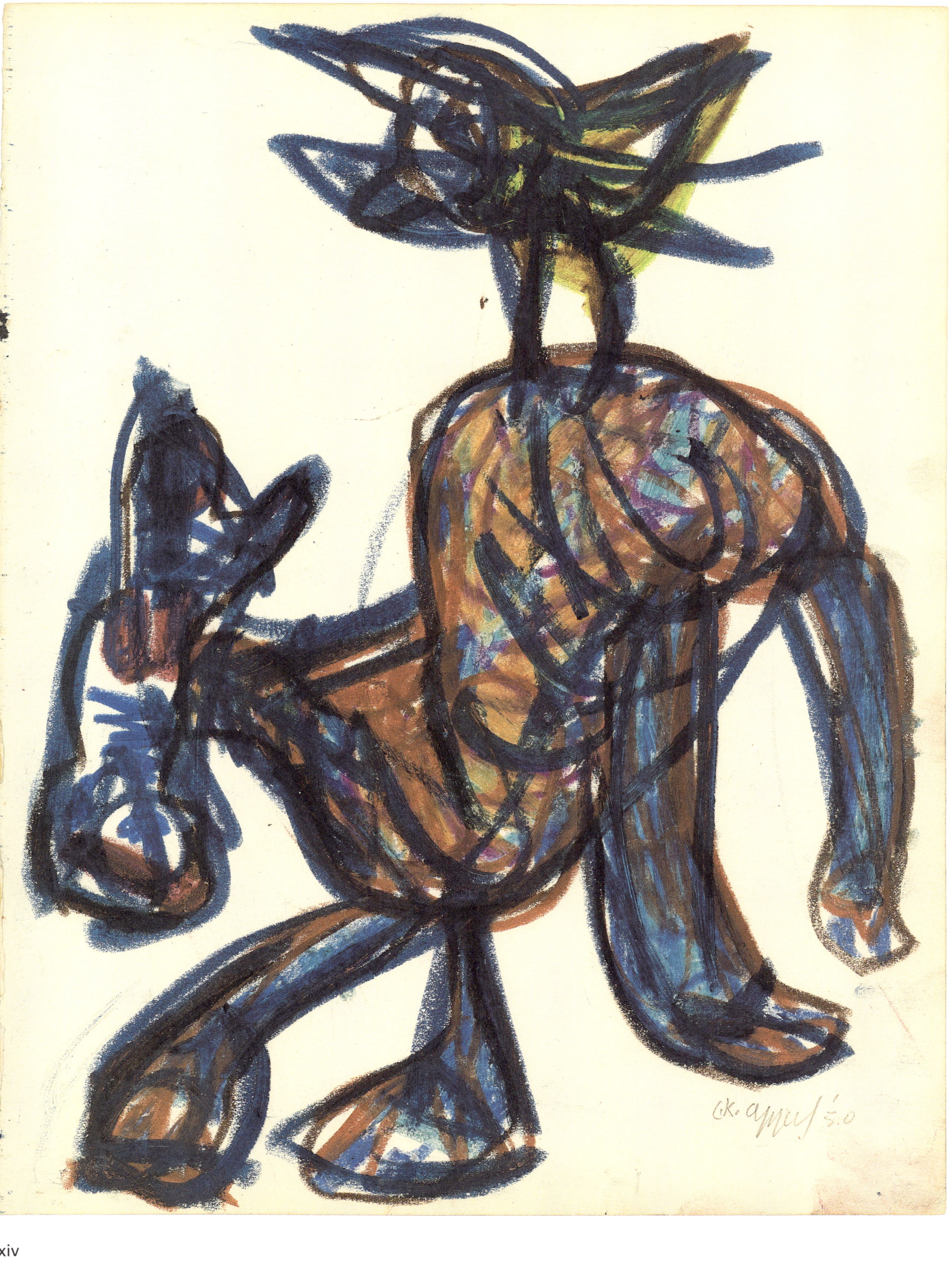

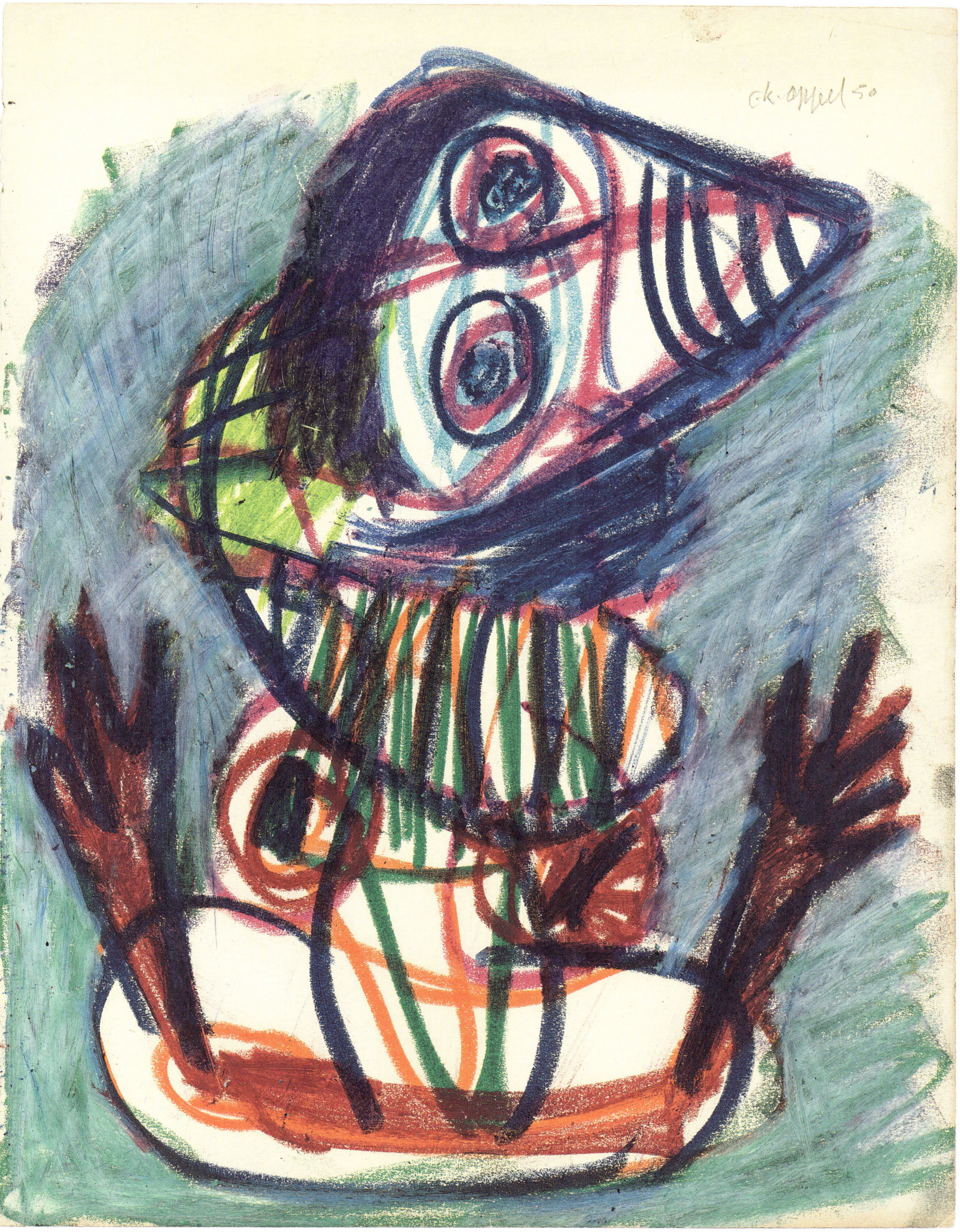

XXV

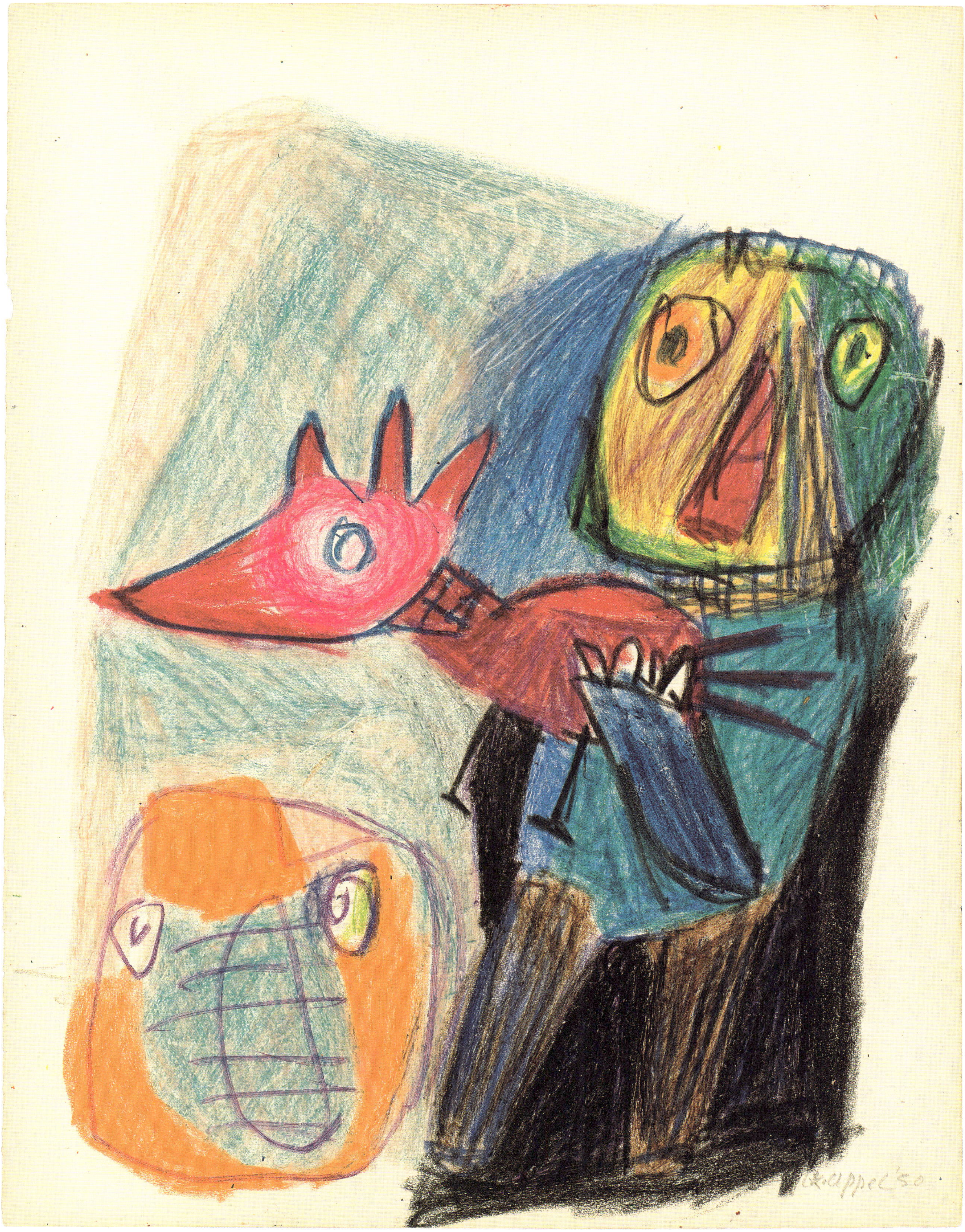

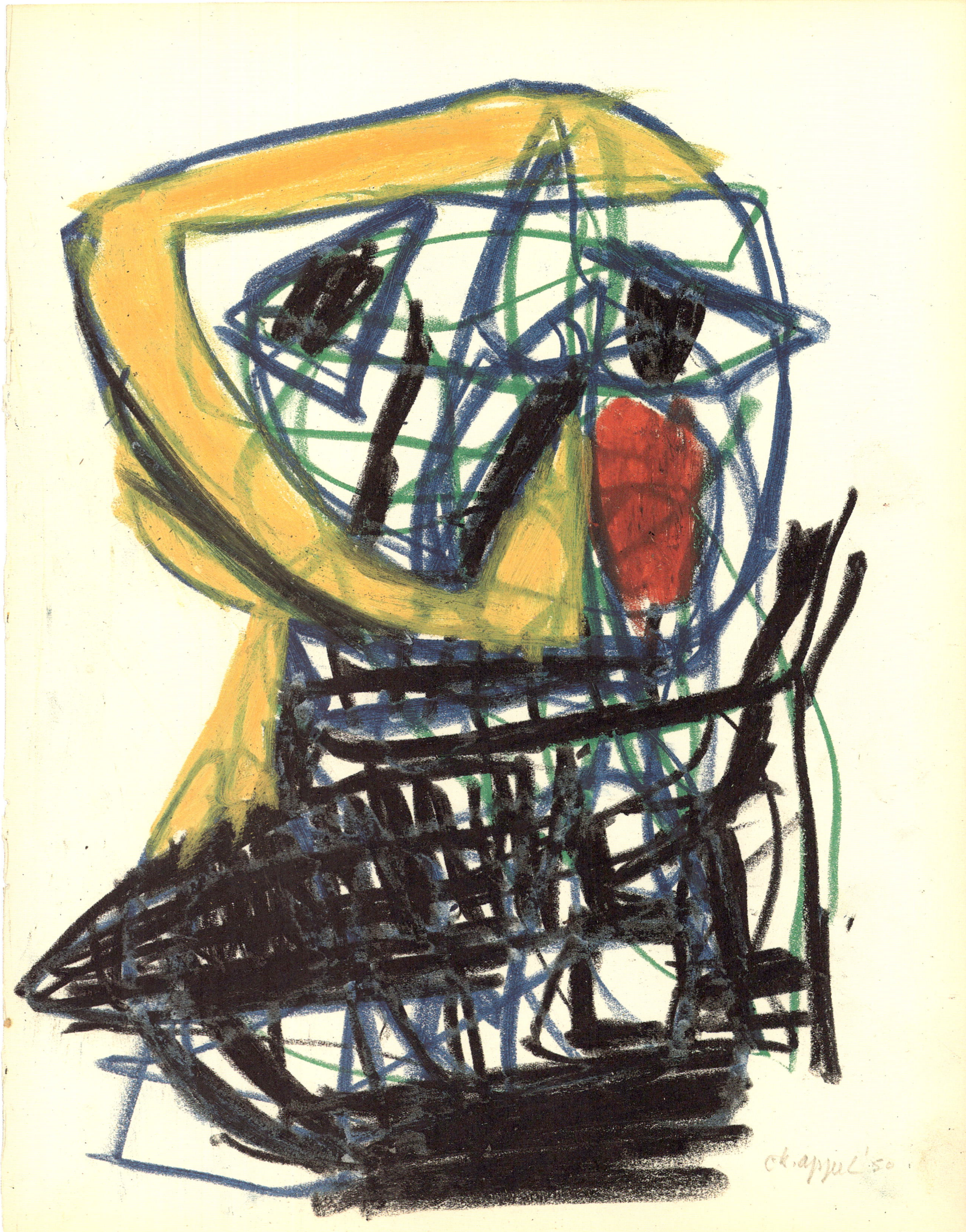
ck.appel '50

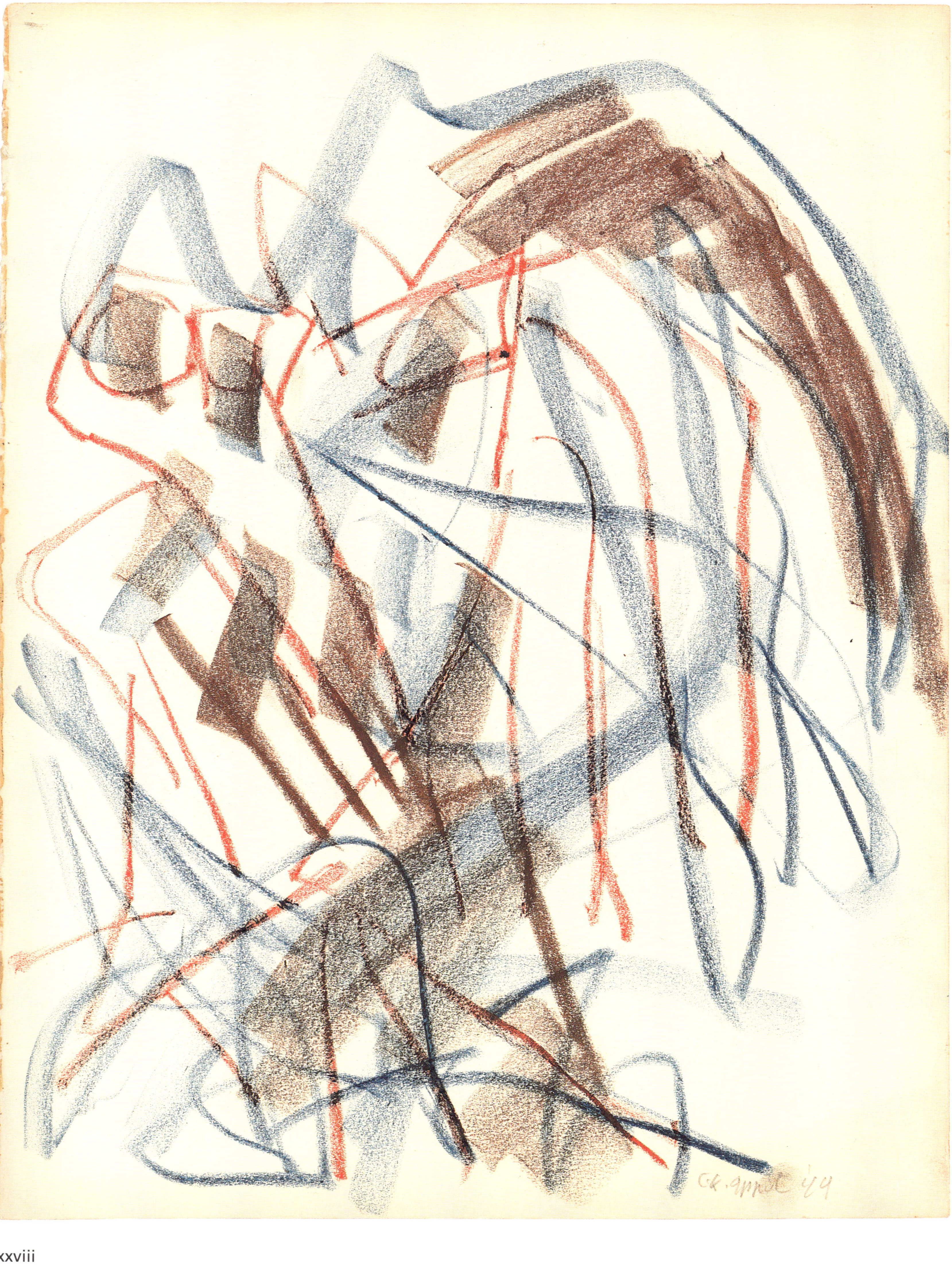

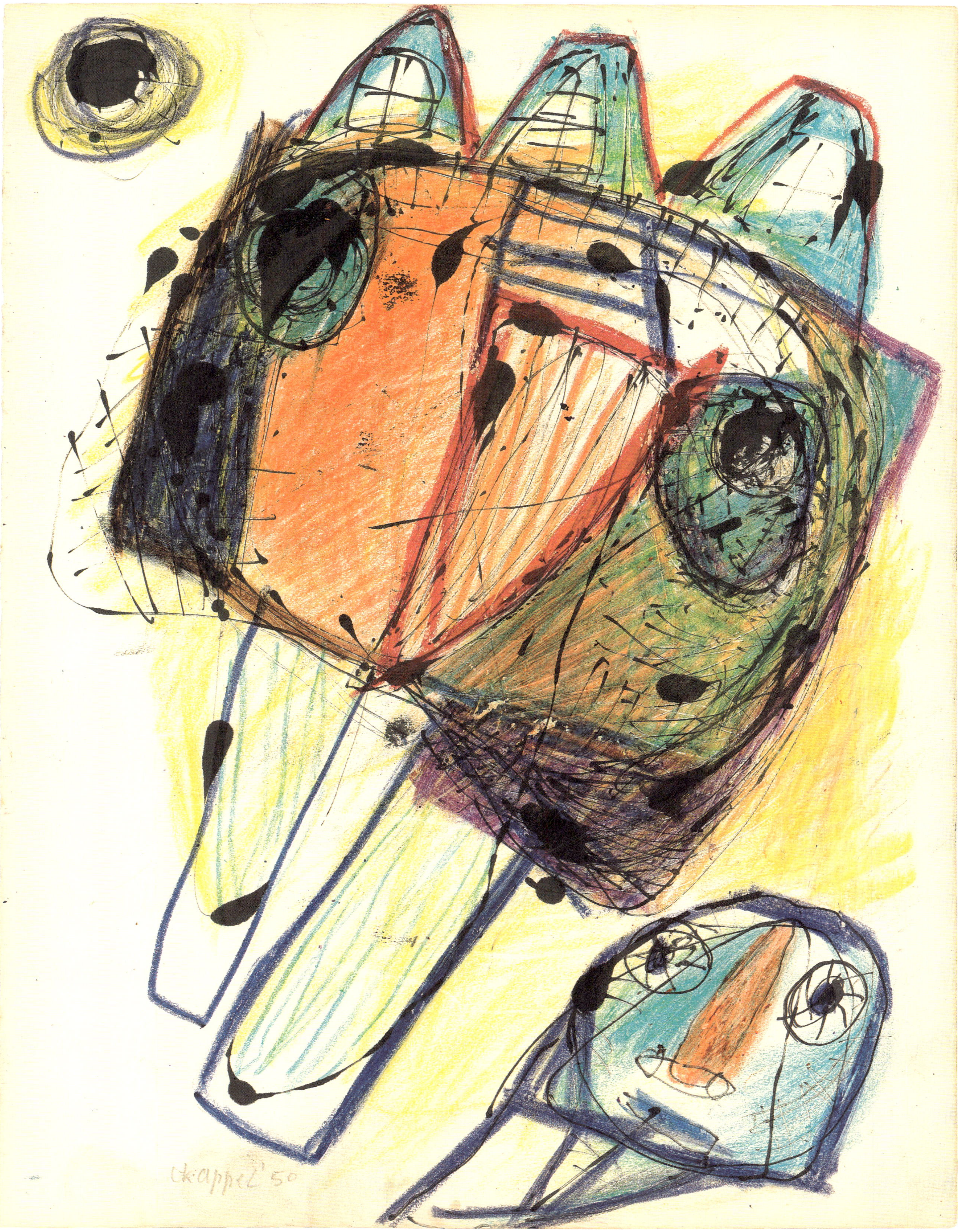
ck.appel '50

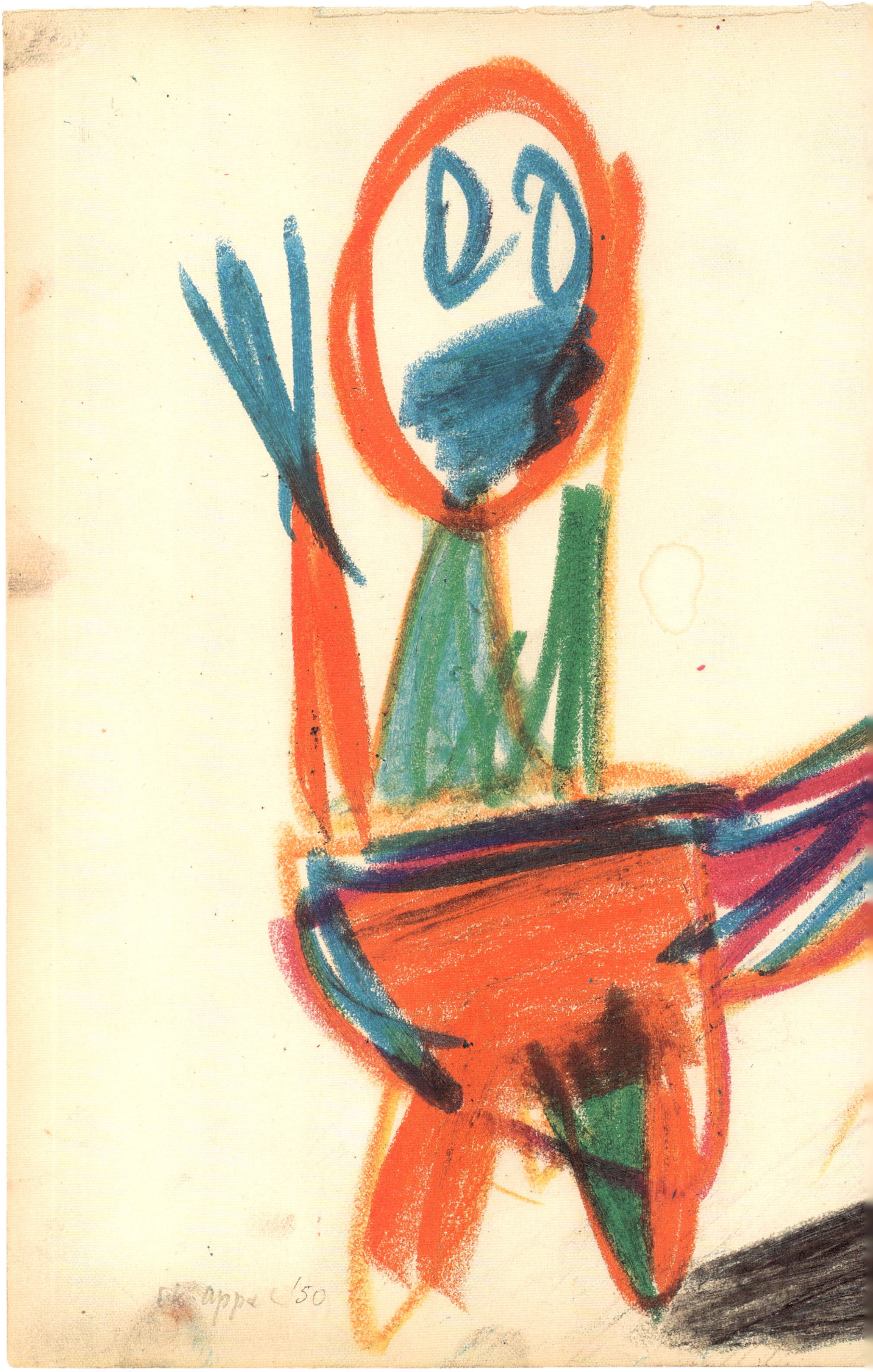
appel '50

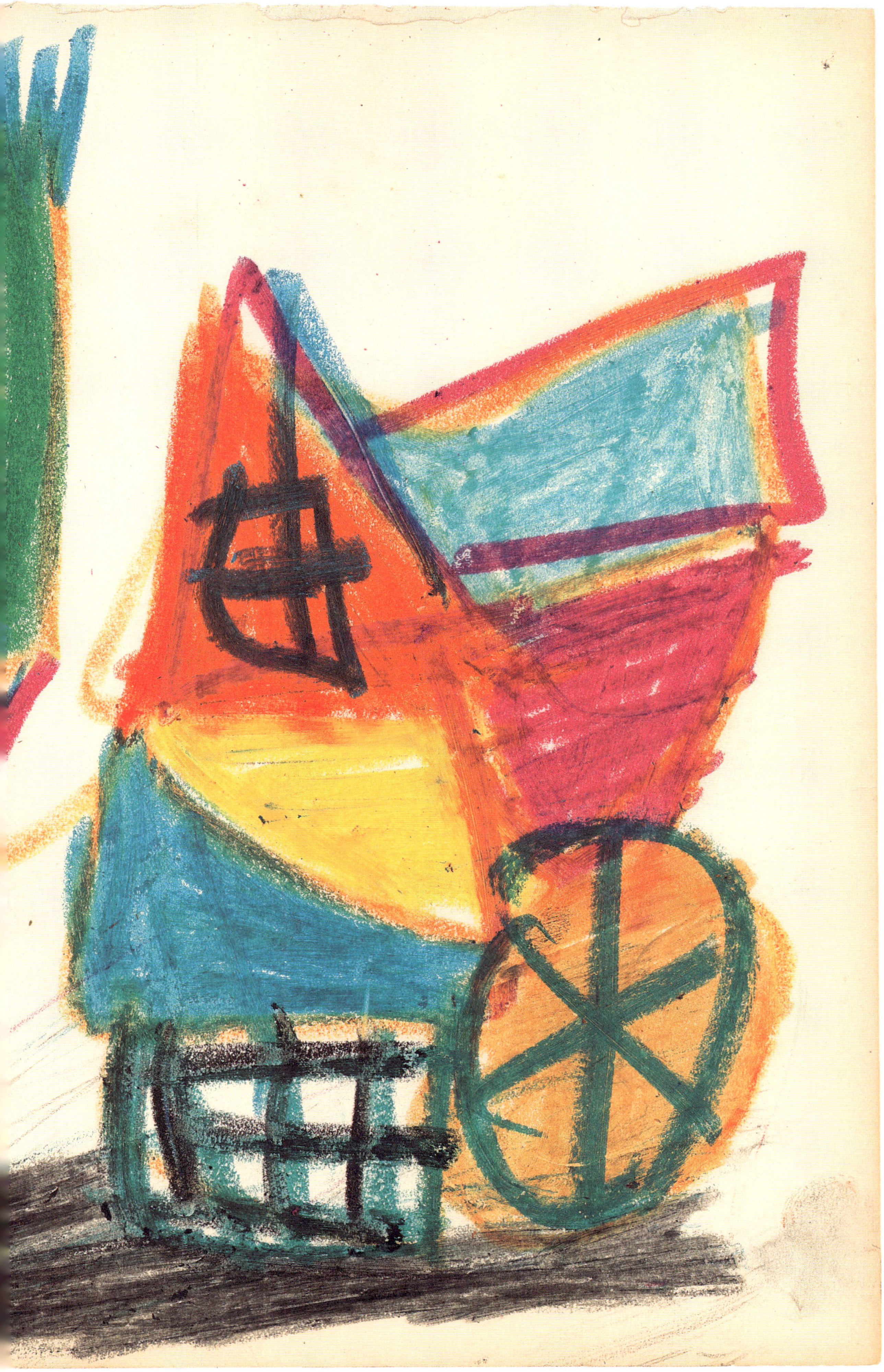

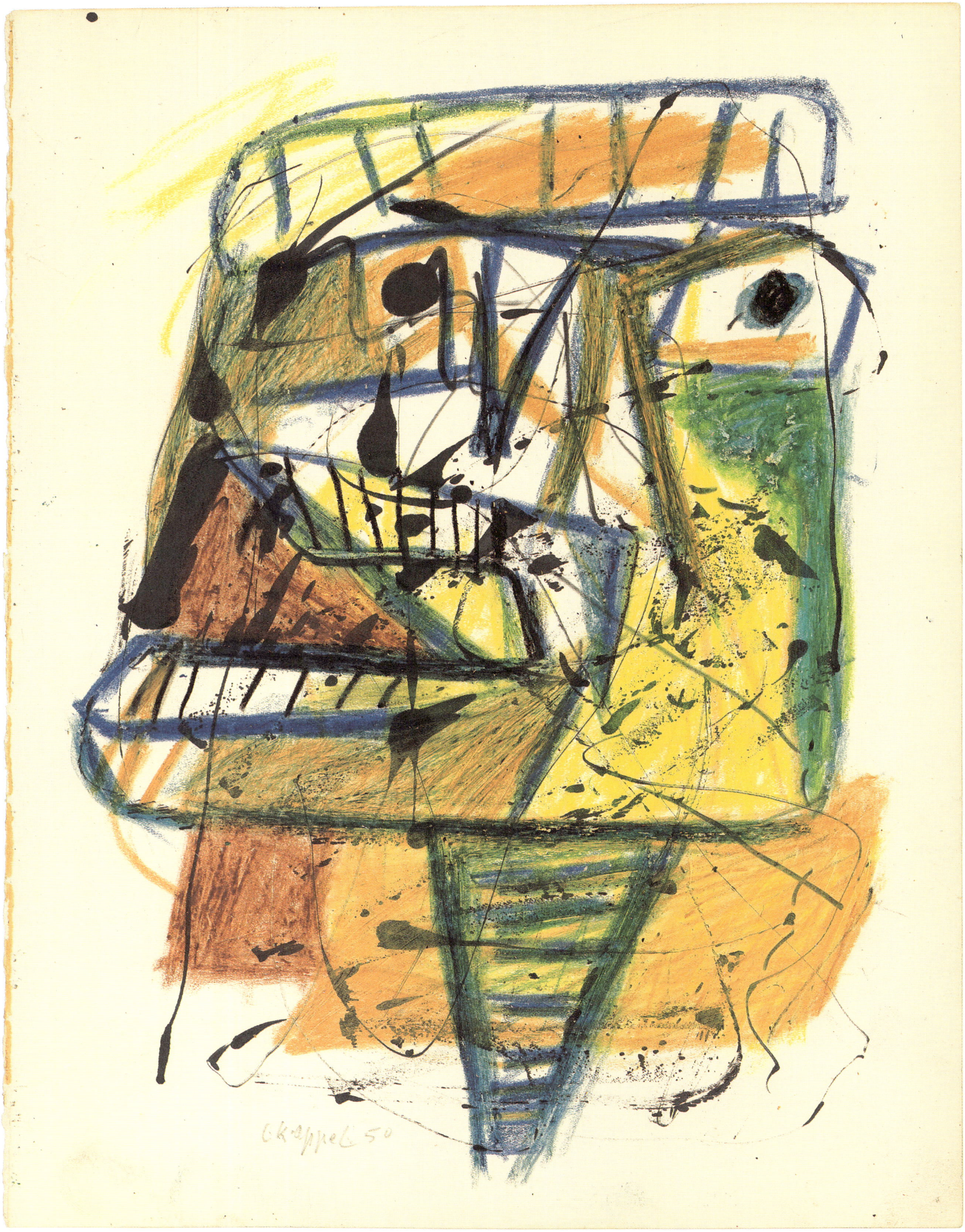

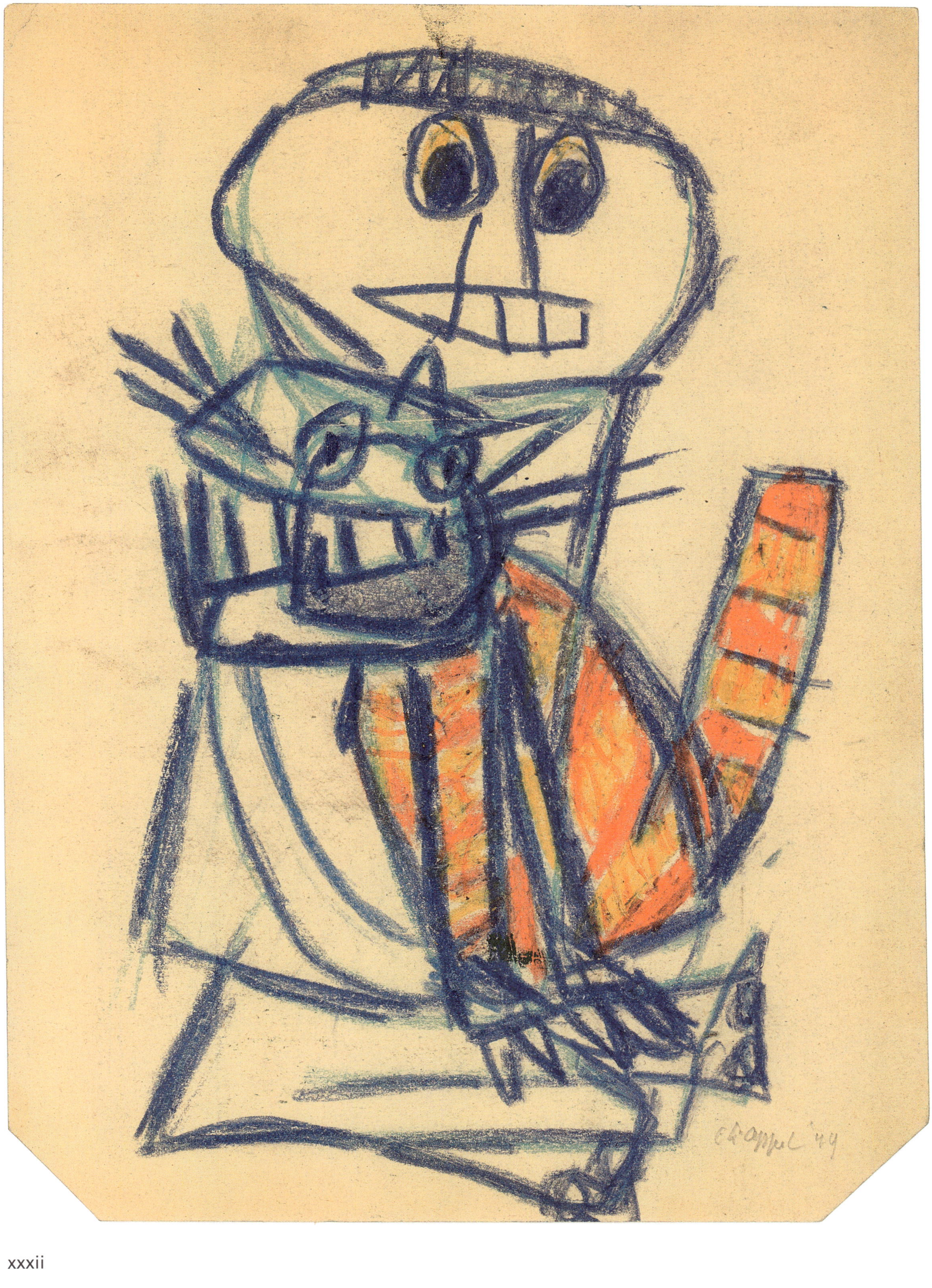

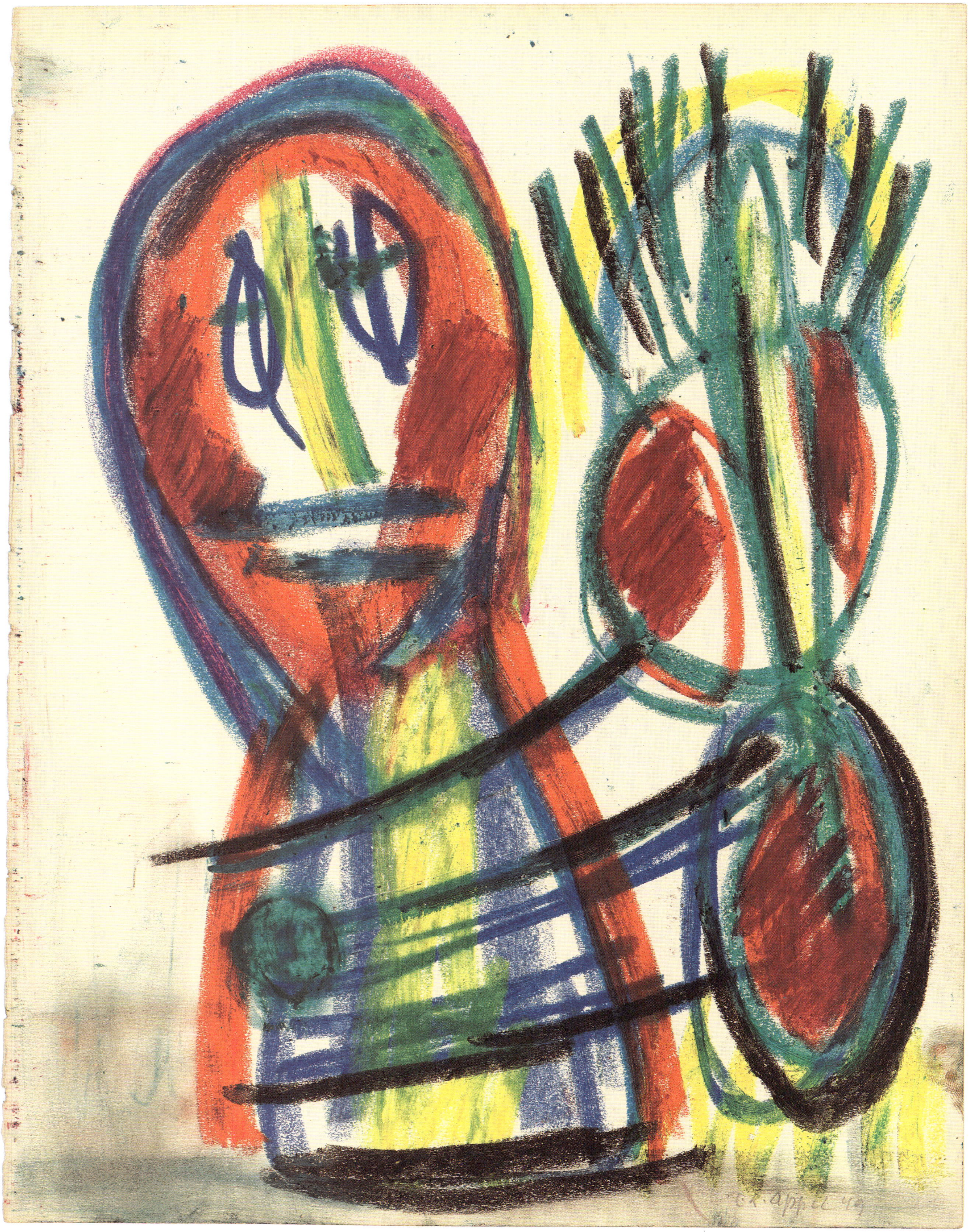

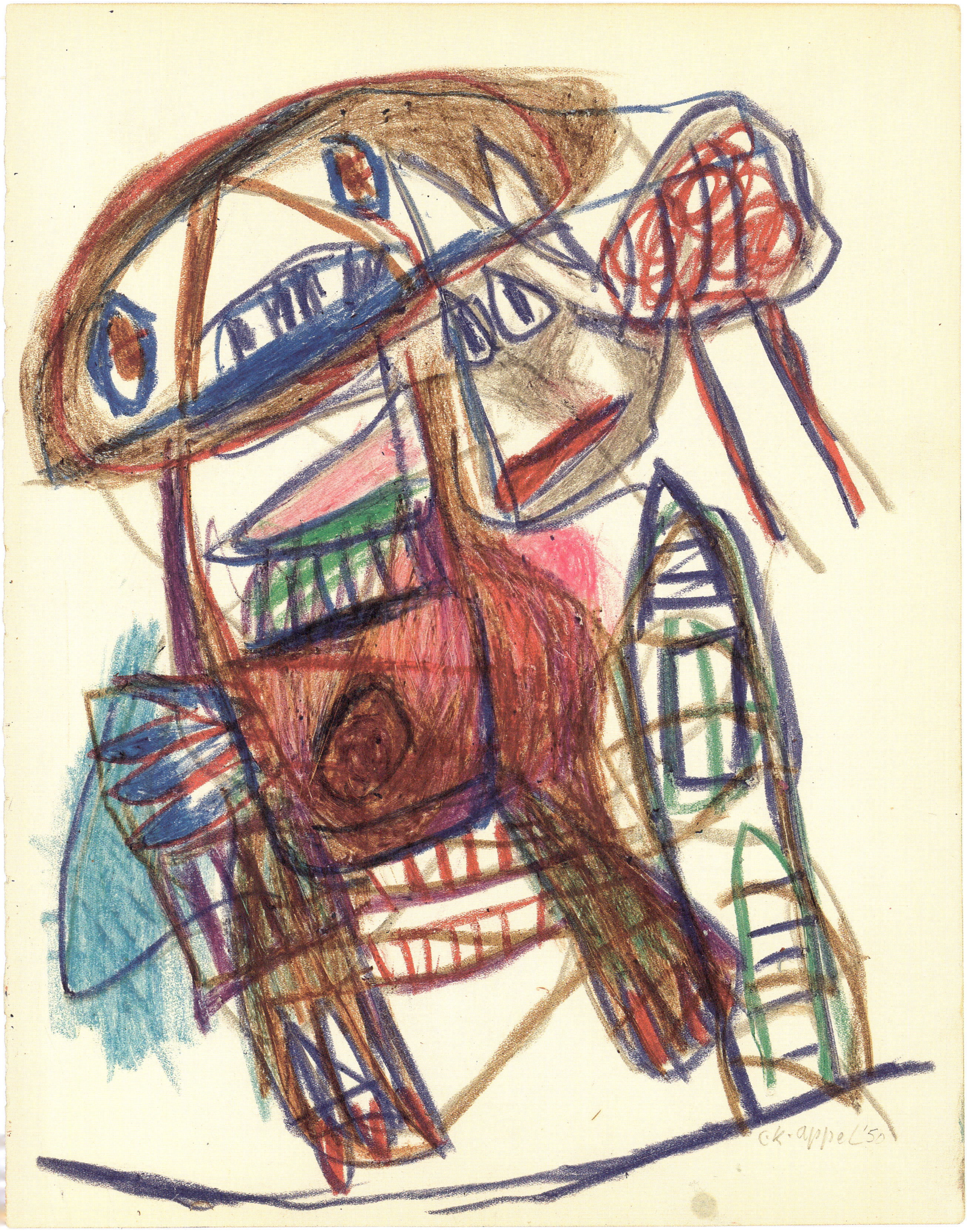
c.k. appel '50

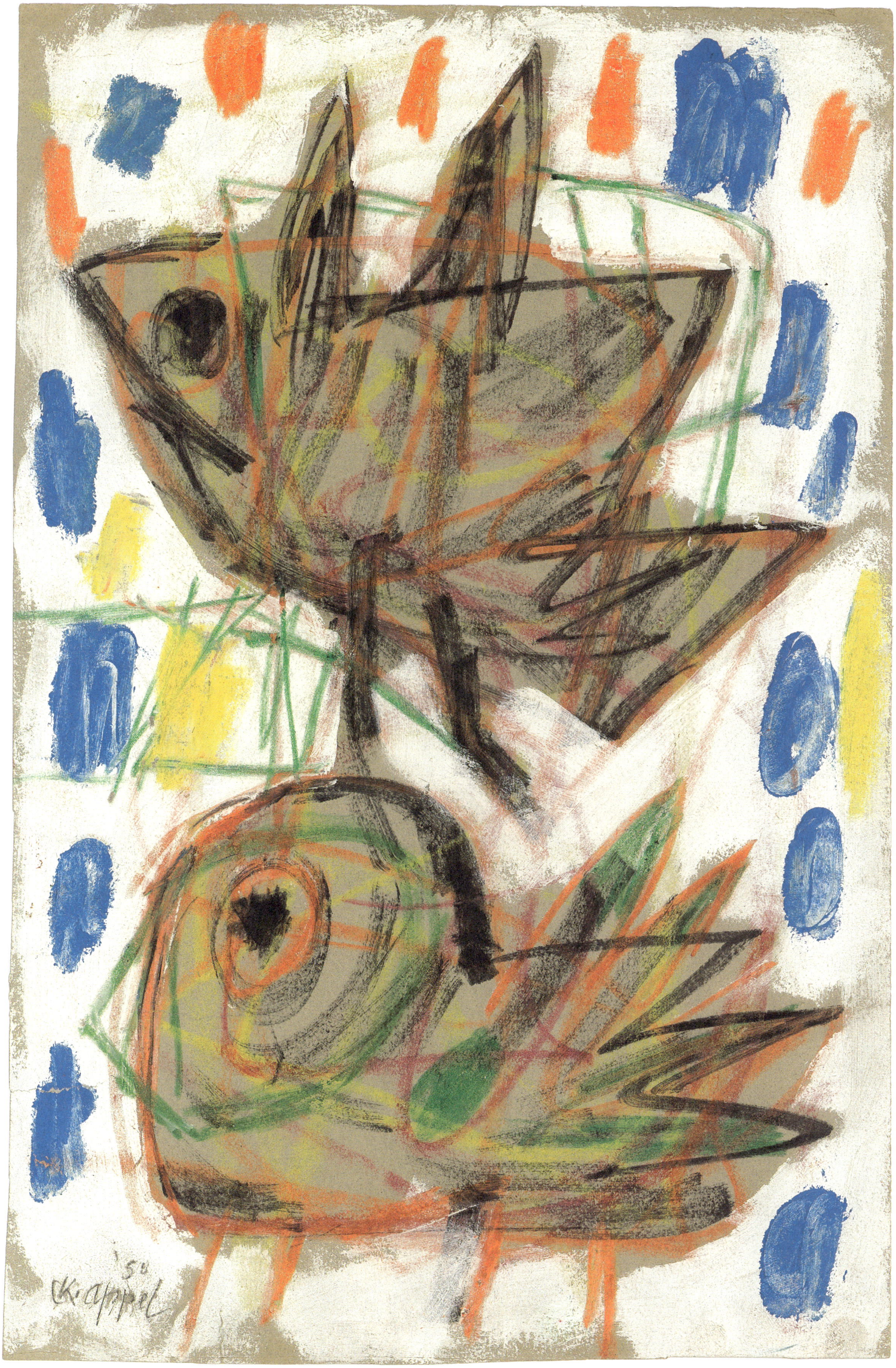
'50
K. appel

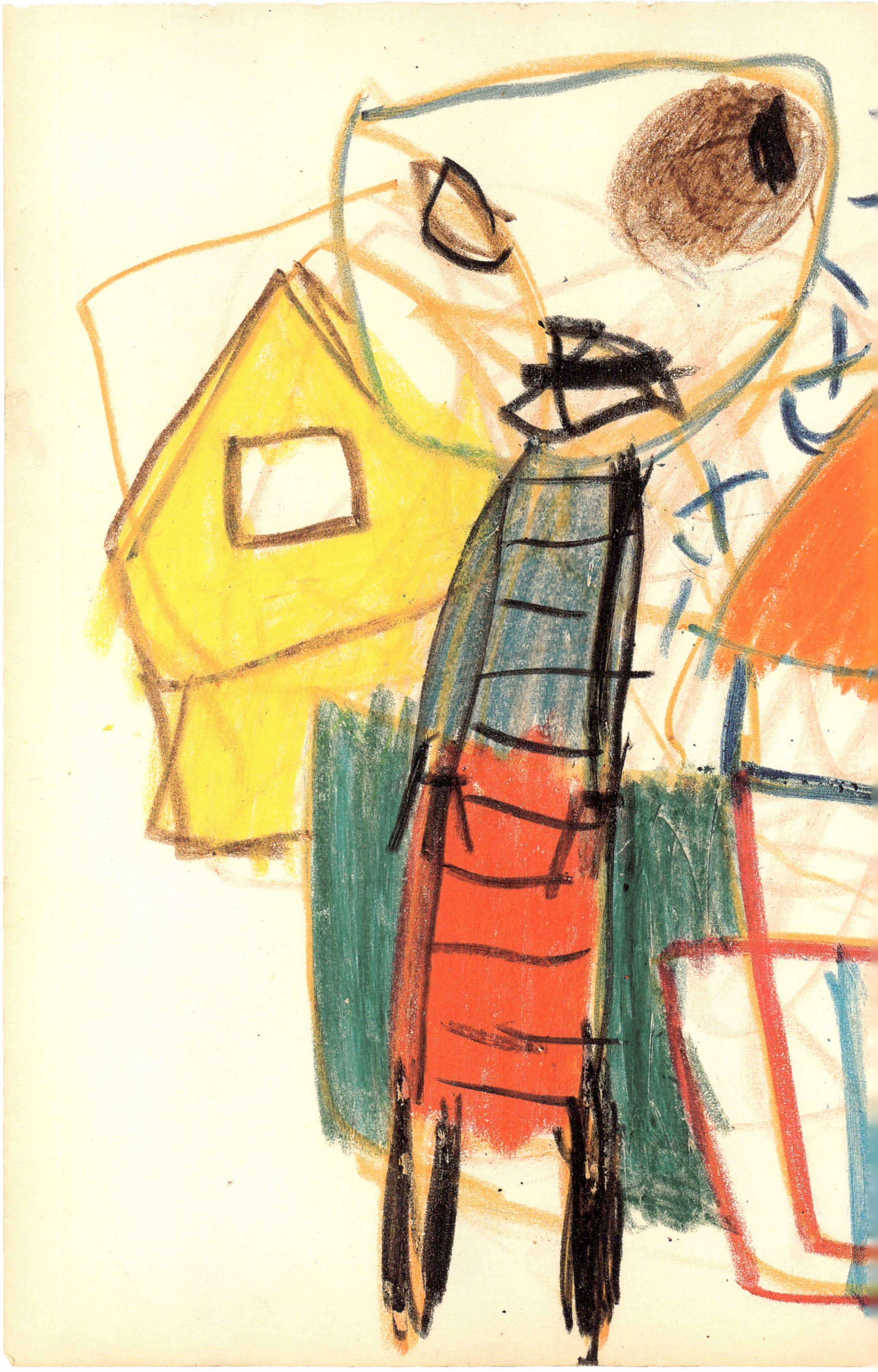

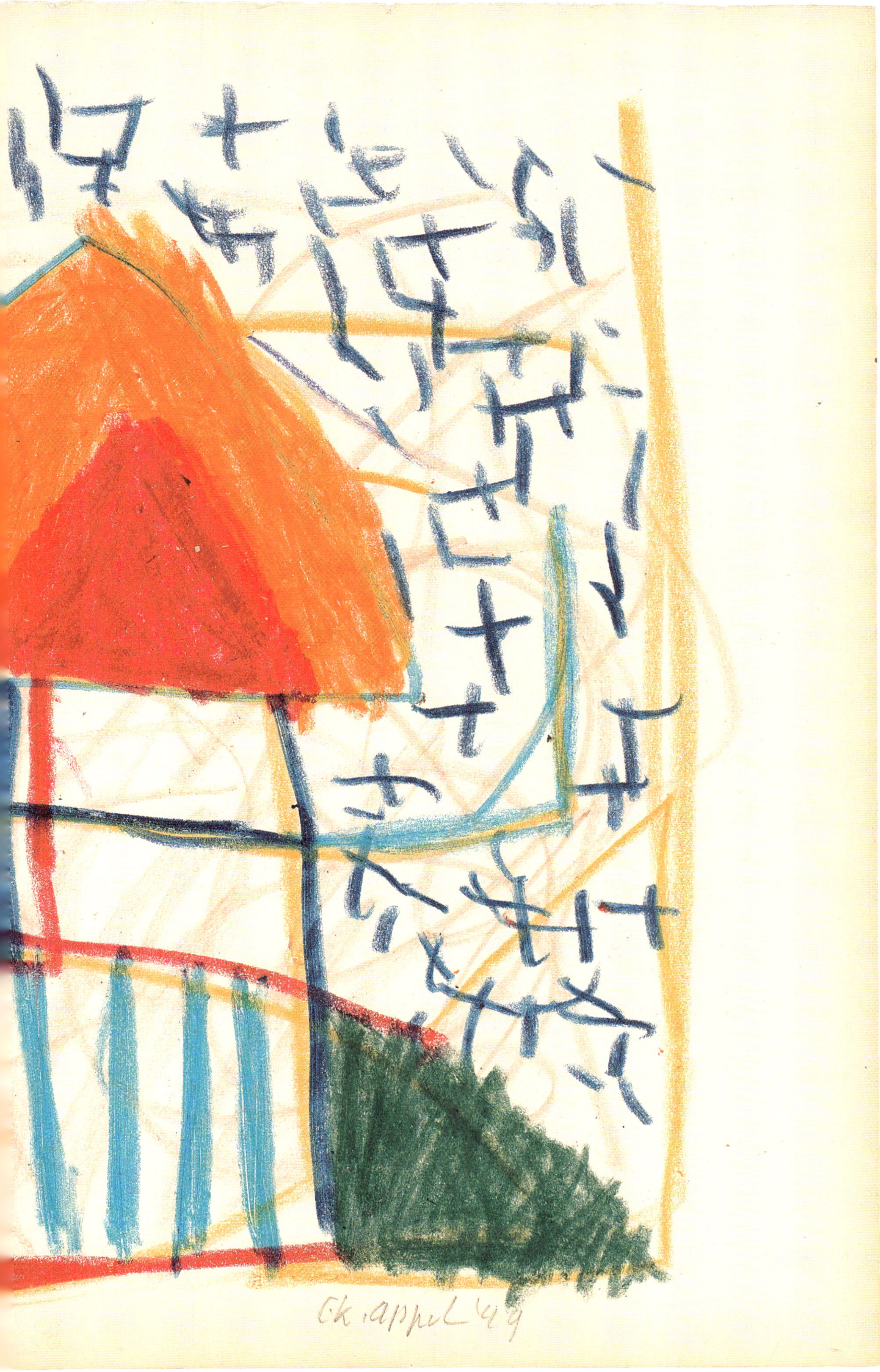
Ck.appel '49

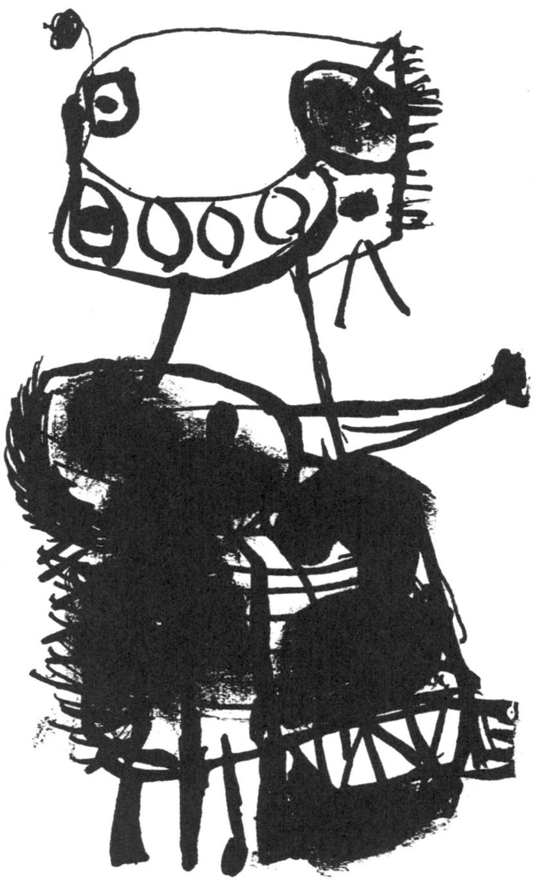

Gambits between Generations

Johannes Gachnang

As a publisher, I should call this book a stroke of pure luck. Its publication brings a series of open circles to a close within a specific context. I take the liberty, in the following lines, of circumscribing the geometry of its evolution, for it has much to do with the history of this publishing house and in particular with the artist Karel Appel.

"Life is little more than a dream, but please don't wake me up," a Jewish saying tells us. We have looked for a great many things and have found some of them, but there was no way we could have come upon these drawings, published here for the first time. Made by Appel in the years 1948–1950 for the "Psychopathological Notebook," only a few of them have ever been on view. And those were seen in a glass display case in 1992/93 in Los Angeles and other places, as part of the exhibition "Parallel Visions—Modern Artists and Outsider Art." The technique used, that of the collage, is still modern today, but it also recalls the attempts of Breton and Eluard in the early thirties to renew literature by simulating the manias of the mentally disturbed; Karel Appel followed a similar path in seeking new visual solutions. In December 1995, I was in Amsterdam with Rudi Fuchs, when the artist showed me the brochure *Psychopathological art* "improved" with his drawings as well as additional related drawings in a slightly larger format. I was astonished by the freshness of these near fifty-year-old works executed in crayon and ink. And I was reminded of what the Polish writer and draftsman Bruno Schulz said in his story "The Age of Genius": "How often I still dream about finding them, after so many years, at the bottom of old drawers, radiant and fresh like dawn—still damp from the first dew of the day: figures, landscapes, faces!"

The interest that motivated 29-year-old Karel Appel in 1950 to visit the exhibition at the Sainte-Anne Clinic in Paris must have been comparable at the time to that of the circle around Baselitz in Berlin ten years later. In both cases, it was the quest for the unseen picture that is dormant in all of us but can only be aroused by the artist.

After walking through the above-mentioned exhibition of the "Société internationale de psychopathologie de l'expression," Appel bought the brochure with details regarding the individual cases—as a reminder of what he had seen and for future reference. His visit to the psychiatric clinic of Sainte-Anne was anything but accidental; it was the outcome of research undertaken at the time by the CoBrA group (Copenhagen–Brussels–Amsterdam). This had been brought to the attention of the public in 1949 through the exhibition mounted by Willem Sandberg at the Stedelijk Museum in Amsterdam. The origins of this art, made manifest in Sandberg's show, are, of course, found in Nordic folk art, but they also derive from the output of children and the mentally ill: important territories outside convention, reflected in the academic efforts of the *Ecole de Paris* to overcome the heritage of Cubism in accord with history.

The trolls from northern Europe did not resort to an existing style to elaborate on these stimuli, but rather recurred—as already mentioned—to their own cultural heritage around the North Sea. In working out their own pictorial idiom, they did not turn to the Cubists but logically to artists like Paul Klee, whose artistic significance did not make an impact in the trendsetting art capital on the Seine until much, much later. In addition Appel and his friends initially found inspiration from the Surrealists in shaping their own manifestos and artistic agendas, even though the Surrealist movement lost much of its drive and influence after 1945. Nor did their spokesman, André Breton, remain idle. He too sought new means of reactivating his followers. To this end, he removed to the margins of cities and towns, where he discovered interesting objects unmarred by artistic concepts, indebted to no schools, unrelated to folklore, and yet still very close to the mystery of art. Such mysteries, as mentioned, are found in the work of children and mental patients, investigated and artistically exploited in the early thirties at Salvador Dalí's instigation by the psychiatrically schooled Breton and consorts.

My interest in writers and artists from the *other* side was awakened in Paris in 1960 after a first reading of Alfred Kubin's illustrated fantastic novel of 1908, "The Other Side." The moods and the reports on the Balkans, so eagerly absorbed, have since been my discreet companions on travels eastwards, thanks as well to the echo from a younger poet of the Viennese group, H. C. Artmann. Another novel of 1907, Guillaume Apollinaire's "Les onze mille verges" (Eleven Thousand Rods), was also eagerly absorbed half a century later to sustain the moods imbibed so far of Transsylvania. The large field on the *other* shore was thus already richly endowed with the best of minerals and, in the years that followed, enjoyed an unmitigated boom in the highly conducive climate of Berlin, my place of residence for many years.

As a young person with serious artistic ambitions and budding independent ideas, I sought allies whose accomplishments might be of use in the development of my own strategies, particularly if these had been si(gh)ted on the other shore—above all, people like Artaud, Soutter, Hill, and Wölfli. I acquired valuable insight into Adolf Wölfli through the observations of his psychiatrist, Walter Morgenthaler, from Bern. The work of this patient was also included in studies on the visual output of mental patients by Morgenthaler's colleague from Heidelberg, Hans Prinzhorn. Both physicians had already produced compelling and conclusive analyses in important, fundamental writings of the early 1920s that summarized their experiences with this manner of creative work. The role of contemporary art is manifest in the title of Morgenthaler's book, "Madness and Art, The Life and Works of Adolf Wölfli." A year later, Julius Springer published Prinzhorn's book, "Bildnerei der Geisteskranken" (The Visual Output of the Mentally Ill) in Heidelberg.

My partner Rudolf Springer, born in April 1909 in Berlin, is in fact the son of the Heidelberg publishing family and it was he who sold one of the first editions of Prinzhorn's work in the sixties. In addition, Springer opened his first gallery in Berlin in 1949 and significantly devoted his opening exhibition to an outsider with the wondrous name of Friedrich Schröder-Sonnenstern. Later, in addition to current art by the likes of Max Ernst and others, the gallery also showed Unica Zürn and Hans Bellmer. But professional interest in this kind of art was at a low ebb in the fifties, which may seem surprising considering that first attempts to bridge the gulf had long been made. For instance, Wassily Kandinsky presented examples from the *other* side in pictures and words as early as 1911 in the almanac of the "Blue Rider," with Paul Klee and the Surrealists following suit.

These basically alien worlds of imagery captivated me, and in 1960 they were complemented by further important issues addressed at the Parisian exhibition "Les sources du XXe siècle: 1884–1914" through the work of such artists as Ensor, Schönberg, Hill, and Josephson. With accounts of these territories, I later succeeded in capturing the mind of a young artist in Berlin, Georg Baselitz, who in turn came up with detailed reports of his own discoveries. In 1963 on the occasion of his first exhibition at the newly opened Galerie Werner & Katz, this artist provoked the wrath of the district attorney, resulting in an order for two paintings to be confiscated. The district attorney's verdict may well have been motivated not so much by the subject matter of the two confiscated works as by the title of the larger painting: "Die grosse Nacht im Eimer" (literally: the big night in the bucket, meaning, the big night in vain or for nothing). Baselitz's reference to the political and cultural situation facing young artists in a divided Germany was evidently intolerable to the powers that be when presented in this form. I saw the exhibition at the time without the two confiscated paintings. And in it I discovered an exceptional œuvre that captivated me because the discourse, though still new to me, undoubtedly spoke of the *other* side. Being Swiss, I was only surprised at the vehemence with which the Kulturkampf was being conducted, for it obviously had nothing to do with the issue of art, which had, after all, occasioned the exhibition.

And it was Baselitz who came back to Berlin in 1965 after a stay at the "Villa romana" in Florence with news of pictures and prints by Italian Mannerists like Pontormo or Rosso Fiorentino and held forth on the intensity of their coloring. In this newly discovered art world with all its distorted representations of human nature, he had found not only the sources of modernism but also his own project. In elucidation of his recent discoveries, he recommended a book entitled "Die Welt als Labyrinth – Manier und Manie in der europäischen Kunst" by Gustav René Hocke, first published in Hamburg by Rowohlt in 1957. The numerous, though small, black-and-white reproductions were extremely stimulating and ultimately showed us visually sensitized people the path to the great mysteries of art. Ten years later, in 1973, we went together to the exhibition "Ecole de Fontainebleau" at the Grand Palais in Paris and delighted in the unabated freshness of the prints on view with their frequently brassy representations of exalted, courtly custom.

Baselitz's indefatigable quest and study of this imagery in the past three decades has resulted in a unique collection of masterpieces of Italian Mannerist prints and the "Ecole de Fontainebleau." Fitting tribute has been paid to this collection in our publication of 1994, significantly titled "La bella maniera," which has met with acclaim from both art lovers and specialists.

From Holland, Michael Werner brought a catalogue back to Berlin of the far ranging exhibition "CoBrA—1948/51," hailed as an historic event in 1966 at the Boymans van Beuningen Museum in Rotterdam. Reproductions of works already familiar were enhanced by interesting new documents. References to the activities around group members Appel, Constant or Jorn piqued our curiosity because they cast considerable light on what my teacher in Berlin, the architect Hans Scharoun, tried to capture in the phrase *Nordic space*. Although on the geographical margins as a German-speaking Swiss person, I was also moved by this culture. It dawned on me that, during the decisive years of my aesthetic education, I had in fact matured at the heart of this culture. This was what I had to study, because hitherto my dreams had been fulfilled elsewhere, namely in Paris, the capital city of the 19th century, where art was understood to *embellir les choses* (beautify things) and the attempt was made to intellectualize the *aesthetics of ruptures* from the Protestant north. The words of the Cartesian Structuralists were designed to domesticate imminent phantasms and make them comprehensible in the form of an intellectual experience. They cavorted on the verge of the abyss without really getting closer to the *other* side. Not so in Berlin, where initially so much seemed repelling, ugly, even insulting, and the pictures that emerged were out to make a conquest or, conversely, demanded to be conquered. This was exciting and new; it exerted a great fascination and, in retrospect, I realize that these challenges belong to my own age and culture.

But back to Paris in the fifties. In pursuit of a signature of his own, Jean Dubuffet followed hard on Breton's heels after 1945 and seized his latest discoveries, conceived as possible stimulants for the Surrealist movement. With Cartesian zeal, Dubuffet tried to complete the palette of possibilities, finally subordinating them to his own interests. These efforts, known today as "l'art brut," are inseparably intertwined with his name. As early as 1947, writer and friend Jean Paulhan described the fixation of the painter Limérique in his essay "Guide d'un petit voyage en Suisse." Limérique was obsessed with spontaneous, unspoiled art, *raw art* as he called it, to be found, he believed, above all among the mad and the incarcerated. And if he were to receive news of a painting bear from a Swiss canton, he would not hesitate to embark instantly on hunting it down. Paulhan is undoubtedly speaking about his friend Dubuffet, for the two traveled together through Switzerland shortly after the war. The former had been invited to give several lectures on literature and art while his companion not only pursued his fixation but also—as maliciously rumored—looked into the continuing existence of his Swiss bank accounts...

The artistic side of these facts will hardly have escaped the notice of such a young, talented artist as Karel Appel, and the rebellion of

French colleagues like Dubuffet or Fautrier must have piqued his curiosity, especially inasmuch as they provided a broader base for his own efforts. He himself subsequently sidestepped the debate on content and devoted all his energies to his painting, fully aware that a painter can only solve his artistic problems by painting. Michel Leiris quoted Picasso as having supposedly remarked that since everybody had now turned sixty, they finally had time to devote themselves to tinkering with their own careers. And as history shows, Appel solved his artistic problems with remarkable bravura. International recognition in the years around 1960 was his well-deserved reward. His attitude today permits him to accept the responsibility of carrying out his self-imposed project.

Appel's "Psychopathological Notebook" arose primarily out of the then current debate among artists in Paris in the fifties. His personal efforts and investigations coincided with theirs, but he gave them shape with an intensity all his own. He effectively transformed the quest for inimitable expression into a fully matured fact, which assisted him in molding, in coming to terms with the ups and downs of a lifework and communicating its mysteries to us. The artist waited before publishing these drawings; he allowed half a century to pass before revealing the beginnings of his artistic journey and also documenting his vocabulary. The art historical assessment of this œuvre may well require adjustment upon examining and elaborating the new light cast on work already known.

Karel Appel's "Psychopathological Notebook," originally published by us in German, is here issued in an English edition that will be a valuable addition to the libraries of English-speaking friends of the arts. The publisher's gratitude towards the artist is colored with an additional thought: I thank him for permitting me to be godfather to this archaeological enterprise.

Translation: Catherine Schelbert

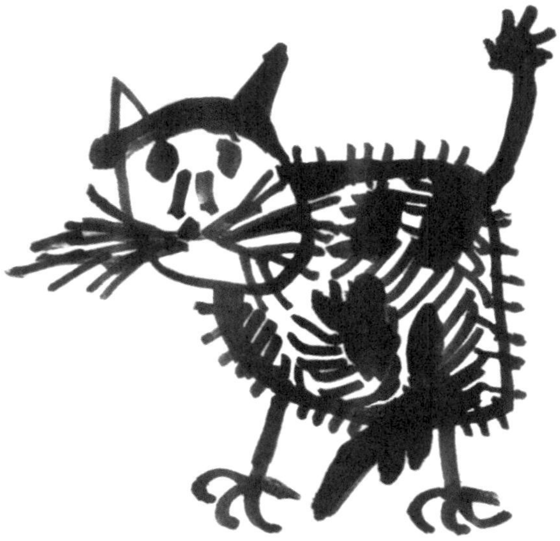

Notes and Materials

On the plates

The brochure "Psychopathological art / International Congress of Psychiatry / September 1950 / Paris France," which Karel Appel re-worked and "extended" by adding his own drawings, was published on the occasion of the exhibition "Exposition internationale d'art psychopathologique" which ran parallel to the above-mentioned congress. The exhibition included approximately 2,000 works of art by 350 mentally ill people, selected by 29 psychiatrists from 16 different countries. Both the congress and the exhibition took place on the premises of the "Centre psychiatrique Sainte-Anne" in Paris. The exhibition was opened on 21 September 1950 in the presence of the congress participants, renowned public personalities, and interested people from the world of art. It was accessible to the public until 14 October 1950. More than 10,000 people, including Karel Appel, visited the exhibition, which was highly acclaimed both in the French and the international press, although it also elicited a number of polemical reactions.

Despite inquires which the editors of this book made of congress participants and institutions familiar with the material, it has not been possible to see an original copy of the brochure Karel Appel used for his work; it was published in four languages, English, French, Italian and Spanish.

The content of the brochure appeared again in 1956, but then only in French. It was published in Paris by "Presses universitaires de France" as part of the book "L'art psychopathologique" in the series "Bibliothèque de psychiatrie," edited by Robert Volmat. On pages 3 to 135 of the first part of the book, subtitled "Les collections," the notes by the responsible psychiatrists—grouped according to countries and clinics—are listed once again for the benefit of specialists, with references to and descriptions of the individual "cases". The other parts of the book deal with the material under discussion from specific viewpoints. As a creative artist, Karel Appel used the means at his disposal to provide a further interpretative dimension. At the same time, he guided the specific discussion in a totally different direction, his aim being to highlight man's deep-rooted creativity. Another artist, namely, Jean Dubuffet, also tuned in to the discussion that was being carried on at the time, polemicizing against the procedures of psychiatrists. Dubuffet was of the opinion that there was as little genuine talent to be found among the sick as there was among the healthy.

A. Brochure "Psychopathological art/International Congress of Psychiatry/September 1950/Paris France" 92 pages, text only, no plates, format 10¼ x 7⅞"

Reproduced in the original size, height by width.

1. Front cover: ball-point pen, gouache and chalk over type

2. Inside cover: chalk on blank page

Title page:
Ball-point pen and gouache over type

Dedication page: gouache over type

1 Gouache over type
2 Tipped-in gouache, silhouetted, 9¼ x 7½", and gouache over type
3 Gouache over type
4 Gouache over type
5 Gouache over type, signed top right: c. k. Appel 50
6 Ball-point pen, gouache over type
7 Gouache over type
8 Tipped-in ink drawing, 8⅛ x 5¼", and gouache over type
9 Tipped-in ball-point pen drawing, 8 x 4 15/16", and gouache over type
10–11 Tipped-in drawing, ball-point pen, chalk and gouache, 8¼ x 12 11/16", over two pages, completed with gouache, over type
12 Tipped-in ink drawing, 9 5/16 x 5", and gouache over type
13 Gouache and chalk over type
14 Felt pen drawing, silhouetted, 6⅝ x 6", over type
15 Felt pen drawing, silhouetted, 5⅝ x 5 9/16", over type
16 Untitled, Indian ink on paper, 9¾ x 5 7/16", landscape format tipped-in as upright format, signed bottom right: CK Appel '50, mounted specially for this publication
17 Untitled, Indian ink on paper, silhouetted, 11 x 6 11/16", signed lower edge: CK Appel '49, mounted specially for this publication
18 Two tipped-in ink drawings, 5 1/16 x 2 15/16" and 5 1/16 x 2 11/16", completed with gouache, over type
19 Two tipped-in ink drawings, 5⅛ x 2⅞" and 4 9/16 x 3⅜", completed with gouache, signed bottom right: CK Appel '48, over type
20 Tipped-in lead pencil drawing, 8⅝ x 7 5/16", over type
21 Tipped-in ink drawing, 7¼ x 3⅛", and gouache, over type
22 Tipped-in gouache / chalk drawing, 10 1/16 x 5⅛", and watercolor, over type
23 Tipped-in gouache, 9 13/16 x 4 5/16", and gouache over type
24 Untitled, gouache on paper, 11⅝ x 8 13/16", signed below centre: CK Appel '48
25 Untitled, Indian ink on transparent paper,

10 5/8 x 8 3/16", signed bottom right: CK Appel, mounted specially for this publication

– Untitled, chalk and gouache on cardboard, 9 3/8 x 12 3/4", signed bottom right: CK Appel '48, mounted specially for this publication

26–27 Tipped-in gouache, 11 13/16 x 4 3/16", over two pages, and gouache over type

28 Tipped-in chalk / felt pen drawing, 9 3/8 x 5 1/4", over type

29 No re-working, just type

30 Tipped-in chalk drawing, 4 1/8 x 6 1/2", over type

31 Tipped-in ball-point pen drawing (cover of a school copybook), 8 5/8 x 6 11/16", over type

32 Tipped-in felt pen drawing, 8 3/8 x 4 5/8", and gouache over type

33 Tipped-in felt pent drawing, 4 3/4 x 3 7/8", and gouache and chalk on type

34 Tipped-in ink drawing, 5 x 3 1/16", signed top right: CK Appel, and gouache and chalk over type

35 Two tipped-in ink drawings, 5 3/16 x 3 9/16" and 5 5/16 x 3 7/16", and gouache over type

36 Two tipped-in chalk drawings, 4 1/8 x 6 1/2" and 4 1/8 x 6 9/16", and gouache over type

37 Two tipped-in chalk drawings completed with ink, 3 7/8 x 5 5/16 " and 3 15/16 x 6 5/16 ", signed bottom left: Appel, and gouache over type

38 Tipped-in chalk drawing, 8 1/2 x 2 1/8", and Indian ink over type

39 Tipped-in ink drawing, 5 1/16 x 5 11/16", and chalk over type

40 Tipped-in indelible pencil drawing, 4 1/8 x 5 3/8", and chalk over type

41 Tipped-in ink drawing completed with chalk, 3 7/8 x 5 15/16", and chalk over type

42 Tipped-in lead pencil drawing, 5 13/16 x 3 5/8", on page with type

43 Tipped-in chalk drawing, larger in format than the brochure, 11 7/16 x 9 5/16", monogrammed bottom left: CKA, over type

44 Gouache silhouetted, 8 15/16 x 5 5/8", and chalk over type

45 Gouache silhouetted, 8 9/16 x 5 1/16", and chalk over type

46–47 Tipped-in drawing, felt pen, chalk and watercolor, 8 5/8 x 12 13/16", extending over two pages, monogrammed bottom left; CKA, and gouache over type

48 Tipped-in ink drawing, 8 1/8 x 5 1/8", extending beyond lower edge of page, on page with type

49 Tipped-in chalk drawing, 7 5/8 x 8 11/16", extending beyond right edge of page, on page with type

50 Tipped-in lead pencil drawing, 4 15/16 x 3 9/16", and Indian ink over type

51 Doubled chalk drawing, 8 11/16 x 7 7/16", pasted over type

52 Chalk and gouache over type

53 Tipped-in chalk collage, 8 5/8 x 7 13/16", extending beyond right edge of page, over type

54 Tipped-in felt pen drawing, 6 x 6 11/16", monogrammed bottom right: CKA, over type, completed with chalk

55 Tipped-in felt pen drawing, 6 x 6 9/16", monogrammed bottom right: CKA, over type, completed with chalk

56 Chalk, Indian ink and felt pen over type

57 Tipped-in ink drawing, 8 9/16 x 3 7/8", over type

58 Tipped-in silhouetted ink drawing, 8 9/16 x 4 1/2", and gouache over type

59 Felt pen/ chalk drawing on blank page

60 Tipped-in doubled felt pen drawing, 6 x 7 3/8", monogrammed bottom right: CKA, over type, completed with chalk and felt pen

61 Tipped-in chalk drawing extending beyond the edges of the brochure, 10 11/16 x 9 5/16", over type

62 Tipped-in fold back chalk drawing, folded parallel to binding, 9 5/16 x 12 3/4", over type

63 Type, completed with felt pen and lead pencil

64 Tipped-in fold back chalk drawing, folded parallel to binding, 8 13/16 x 11 13/16", over type, completed with chalk

65 Type, completed with chalk and lead pencil

66 Type, completed with chalk

67 Tipped-in chalk drawing extending beyond the edges of the brochure, 9 15/16 x 9", over type

68 Felt pen over type

69 Felt pen over type

70 Tipped-in chalk drawing, 9 3/8 x 6 1/2", signed bottom right: Appel, over type previously re-worked with felt pen

71 Tipped-in gouache, extending beyond right edge of page, 9 3/8 x 9 7/16", over type

72 Felt pen over type

73 Felt pen over type

74 Tipped-in chalk drawing extending beyond left edge of page, 6 3/8 x 12", over type

75 Tipped-in lead pencil drawing, completed with gouache, 6 7/16 x 3 15/16", over type

76–77 Stamp ink drawing completed with chalk, pasted over two pages, 10 1/2 x 8", over type, completed with chalk

78 Tipped-in chalk, pencil and felt pen drawing, 10 3/16 x 3 11/16", over type

79 Tipped-in chalk drawing, completed with felt pen, 9 5/16 x 7 5/8", over type

80 Three tipped-in ink drawings, 5 3/8 x 7 7/16", 5 3/8 x 7 7/16", 3 3/16 x 4 1/8", the lower one signed bottom right: CK Appel, over type, completed with gouache

81 Three tipped-in ink drawings, 5 3/16 x 3 9/16", 5 5/16 x 3 7/16", 3 1/16 x 5 1/16", the lower one signed top right: CK Appel, over type, completed with gouache

82 Tipped-in ink drawing, 5 3/16 x 3 9/16", over type, completed with Indian ink and gouache

83 Tipped-in ink drawing on printed paper, 9 3/4 x 7 13/16", over type

84 The aforementioned ink drawing also covers part of this page, though neither folded nor tipped-in, 9 3/4 x 4", over type, completed with gouache. Format of the whole drawing: 9 3/4 x 11 13/16"

85 Tipped-in gouache on printed paper, 9 5/8 x 5 13/16", and gouache on type

86 Indian ink over type
87 Tipped-in gouache silhouetted, 9 15/16 x 5 5/16", and gouache over type; traces of adhesive visible in the binding
88 Untitled, chalk and gouache on paper, 11 7/8 x 9 3/4", signed bottom right: CK Appel '50; mounted specially for this publication
89 Untitled, felt pen on paper, 11 15/16 x 9 1/16"; mounted specially for this publication
90 Tipped-in felt pen drawing, 5 15/16 x 6 11/16", monogrammed bottom left: CKA, on blank page

3. Back inside cover: blank page, not re-worked

4. Back cover: ball-point pen on blank page

B. The following drawings were done at the same time as the "re-working" of the *Psychopathological art* brochure and were selected specially by the artist for this publication.

Reproduced in reduced format except for those marked with an asterisk.

i Untitled, felt pen on paper, 10 11/16 x 14", signed bottom right: CK Appel '49*
ii Untitled, Indian ink and watercolors on paper, 8 3/8 x 10 15/16", signed bottom right: CK Appel '48*
iii Untitled, watercolors on paper, 8 3/4 x 11 11/16", signed bottom right; CK Appel '48*
iv Untitled, Indian ink and watercolors on paper, 8 7/16 x 10 15/16", signed bottom left: CK Appel '48*
v Untitled, felt pen on paper, 12 13/16 x 8 3/16", signed bottom right: CK Appel '50
vi Untitled, watercolors on paper, 11 3/4 x 8 7/8", signed bottom left: CK Appel '48
vii Untitled, felt pen on paper, 14 x 10 11/16", signed bottom left: CK Appel '49
viii Untitled, watercolors on paper, 11 11/16 x 8 11/16", signed below centre: CK Appel '48
ix Untitled, felt pen on paper, 14 x 10 11/16", signed centre right. CK Appel '49
x Untitled, felt pen on paper, 14 x 10 11/16", signed bottom left: CK Appel '49
xi Untitled, watercolors and gouache on paper, 14 x 11", signed bottom right: CK Appel '49
xii Untitled, felt pen on paper, 14 x 10 11/16", signed bottom right: CK Appel '49
xiii Untitled, felt pen on paper, 12 3/16 x 9 13/16", signed bottom left; CK Appel
xiv Untitled, Indian ink on paper, 14 x 10 5/8", signed bottom right: CK Appel '49, and, top left: 29 x 32.5"
xv Untitled, felt pen and chalk on paper, 9 3/4 x 12", signed bottom left: CK Appel '48*
xvi Verso of previous page, untitled, felt pen on paper, 9 3/4 x 12", signed bottom left; CK Appel '48*
xvii Untitled, chalk on paper, 10 11/16 x 14", signed bottom right: CK Appel '49*
xviii Untitled, chalk on paper, 10 5/8 x 14", signed bottom left: CK Appel '49*
xix Untitled, chalk on paper, 14 x 10 5/8", signed bottom right: CK Appel '49
xx Untitled, chalk on paper, 14 x 10 5/8", signed bottom right: CK Appel '49
xxi Untitled, chalk on paper, 14 x 10 5/8", signed bottom right: CK Appel '50
xxii Untitled, chalk and felt pen on paper, 14 x 10 5/8", signed bottom right: CK Appel '49
xxiii Untitled, chalk on paper, 14 x 10 5/8", signed bottom right: CK Appel '49
xxiv Untitled, chalk on paper, 14 x 10 11/16", signed bottom right: CK Appel '50
xxv Untitled, chalk on paper, 14 x 10 11/16", signed top right: CHK Appel '50
xxvi Untitled, chalk on paper, 14 x 10 5/8", signed bottom right: CK Appel '50
xxvii Untitled, chalk on paper, 14 x 10 5/8", signed bottom right: CK Appel '50
xxviii Untitled, chalk on paper, 14 x 10 5/8", signed bottom right: CK Appel '49
xxix Untitled, chalk and Indian ink on paper, 14 x 10 11/16", signed bottom left. CK Appel '50
xxx Untitled, chalk on paper, 10 5/8 x 14", signed bottom left. CK Appel '50*
xxxi Untitled, chalk and Indian ink on paper, 14 x 10 5/8", signed bottom left. CK Appel '50
xxxii Untitled, chalk on cardboard, 12 11/16 x 9 3/8", signed bottom right: CK Appel '49
xxxiii Untitled, chalk on paper, 14 x 10 11/16", signed bottom right: CK Appel '49
xxxiv Untitled, chalk on paper, 14 x 10 5/8", signed bottom right: CK Appel '50
xxxv Untitled, chalk on paper, 15 3/8 x 9 7/8", signed bottom left: CK Appel '50
xxxvi Untitled, chalk on paper, 10 5/8 x 14", signed bottom right: CK Appel '49*

Biography

Karel Appel was born in Amsterdam in 1921, not quite a hundred years after the publication of Balzac's "Le chef-d'œuvre inconnu" (1831), and almost ten years after Kandinsky produced his "First Abstract Watercolor," which heralded the beginning of abstract art. In other words, Appel's artistic career began at a point in time when abstract art was calling traditional values and agreements into question.

1942–44 Studied at the Royal Academy of Fine Art in Amsterdam. Visited Denmark, where he met the Danish artists belonging to the later CoBrA (Copenhagen-Brussels-Amsterdam) group.

1948 Together with Constant and Corneille, founded an experimental artists' group which also edited the magazine "Reflex." Six months later in Paris, the Dutch group met up with their Danish and Belgian colleagues in CoBrA; the group was particularly interested in folk art and sculptural works by children and the mentally ill.

1949 Willem Sandberg organised the "International Exhibition of Experimental Art" at the Stedelijk Museum in Amsterdam, the first large-scale presentation of CoBrA works, designed by architect Aldo van Eyck.

1950 Appel left Amsterdam and set up a studio in Paris, the center of the art world at the time. It was there that he produced the "Psychopathological Notebook."

1953 First solo exhibition at the Palais des Beaux-Arts in Brussels.

1954 Awarded the UNESCO prize at the Venice Biennale. Showed his works for the first time in New York at the Martha Jackson gallery.

From 1955, various commissions for works for public buildings, first in Holland, then abroad.

1959 Awarded the major prize for painting at the Fifth São Paulo Bienal.

1960 Received first prize on the occasion of the "Guggenheim International Art Award" in New York.

1961 "La Réalité de Karel Appel," color film by Jan Vrijman with music by Dizzy Gillespie and Karel Appel.

1961 Theater work in the Netherlands.

1964 Invitation to documenta III in Kassel. As his works were not released from customs in time, Appel painted a large-format work specially for the exhibition in one sitting the night before the opening.

1970 Recordings in San Francisco together with Merril Sanders, Chet Baker and other musicians and vocalists from the jazz scene.

1987 Carte Blanche at the Opéra de Paris: together with Japanese dancer and choreographer Min Tanaka and the Vietnamese composer Dao, Appel directs the piece "Peut-on danser le paysage?"

1988 Publication in Paris of the first part of a survey of his works entitled "Karel Appel—The early years (1937–1957)."

1994–95 Further theater productions and stage sets commissioned by the Dutch Opera House in Amsterdam, including "The Magic Flute," which he adapted jointly with Min Tanaka.

VENDREDI 22 SEPTEMBRE 1950

FONDÉ EN 1859

NOUVELLE SERIE. — N° 277

PARAIT LE VENDREDI

ABONNEMENTS

FRANCE : 1 an .... 900 fr.
— 6 mois .. 475 fr.
ETRANGER : 1 an .. 1.500 fr.

POUR TOUT CHANGEMENT D'ADRESSE

joindre la dernière bande et la somme de 25 fr. en timbres-poste ou mandat.

140, Faubourg Saint-Honoré
PARIS-8e
Téléph. : ELY. 21-15 et BAL. 32-34

ARTS

BEAUX-ARTS
Journal des Arts

LITTERATURE
Chronique des Arts

DIRECTEUR : Georges WILDENSTEIN

SPECTACLES
et de la Curiosité

8 PAGES. — 20 FRANCS

DANS CE NUMERO :

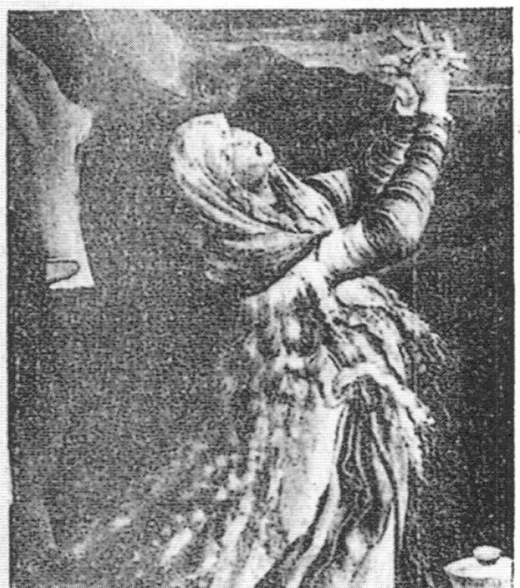

SAINTE-MADELEINE
Détail du polyptique exécuté pour les antonistes d'Issenheim par Grünewald qui se cloîtra entre 1490 et 1510 au monastère consacré à la guérison du Mal des Ardeurs et y choisit ses modèles.

Au Congrès International de Psychiatrie

L'ART psychopathologique

par le Dr René BESSIÈRE
Médecin-chef de l'hôpital Sainte-Anne

EN 1946 une première exposition de peintures, dessins, sculptures, exécutés par des malades mentaux était ouverte à l'hôpital Sainte-Anne et connaissait un grand succès. Cette année l'assemblée qui peut être appelée le premier congrès mondial de Psychiatrie, et qui se tient en ce moment à Paris, a voulu réunir dans une exposition, ouverte au public à partir du 29 septembre, les productions artistiques les plus diverses et les plus significatives, recueillies auprès des malades par les psychiatres français et étrangers appartenant à quinze nations. C'est dire l'intérêt que suscite partout dans les milieux psychiatriques, l'art psychopathologique.

Contrairement à ce que l'on pourrait penser, les tableaux, les dessins, et surtout les sculptures que l'on peut rassembler dans les hôpitaux psychiatriques sont relativement assez rares.

Ces œuvres exécutées par des convalescents ou des malades chroniques calmes sont de deux ordres. Elles émanent de peintres professionnels qui s'efforcent de reprendre leurs occupations antérieures, ou de ceux qu'on peut appeler les « illettrés » de la peinture qui dessinent ou peignent pour se distraire.

La psychose ne modifie guère la technique des peintres professionnels. Ils continuent à peindre suivant leur manière habituelle. Les uns sont des spécialistes du chromo commercial exécuté en série. Les autres sont influencés par la mode de l'époque. Et l'on verra des toiles parfaitement académiques ou manifestement dans la même ligne que le cubisme, le fauvisme, ou Picasso, Rouault, Matisse, etc.

(*Suite en page* 5.)

LE GÉNIE dans la création

par
Jean BOURET

« Ils estiment qu'un homme est fou quand il entend ce que les autres n'entendent pas et voit ce que les autres ne voient pas ; pourtant Socrate consultait son démon et Jeanne d'Arc entendait des voix. Et d'ailleurs ne sommes-nous pas tous des visionnaires et des hallucinés ? »
ANATOLE FRANCE
« La Vie littéraire »

C'EST une bien excellente page que celle d'Anatole France sur la folie dans la littérature lorsqu'il analyse « *le Horla* » de Guy de Maupassant. Elle vient certes après des centaines d'autres car le sujet est inépuisable et si Aristote fut le premier à traiter des rapports de l'art et de la folie, nous nous trouvons aujourd'hui devant un nombre considérable d'ouvrages tant littéraires que savants lorsqu'on veut faire le point. Mais pour ancienne qu'elle soit cette page de France a le mérite d'insister sur ce fait, qu'entre un fou et un être normal il n'y a pas une telle différence qu'on le croit communément, et que le fou n'est pas toujours un épileptique ou un furieux, ce qui laisse une belle marge à la création. C'est cette distinction du « seuil » qui est l'objet des travaux des savants, et bien souvent le dessin est un test qui ne trompe guère d'où cette Exposition Internationale d'œuvres de malades mentaux organisée cette semaine par le Congrès International de Psychiatrie qui se tient à l'hôpital Sainte-Anne.

La rareté des œuvres des fous a rendu difficile les tâches de classification des psychiatres et c'est aux travaux de Rogues de Fursac, de Réja, de Max Simon, et pour la partie la plus constructive de Jean Vinchon qu'on doit le plus essentiel.

C'est vers 1880 que la mode (car il y eut très exactement mode) de la folie en littérature et en art prit corps sous l'impulsion des disciples des Goncourt. Lombroso considéra les trois quarts des artistes comme fous.

(*Suite en page* 5.)

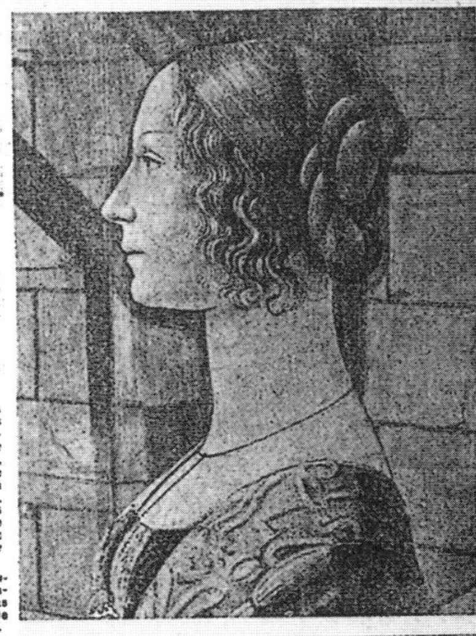

Giovanna Tornabuoni qui figure dans le groupe de la Visitation du Ghirlandajo est un cas d'endocrinonévrose selon le professeur Laignel-Lavastine.

LES FRESQUES DU MOYEN AGE en FINLANDE

par J.-A. KEIM

QUAND on parle de la peinture finlandaise, on pense toujours à la période contemporaine, qu'une exposition a présentée cette année à la Galerie Beaux-Arts : l'intérêt certain que peuvent présenter ces tableaux, est cependant loin d'égaler celui des fresques du moyen âge finlandais, qui demeurent complètement inconnues en dehors du pays.

Ces œuvres ont été inspirées par le christianisme, qui a fait son apparition en Finlande au XIe siècle ; un Anglais, l'évêque d'Upsal, y subit le martyre dans la deuxième moitié du XIIe. De nombreuses croisades furent entreprises pour convertir les païens ; après celle dirigée par le Suédois Birgel Jarl en 1249, la Finlande peut être considérée comme complètement évangélisée. De nombreuses églises s'élevent, couvertes de fresques et ornées de sculptures en bois remarquables. Quand au XVIe siècle la doctrine de Luther s'impose sans lutte, les sanctuaires sont respectés et sont utilisés par le culte réformé ; mais la peinture sacrée est définitivement morte.

Près de soixante-dix églises du moyen âge subsistent encore en Finlande ; la plupart ont conservé leurs riches décorations et portent un témoignage vivant d'un art de grande classe.

D'une façon générale ces peintures sont faites al secco sur la chaux. Le maître a dessiné en blanc les principaux traits et a indiqué d'un coup de pinceau les couleurs, qui seront l'œuvre de ses assistants ou de ses élèves. Un seul nom nous est connu : Kort Morare, Connadus Pictor, qui travaillait au début du XIVe siècle. Aucune fresque n'est datée et cet art, malgré les travaux intéressants des historiens finlandais (1), pose encore de nombreux problèmes non résolus.

Il est à peu près établi que des fresques existaient déjà vers le XIIIe siècle ; mais aucune n'est parvenue jusqu'à nous. Les deux premières couleurs utilisées étaient le brun rouge et le noir, les deux couleurs magiques ; plus tard apparaît le vert, puis le jaune. Les dessins commencent par être complètement schématiques ; la perspective n'existe pas ; il n'y a que deux dimensions. C'est un art purement décoratif, plein d'étoiles, de spirales, de palmettes, de feuilles, de branches, de rameaux ; plus tard viennent s'ajouter à l'ornementation des trèfles à trois et quatre feuilles et des roses à cinq pétales. Tous les murs, les plafonds, les colonnes sont couverts de motifs, qui s'harmonisent entre eux, savamment disposés pour constituer un tout avec l'architecture de l'église. Ces décors font penser aux ryujy, tapisseries nouées à long poil dont les musées conservent de splendides exemplaires et dont la tradition s'est perpétuée jusqu'à nos jours.

Les premières figures sont très primitives. A Finström ont été retrouvés quelques dessins, qui semblent l'œuvre d'enfants, comme ces bateaux avec passagers dont le charme est certain. A Nousiainen les cavaliers et les chiens demeurent encore bien schématiques, parfaites reproductions des textiles de l'époque ; à Maaria les traits et les couleurs affirment lentement une maîtrise.

Dans les peintures postérieures de ces mêmes églises, à Jomala, à Sund, dans la cathédrale de Turku apparaissent des personnages d'abord figés, qui prennent peu à peu de l'aisance et de la grâce.

Dans la deuxième moitié du XVe siècle apparaît une ornementation luxuriante, qui atteint son apogée à Kalani. A côté du noir, du rouge brun, du rouge jaune, du jaune et du vert viennent s'ajouter le bleu, le rouge vif et le blanc.

(*Suite en page* 6)

(1) L. Wennervirta. — Suomen Keskiaikainen Kirkkomaalaus.

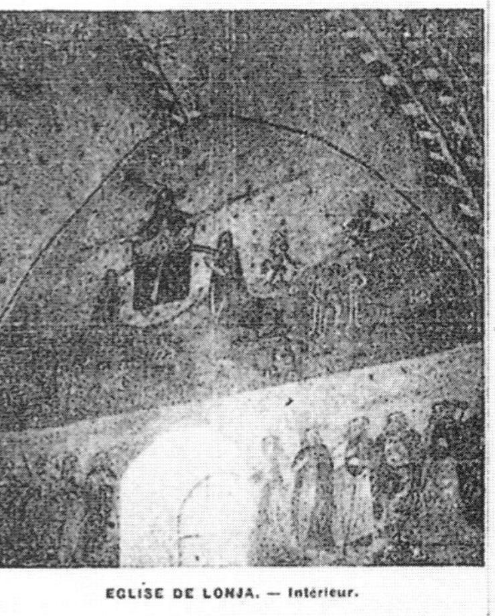

EGLISE DE LONJA. — Intérieur.

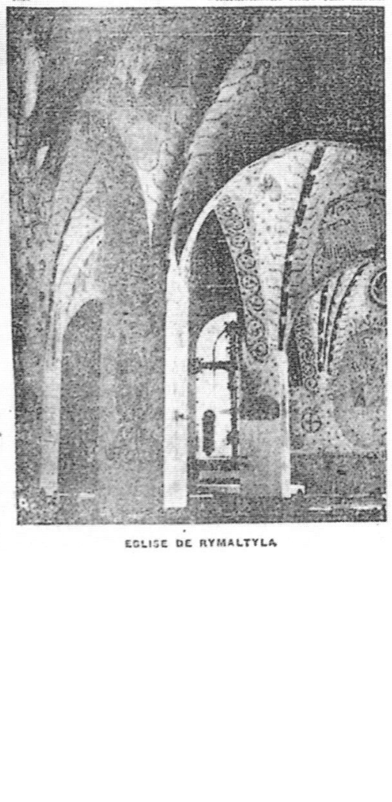

EGLISE DE RYMALTYLA

L'Exposition
LA VIERGE DANS L'ART FRANÇAIS
au Petit-Palais
Fermeture le 1er Octobre

LA FRANCE remporte un nouveau Prix de peinture

LE prix italien qui vient d'être attribué cette semaine et qui porte le nom du sculpteur Pietro Costa (Celle 1849, Rome 1901) a été promu par la Commune et l'Azienda Autonoma di Soggiorno de Celle, avec la collaboration de la Société des Beaux Arts de Savone et sous le patronage de M. Luigi Einaudi, président de la République italienne. Il se composait de quatre concours : un pour la sculpture et trois pour la peinture, ainsi subdivisés : concours à sujet libre ; concours dont le sujet s'inspirait du paysage de Celle ; concours pour la peinture étrangère. Le concours dont les peintres ont tiré du paysage de Celle se mit sur un Raduno de peintres italiens et étrangers, qui ont été invités par le Comité organisateur à demeurer gratuitement dans les meilleurs hôtels de Celle, du 18 juin au 30 juin 1950.

Ont participé au Raduno les meilleurs peintres italiens et les peintres français Kostia Terechkovitch, Christian Caillard, Gustave Singier.

(*Suite en page* 6)

GRAND'MA MOSES sera exposée à Paris

A l'automne aura lieu à l'Ambassade des Etats-Unis une exposition de 50 graveurs américains. Ensuite, au mois de décembre, seront présentées une quarantaine de tableaux du peintre naïf Grandma Moses qui, ainsi que chacun sait, est une femme âgée de plus de quatre-vingt-dix ans. On pourra voir à Paris une exposition de cette artiste dont les œuvres excitent la plus vive curiosité. Ceci grâce au Service des Relations culturelles de l'Ambassade pour lequel Miss Dorthea Speyer se montre une infatigable animatrice.

UNE CURIEUSE TAPISSERIE du XVIIe SIÈCLE

par Jean DAUTZENBERG-BRAQUENIÉ

L'OCCASION nous a été donnée récemment de voir, dans une collection particulière, la tapisserie ancienne reproduite ici. A droite, une femme, le buste nu, prend un bain, tandis qu'un Amour lance des flèches dans l'eau de la baignoire. A gauche, dans un nuage, Diane, la tête ornée du croissant, mène un jeune homme coiffé d'une couronne de fleurs. On pourrait prendre celui-ci pour Apollon ou pour Bacchus.

Mais rien dans la mythologie concernant Diane, Apollon ou Bacchus n'explique le sujet représenté.

Le possesseur de la tapisserie supposait, d'après une tradition de famille, que la baigneuse était Diane de Poitiers.

Cela nous laissant sceptique, nous nous sommes livré à des recherches dont le résultat nous a semblé digne d'être publié.

Le sujet de la tapisserie est tiré du roman : « l'Ariane de Monsieur Des Maretz (de Saint-Sorlin), Contrôleur général de l'extraordinaire des guerres. A Paris, chez Mathieu Guillemot, rue Saint-Jacques, près la Porte, avec privilège du Roi, 1639 ». (Bibliothèque Nationale, Réserve, Y. 2.720).

Cet ouvrage est illustré de 17 planches gravées par Abraham Bosse, d'après Claude Vignon.

Le frontispice du chapitre III est intéressant à comparer à la tapisserie, en raison des quelques variantes qui y ont été apportées :

Voici le texte du roman (page 105) :

(*Suite en page* 6)

LE DESSIN INTERNATIONAL TRIOMPHERA A BERGAME

UNE exposition internationale de dessin sera présentée à Bergame à partir du 24 septembre par les soins de l'Ente Provinciale per il Turismo et le College des Professionistes de la ville de Bergame.

Cette exposition rassemblera les meilleures expressions de l'art international de notre siècle.

Pour la participation française, notons après les grands noms de nos chefs de file, ceux de Bazaine, Borès, de Staël, Estève, Hélion Lapique, Le Moal, Marchand, Masson, Pignon, Tal Coat, Villon.

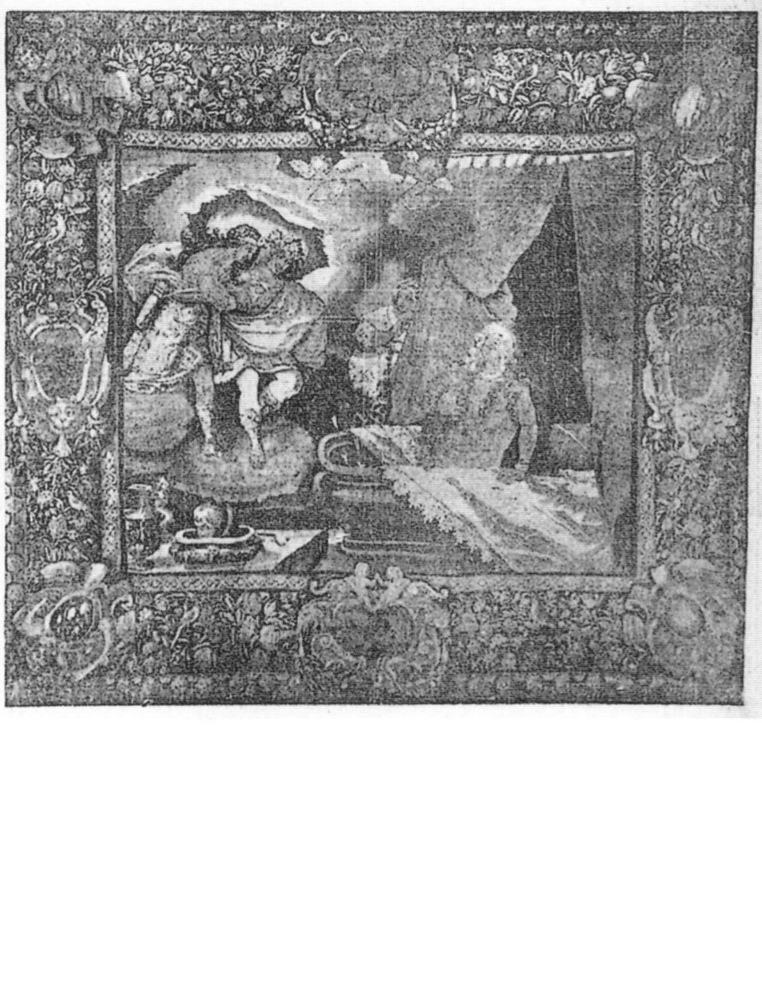

L'ART ET LA FOLIE

L'art psychopathologique

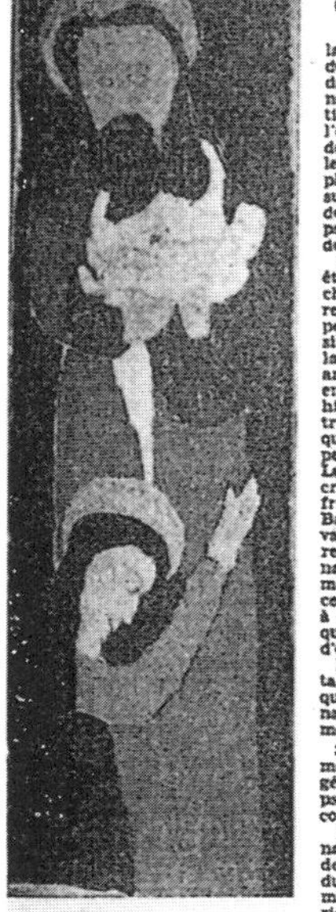

Peinture d'un paranoïaque avec manie des grandeurs (Hôpital de Bassens.)

(Suite de la première page.)

Dans quelques cas cependant la dissolution de la personnalité de l'artiste s'accuse et se traduit dans ses œuvres où l'on reconnait pourtant toujours le « métier », la « patte ». On verra à l'exposition quelques exemples de cette transformation picturale dont les deux plus beaux exemples sont ceux de deux peintres suédois, Hill et Stephenson, tous deux traités dans des hôpitaux psychiatriques après une période de production artistique normale.

Les « illettrés » de la peinture, êtres frustes et sans culture sachant souvent à peine lire et écrire, cherchent à exprimer leur pensée sous une forme graphique simplifiée comme un schéma maladroit. Leurs productions sont analogues aux dessins de jeunes enfants, à l'art des grottes préhistoriques, à l'art nègre. D'autres sont plus évolués. Bien qu'autodidactes ils se sont peu à peu éduqués et perfectionnés. Leurs œuvres rappellent l'art crétois ou byzantin, les primitifs français de la tapisserie de Bayeux, ou des fresques de Tavant ou de Saint-Savin, les préraissants italiens, l'art japonais ou chinois, ou tout simplement les images d'Epinal. Parfois cependant, s'ils sont « doués », à la lueur d'une étincelle de génie, quelques-uns réalisent leur chef-d'œuvre naïf.

Il est ainsi intéressant de constater que quelle que soit l'époque ou la latitude, l'art pictural naît, s'exprime et évolue de la même façon.

Si le technique des malades mentaux ne peut apprendre, en général, que peu de chose au psychiatre, en est-il de même du contenu, du sujet du tableau ?

Assez souvent ce sujet est banal et peu significatif, mais dans de nombreux cas le malade traduit sur ses toiles, ses cauchemars, ce que nous appelons l'onirisme. Les tableaux répondent alors parfaitement à la description qu'en donnait Tardieu, le premier psychiatre, croyons-nous, qui ait écrit quelques pages sur les dessins des aliénés. Tardieu écrivait : « Les associations de couleurs les plus folles, des lignes vertes ou écarlates, des proportions inusitées, des ciels jaunes, des effets de lumière impossibles, des êtres monstrueux, des animaux fantastiques, des architectures inconnues, des flammes infernales, réalisent sous des formes inimitables les rêves les plus indescriptibles ».

Est-il moins violent, le rêve se conceptualise et le malade s'efforce de traduire d'une façon plus concrète son monde intérieur. C'est alors que l'on observe la figuration claire ou estompée des conflits enfantins ou juvéniles, de l'agressivité ou de la passivité, des complexes obsédants ou anxieux : complexes d'infériorité ou de supériorité sous toutes leurs formes, préoccupations mystiques ou métaphysiques, conscience partielle de la déchéance mentale. Bien entendu les thèmes sexuels, sous des formes parfois trop précises mais parfois maquillée, transposées, symbolisées, sont presque toujours présents : pureté, impuissance, érotisme déchaîné, homosexualité, sadisme, masochisme, fétichisme, voire même bestialité.

Le dessin ou le tableau est aussi la traduction par le malade de sa perception originale du monde où il vit. Or la déformation du monde extérieur est fréquente dans les œuvres des malades. C'est ainsi, pour me borner à un exemple, que le schizophrène montre dans ses dessins sa personnalité pathologique et sa perte de contact avec la réalité par l'abstraction de l'ensemble, le remplissage systématique de la toile ou du papier par la multitude de petits détails minutieux, fragmentés, isolés, séparés ; les formes statiques, figées, géométriques, anatomiques, les répétitions stéréotypées de sujet ou de motif, le penchant pour la déformation et la caricature ; le symbolisme constant.

Le contenu du dessin du tableau est ainsi une confession intime, une sorte de psychanalyse graphique, un reflet de la personnalité totale de l'auteur, de telle sorte que la vie, la personnalité, la psychose et l'œuvre sont intimement liées.

L'étude de ces œuvres, parfaites à cet égard, constitue alors un moyen important, non de faire à lui seul le diagnostic de la psychose, mais de le compléter et d'en préciser les composantes. Le tableau, le dessin doit être considéré comme un test.

Mais, outre cet intérêt, c'est par leur aspect profondément humain, plus que par leur pittoresque ou leur valeur artistique dont on peut discuter, que les œuvres spontanées, sincères, désintéressées, des malades mentaux sont belles et émouvantes.

Dr René BESSIERE.

COMMENTAIRES SUR UNE EXPOSITION CONSACRÉE A LA PSYCHOPATHOLOGIE

« Il n'y a pas de ligne nette de démarcation entre la vie psychique normale et l'anormale », ni de rideau de fer entre l'asile des malades mentaux et le reste de l'Univers. Dans l'asile, en dehors, c'est de la même façon que la même catégorie de gens suit les mêmes événements artistiques ou autres.

La peinture du valet de ferme interné aujourd'hui et libre demain (environ 75 % des malades mentaux sortent guéris temporairement ou définitivement) n'est pas plus fantastique aujourd'hui qu'elle le sera demain.

Peintre ou valet de ferme, pendant la dissociation, la confusion, la désagrégation mentale, ne griffonnera que sur commande et à peine quelques lignes floues, confuses, même pas abstraites.

Artiste professionnel, peintre du dimanche mis à part, à l'asile comme en dehors, un dilettante sur cent seulement créera une œuvre d'un intérêt exceptionnel. Ce faible pourcentage provenant d'asiles constitue la base de la présente exposition.

Certes, au point de vue « Art et Folie », etc..., d'une exposition sans triage incluant aussi l'amas d'œuvres banales, on tirerait d'autres conclusions, plus générales, plus définitives et plus objectives.

Toutefois, le groupement d'un nombre si important de ces œuvres, la possibilité de comparaisons permettront d'ouvrir le débat contre ou pour les propositions écrites sur ce sujet jusqu'à nos jours.

Et, qui sait ? peut-être donnera-t-il naissance à une science nouvelle, surprenante, insoupçonnée.

SCHWARZ-ABRYS.
Secrétaire de la Section Française de l'Exposition.

Génie, folie, et à-cotés...

(Suite de la première page.)

« Le génie, dit-il, est le fait d'une inconscience étonnante, d'une création instantanée et d'une intermittence analogue aux états de l'épilepsie. » Lombroso allait un peu loin et l'école française remit les choses en place.

Il est inutile de reprendre ici les travaux du docteur Vinchon dont une plaquette parue chez Stock en 1924 et un ouvrage récent ont contribué à vulgariser intelligemment l'essentiel des théories. Il est même dangereux de se hasarder à exposer ces théories, les écoles n'ayant encore pu établir scientifiquement le diagnostic des psychopathologies multiples. Ce qui nous intéresse davantage, c'est la qualité plastique des œuvres des malades mentaux.

Il faut tout d'abord éviter de crier au génie et bien que Cocteau écrive dans le « Secret professionnel » que le docteur Vinchon n'a eu garde d'oublier qu'« Enfants et fous coupent ce que le poète met une vie de patience à dénouer », il ne faut pas croire que la folie résout comme par enchantement les problèmes de la forme et ceux de la couleur.

De la visite à cette excellente exposition (disons tout de suite que les docteurs Grolle et Bessières ont réalisé des prodiges en équipant comme nos musées ne le sont pas, un ancien garde-meubles) on déduit que le psychopathe à les mêmes défauts que le peintre non malade...

Au départ une naïveté adorable, puis avec l'acquisition assez rapide du métier un insupportable cabotinage, un emploi fastidieux du procédé et de la cuisine. Les Américains en sont l'exemple le plus significatif. Les œuvres abstraites ou prétendues telles de certains vétérans sentent diablement le faux.

Il faudrait ouvrir un chapitre spécial, le portrait du psychopathe exécuté par le non-fou est presque toujours un non-sens et l'on ne peut guère se baser sur lui pour l'étude sérieuse des cas, l'artiste transposant son modèle le détruit, c'est ce qu'a compris Schwarz-Abrys à qui l'on doit le collectage le plus érudit d'œuvres de fous et une fort excellente fresque à l'intérieur de ce petit musée.

Sujet trop grave et trop grand pour la vulgarisation hâtive, « L'Art et la Folie » demande la patience et surtout la foi des chercheurs.

Jean BOURET.

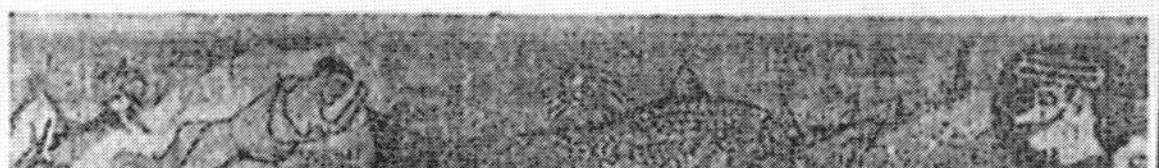

SCHWARZ-ABRYS. — Fresque pour le Musée de la folie.

Panorama des salles

PLUS de vingt nations doivent participer à cette manifestation qui pose un double problème scientifique et médical. Mais au moment où nous mettons sous presse, plusieurs envois étrangers ne sont pas encore parvenus à l'Hôpital Sainte-Anne et arriveront peut-être trop tard pour y figurer.

Voici cependant, sauf modification de la dernière minute, comment se présentera l'exposition.

LA SALLE 1

LA SALLE 1 (à droite en entrant) est consacrée à la Suisse, représentée ici par les collections des docteurs Ladame, Weber et Steck, qui réunissent les œuvres de quatre artistes. On connait déjà l'œuvre mystérieuse de Woelfly qui a séjourné rue Sébastien-Bottin, dans les locaux de l'Art Brut. C'est le monde d'un obsédé qui s'abime farouchement dans un puzzle infini. Mais sa réussite n'est pas sans charme. On remarquera le curieux graphisme de la bouche, des yeux et des seins des multiples femmes toujours semblables qui figurent ici, mais notre préférence ira à ces dessins sombres et émouvants qui retracent une indicible atmosphère d'angoisse.

LES SALLES 2 ET 3

LA SALLE 2 ou SALLE DE PROJECTION abritera les envois des hôpitaux belges.

LA SALLE 3 sera consacrée aux

LA GRANDE SALLE

LA GRANDE SALLE offre l'aspect général d'un excellent salon d'amateurs et nul ne devinerait qu'il s'agit d'œuvres de malades mentaux sans les tableaux explicatifs, les notices biographiques ou cliniques (d'une valeur relative d'ailleurs) qui jalonnent tous les panneaux et surtout ceux de la section américaine. A droite, la collection du docteur Agerberg rassemble l'œuvre de trois authentiques artistes : Ernst Josephson (1851-1906), tourmenté et minutieux comme le sont souvent les Germains et les graveurs ; Fredrik Hill (1849-1911), dont les reproductions fort fidèles respectent le caractère mystique et l'atmosphère un peu trouble, Primus Pettersson, enfin, un extraordinaire et exubérant naïf.

L'Espagne reste elle-même jusque dans la démence : mystique, soucieuse de l'effet décoratif et non sans une trace d'inquisition...

Avec la collection du Maintenon State Hospital, de grande qualité plastique tout comme celle de Wilfred C. Hulse, l'une fauve de couleurs et de formes, l'autre sombre comme nos modernes réalistes, nous pénétrons dans le domaine américain qui occupe tout le centre avec des tableaux rassemblés par la Veterans Administration. Nous rencontrons là une tentative de démonstration par l'analyse de la désintégration des formes, des lignes, des plans, de la perspective et des couleurs. Un peu pédante, cette science, aussi idéaliste, est un cas intéressant. Et les malades yougoslaves — présentés par le docteur Julius — font preuve d'une angoisse vraiment « dostoïewskienne ». Enfin le docteur Kuneberg amène de Finlande de somptueuses broderies. Ainsi s'achève le tour de cette grande salle.

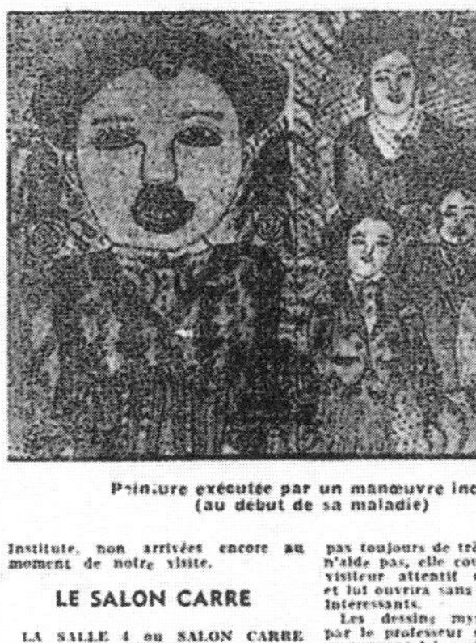

Peinture exécutée par un manœuvre inculte (au début de sa maladie)

Institute, non arrivées encore au moment de notre visite.

LE SALON CARRE

LA SALLE 4 ou SALON CARRE sera un des centres d'attraction. Outre les envois du Burden Institute, les œuvres surréalisantes qui sortent du Napsbury, celles très caractéristiques qui viennent du Powers Hospital, on pourra observer dans la participation du Netherne Hospital des exemples fort intéressants sinon toujours concluants de peintures et de dessins exécutés par des patients avant et après une lobotomie et à des dates successives, une semaine, quinze jours, trois mois après cette grave opération qu'est l'ablation du lobe frontal du cerveau.

Je doute que le profane puisse, en sortant de ces salles, distinguer les œuvres d'un paranoïaque de celles d'un schizophrène. Pourtant, l'exemple d'un géométrisme poussé à l'extrême, peint par le grand danseur russe Nijinsky dans une crise de schizophrénie, tout comme cette série de chats qui se perdent dans les ornements jusqu'à des dessins d'un décorativisme byzantin, se montrent très significatifs.

Dans ce salon carré, on verra enfin deux œuvres envoyées de Grèce qui, dans leur surréalisme, dénoncent une profonde obsession sexuelle, et un tableau venu d'Indonésie qui nous offre un curieux mélange du style de Gauguin et de l'Art asiatique.

pas toujours de très bon aloi. Si elle n'aide pas, elle couragera du moins le visiteur attentif dans son examen et lui ouvrira sans doute des aperçus intéressants.

Les dessins mystérieux recueillis par le professeur sarrois, K. Conrac, ne peuvent laisser indifférent. La reproduction de thèmes stéréotypés chez cet Hindou qui reproduit dix fois sa mère, d'une façon toujours

LA FRANCE ET LE BRESIL

AU PREMIER ETAGE, la France et le Brésil se partagent équitablement une longue salle mansardée.

Disons tout de suite que les envois de ce dernier pays, s'ils ne manquent pas souvent d'une sauvagerie « rassurante », oserait-on dire, semblent manquer parfois de spontanéité. Et sans doute faut-il voir là le résultat de méthodes thérapeutiques employées d'une façon extensive à des fins psychanalytiques. Il faut pousser le malade à dessiner pour confirmer le diagnostic ! Si on retrouve dans ces œuvres sur commande les traces de délire ou d'obsession, si celles-ci ne sont pas dénuées (il s'en faut de beaucoup) de qualités artistiques, il leur manque un je ne sais quoi, la spontanéité sans doute, qui justement se déploie librement dans la section française. Citons pourtant les importantes participations de Mauricio de Madeiros, du docteur Yahn, de Heitor Peres et de Osoria Cesar.

De tous les asiles de France ont convergé vers Sainte-Anne les pièces les plus significatives. Au-dessus d'une lettre d'un interné (de 170 mètres de longueur) se plaignant du régime des hôpitaux, et qui fait le tour de la salle, on sera plus d'une fois séduit (et si rarement choqué) par la naïveté, la franchise et la pureté (malgré les complexes) de ces dessins où apparaissent comme des « leit-motiv » non les obsessions morbides (assez exceptionnelles), mais les désirs de liberté, de campagne et d'amour. Nombre des toiles sont de véritables « ex-voto ». Dans son désœuvrement, artiste malgré lui, l'interné s'est efforcé de donner corps et réalité à son rêve. Ils font preuve de plus ou moins d'habileté, de plus ou moins de technique. Il y a beaucoup de très authentiques naïfs — d'autres plus influençables — comme tous les malades mentaux se laissent gagner par les facilités (en sont-ce vraiment ?) d'un modernisme où ils excellent et où les réussites sont nombreuses. Chacun prendra beaucoup d'intérêt à mieux connaître ces artistes anonymes en parcourant les notices qui accompagnent leurs œuvres. Citons enfin ces petits santons, ces étranges cailloux qu'on ramasse et qu'on grave dans un style si proche du roman et des primitifs, ces moutons à cinq ou six pattes et ce misérable sac fait de lambeaux de tissus qui semble échappé des mains de la Folle de Chaillot. Et puisqu'on ne peut publier les noms de ces exposants involontaires, mentionnons du moins ceux du docteur Graulle, directeur de Sainte-Anne, et du docteur Bessières, qui ont apporté leur précieuse contribution à cette manifestation qui ne manquera pas de trouver le plus large retentissement.

Enfin signalons que simultanément seront exposés à la Sorbonne des dessins d'enfants prêtés par Mme Minkovska et par Miss Margaret Naumburg.

G. B.

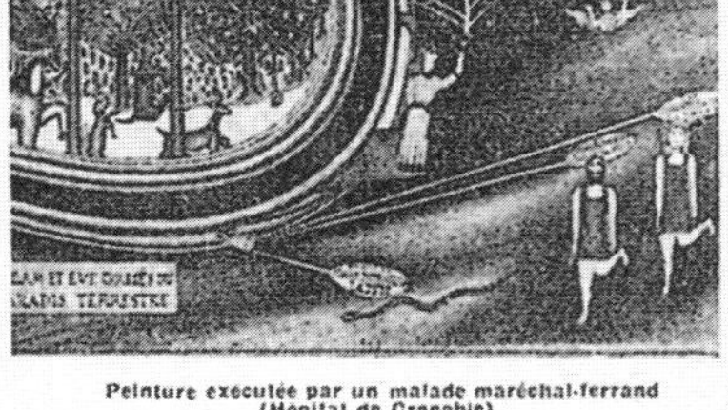

Peinture exécutée par un malade maréchal-ferrand (Hôpital de Grenoble)

LES GALERIES

LA GENTILHOMMIERE, 67, bd Raspail (Lit. 35-14) : Peintures modernes.

KATIA GRANOFF, 13, quai Conti (Odé. 41-02) : Maîtres contemporains.

LE GARREC, 24, rue du Four (Dan. 43-38) : Dessins, gravures, tableaux des XIXe et XXe siècles.

LA HUNE, 170, boulevard Saint-Germain (Lit. 25-85). Dessins, gravures et estampes contemporains. Le 3 octobre : Johnny Friedlaender.

MAX KAGANOVITCH, 99, boulevard Raspail (Lit. 53-42). Tableaux modernes et sculptures de Degas.

GALERIE-LIBRAIRIE PALMES, 3, place Saint-Sulpice (Odé. 40-73).

VITRINE PAUL PROUTE ET SES FILS, 74, rue de Seine (Dan. 89-80) : Le Chien, dans l'estampe ancienne et moderne, jusqu'au 30 septembre.

MITIA KOLESAR, peintures, dessins, gravures. Du 22 septembre au 6 octobre.

GALERIE DU SIECLE, 168, bd Saint-Germain (Dan. 93-09) : Peintures contemporaines.

GALERIE SAINT-PLACIDE, 41, rue Saint-Placide. Les jeunes de la Galerie.

GALERIE ZAK, 16, rue de l'Abbaye (Dan. 94-56). Tableaux modernes : Renault, Utrillo, Degas, Soutine, Edzard.

7e ARRONDISSEMENT

GALERIE DE BEAUNE, 5, rue de Beaune. Œuvres de Chapoval, Fahrel, Nissa Zeid, Gillet, Loubchansky, Marie Raymon, Nejad, etc...

GALERIE POMONE « Bon Marché », rue du Bac. Sous le patronage de l'U.A.P. Rues et routes de France.

GALERIE RASPAIL, 7, boulevard Raspail (Métro : Bac) : Astelin, Bouche, Charmy, Dufresnoy, Lacoste, Lenset, Mainssieux, Picart-Le-Doux, Signal.

14e ARRONDISSEMENT

L'ART PICTURAL, 5, rue Campagne-Première : Peintures de Beaulieu, Bosse, Calmettes, Clavé, Cortot, Daimbert, Dominiquez, Flores, Guignebert, Parmeste, Pattis, Votensky ; sculptures de Alonso Condor, Kahn, Longuet, Margot, Veyssel.

LES MUSÉES

ARCHIVES NATIONALES, 60, rue des Francs-Bourgeois, Paris 3e (Palais Soubise) : L'Art et la Vie au Moyen-Age dans les blasons et les sceaux. Tous les jours, sauf mardi, de 14 à 17 heures. Entrée : 50 francs.

BIBLIOTHEQUE NATIONALE, 58, rue de Richelieu : Galerie Mazarine, Trésors des Bibliothèques d'Italie. Manuscrits et livres du IVe au XVIe siècle. Dessins des Cabinets de Florence et de Rome, de 10 à 17 heures.

GALERIE MANSARD : « Villégiatures d'autrefois ». Entrée libre, jusqu'à fin septembre.

MUSEE DES ARTS DECORATIFS, 107, rue de Rivoli (Me Palais-Royal, Opé. 60-63) : Exposition permanente de meubles du XVe au XXe siècle et Ve Salon des Arts de la Table. Ts les j., sauf mardi, de 10 à 12 et de 14 à 17 h. Entrée : 100 francs.

MAISON DE VICTOR-HUGO, 6, place des Vosges : de 10 à 12 h. 30 et de 14 à 17 heures, sauf mardi.

MUSEE NISSIM DE CAMONDO, 63, rue de Monceau (Lab. 12-32). Mardis, jeudis, samedis, de 13 à 17 heures. Dimanches, de 10 à 12 h. 30 et de 14 à 17 heures : Meubles et objets d'art du XVIIIe.

MUSEE CARNAVALET, rue de Sévigné : de 10 à 12 h. et de 14 à 17 h., sauf mardi : Collection historique de la Ville de Paris et nouvelles salles de l'Echevinage Parisien. Entrée 25 francs.

MUSEE COGNACQ-JAY, 25, bd des Capucines (Opé. 55-66). Trésors d'Elégance du XVIIIe : tabatières, bonbonnières, etc. Tous les jours sauf mardis, de 10 à 12 heures et de 14 à 18 heures. Entrée 50 francs.

MUSEE DE LA FRANCE D'OUTRE-MER, 293, av. Daumesnil (Porte Dorée). Tous les jours, sauf mardi de 14 à 17 heures.

MUSEE GUIMET, 6, place d'Iéna : Exposition d'art asiatique : Afghanistan, Asie Centrale, Chine, de 10 à 17 heures et présentation nouvelle de la collection GRANDIDIER et des collections chinoises et japonaises des Musées nationaux. Entrée 30 francs, dimanche 15 francs.

MUSEE DES INVALIDES, Esplanade : Musée et Chapelle, ts les jours de 10 à 12 et de 13 h. 30 à 17 h. : Tombeau de Napoléon, de 12 à 18 h., sauf mardi.

MUSEE JACQUEMART ANDRE, 158, bd Haussmann. Tous les jours, sauf vendredi, de 13 à 16 h. : Renaissance italienne et XVIIIe.

MUSEE DU JEU DE PAUME : Les Maîtres de l'Impressionnisme, tous les jours, sauf mardi, de 10 à 12 h. 45 et de 14 à 17 heures.

MUSEE DU LOUVRE, Palais du Louvre : Entrée : porte Denon. De 14 à 17 h. : les visites en français, sous la direction des conférenciers officiels des musées nationaux, ont lieu tous les jours, à 15 h., sauf dimanches et mardis. Prix : 100 fr. entrée comprise.

MUSEE DE LA MARINE, Palais de Chaillot. Tous les jours, sauf samedi, dimanche et lundi, de 10 h. 30 à 12 h. 30 et de 15 h. 30 à 17 h. 30.

MUSEE DE L'HOMME, Palais de Chaillot, Trocadéro. (Pas. 74-46). L'art rupestre en Afrique du Sud. Tous les jours sf mardi, de 9 à 18 heures. Entrée 40 francs.

ORANGERIE DES TUILERIES (Opé. 99-48) : Louis XV et Rocaille. Sculptures, peintures, mobilier, arts décoratifs. Tous les jours, sauf mardi, de 10 à 17 heures.

MUSEE POSTAL, 4, rue Saint-Romain. Métro : Duroc. Histoire postale, de 14 à 18 h., ts les jours, sauf mardi.

PETIT-PALAIS : Exposition permanente des chefs-d'œuvre de la Peinture Française du Louvre. Ts les j., de 10 à 18 h., sauf vendredi. Exposition « La Vierge dans l'Art français ». Ts les j., de 10 à 18 h. Entrée : 100 fr. la semaine, 120 fr. vendredi, 50 fr. dimanche.

MUSEE RODIN, 77, rue de Varenne, Paris (7e) : Œuvres du grand sculpteur. De 13 à 17 heures, tous les jours sauf mardi.

MUSEE D'ART POPULAIRE JUIF ET ARCHIVES, 12, rue des Saules (18e). Dimanches et jeudis, de 15 à 18 heures.

LA SAINTE-CHAPELLE, Cour du Palais de Justice. Tous les jours, sauf mardi, de 10 à 12 et de 13 h. 30 à 16 heures.

CINEMATHEQUE FRANÇAISE, 7, av. de Messine. Tous les jours, sauf mercredi et jeudi, de 13 à 20 heures et après 20 h. 30.

MUSEE DE CLUNY, 6, place Paul-Painlevé (Odé. 24-21). Tous les jours, sauf mardi, de 10 à 12 h. 45 et de 14 à 17 h. Entrée semaine : 30 fr. ; dimanche : 15 francs : Collection du Moyen Age.

PALAIS DE LA DECOUVERTE, avenue F.D. Roosevelt (Bal. 17-24). Exposition Internationale d'Histoire et Progrès de la Psychiâtrie. Documents anciens et originaux, appareils, livres, etc... Ts les j., sauf vendredis, de 10 à 12 h. et de 14 à 18 h. Entrée : 50 fr.

VERSAILLES, Château, Trianon et Musée des voitures. Ts les j., sauf mardi, et Nouvelles salles des XVe et XVIe siècles. De 10 à 18 h. Entrée 50 fr.

CHANTILLY, Musée Condé. — Tous les jours, de 13 h. 30 à 17 h. 30, sauf mardis, vendredis et jours fériés.

CHAALIS, Musée et parc d'Ermenonville. — Tous les dimanches, jeudis et samedis, de 13 h. 30 à 17 h. 30.

MEUDON, Villa des Brillants : Musée Rodin, av. Auguste-Rodin. Ouvert le dimanche de 13 à 18 h., du 1er avril au 1er novembre.

ATELIER D'EUGENE DELACROIX, 6, rue de Furstenberg. M[e] St-Germain-des-Prés : Delacroix et le Portrait Romantique (Delacroix, Chassériau, Ingres, Corot, Deveria, Helm, etc.). Ts l. j. sans exception, de 10 à 12 h. et de 14 à 17 heures. Entrée 30 francs.

LES MANUFACTURES NATIONALES, 17, rue de la Paix (Opé. 55-47) : Sèvres, Gobelins, Beauvais, chalcographie, moulages.

ATELIERS D'ANTOINE BOURDELLE, 16, rue Antoine-Bourdelle (avenue du Maine, Me Montparnasse) : Œuvres monumentales. Tous les jours, sauf mardi, de 10 à 12 h. et 14 à 17 h. Entrée : 25 francs.

ACADEMIES

ACADEMIE JULIAN, 5, rue de Berri (Ch.-Elysées), Me George-V : Cours sculpture, prof. Gimond et Yencesse ; peinture : Cavailles et Sabouraud ; dessin : Zuohada. Atelier libre de croquis : tous les jours, de 14 à 19 h. Deux modèles à chaque séance.

ACADEMIE DES ARTS MODERNES, L.-K. Derryx, directeur, 66, rue de la Pompe (16e) (Tro. 69-65) : Ecole Supérieure d'Arts Appliqués, agréée par l'Etat : Dessin, peinture, décoration, figurine de mode, haute couture, art publicitaire, illustration et gravure sur bois. Cours sur place : Brochure n° 1, Cours par correspondance : Brochure n° 2 sur demande.

ACADEMIE DE LA GRANDE-CHAUMIERE ET COLAROSSI, 12 et 14, rue de la Grande-Chaumière : Peinture : Brayer, Goerg, Mac Avoy, Aujame, Picard-Le Doux ; Sculpture : Zadkine, Raymond Martin ; Dessin et Modelage : Kretz ; Croquis De 14 à 19 h. et de 20 à 22 h.

ATELIERS GEORGES MUGUET. Dessin, sculpture, modèle vivant. T. les j.

COURRIER DES ARTS

FRANCE

LEGION D'HONNEUR

Nous avons eu le plaisir de trouver dans les récentes promotions de la Légion d'honneur, au titre du ministère des Affaires étrangères, les noms de : M. Fouques-Duparc, ambassadeur de France à Rome, élevé au grade de commandeur, et de Jacques Maritain, promu officier. D'autre part, la Présidence du Conseil pour l'Information a promu commandeur : Emile Servan-Schreiber, co-directeur des « Echos », et officier

ÉTRANGER

PREMIER SALON du Tourisme et de l'Industrie hôtelière

LES BONNES ADRESSES

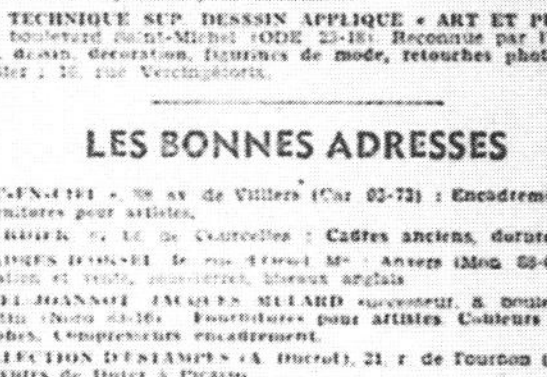

CLAUDE ARPELS. — Paysage de New-York (Galerie Cardo)

Translation of the two articles from: *Arts*, Paris, September 22, 1950

International Congress of Psychiatry

Psychopathological Art

by Dr. René Bessière, Head of the Sainte-Anne hospital

A first exhibition of paintings, drawings and sculptures by mentally ill patients was organized at the Sainte-Anne hospital in 1946 and won considerable acclaim. This year (1950), those responsible for the first International Congress of Psychiatry have brought together works of art selected by psychiatrists from France and fifteen other countries, making them accessible to the public from 29 September. Once again there is simply no overlooking the keen interest which psychopathological art awakens in psychiatric circles.

Contrary to what one might assume, the number of paintings, drawings, and in particular sculptures which one is likely to be able to find in psychiatric hospitals is relatively small.

The works produced by convalescents or chronically ill patients can be subdivided into two categories: either they are by professional artists striving to return to their former activities again, or they are the work of people regarded as "uneducated" in matters of art, and who draw and paint for their own diversion. The techniques used by the professional artists are scarcely influenced by their psychosis; they continue to paint in the style they had once acquired. Some are specialists in color prints, which they produce in series for commercial purposes; others are influenced by trends and fashions in art. Their works include not only thoroughly academic paintings, but also ones that tend in the direction of the Cubism or Fauvism of Picasso, Rouault, Matisse etc.

In some cases, the disintegration of the artist' personality is clearly evident in the paintings, even if they still betray a certain amount of "professionalism" and "talent." The exhibition contains several such paintings: the two best examples are by Swedish artists Hill and Josephson [sic], both of whom are now undergoing treatment in psychiatric hospitals, having once led normal lives as artists.

The "uneducated," simple, uncultured artists, who can often scarcely read or write, attempt to lend expression to their thoughts in an unwieldy schema and a simplified graphic form. Their works resemble drawings by young children, prehistoric cave drawings, or "Art Nègre." By contrast, the works by self-taught artists who have trained and improved their skills over a period of time are obviously more mature. These are reminiscent of Cretan or Byzantine art, of the primitive craft associated with the French Bayeux Tapestry, of the frescoes in Tavant or Saint-Savin, of the Italian pre-Renaissance, of Japanese or Chinese art, or simply of generally intelligible pictorial worlds. If they are "equipped" with a spark of genius, the mentally ill occasionally manage to produce veritable masterpieces of naive art.

It is interesting to realize that fine art emerges, expresses itself, and develops at all times and in all places, regardless of when or where in the world.

Whereas the painting and drawing techniques used by the mentally ill may be largely inconclusive for the psychiatrist, the content and theme of the works are definitely of more consequence.

Often the theme of the work is banal and insignificant, yet in many cases the images created by the mentally ill lend expression to their nightmares, what we call "oneirism." These works comply with the description given by Tardieu, in our opinion the first psychiatrist to write about drawings by the insane: "The wildest color associations, green or scarlet lines, unusual proportions, yellow skies, impossible light effects, monstrous creatures, fantastic animals, unimaginable architectural constructs, and hellish flames render the most inexpressible dreams tangible in inimitable forms."

If the dream is not too violent, it is conceptualized, and the insane person tries to translate his inner world into a concrete form. Here one encounters either a very graphic, or a more camouflaged pictorial transposition of the conflicts of childhood or adolescence, of aggression or passivity, of oppressive or anxiety-driven complexes: inferiority or superiority complexes in all their manifestations, mystical or metaphysical inclinations, the person's partial awareness of his own mental disintegration. Needless to say, these works often involve sexual themes, sometimes glaringly evident, sometimes disguised as their opposite, overlaid, or else laden with symbolism: compulsive cleanliness, impotence, heightened eroticism, homosexuality, sadism, masochism, fetishism, and now and then, plain bestiality.

A painting or drawing can also bring to light how the insane lend graphic expression to their original perception of the work in which they live. Yet one often finds a distortion of the exterior world in paintings by the mentally ill. In the case of one schizophrenic, to provide just a single example, his pathological condition and loss of contact with reality showed up in his drawings as a general tendency towards abstraction, with the whole pictorial plane systematically filled with myriad minute, fragmented, isolated details; also in static, fixed geometric or anatomical forms, the stereotypical repetition of themes or motifs, a leaning towards distortion and caricature, and finally, in the omnipresent symbolism.

The content of a picture is such an intimate confession—a kind of graphic psychoanalysis, a mirror of the total personality of the author—that life, personality, psychosis, and work meld into one another.

One cannot arrive at a diagnosis of a psychosis just by

examining these highly revealing works, but such an examination can complement a diagnosis and highlight its components. The painting or drawing should be looked upon as a test.

Produced as these works by the mentally ill are with such spontaneity and with no ulterior motive, it is their intensely human aspect, rather than their picturesque character or their debatable artistic value, that makes them so beautiful and moving, quite apart from their interest for psychiatry.

The Creative Genius

by Jean Bouret

"People think a person is insane when he hears what others do not hear, and sees what others do not see; and yet Socrates consulted his daimon, and Jeanne d'Arc heard voices. What is more, do we not all have visions and hallucinations?" Anatole France, "La Vie littéraire"

What exquisite lines by Anatole France, in a text on insanity in literature, in which he undertakes a marvellous analysis of Guy de Maupassant's short story "La Horla." Admittedly, he is just one of hundreds, for the theme is inexhaustible. And if Aristotle was the first to examine the relationship between art and insanity, today we find ourselves confronted with a mountain of literary and scientific books on the topic, that is, if we really want to know more about it. And although that time is well past, it at least serves to show that the difference between an insane and a normal person is not as clear as we generally assume. By the same token, an insane person is not necessarily an epileptic or crazed, and in any case, there is room enough for the creative. The efforts of the researchers are concentrated on examining this "threshold," whereby for them, drawings represent a test, the results of which are only seldom deceptive. This is something one can confirm by visiting the international exhibition of paintings by the mentally ill organized by the first International Congress of Psychiatry at the Sainte-Anne hospital this week.
The uniqueness of the works by the insane has not facilitated the psychiatrist's task of classifying them. Rogues de Fursac, Réja, Max Simon, and above all, the highly constructive work of Jean Vinchon, can be appealed to as indispensable sources.
The fashion (for it was actually a fashion) surrounding insanity in literature and art emerged around 1880 under the influence of the Goncourt brothers and their circles. Lombroso regarded three quarters of artists as insane.
"Genius," he claimed, "is the consequence of an astonishing unconscious, of a spontaneously occurring act of creation, and of a state that occurs much like an epileptic fit." Lombroso was probably exaggerating somewhat, and the French school subsequently straightened out the matter.
It is not necessary to go into the works of Dr. Vinchon here, especially as a book published by Stock in 1924 and another more recent one have succeeded in presenting the theories in a generally intelligible manner. It may even be somewhat daring to disseminate these theories, in view of the fact that, for the moment, the schools have not managed to make a scientifically founded diagnosis of the various psychopathologies. Of greater interest to us is the graphic quality of the works produced by the insane.
First and foremost, one should of course avoid speaking of genius straight away. Despite what Cocteau writes in his "Professional Secret" (and what will always be present in Dr. Vinchon's mind), namely, that "children and lunatics emit what the poet tries patiently to unravel his whole life long," one should not believe that in no time at all madness could simply eliminate all problems of form and color.
After visiting this excellent exhibition (Dr. Grolle and Dr. Bessière have really worked wonders, transforming an old furniture storeroom into something that is seldom to be found in our museums), we can draw the conclusion that the psychopath has the same defects as the healthy artist ...
Initially there is a charming naivety, then the trade is learnt relatively swiftly, only to be followed by a completely unbearable masquerading, a burgeoning use of one procedure and the techniques this entails. The Americans are the best examples of this. The abstract or supposedly abstract paintings of some of the veterans give off a devilishly strange odor. One would really have to go out on a tangent here and examine, for example, the portrait of a psychopath carried out by a sane person, which is almost always nonsense. At any rate, one cannot rely on this in serious case studies, for when the artist transfers his model, he destroys it. Clearly this has been understood by Schwars-Abrys, whom we have to thank for the most important collection of works by the insane, as well as for an outstanding fresco in the interior of the small museum.
"Art and Madness" is much too serious and wide-ranging a theme to allow hasty generalisations to be made. On the contrary, it demands a lot of patience, and above all, strong convictions on the part of the researchers.

Translation of Rudi Fuchs' text from Dutch: Beth O'Brian
Translation of Johannes Gachnang's text from German: Catherine Schelbert
Translation in chapter "Notes and Materials" from German: Pauline Cumbers
Editing: Constance Lotz

Photolithographs: Henzi AG, Bern
Design: Peter Sennhauser, Stämpfli AG, Bern
Printed by Stämpfli AG, Bern
Printed in Switzerland

ISBN 3-906127-57-5